A History of Global Consur

In *A History of Global Consumption: 1500–1800,* Ina Baghdiantz McCabe examines the history of consumption throughout the Early Modern period using a combination of chronological and thematic discussions, taking a comprehensive and wide-reaching view of a subject that has long been on the historical agenda. The title explores the topic from the rise of the collector in Renaissance Europe to the birth of consumption as a political tool in the eighteenth century.

Beginning with an overview of the history of consumption and the major theorists, such as Bourdieu, Elias and Barthes, who have shaped its development as a field, Baghdiantz McCabe approaches the subject through a clear chronological framework. Supplemented by illustrations in every chapter and ranging in scope from an analysis of the success of American commodities such as tobacco, sugar and chocolate in Europe and Asia to a discussion of the Dutch tulipmania, *A History of Global Consumption: 1500–1800* is the perfect guide for all students interested in the social, cultural and economic history of the Early Modern period.

Ina Baghdiantz McCabe is Professor of History and the Darakjian and Jafarian Chair of Armenian History at Tufts University, USA. Her publications include *The Shah's Silk for Europe's Silver: The Eurasian Silk trade of the Julfan Armenians in Safavid Iran and India, 1590–1750* (1999), *Diaspora and Entrepreneurial Networks 1600–2000,* co-editor (2005) and *Orientalism in Early Modern France: Eurasian Trade, Exoticism and the Ancien Régime* (2008).

A History of Global Consumption

1500–1800

Ina Baghdiantz McCabe

Routledge
Taylor & Francis Group

LONDON AND NEW YORK

First published 2015
by Routledge
2 Park Square, Milton Park, Abingdon, Oxon OX14 4RN

and by Routledge
711 Third Avenue, New York, NY 10017

Routledge is an imprint of the Taylor & Francis Group, an informa business

British Library Cataloguing in Publication Data
A catalogue record for this book is available from the British Library

Library of Congress Cataloging in Publication Data
A catalog record for this title has been requested

ISBN: 978-0-415-50791-2 (hbk)
ISBN: 978-0-415-50792-9 (pbk)
ISBN: 978-1-315-76389-7 (ebk)

Typeset in Times New Roman
by Taylor and Francis Books

MIX
Paper from
responsible sources
FSC
www.fsc.org   FSC® C013604

Printed and bound by CPI Group (UK) Ltd, Croydon, CR0 4YY

I would like to dedicate this book to my students and especially to Lara Danguillecourt (Tufts class of 2011).

Contents

List of Illustrations

Acknowledgements

If writing is a lonely endeavor, no book is ever written alone. This book could not have taken shape without the enthusiasm of my Tufts students. It would never have been written without the close collaboration of one of them: Tufts undergraduate Lara Danguillecourt, my research assistant. Lara continued to work with me after graduating and leaving for San Francisco, where Skype and other forms of new technology kept us in constant contact. Every phase of this book was shared with her. It is difficult to express the importance of her enthusiastic and efficient participation. It would have been impossible to undertake this project without her. James S. Schmidt, graduate student in the history department, a teaching assistant in my class on the history of consumption, read the entire manuscript before it was sent off. Michael McKinnon and Sairah Husain also gave some of their time to this book project while they were at Tufts.

I started to teach history of consumption in 1998; I thank the history department and my colleagues in International Relations at Tufts for helping me make it a popular course. I am very grateful to Deans Joanne Berger-Sweeney, Andrew McClellan and Nancy Bauer for the spring leaves that made research and writing possible. Andrew McClellan's faith in the book project was invaluable when it seemed a very difficult one to undertake. My colleague Sylvia Marzagalli offered me warm hospitality, support and participation in their seminars at Nice University during my leave. Her expertise will be invaluable for the next volume, which begins with the nineteenth century.

Without Eve Setch, Senior Editor at Routledge who commissioned this book, *A Global History of Consumption* would never even have reached the project stage. I thank her for her faith in me; a general book on the history of consumption is a bold move. A special thanks to her editorial assistant Amy Welmers, who went out of her way with grace and incredible speed to help me with the illustrations and other aspects of the production of this book. I thank the readers who were sent the manuscript for their time and careful reading.

The support of friends and family has been not only an inspiration but a source of strength and continued enthusiasm. My daughter listened to several parts of the manuscript and contributed ideas. I thank her and my husband for their support, patience and love. My husband's daily reading from the definitive edition of the *Diary of Samuel Pepys* in nine volumes continues to fill me in on the details of daily life in the seventeenth century. Nothing I can write can ever express how much I do in life is also his. This volume could not contain all the details that amaze the contemporary reader, but I hope it gives some life to the past; history is about people. I thank Amy Welmers for the illustration of Christopher Columbus by Theodor de Bry; no one knows what Columbus actually looked like, we have vague general descriptions but no portraits made during his lifetime. This book is not about heroes or even about events; it is more about the food handed to the Spanish by natives in Hispaniola in Figure 1.1. This volume is about exchanges and the impact of global exchanges; here I have too many colleagues to thank. Without their work in their own areas of expertise it would have been an impossible task. Their names are in the bibliography and I send each and every one of them my thanks.

The publishers would like to thank Berg Publishers, by permission of Bloomsbury Publishing Plc., for approving the use of material from *Orientalism in Early Modern France: Eurasian Trade, Exoticism and the Ancien Régime* (2008) by Ina Baghdiantz McCabe.

Introduction

WANG: Elder brother who sells satin, [do you have]: sky blue sleeveless jackets, willow blue knee-wraps, duck green edging, with clouds, parrot-green floral designs; dark-green heavenly flowers inlaid with eight treasures, grass-green-bees with clouds; peach-red capes; blood-red peony with entwined branches, glittering yellow Chinese writing brush flowers, goose-yellow with four clouds, willow-yellow threaded with colourful male phoenixes, musk-deer brown knee-wraps, moxa-brown jade bricks and steps, shimmering honey-browns, eagle-back brown hippocampus, and dark tea-brown flowers? Do you have all these types of thick silks and thin silks?

SHOPKEEPER: Customer, do you want it from Nanjing, from Hangzhou, or from Suzhou?[1]

This is dialogue from a handbook of spoken Chinese that circulated in late fourteenth-century Korea written for Koreans visiting Beijing. Craig Clunas uses this passage, which casually trumpets the customer's list of demands, to give a picture of China as an almost "inexhaustible source of profusion and variety of the material world".[2] Yet he stresses that the concepts of "consumption", "consuming" or the "consumer" are anachronistic for China in the Ming period (1368–1644), just as they are in Early Modern Europe. What is present in Ming texts is a juxtaposition of positive words such as *sheng*, "prosperity", or *fan*, "splendor". The negative side of consumption in Ming texts is expressed with the word *chi*, "wasteful excess" and *she*, "luxury and extravagance". Like many European texts, Ming writings expressed anxiety over inappropriate consumption and behavior, which might have caused instability in the social order.[3] The analogy between ranking things and ranking people is made very explicit in several texts examined by Clunas. A handful of scholars have studied consumption in China, most famously Kenneth Pomeranz who has argued against the exceptionalism that consumption was a Western phenomenon. With the exception of China, studies on consumer culture in the Early Modern period cover the world very unevenly, making it quite premature to write a global history of consumption. An effort has been made to balance the over-representation of Europe by including groups never discussed such as Native Americans and both the African and white settlers in the Caribbean and North America. This volume attempts to integrate whatever is available on the Early Modern period in chronological order.

Pioneering Theories and Works

Social emulation and imitation have been favorite ways to explain the importance of consumer culture whether in China or in Europe. Chief among the books that have marked the study of consumption in Europe is *The Civilizing Process* by Norbert Elias.[4] The book examines the changes in the behavior of the secular upper classes, such as the behavior at the table, the eating of meat, a survey of courtly society, manners, foresight and self-constraint. It diverges on many subjects and gives many insights into what Elias calls "the civilizing process". The chief influence Elias has had on studies of consumption has been coined the "trickle-down theory" of imitation. Many theories have accepted the assumption that lower social classes imitated the elite. For example, based on that theory, Neil McKendrick argued that "the mill girl" who wanted to dress like a duchess was a form of demand that drove consumption in eighteenth-century England.[5] Elias's model was not simply material. The acquisition of distinction, manners and lifestyle is seen as a whole, what he calls a "civilizing" process, and several scholars have followed his lead in studying "respectability" in eighteenth-century England. McKendrick sought to explain the social transformations that took place in eighteenth-century England by insisting that the traditional approach to production and manufacturing goods gave only half the picture. He stepped away from the long held discourse about the industrial revolution to what he calls a "consumer revolution". McKendrick examines the story of the commercialization of eighteenth-century fashion as a main marker of change. He posits two conclusions that have been questioned by other scholars since he published his work in 1982.[6] The first questioned is that the consumer revolution was a sudden break from the past, and the second is that this revolution took place in the eighteenth century, chiefly in England.[7] One premise is unanimously accepted: fashion and commercialization remain key to defining a consumer society.

It is in England that studying consumption in the field of history was born. A pioneering study by McKendrick argues that consumption in the modern sense originates in eighteenth-century England. Among the eighteenth-century partisans for the origins of Early Modern consumption, two colleagues have joined him for a seminal study in the field, *The Birth of a Consumer Society: The Commercialization of Eighteenth-Century England*, edited by Neil McKendrick, John Brewer and J. H. Plumb.[8] The book *Consumption and the World of Goods* was the next major contribution that changed the field by bringing in more scholars, such as Jan de Vries.[9] Jan de Vries argued for another starting point in another part of the world; the long seventeenth-century Dutch Republic is key in his *The Industrious Revolution: Consumer Behavior and the Household Economy, 1650 to the Present*.[10] Other scholars have also argued for the eighteenth century in England as a turning point, such as Maxine Berg and Elizabeth Eger in *Luxury in the Eighteenth Century: Debates, Desires, and Delectable Goods*.[11] The consumption of calicoes from India and their imitations is seen as a crucial moment to cement the argument for transformation. Even for England alone, the birth of consumption as posited by Neil McKendrick in the eighteenth century has been debated. For the earlier seventeenth-century origins of consumerism in England, one can consult Linda Levy Peck who studied luxury in *Consuming Splendor: Society and Culture in Seventeenth Century England*.[12]

This starting date for the birth of consumption in Europe has been further challenged by works researching life in the Italian cities. For the Renaissance as a start for modern consumption, which is centered on Italy, see among others: Richard Goldthwaite, *Wealth and the Demand for Art in Italy, 1300–1600*, and *The Building of Renaissance Florence: An Economic and Social History*; Chandra Mukerji, *From Graven Images: Patterns of Modern Materialism*; Lisa Jardine, *Worldly Goods: A New History of the Renaissance*; and Paula Findlen, "Possessing the Past: The Material World of the Italian Renaissance", and many works after that among them the recently edited compendium of articles, *Early Modern Things*.[13] A serious study by Evelyn Welch of shoppers and shopping for the period makes a strong argument for consumerism being alive and well by the fifteenth century in *Shopping in the Renaissance: Consumer Cultures in Italy 1400–1600*.[14]

If it is true that Fernand Braudel was the first to focus on material life and the *Annales* school focused on material culture, the word consumption did not arise in French scholarship until the work of Daniel Roche. For both fashion and consumption in France, seminal works have been written by Daniel Roche including *Histoire des choses banales: naissance de la consommation dans les sociétés traditionnelles (XVIIe–XIXe siècle)*.[15] In 1989, Roche wrote a history of clothing well before any other serious historian approached the subject, entitled *La culture des apparences: une histoire du vêtement (XVIIe–XVIIIe siècle)*.[16] More recent scholarship on the subject about France is in English, such as key works by Joan DeJean, Jennifer Jones and Caroline Weber.[17] Most of this scholarship would argue for seventeenth-century France as a turning point for consumerism in France. I think these examples suffice to make it clear that the birth of consumption is neither a clear turning point nor a straight line to the twenty-first century, nor does it have a linear evolution within Europe itself. Each society, even every city, has its own history and so to make generalizations is a rather futile exercise. The history of consumption is a history of discontinuity. Even for Europe more work is necessary, as most studies concentrate on capital cities. Focusing on the elite is another large problem, as very often work has only been done on the habits of the wealthy in capital cities. Since consumption concentrates in great part on food and clothing, the regional aspects of eating and dressing are key in Europe. Save for a few exceptional articles, the history of consumption has remained a history of elites. Recent efforts to address this issue have been made with articles such as Anne E. C. McCants' recently published "Porcelain for the Poor: the Material Culture of Tea and Coffee in Eighteenth Century Amsterdam".[18] The least studied subject is the under-consumption of the poor during times of plenty, let alone during the many famines that mark Early Modern Europe's history.

Debating the Beginning of Consumerism

Another major debate in the field concerns the social origins of consumer society. It concerns the bourgeois versus aristocratic origins of modern consumption; the classic debate was between Werner Sombart, who argues for the aristocrats as models, and Max Weber, who has famously written about merchants.[19] Furthermore, depending on which society is studied, the divide widens further; scholars who see the locus of the consumer revolution in eighteenth-century Britain point to the ascending middle classes, while those who locate it earlier focus on the French courts and point to the aristocratic origins of consumption. For Jan de Vries, in the urban society of the Golden Age Dutch Republic, a republic with no aristocrats, the Early Modern household had a new efficiency that was key to modern consumer behavior.[20]

Far from hoping to solve such major debates, this book tries to incorporate them to point to the problems that are thought provoking in the field. One main question to be addressed in the global context is whether consumption is an exceptional and unique western phenomenon as most scholars have assumed. To counter this, Kenneth Pomeranz's argument for consumption in China is tied to an argument that consumption did not really exist in European society until the nineteenth century.[21] His work, as well as those of the scholars who have argued against him, has been presented to give the reader an awareness of the debates. Elias' trickle-down theory of social imitation has been much amended by other theories. A number of these new theories have been critical tools in recent scholarship.

Theories Used by Historians and Anthropologists

Thorstein Veblen has argued that consumption has existed since the earliest phases of predatory culture. Author of *The Leisure Class*, he drew a sharp distinction between two social groups.[22] He contrasted the productivity of nineteenth-century industries run by engineers who manufactured goods, to the parasitism of a second group of "business" men who existed only to make financial profits for the leisure class. The chief activity of the leisure class was what he labeled "conspicuous consumption", which is lavish spending on goods and services acquired mainly for the purpose of displaying income or wealth. Today the usage of the term "consumption" clearly evokes Veblen's nineteenth-century definition. The term "consumption" in economics denotes the use of goods and services by households. The economist John Maynard Keynes was the first to stress that up to 90 percent of any increase in household income would translate into an immediate increase in consumption expenditure.[23]

Historians not only integrate findings from the field of economics, but also from the field of semiotics, which has become key to writing about the history of consumption. Ferdinand de Saussure is one of the founders of semiotics. Semiotics is a tool used by historians as way to classify signs and describe how they are socially communicated by social groups. Communities of people must agree on the meaning of a sign, whether it is a word, a gesture, an object or a piece of clothing. Since Saussure, and sometimes independently of him, a whole section of contemporary researchers have grappled with the problem of meaning and how it is communicated. Their fields are psychoanalysis, structuralism, eidetic psychology and some new types of literary criticism; these are all sciences dealing with social values. Semiology is a science of forms since it studies significations apart from their content. Edward Saïd's quotation below clearly summarizes the thoughts of the French semiotician Roland Barthes in his analytical work *Mythologies*.

> [Mythologies] illustrates the beautiful generosity of Barthes's progressive interest in the meaning (his word is signification) of practically everything around him, not only the books and paintings of high art, but also the slogans, trivia, toys, food, and popular rituals (cruises, striptease, eating, wrestling matches) of contemporary life. For Barthes, words and objects have in common the organized capacity to say something; at the same time, since they are signs, words and objects have the bad faith always to appear natural to their consumer.[24]

In the 1950s Roland Barthes observed daily life around him in Paris. He took a page from semiotics to study objects, events and images as collective cultural representations. While Roland Barthes is most famous for the semiotic structures behind the visual culture of his time and for his deconstruction of everyday life in Paris in *Mythologies*, it is in the field of fashion and clothing studies that he developed a very complex and influential framework for clarifying the mechanisms behind the fashion system. Many of the pieces he wrote were essays published in *Marie Claire* and *Vogue,* and just like his *Mythologies,* he was well known by the general public. One wonders what the readers of *Vogue* or *Marie Claire* thought of some of his elaborate theories. His book on the language of fashion is divided into three sections: the first is a history of clothing, the second is called "Systems and Structures" and the third is "Fashion, Debt and Interpretation". This last section shows his strength as a public intellectual as he talks about Chanel and Courrèges and criticizes hippies for appropriating poverty as a style. He argues that this mirrors *petite-bourgeoisie* values instead of challenging them. In most of his work, he is keen to demonstrate the aesthetics of a class such as the *petite-bourgeoisie*. One of his most striking pieces in *Mythologies* is about the recipes and pictures in the women's magazine *Elle* called "Ornamental Cooking".

Barthes analyzes the photographs of food, notes the predominant colors as pink and light yellow, and looks at how food is disguised and then ornamented with lemon wedges or a pinch of parsley to hide the fact that it is food. He argues that *Elle* is creating the myth of "chic" for its readers who were predominantly working class women. This was "aspirational cuisine" he argued, it did not have the "brutality of meat or the abruptness of shellfish".[25]

Barthes remains most famous for his book *The Fashion System*. Fashion is key to the study of consumption. In the book, he outlines how the text that always accompanies fashion images creates a connotation in the photographic images. Barthes is interested in looking at the way in which the sign system produces neither clothing nor women, but a totally abstract notion of fashion. He argues that fashion is an independent autonomous system and that it is an inscription that is normalized by a code. He proceeds to define several levels of analysis: the real or vestimentary code, the written vestimentary code and the rhetorical code.[26] While his influence has mainly been on theory, his presence is felt in many fields concerned with representation, information and models of communication, photography, music, literature, fashion and consumption.

Influenced by Barthes' ideas, the neo-Marxist Jean Baudrillard produced a theory of consumption in which commodities were not valued for their practical use but for their social meaning in a self-referential system of signifiers. According to Baudrillard, the functionality of an object allows it to surpass its primary function to become part of the universal system of signs. This book sees a close correlation between the human urge for collecting and consumption. The main theorist to have looked into collecting objects is Jean Baudrillard:

> Man never comes so close to being the master of a secret seraglio as when he is surrounded by his objects. Human relationships home of uniqueness and conflict never permit any such fusion of absolute singularity with infinite seriality – which is why they are such a continual source of anxiety. By contrast, the sphere of objects, consisting of successive and homologous terms, reassures.[27]

He hastens to add that such reassurance is founded on an illusion, yet that the object is the finest of domestic animals, the only "being" whose qualities exalt rather than limit a person. He argues that everything can be possessed, organized, classified and assigned a place. The object, in his view, is a mirror because the images it reflects won't ever contradict one another because they reflect the owner's desire. He argues that because objects dissipate many neuroses, it gives them their "soul" and makes them "ours". Few theories have made clearer the tie between the owner's identity and the collected or purchased object. His work is an attempt to understand the structure of the system of possession by analyzing the passion of curiosity and the compulsion of collecting.[28]

Collecting is defined as both desire and longing – the longing for the absence of an object. Aspiring to possess is seen as the dynamic behind consumption. Another key idea is going beyond one's means to possess. Baudrillard's section on credit argues that objects appear under the sign of differentiation and personal choice, but that they also appear under the sign of credit.[29] He argues that it is possible to live on credit because this mechanism of debt governs the realm of social advancement. Through credit and debt, advancement consequently becomes a realm of handicapped aspiration. "We are forever behindhand relative to our objects."[30] He means that objects precede us, they are there before us, sometimes a year away located in a final payment or in the next model available. Baudrillard argues that credit transfers the basic psychological situation of possession to the economic plane. He believes that just as the "personalization" of possessed objects makes him conclude that there is far more to them than advertising gimmicks, likewise credit has to be understood as far more than a simple financial arrangement. It is nothing less than a fundamental change that has created a new dimension and a new ethical system. Today, objects exist for us before they are earned and sometimes even before they are produced. He posits that while man once imposed his own rhythm on objects, today objects impose their disjointed rhythms upon us with the sudden manner of being present in our lives. Baudrillard continues to argue that a new morality has been born with credit; the precedence of consumption over accumulation (saving), forced investment, sped up consumption and the obligation to buy have all become the motors of our whole present system of buying first and paying later. Credit has brought back a system that is feudal in character, allocating labor in advance just as serf labor was to a feudal lord. The difference is that the serf had no complicity with his feudal lord, but modern consumers spontaneously embrace and accept an un-ending constraint that is imposed upon them by abstract powers that hold their debt.[31] Although the reader may think credit is a contemporary issue, there existed large amounts of debt accumulated by the wealthy in the Early Modern period. Baudrillard's analysis is based on an earlier model of the feudal system and not on modern times; the argument is that credit takes us back to the earlier constraints of feudal power. Courts, nobility and the bourgeoisie lived with debt and credit. Notwithstanding radical and puzzling statements such as "if non-collectors are 'nothing but morons', collectors, for their part, invariably have something impoverished about them", Baudrillard analyzes the symbolic value, the daily usage and the discourse of objects in order to bring to light the subjective socio-cultural discourse that they create.[32] He argues that the unconscious economy of the system of objects is a mechanism of projection and domestication to control the libido. Baudrillard makes use of both Marxist and Freudian theory in his analysis. In his view, the system of objects is the material embodiment of the problematic exercise of real psychological conflicts. It systematizes the fragility of life – therefore our own ephemerality – and the ever more rapid recurrence of the repetitive compulsion of seeking satisfaction and the disillusion of acquisition and consumption.[33]

Wanting an object is a compulsion in Baudrillard's view. Academic literature has often renamed "want" goods as luxuries and several important books have been written about luxury goods in European history. To clarify needs and wants, authors sometimes refer to Maslow's "Hierarchy of Needs", which classifies human desires into different categories by ascending innate order. The first four (out of six) levels are deficiency needs. These levels include physiological needs for the survival and function of the body (water, food, clothing, shelter), safety and orderly structure (financial, personal and healthy), love and belonging, and finally self-esteem. The last two levels are for individuals who are "meta-motivated" to be better: the fifth level is self-actualization while the sixth is self-transcendence. Maslow's "Hierarchy of Needs" depicts the most basic human needs and those that are more aspirational in character.[34]

What is necessary to stay alive is common to all of humanity. Views about what constitutes necessary consumption vary from one society to another. Within the same society, it may also vary greatly according to class, religion and social customs; it may further be localized to smaller groups such as families. The issue of what is a necessity and what is a luxury has helped define certain commodities as luxury goods. It is these luxury goods that have attracted the attention of most historians. In *The World of Goods,* Mary Douglas and Baron Isherwood "have argued that consumer goods represent a communication system that renders visible and stable the categories of culture and enables individuals to make and maintain social relationships".[35] To the consumption of goods, one must add the category of cultural consumption, as there is an important difference between the two. Material goods are physically visible whereas cultural consumption, save the collection of painting and sculpture, is invisible once it has occurred. Social status may be defined by the consumption of goods but it is no less defined by attending a concert or an art exhibit. This invisible aspect is often left out as most scholars have concentrated on material goods. Anthropologists and sociologists have produced most of the theoretical framework through which one can study consumer society. The study of culture itself, often a focus of anthropologists, enters into the history of consumption because it is impossible to speak about consumer society without speaking about culture. It is impossible to understand the history of consumption without examining different conceptions of culture that are ultimately subjective. In fact, it is the failure to examine culture that has resulted in purely economic understandings of consumption. The anthropologist James Clifford has made us aware of the predicament of "being in culture while looking at culture".[36]

Perhaps the most universal definition of culture has been given by another anthropologist, Clifford Geertz, in his work *The Interpretation of Cultures.* Geertz defined culture as "a system of inherited conceptions expressed in symbolic forms by means of which men communicate, perpetuate, and develop their knowledge about and attitudes toward life".[37] In his view, each culture has specific guiding symbols that the anthropologist has to decipher and interpret. Early in his career, Geertz argued that the drive to make sense of human experience and to give it shape and order is as pressing as biological needs. This is a functionalist view of culture that he left behind in later years as he described the difficulty of ever adequately describing objective reality. Geertz's influence on the social sciences is just as unparalleled as his understanding of the scope of culture. His view that human beings are "symbolizing, conceptualizing, meaning-seeking animals" is the most widely accepted view among social scientists.[38]

One of the newer aspects analyzed by historians of consumption is the "consumption of culture". Historians have looked at the activity of consuming culture as a way that enables individuals to construct social identities. In many cases, these studies have been inspired by the German sociologist and philosopher Jürgen Habermas (1929–) to map the formation of a polite and informed public in the Early Modern period by examining the role of public and private institutions such as coffeehouses, private salons, newspapers, book clubs and libraries. According to Habermas, bourgeois public opinion was formed in the cultural and social spaces of the theatre, the art exhibit and the concert. Frequenting such cultural venues formed a class' social identity and ideas. This process converted art and culture into objects for public consumption and into commodities to be bought and sold.[39] Habermas' theories have been crucial to the main history written on the consumption of culture in Europe: *The Consumption of Culture, 1600–1800: Image, Object, Text.*[40]

One of the seminal studies to address the history of consumption theoretically was made by Jan de Vries in his book *The Industrious Revolution*.[41] In the first chapter about the transformation of consumer desire in the long eighteenth century, he argues for the importance of the household as an economic unit that interacts with markets. He ties Veblen's idea of consumption as a social signal of status to the striving for respectability that arose in the seventeenth and eighteenth centuries according to Woodruff Smith. As consumers respond to the consumption acts of others, no point of satiation can ever be reached. De Vries argues that the decomposition of consumer behavior into basic parts only offers a sketch of the dynamic structure of consumer demand. He argues that it is necessary to do away with the idea of the passive consumer and replace it with an active consumer who interacts with an array of goods that signal meaning. De Vries continues to look at the combinatory possibilities of available goods and looks at consumption bundles. He cites some important bundles that may seem natural to us, such as tea combined with sugar. Bundles can apply to many goods; a famous example comes from the works of philosopher Denis Diderot.[42] Soon after he had replaced his old dressing gown with a splendid one, Diderot found himself looking at his desk that suddenly appeared shabby. The tapestries on the wall seemed threadbare. He found himself ordering new draperies and in this way the study was entirely renovated with new things. This had not been his intention, but his new gown had led him to this result. The point made by de Vries is that the new commodities by themselves did not possess the utility they acquired together, thus goods embedded within the "worlds of goods" acquire marking functions that supply social distinction. As the anthropologists Douglas and Isherwood have argued, "all goods carry meaning, but none by itself".[43] Douglas and Isherwood have also pioneered a study on taste.

Taste as the Dynamic Force behind Consumption

The heart of the issue in the history of consumption is taste. Mary Douglas and Baron Isherwood wrote that goods like aesthetic and artistic taste "are neutral, their uses are social; they can be used as fences or bridges".[44] Conversations about opera, minimalist art and ballet enable individuals to place one another socially and serve as rituals for the elite. These conversations are created about these scarce cultural goods that bind partners within the same social class. As Douglas and Isherwood have argued, these investors in special tastes join together in "the joy of sharing names".[45] Taste is therefore a form of ritual identification and a means of constructing social relations and creating boundaries between classes. Symbols and signs, as studied by sociologists and theorists such as Roland Barthes and Pierre Bourdieu, are increasingly important as social interactions are moved beyond the circles of kinship, neighborhood and small town. This process is marked by the rise of meritocratic ideology and the use of "cultural capital" for strategic mobility within the upper middle classes.[46]

Pierre Bourdieu's greatest contribution to the field is the notion of "habitus". It has been adopted by several historians of the Early Modern period. He posited, "the perception of the social worlds is itself the product of internalization".[47] Human internalization is a product of differences perceived when observing social classes. "Each class condition is defined [both] by its [own] properties and by the [relationships] which it derives from its [social] position" in the class system. A specific habitus is "everything which distinguishes it from what it is not". It is also defined by "everything [that] it is opposed to; social identity is defined and asserted through difference".[48] Within the habitus is contained all of the life experiences of occupying a certain social condition. This was Bourdieu's way of trying to define a social class, its cultural habits, its way of life and its distinction from other groups. "The most fundamental oppositions in the structure (high/low, rich/poor etc.) tend to establish themselves as the fundamental structuring principles" of our own perceptions and practices.[49] The *habitus* apprehends the greatest differences between social conditions when it notices the differences between rich and poor, high and low. Because our social values and views are a product of our differences, these categories seem natural. Bourdieu established the importance of the internalization of our own social values. These internalized values shape our material acquisitions. On the other hand, the existing material order creates what we internalize as true and valuable. For Bourdieu, "taste classifies and classifies the classifier".[50] Taste is at the base of the desire and capacity to acquire, materially or symbolically, a given group of objects or cultural practices that define lifestyle. Acquiring property with which individuals and groups surround themselves – such as estates, houses, furniture, paintings, textiles, books, cars, spirits, cigarettes, perfume, clothing and footwear – symbolizes the unity of this lifestyle. Many historians writing on consumption have adopted the concept of taste as a major driving force for the consumer.

Early Modern Globalization

This book has the title *A History of Global Consumption*. To be sure, it is an ambitious one for the state of the field. The question remains as to just how much one can argue for a global world in the Early Modern period. Successful attempts have been made by the British historian Christopher Bayly to tackle the different definitions of archaic and modern globalization. Modern globalization is defined by nationalism, capitalism, democracy and consumerism, while archaic globalization is defined by cosmic kingship, universal religion and "humoral understandings of the body and the land".[51] The Chinese empire and the pre-modern European countries are the best examples of cosmic kingship, the predecessor to the nation state. These empires not only acquired mass territories but also spread universal knowledge, history, cultural goods, ideals and religion. These empires imported such mass quantities of foreign goods into their treasuries that the consumption and consequent gift giving of foreign goods was passed onto local rulers and wealthy merchants. Consumption became less about the purpose or capitalistic nature of the goods and more about how far away and exotic the goods were. Archaic consumption was essentially collecting diverse cultural goods by people who then became agents of globalization. Christopher Bayly argues that beyond material collection, cosmic religion was the second feature of archaic globalization and that its third feature was the use of scientific systems to attempt to control the body and the landscape.[52] Bayly contends that proto-globalization started with the trade of what many historians have called the drug foods: sugar, tobacco, coffee, tea and opium. In his definition of globalization, the consumption of exotic goods is key. Without espousing *a priori* theories, when writing this book it became clear how collecting the exotic and consuming drug foods were the markers of both domestic and imperial desire in the Early Modern period.

Study Questions

1 What did consumption mean in Ming China?
2 What are some of the times and places scholars have argued marked the beginning of modern consumption?
3 With what socioeconomic classes have scholars argued modern consumption began? Is there a debate about the social origins of consumption?

4 From what sources do consumable objects derive their meaning and value, according to Jean Baudrillard?
5 What is *habitus* and how does it inform taste?

Notes

1 Svetlana Rimsky-Korsakoff Dyer, *Grammatical Analysis of the Lao Ch'i-ta: With an English Translation of the Chinese Text* (Canberra: Faculty of Asian Studies, Australian National University, 1983), 430–431. Cited by Craig Clunas in *The Oxford Handbook of the History of Consumption*, ed. Frank Trentman (Oxford: Oxford Universty Press, 2012), 51.
2 Clunas, "Splendour and Excess in Ming China" in *The Oxford Handbook of the History of Consumption*, 51.
3 Clunas, "Splendour and Excess in Ming China", 52.
4 Norbert Elias, *The Civilizing Process: Sociogenetic and Psychogenetic Investigations*, trans. Edmund Jephcott (Malden, MA; Oxford, England; Victoria, Australia: Blackwell Publishing, 2000).
5 Neil McKendrick, "Home Demand and Economic Growth" in *Historical Perspectives: Studies in English Thought and Society*, ed. Neil McKendrick (London: Europa, 1974), 209.
6 Neil McKendrick, John Brewer, and J. H. Plumb, eds., *The Birth of a Consumer Society: The Commercialization of Eighteenth-Century England* (Bloomington: Indiana University Press, 1982).
7 Grant McCracken, *Culture and Consumption: New Approaches to the Symbolic Character of Consumer Goods and Activities* (Bloomington: Indiana University Press, 1990), 4–7.
8 McKendrick, Brewer, and Plumb, eds., *The Birth of a Consumer Society*.
9 John Brewer and Roy Porter, eds., *Consumption and the World of Goods* (London; New York: Routledge, 1993).
10 Jan de Vries, *The Industrious Revolution: Consumer Behavior and the Household Economy, 1650 to the Present* (Cambridge: Cambridge University Press, 2008).
11 Maxine Berg and Elizabeth Eger, eds., *Luxury in the Eighteenth Century: Debates, Desires, and Delectable Goods* (Basingstoke, Hampshire; New York: Palgrave, 2003).
12 Linda Levy Peck, *Consuming Splendor: Society and Culture in Seventeenth Century England* (Cambridge: Cambridge University Press, 2005).
13 Richard Goldthwaite, *Wealth and the Demand for Art in Italy, 1300–1600* (Baltimore, MD: Johns Hopkins University Press, 1993); Richard Goldthwaite, *The Building of Renaissance Florence: An Economic and Social History* (Baltimore: Johns Hopkins University, 1980); Chandra Mukerji, *From Graven Images: Patterns of Modern Materialism* (New York: Columbia University Press, 1983); Lisa Jardine, *Worldly Goods: A New History of the Renaissance* (London: Macmillan, 1996); and Paula Findlen, "Possessing the Past: The Material World of the Italian Renaissance," *AHR* 103, no. 1 (February 1998): 83–114; Paula Findlen, ed., *Early Modern Things* (New York: Routledge, 2012).
14 Evelyn Welch, *Shopping in the Renaissance: Consumer Cultures in Italy 1400–1600* (New Haven, CT: Yale University Press, 2005).
15 Daniel Roche, *Histoire des choses banales: naissance de la consommation dans les sociétés traditionnelles (XVIIe–XIXe siècle)* (Paris: Fayard, 1997).
16 Daniel Roche, *La culture des apparences: une histoire du vêtement (XVIIe–XVIIIe siècle)* (Paris: Fayard, 1989).
17 Joan DeJean, *The Essence of Style: How the French Invented High Fashion, Fine Food, Chic Cafés, Style, Sophistication and Glamour* (New York: Free Press, 2005);

DeJean, *The Age of Comfort: When Paris Discovered Casual – and the Modern Home Began* (New York: Bloomsbury, 2009); Jennifer Jones. *Sexing la Mode: Gender, Fashion and Commercial Culture in Old Regime France* (Oxford; New York: Berg, 2004); Caroline Weber, *Queen of Fashion: What Marie Antoinette Wore to the Revolution* (New York: H. Holt, 2006).

18 Anne E. C. McCants, "Porcelain for the Poor: the Material Culture of Tea and Coffee in Eighteenth Century Amsterdam", in Paula Findlen, ed., *Early Modern Things* (New York: Routledge, 2012).

19 Werner Sombart, *Luxury and Capitalism* (Ann Arbor: University of Michigan Press, 1967); Max Weber, *Protestant Ethic and the Spirit of Capitalism*, trans. Talcott Parsons (London: G. Allen & Unwin Ltd., 1930).

20 For an overview on the debates, which cannot be addressed in this introduction see: Jean-Christophe Agnew, "Coming Up for Air: Consumer Culture in Historical Perspective", in Brewer and Porter, eds, *Consumption and the World of Goods*, 23–25, and Craig Clunas, "Modernity Global and Local: Consumption and the Rise of the West," *American Historical Review (AHR)* 104, no. 5 (December, 1999): 1497–1511.

21 Kenneth Pomeranz, *The Great Divergence: China, Europe and the Making of the Modern World Economy* (New Jersey: Princeton University Press, 2000).

22 Thorstein Veblen, *The Leisure Class: An Economic Study in the Evolution of Institutions* (New York; London: Macmillan, 1899).

23 John Maynard Keynes, *The General Theory of Employment, Interest, and Money* (London: Macmillan,1936).

24 Edward Saïd on Roland Barthes *Mythologies*, trans. Annette Lavers (New York: Farrar, Straus, Giroux, 1972), back cover.

25 Roland Barthes, *Mythologies*, 78.

26 Roland Barthes, *The Fashion System* (New York: Hill and Wang, 1983).

27 Jean Baudrillard, *Système des Objets* (New York; London: Verso, 1996), 95.

28 Baudrillard, *Système des Objets*, 100.

29 Baudrillard, *Système des Objets*, 169.

30 Baudrillard, *Système des Objets*, 171.

31 Baudrillard, *Système des Objets*, 173.

32 Baudrillard, *Système des Objets*, 114.

33 Baudrillard, *Système des Objets*, 141–142.

34 Colin Campbell, "Consumption and the Rhetorics of Need and Want", *Journal of Design History,* Vol. 11, No. 3 (Oxford University Press, 1998): 235–246, 239.

35 Mary Douglas and Baron Isherwood, *The World of Goods: Towards an Anthropology of Consumption* (New York: W.W. Norton, 1979), 59–60.

36 James Clifford, *The Predicament of Culture: Twentieth Century Ethnography, Literature, and Art* (London: Yale University Press, 1988), 8.

37 Clifford Geertz, *The Interpretation of Cultures: Selected Essays* (New York: Basic Books, 1973), 89.

38 Clifford Geertz, "Ethos, World-View and the Analysis of Sacred Symbols", *Antioch Review* (Winter 1957–1958), 436.

39 Jürgen Habermas, *The Structural Transformation of the Public Sphere: An Inquiry into a Category of Bourgeois Society*, trans. Thomas Burger (Cambridge, MA: MIT Press, 1989), 41.

40 Ann Bermingham and John Brewer, *The Consumption of Culture, 1600–1800: Image, Object, Text* (London, New York: Routledge, 1995).

41 De Vries, *The Industrious Revolution.*

42 De Vries, *The Industrious Revolution,* 33.

43 Douglas and Isherwood, *The World of Goods,* 49. As quoted in De Vries, *The Industrious Revolution*, 33.

44 Douglas and Isherwood, *The World of Goods,* 12.

45 Douglas and Isherwood, *The World of Goods*, 75.
46 Pierre Bourdieu, *Reproduction in Culture, Education, Society* (Beverly Hills, CA: Sage, 1977).
47 Pierre Bourdieu, *Distinction: A Social Critique of the Judgment of Taste* (London: Routledge and Kegan Paul, 1984), 169–177.
48 Bourdieu, *Distinction*, 172.
49 Bourdieu, *Distinction*, 169–177.
50 Bourdieu, *Distinction*, 6.
51 C. A. Bayly, "'Archaic' and 'Modern' Globalization in the Eurasian and African Arena, ca. 1750–1850", in A. G. Hopkins, ed. *Globalization in World History* (New York, NY: W. W. Norton & Company, 2002), 45–72, 50.
52 C. A. Bayly, "'Archaic' and 'Modern' Globalization" in *Globalization in World History,* 50–51.

Figure 1.1 Christopher Columbus, Genoese explorer, discovering America, 12 May 1492 (1590). Artist: Theodor de Bry. © Print Collector/Getty Images.

1 Collecting the World

> For you must know that all the spicery, and that cloths of silk and gold, and the other valuable wares that come from the interior, are brought to that city [Ayas]. And the merchants of Venice and Genoa, and other countries, come thither to sell their goods, and to buy what they lack.
>
> Marco Polo[1]

The spices, silk and gold described by Marco Polo in the thirteenth century marked the imagination of Europe's merchants and explorers for centuries to come. The quest for rare goods and expensive spices was the object of cross-cultural exchanges and exploration since antiquity, but it became a global phenomenon after the fifteenth century. Until then Europe's economy has been described as a "gift economy". Both trade and gift giving were very important aspects of medieval culture. Gifts and gift-giving practices have been studied since the late 1950s, inspired by the work of the French sociologist Marcel Mauss. Under his influence, several scholars have argued that gift giving was a special form of transaction that took place for social prestige alone and not for material or tangible profit. The famous historian of medieval France, Georges Duby, pushed Mauss' ideas even further by making a fundamental difference between gifts and trade. In his view, gifts were given and reciprocated because of social obligation. Other scholars have pushed this dichotomy even further by dividing medieval history into an earlier period, that of a "gift economy", and a later period, that of a "profit economy". In this view, in the early period, gifts were exchanged as an expression of power and social prestige without a specific calculated economic value. For Duby and his followers, society in the early Middle Ages was founded on networks that circulated the gifts of dependants to their political protectors, of magnates to kings, of kings to aristocrats and of the rich to the poor.[2] Although most of this book examines consumption during a "profit economy", a brief examination of gift giving is in order, as the early collections of luxury goods and gift giving are entwined.

Travel Accounts, Letters and Gifts

Even though Marco Polo belonged to a trading family, his descriptions are also devoted to gifts. In his description of the court of the Mongols in China, the Venetian traveler Marco Polo wrote that the Mongol Great Han received gifts of more than 10,000 white horses of great beauty and price. He also describes that on the same day there was a procession of the Han's elephants, 5,000 of them all draped in fine cloths embroidered with decorations of beasts and birds. According to Polo, each one of these elephants bore on its back two strong boxes filled with the Han's plates and apparel for his white-robed court. Following the elephants came innumerable camels draped with cloths and laden with provisions for a courtly feast. Marco Polo described how the Han had organized thirteen feasts, one for each of the thirteen lunar months, attended by 12,000 barons who were his dependants. Polo continues to describe the treasures of the Han, such as gold belts and shoes of fine leather and precious embroidered robes. Starting with Polo's travel account, Asia became the site of luxury in Europe's imagination. Whether it was for gift giving or for trade, European merchants undertook long journeys to reach the objects, textiles and gems that would be displayed by the European elites.[3]

The port of Ayas in Little Armenia was Marco Polo's port of departure and the hub of Mediterranean maritime trade at a time when the Mediterranean dominated the Oriental goods trade to Europe. If the fifteenth century marked a turning point as the discovery of the Americas permitted global exchanges for the first time, this exchange had longer Eurasian antecedents that prompted Columbus's departure. When Columbus set out to find the road to India and China's riches and accidentally "discovered" the Americas, the book he had read was Marco Polo's thirteenth-century travels to China. A merchant by profession, Polo was made famous by his travel narrative to China. Few knew of a thriving community of Italian traders, merchants much like the Polo brothers, living in China by the mid fourteenth century. A 1342 tombstone of a young child, Katarina Villionis, carved in Latin, was discovered in the early twentieth century. It suggested the existence of children in a thriving foreign merchant community. The tombstone also bore the oldest surviving image of the Virgin Mary in China. Much of China's medieval relationships with the West have been buried by centuries of scholarly neglect, making Marco Polo's example seem exceptional.[4]

In 1288, China was about to become a destination of choice for the Franciscans. Among the friars, who walked to China, the best known are Giovanni dal Pian del Carpini (c.a. 1282–1252) and Guilloume de Roubrouck (1215–1270). The accounts of their travels, Carpini's *Ystoria mongalorum* and Roubrouck's *Itinera*, are early descriptions of the Mongol realm that became the basis for illustrated compendia of travel accounts that were popular objects for wealthy collectors in the late fourteenth and early fifteenth centuries. Their firsthand accounts were circulating amongst the elite at a time when there was a diplomatic relationship between the ruling Mongol Khans in European accounts in their new capital of Beijing and the Pope in Rome. Therefore any notions of the medieval world as a closed and static society should be left behind; nevertheless until the Americas were part of the European itinerary, exchanges were simply Eurasian and not global.

An exchange of letters and gifts was an important part of diplomacy between Beijing and Rome; both sides persisted in this exchange for almost a century, even when cultural differences and languages were almost insurmountable barriers. Gifts were an important aspect of social relations among the elite and their collection was associated with status.[5] Inventories of objects collected by the popes indicate that by 1295 there were one hundred exotic items identified as *tartarico*: silk, metal work and other precious objects of Mongol or Chinese origin. European merchants were usually the companions of choice for the traveling friars on the road to Beijing because they were experienced go-betweens. The language of commerce never lent itself to the nuances of spirituality and the local interpreters and merchants in Beijing never really had any interest or capacity to fully translate papal messages. The Mongols had similar problems communicating with the Franks, as the Europeans were called. A letter from Arghun Khan dated 1285 was written "in a Latin so barbarous" that it was almost untranslatable in the Vatican. In this difficult manner of exchange, objects and gifts had exceptional power.[6]

The China unified under the Mongol Kublai Khan in 1279 had suffered more than a century of domestic turmoil, but contacts were now a priority and gifts continued to be a major aspect of these contacts. Collecting rare objects was an important symbol of status for the European elites in medieval times. The Crusades had already brought in exotic spices, sugar and expensive textiles, the last of which became the most important marker of wealth. Most expensive among them was silk, and within the silks, the most precious was gold or silver embroidered brocade. Records indicate that Chinese silk and objects became part of the European elite's collections as early as the thirteenth century.[7]

Peace after the Mongol conquest of a large part of Asia brought a new order that made these exchanges possible. In China, as in Europe, a new class of merchants, many of them foreign, became socially important. In China this was unprecedented and eliminated much of the power of the Chinese elite as the Mongols extended patronage to foreigners. The Chinese Song aristocracy had settled in the city of Hangzhou, which had become the artistic center of China. Kublai Khan overran the city of Hangzhou and abolished the traditional Confucian based rules of advancement within the government. He promoted foreigners or Mongols rather than the native Chinese. One of the first official acts of Kublai Khan after the fall of Hangzhou was to remove the imperial library, move it to his imperial capital of Beijing, and open it to viewing by artists. This imperial library was the repository of many objects of China's long and rich cultural past; it contained writings, scrolls and antique paintings by venerated masters. Even if many artists withdrew from public life under the Mongols, as it has been argued, others accepted official positions at the library and the tradition of producing paintings and precious scrolls continued, as they were then allowed to draw inspiration from the finest examples of China's past. A major change under Mongol rule was key: there were crowds of *nouveau riche* pouring into the new capital of Beijing to become patrons of the arts. This new elite was consuming the highest form of luxury goods: art objects. Under the Song dynasty, only imperial patronage had flourished but now a new artistic school burgeoned as merchants, foreign traders and city dwellers became patrons of the arts and profited from the new trading policies of the Mongols.[8] Merchants had been very low in the social hierarchy of Chinese society but the new international trade, facilitated by the *pax Mongolia*, transformed the previous social hierarchy.

The study of the history of consumption examines the habits of this rising elite, composed of both wealthy merchants and well-established aristocrats, that was new to both China and Europe. The rise of merchants in international trade was at the basis of the creation of a "profit economy". However, travel and cross-cultural contact were facilitated by this new world of exchange, although at first exchanges, mainly gifts, remained rare by modern standards. When Rabban Sauma, a Nestorian Christian envoy of the Arghun, arrived in Rome in 1287, he brought princely gifts for the Pope. After a journey of thirteen years, he arrived to the unfortunate news that Pope Honorius IV had just died and no successor had been chosen.[9] After a long wait, Rabban Sauma's diplomatic contact was Pope Nicholas IV who belonged to the Franciscan order. The new Pope was trained in Assisi, had diplomatic skills and a gift for languages. Nicholas IV had a taste for glowing mosaics and rich liturgical fittings that probably came from his sojourn in the rich Byzantine capital of Constantinople in the 1270s. Nicholas IV was to initiate a strong tradition of travel for his order; he sent missionaries to the Bulgarians, Ethiopians, Tatars, Chinese and Mongols.[10]

Travel was rarer in the other direction. The itinerary of Rabban Sauma from Beijing, the new Mongol capital, was daunting considering that he was a monk in his mid sixties when Arghun, Kublai Khan's great nephew, ordered him to take the long journey to Rome. We know that Pope Nicholas IV sent Rabban Sauma home to Beijing richly laden with gifts and relics. Pope Nicholas's generosity was legendary within his own order but the exact nature of Rabban Saumas's reciprocal gifts can only be guessed. Inventories taken over the following years, after the visit of 1287, document the wealth of luxury items from Mongol-dominated China in the treasury of the Vatican and at Assisi. The first comprehensive inventory of papal treasures in 1295 had an entire rubric devoted to cloth from Tartary, *nasij*. *Nasij* is a brocaded silk embroidered with gold thread. This was a luxury item desired by the Mongols for both wearing and gift giving, so much so that they enslaved whole villages of Muslim weavers deported to northern China to produce this fine fabric. In Assisi the most important piece, a cloth to drape around the high altar, a *dossale*, was a spectacular piece of embroidered scarlet silk over twenty feet long. Lauren Arnold speculates that the silk *dossale* might have been one of the gifts brought to Rome by Rabban Sauma.[11] Precious oriental objects and textiles such as the *dossale* spoke to a vibrant medieval inter-change of luxury goods, but collection of these exotic luxury items remained only possible for the very top of the elite within this traditional "gift economy".[12]

Sartorial Splendor and Social Rank in the Sixteenth Century

Even if Thorstein Veblen used the term "conspicuous consumption" for the nineteenth century, it has been argued that consumption to display rank was already a familiar habit for the wealthy during the Renaissance. The self-promoting and propaganda value of appearance was not lost on the European elites. Some chose to dress to impress to enlarge their prestige. The influence of a royal house or lord was reflected not only by the clothing of the ruler but that of his retinue, who often wore the colors of the house in a livery. Initially because of sumptuary laws, silks and brocades were reserved in many societies for the nobility and for the high-ranking ecclesiastics. The merchant families in the Italian cities of Florence and Venice would be influential in having their merchant class participate in this forbidden sartorial splendor through wealth alone. The Medici, who eventually became bankers, had been involved in the cloth trade. Most of the heavy state dresses worn by Europe's princes and lords were of exotic brocade, velvet and silk. They were trimmed with gold, silver and precious stones and could be obtained by the courts of Europe only through imports. Giorgio Riello argues that fashion in the Italian cities was greatly influenced by contact with these imports.[13]

The Ottoman markets were crucial to these imports. Silk was a major import during this period. Silk cloth was the central commodity consumed by elites in all of Eurasia. It was not this high quality cloth reserved for the elite that made the greatest share of the total European cloth trade. Ordinary cloth, broadcloth, dominated in terms of commercial value. Broadcloth was consumed by a larger group of people, mostly in Northern Europe. At this time, the production of broadcloth had been perfected in Flanders and England so that the buyer could have a reasonable idea of what quality to expect. These advantages helped to bring about the usage of imported broadcloths from places as far north as medieval and early modern Sweden by both the clergy and the military. Mercenaries have a traditional claim to be supplied with broadcloth because there were important considerations involved in the provision of their parade dress. Imports were not reserved to the elites. The lower orders of society also demanded textiles that could not be supplied locally. In Russia, in the fifteenth to seventeenth centuries, only the upper class, the *boyars* and the rich merchants were consumers of Flemish or English broadcloth while the lower classes used cheaper cloth imported from Bohemia. During the sixteenth century, the Italian cities and Flanders held dominance in cloth production, although that dominance would shift to northwestern Europe in the seventeenth century. Many of the finer fabrics regarded as luxury goods were imported to Europe via the Ottoman markets and came from as far as China.[14]

The rise of Italian city-states has been studied by Richard A. Goldthwaite. The city of Florence had a well-established textile industry that produced a limited quantity of silk but wool was its main early production; more than any other activity, textile production generated the city's wealth. As early as 1321, the highest sources of city taxes came from the wool guild followed by the guilds that manufactured silk and silk products. Guilds, or corporations, were an organized body of craftsmen that would have immense importance in the political life of the city-states both in the Flanders and in the Italian cities. Among the guilds, the most powerful were the craftsmen who were involved in the production of textiles. By 1587 in Florence, a report meant for the Grand Duke who ruled the city recognized the wool and silk industries as "two beautiful eyes in front of the head" of the city of Florence.[15] The organization of the political life of the city-states was run by the guilds and the idea of citizenship was based on one's affiliation to a craft or profession. Florence was an independent city-state and in 1425 the city had a population of 60,000 and was self-governed through the guilds. Twelve artist guilds that regulated the main trades were the basis not only of Florence's commercial success but of its political system. Members of the guilds held positions in government. In the many city-states that were governed by merchants, since the bourgeoisie ruled, commerce and politics went hand in hand.[16]

Consumerism and display played a large role in the rise of merchant families. Most of the silk consumed by the Florentine silk industry was imported from abroad, as raw silk was not produced anywhere near Florence even as late as the sixteenth century. The wool and silk textile industries required merchants to go far afield to find all the necessary raw materials and bring them home in order to sell finished luxury goods on international trade routes. The production processes of wool and silk from raw materials were completely different. Wool derives from sheep and silk derives from the cocoon of the silk worm. The former passed through the hands of workers with a wide range of skills while the production of silk passed more directly through the cheapest type of labor, often women and children, to highly skilled weavers. Despite fundamental differences, the two industries were organized around the same basic structures. The guild incorporated all the workers within the industry and subordinated the work force to the owners of the firms who ran the business enterprise and were the capitalist investors. There was a clear division of the workers from the investors and managers of both the trade and production of these textiles.[17]

An important market for wool and silk opened up in the Ottoman Empire's capital of Constantinople. Venetian woolen cloths, probably somewhat inferior to what was produced in Florence, were directed almost entirely to Near Eastern markets where the Venetians had a much stronger trade network. By 1560 the Venetians had largely eliminated the competition from Florence. Florence started exporting its fabrics north, chiefly to the emporium in Antwerp. These fabrics, mostly black in color, enjoyed prestige in northern markets because they were regarded as a luxury good. Florentine cloth also sold well on the Italian markets and, along with Venetian cloth, they were virtually the only products that show up in the Pope's accounts throughout the sixteenth century.[18]

The history of the development of the silk industry in northern Italy was largely centered on its diffusion from Lucca in the fourteenth century. While the diffusion of this new industry that had been imported from the Byzantine Empire was a general Italian phenomenon, the city of Florence had a head start. It is within the structures of the Florentine textile economy that a banking network would be built up by Florentine merchants. The city's wealthy merchants had the capital necessary for investment in the luxury good and had a commercial network to facilitate the transport of raw silk from the Ottoman markets. Legislation was enacted to promote sericulture, the cultivation of silk, in the countryside nearby. In 1441, the city of Florence ordered peasants to plant a minimum of five mulberry trees, the leaves of which are food for silk worms, on the land they farmed. In the fifteenth century, some wealthy individuals planted between 3,000 and 4,000 trees in two or three years on their estates.[19] Although we do not know how much silk was consumed locally, the total production figures for silk textile that exist for the period 1430–1447 show a fourfold increase from 498 to 2,002 pieces. It is not clear what was meant by a piece of silk, since this luxurious fabric varied much in length and value. According to Italian scholars, production was boosted by the increasingly rapid changes in fashion in the city-states that had never existed anywhere in Europe. This created competition among many producers who operated in an efficient international market for luxurious velvets and brocades enriched with gold and silver threads.[20]

Consumer demand from the French elite for Italian silks drove the market. In 1546, the Venetian ambassador to France remarked on the large profits of the Florentines and the Genoese from the sale of silk damasks and satins, that "they produce ... to suit the desires and taste of the French, that is, cloths that cost little and last even less, which is exactly what that nation wants, because it would get bored if a garment lasted too long".[21] By the end of the sixteenth century, to suit this new consumer demand for change, Florentine production had descended to crafting even simpler fabrics, such as plain satins and taffetas that were directed toward the lower end of the luxury market. For the first time, in reaction to the demands of a new group of less well-heeled consumers, standardized products started to appear on the market.

Consumer demand had a systemic effect as it began to shape the clothing industry itself. Standardization was a new step driven by consumer pressure. Textiles started being produced in only a few varieties that required less complex looms. This was especially true for wool but it also affected the silk cloth production. With standardization, the industry did not have to adjust its equipment or skills to meet a demand that arose from continual change in fashion. The industry also produced lower quality cloths with wool it imported from as far away as northwestern Africa. Northern Europe produced a heavier wool cloth that sold successfully. It has been argued that the production of woolens in Flanders was a precursor of "Proto-Industrialization". The Florentine wool trade could not have reduced costs by moving to cheaper labor costs in the countryside. The production of raw silk by the peasants was relatively unsuccessful and imports of raw silk remained key. The city's protectionist policies had long precluded the rise of rural industry around the city. In contrast, the search for cheaper labor in the countryside and outside the city gave new life to textile production in the north.[22]

Giorgio Riello has argued that fashion was born in the Italian cities of the fourteenth century. Patricia Allerston, in "Clothing and Early Modern Venetian Society", has argued that clothing was key to social ranking.[23] During this period, sumptuary laws regulated the use of clothing to maintain rank. The category "sumptuary laws" could be diffuse and vague. Among the ancient Romans, the *leges sumptuariae* concentrated on the regulation of dining habits and were centered on eating. Etymologically, these laws regulated expense (*sumptus*), not just expenditure, but more specifically expenditure on luxury goods. Nevertheless, Italian lawmakers also grouped other concerns under these laws that were not strictly concerned with luxury consumption at all. Loud wailing and weeping at funerals, for example, or disorderly conduct at weddings or banquets were forbidden according to sumptuary laws. This European legislation was created to deal with various manifestations of excess, such as curbing excessive displays of wealth and the consumption of luxury goods. The high frequency and fervor of sumptuary legislation in Renaissance Italy was such that historians never failed to notice them. Antonio Bonardi wrote "for the Middle Ages and for several centuries of the modern era no other historical source, in my opinion, gives a better understanding of the private life of the various social classes than the sumptuary laws".[24] These sumptuary laws provided information about clothing, fashion, interior furnishings, funerals, baptisms and wedding customs. They have served in the study of the private lives of the elites in Italian towns.

There remains a great problem for the study of sumptuary laws in Europe; while the laws themselves could be examined, the records of enforcements were rare. Therefore we know more about policy than reality. There were some records of enforcement such as in Elizabethan England where gentlemen entering the city of London had their swords measured and broken if they were too long for their status.[25] A 1562 statute addressed the making of ruffs, hosiery and the allowable length of swords and daggers and it applied penalties to hosiers, tailors and cutlers who made or sold prohibited items. In this case, it was not simply the wearer who paid the penalty, but the maker or seller. One can generally say that sumptuary legislation failed almost everywhere.[26] Whether it was in the Italian cities or in France, China or Japan the laws failed to limit luxury consumption and despite being aware of this constant failure, lawmakers continued to enact new laws.

Some historians have concluded that the impulse to legislate the consumption of luxuries was irrational and that lawmakers in fact had no real desire to see these laws succeed. Some have said that sumptuary laws led to nothing except to forbid in order to tolerate, to threaten in order to pardon; they were created in order to be abused and ridiculed and some say they were erroneous, absurd, unjust and immoral.[27] They were often class-based and reserved the fineries to the elite. It can be said that perhaps they created a form of aspiration, one that Baudrillard's work could explain theoretically: Forbidding means the absence of a desired good. For example, forbidding anyone but an aristocrat to wear pearls might have created a hope to own pearls in wealthy merchant classes. As previously mentioned, Baudrillard's work was an attempt to understand the structure of the system of possession by analyzing the passion of curiosity, the compulsion of collecting and the longings created by the absence of desired objects.[28] Aspiration to possess was key in the rise of new merchant elites, who were excluded from wearing silk or owning gems by sumptuary laws in most of Europe and in China.

It may come as no surprise that Sparta seemed to have been the earliest Western society to enact sumptuary legislation. This unfortunately un-datable law forbade women to wear jewelry, cosmetics, perfume or any dyed clothing. This legislation was so well known that Greek writers later blamed Spartan women for the creation of sumptuary legislation itself. Some wrote that in the fourth century BC women controlled two-fifths of Sparta's land and neglected their role as mothers and spouses to devote their money and time to acquiring racehorses and clothing. In Plutarch's view, the law failed because of these women's refusal to abandon their newfound luxury. Spartan women were also criticized by Aristotle, who directly blamed their love of luxury and leisure for Sparta's decline. Linking political decline to the over-consumption of luxury equated with moral degeneracy was to be echoed by political literature for centuries. During the Reformation, the Catholic Church would be attacked by Martin Luther for selling indulgences and for its love of material rewards.[29] However, brutally sacking cities during wars was customary and luxuries as booty were a social norm.

War: Religion and Consumption

The Italian city-states, especially Venice, were accustomed to collecting luxurious oriental goods, though sometimes this acquisition was through force. War booty was a traditional means of acquiring luxury goods since antiquity. Some wars are the root of major collections. Most notoriously when the Venetians underwrote the Fourth Crusade by paying for it, they recouped their expenses by sacking the richest city in the world, the Byzantine Empire's capital of Constantinople:

> Constantinople had become a veritable museum of ancient and Byzantine art, an emporium of such incredible wealth that the Latins were astounded at the riches they found. Though the Venetians had an appreciation for the art that they discovered (they were themselves semi-Byzantines) and saved much of it, the French and others destroyed indiscriminately, halting to refresh themselves with wine, violation of nuns, and murder of Orthodox clerics.[30]

In 1204, the aristocratic Doge of Venice, Enrico Dandolo, sent the horses that were long displayed at the Hippodrome of Constantinople to Venice. These precious horses would be taken by Napoleon to Paris in 1785 and returned to Venice in 1815. Since the 1990s, they have been kept in St Mark's Museum; the famous horses were only one of the many objects "collected" by Venice as war trophies.

War trophies were a means of collection, but at times acquiring new objects could help change the course of history. The fall of Constantinople to the Turks has rarely been described in material terms but rather as a power struggle between the Christian northwest and the Islamic southeast. The year 1453 was always seen as a turning point for Eurasia but the debates about it are continuous and sometimes contentious. The technical superiority of the Ottoman army was central to its conquest. In 1452, a Hungarian engineer named Urban presented the idea of a super powerful cannon to the Byzantine Emperor of Constantinople but was rejected because of the Emperor's meager financial resources. When he later presented the new super cannon to the Ottoman Sultan, Byzantium's enemy, it was enthusiastically adopted. Urban boasted that his new secret armament could blast the walls of Babylon itself. Urban was immediately given four times the salary that he had hoped to obtain and all the technical help he needed to produce it within three months. It was so heavy it had to be pulled by sixty oxen and two hundred men marched beside it. The "monster" cannon and the many weapons Urban built for the Sultan were very effective; the Byzantine capital became an Ottoman one.[31]

Nevertheless, the cannon was far from the only reason for the fall of the city. The quest for material wealth, the accumulation of luxury goods, and the collection of the rare and exotic marked the fifteenth century. In a deeply religious world where the Pope forbade trade with the "infidel", as he referred to Muslims, Christian merchants, despite many wars, continued to trade with the Ottomans in what was clearly a "profit economy". The fall of Constantinople happened in part thanks to the neutrality of well-established merchants within Constantinople. The arms race that brought about new technology was instrumental in winning the war, but in addition to Urban's super cannon, the Venetian and Genoese traders chose not to defend or aid the Greek rulers of Constantinople against the new conquerors due to their own commercial interests with the Ottomans. Lisa Jardine highlights the importance of money and wealth over religion, specifically for Christianity; "Indulgences" or papal exoneration for trading with the aggressor was "money well spent" for these international merchants. In Istanbul, an imperial *firman* allowed Italian cities the right to trade with the Ottoman Empire whilst remaining a practicing Catholic. Venetian merchants, despite their Catholicism, traded and remained neutral because they knew they could reap the financial benefits from trade between Christians, Muslims, and Jews.[32]

During the Renaissance, the Church itself entered the world of commerce. Jardine cited Cardinal Francesco Gonzaga's over-the-top spending and collecting as an example of how churchmen entered the world of commerce alongside notable politicians. Even ecclesiastics were socially admired for their material collections. The presence of oriental and oriental-influenced objects among Cardinal Gonzaga's treasures attested to the fact that, contrary to what used to be argued, the fall of Constantinople never blocked any trade routes. In 1455, the Ottoman sultan Ahmed I began to build a grand bazaar and repopulated the city with skilled artisans, many of them deported Armenians and Jews, to have and produce goods in the key luxury industries. Textiles, glassmaking, porcelain, ceramics, and copper work were among the many practices and objects that were bought by Europeans.[33] Istanbul was an international center of around 100,000 people. In the city itself only 60 percent of the population was Muslim, the rest being Armenian, Greek, Jewish and Catholic, while in the district of Galata, where many Europeans had embassies, only 35 percent of the population was Muslim.[34]

Despite the formal trade concessions given to the French by the Ottomans, the Genoese and the Venetians would also populate other cities in the Ottoman Empire with Europeans and other Christians; Istanbul nevertheless remained the major center. Merchants from Venice and Genoa started exchanging European silver for silk, cotton and other luxury goods that sometimes came all the way from India or China on the Ottoman markets.[35] Elites did not always rely on merchants. Collectors, such as Cardinal Francesco Gonzaga and his nephew the Marquis of Mantua, maintained a direct correspondence with the Ottoman sultan Bayezid II. Lisa Jardine noted that the reason for this correspondence was Gonzaga's collection of horses. The Ottoman sultan had a collection of the best Arab horses on the planet and the Gonzaga family imported them in order to breed them in Europe. Their close ties to the Ottoman court allowed them to do this. Europe's grandees had direct contact with the Ottoman court in order to collect exotic goods. Throughout his life, Cardinal Francesco Gonzaga spent lavish sums of money to acquire precious goods such as gems, tapestries, rare books and manuscripts. His probate in 1433 listed 500 gems and cameos, 272 of the gems being unset stone. His collection of tapestries alone was unmatched. His entire collection of treasures established him as a cultured man of discerning taste.[36]

The goods that were sold on the Ottoman markets came from Africa, India, China, Russia, Iran and many other faraway markets. This made the Ottoman Empire the central point of exchange for high-end consumer goods in the fifteenth, sixteenth and well into the seventeenth century, despite the rise of Atlantic maritime commerce. Wealthy customers in Venice, Genoa, Paris or Marseilles were ready to pay large sums for rare and particular goods. Many historians have argued that the collection of rare and exotic goods marked class distinction and differentiated levels of power and wealth within an elite of churchmen and wealthy merchants. Even for this early period, collection closely reflects Pierre Bourdieu's twentieth-century argument that accumulating cultural capital is a marker of class distinction.

The Medici: From Merchants to Bankers

The quest for luxury goods and exotic imports created the need for more flexible means of payment. The fifteenth century saw a development in the world of banking including bills of exchange, customs duties, levies, debts, interest payments and loans. Double entry bookkeeping became common in Europe in this period, although now it is argued that it most probably existed as a method of accounting in Asia. The feudal nature of most European societies afforded little opportunity for social climbing or change. The accumulation of merchant wealth in the fifteenth century, and some scholars even argue the fourteenth century, led to a new form of social mobility where merchants began to form a new elite. The fact that acquired wealth could compete with birth rank was a new element in both China and Europe. An opportunity for social mobility was created through wealth thanks to the world of international commerce and finance. Merchants and bankers became the new elite with the rise of the bank.

At the start of the fifteenth century, a Florentine merchant family by the name of Medici became Europe's greatest banking dynasty. Their wealth came from one of the textile guilds, the wool trade, the *Arte Della Lana*. The Medici became dukes of Florence through their fortune. The Medici Bank (1397–1494) was a financial institution that became the largest bank in Europe.[37] As the wealthiest family in Europe, the Medici family later included four popes and two regent queens of France. Niall Ferguson has described the Medici's secret book of accounts, a book where money lending was recorded. He argues that decentralization of their lending and reaching out internationally was the key to their rise.[38] The Medici's role as leading bankers was soon usurped by the German Fugger family. The papacy was central to both fortunes. Like the Medici, the Fuggers amassed vast wealth by managing the finances of the papacy and of great princes. The Fuggers made their first loan to a Habsburg archduke in 1487, taking as security an interest in silver and copper mines in the Tirol. This initiated extensive family involvement in mining silver and copper. In 1491 a loan was made to the Holy Roman Emperor Maximilian. If defaulted, the loan could open the door to political might for the Fuggers. The loan was secured by the feudal rights to two Austrian counties. Far more notorious was the Fugger project that was undertaken in 1519 on behalf of Emperor Maximilian's grandson, Charles V.

The Habsburgs had led Europe for generations as emperors, but Charles V would have a well-known rival, France's Francis I, who fought and hoped to be elected as Holy Roman Emperor of Europe in his stead. This political rivalry ironically led to an unusual alliance and a commercial contact with the Ottomans that made France an important importer of exotic luxury goods in Europe. France's first diplomatic contact with a Muslim potentate after the Crusades was codified by a treaty between Francis I and Suleiman the Magnificent, the most renowned of all the sultans of the Ottoman Empire. To the horror of all of Catholic Europe, and despite papal bans on trade and contact with the "infidel", the Ottomans became the allies of the French king.[39] Many ties existed between France and the Ottomans before the treaty of 1535 and the capitulation that opened Ottoman markets to French trade. At first, the contacts were informal and secret. In 1526 Louise de Savoie, Francis I's mother, sent a letter to the Ottoman Sultan asking for help. Her son was a prisoner of Charles V in Spain because two monarchs were tied in a struggle over supremacy over Europe and title of Emperor. Sultan Suleiman responded to the secret letter. His response remained in the archives of the *Bibliothèque nationale*, and it diplomatically stated: "It is not unusual for Emperors to be defeated and imprisoned, do not lose your courage."[40] This form of long-distance recognition (albeit non-committal) from the powerful Sultan notwith-standing, a decade later, Francis was still not the Holy Roman Emperor of Europe but was Charles V's prisoner. Yet, King Francis I had accomplished an important feat by being granted unprecedented commercial concessions by the Ottomans. France prepared her first formal embassy to the most powerful empire in the world and was granted a formal presence in the capital of Istanbul even before the powerful merchants of Venice.[41]

What was never made public about Francis I's defeat was the fact that bankers were behind Charles V's election. Charles V borrowed from the Fugger family for his election expenses. Out of a huge amount of money spent on bribing seven electors, Jacob Fugger provided nearly two-thirds, or half a million Rhenish gold gulden.[42] By the time Charles V was elected, banking was becoming important in France, Germany and the Italian cities. Interest rates at the time were never less than 12 percent per annum and the Fuggers expected a return of 12.5 percent on the money advanced.[43] Loans were often for wars. War and politics were closely tied to this form of financing. Charles V granted the Fuggers his protection on the monopoly of mining silver and copper. His demands for money were continuous and there was no repayment of his debt. In a famous letter from Jacob Fugger to Charles V, the banker reminded Charles V of his debt:

> It is also well known that Your Majesty without me might not have acquired the Imperial Crown, as I can attest with the written statement of all the delegates of Your Imperial Majesty. And in all this I have looked not to my own profit. For if I had withdrawn my support from the House of Austria, and transferred it to France, I should have won large profit and much money.[44]

The bankers therefore became, in a sense, not only managers of state assets but also revenue collectors. In 1525 the Fuggers were granted the revenues from the Spanish orders of knighthood, together with the profits from mer-cury and silver mines. By the end of the sixteenth century the Fuggers eschewed risk-taking, as did the Medici before them, and used their wealth to lead an aristocratic existence that their wealth had bought them. If getting rich from political struggles and war seemed modern, it was. The birth of the modern bank lay in the power struggles of the early Renaissance but a more peaceful business was also at the root of the banking industry. The printing press would bring about a small revolution in the world of consumption as it demanded a new business system.

Books as the First Mass-produced Objects

Even if manuscripts were still avidly collected by the sixteenth century, there were between 500 and 1,000 printing presses at work in France alone and paper manufacturers had to supply anywhere between 1,500 and 3,000 reams of paper a day to keep them in production. Printers had prominent patrons: the best-known case was Philippe II's sponsorship of the famous printers Christophe Plantin and Jan Moretus in Antwerp, who produced print runs of between 1,250 to 1,500 copies.[45] Beyond patronage, a new system of financing came into being with the printed book. The complex financing behind book production played an important role that helped launch banking.[46] Printed books became history's first mass produced object because each copy was exactly the same. Raymond de Roover has argued that early printing faced market and financial problems not unlike industries today; it needed to attract capital. To commit oneself to a print run meant putting up substantial money in advance, which could only be retrieved after the book was sold.[47] The comparative speed and efficiency of the production of the typeset book meant that new material could be made available to the reading public much more rapidly than manuscripts and distributed to diverse locations. Unlike woodblock printing, which had existed since the ninth century in China and had been transferred to Europe, typeset was a much faster and more precise printing technique. It produced clear and accurate editions. Scholars and intellectuals were often closely associated with successful printing houses. But the printing of books took far more financing than any printer, university, king or even the Church could afford. Universities and churches sometimes sponsored a book, but books with a new and wider circulation demanded serious capital. In terms of overall cost to the customer, the acquisition of a text was comparatively modest compared to the outrageous prices that manuscripts had commanded. Nevertheless they were not accessible to the masses and collecting books demanded a certain income. The production of printed books remained expensive, not so much because of the equipment, but because of the price of the paper on which texts were printed. Paper costs represented two-thirds of the total cost of book production.[48]

As printing became a profitable commercial undertaking, with an established fair at Frankfurt to promote printed books, printing houses began to draw upon different expertise on the part of their employees.[49] Lisa Jardine argued that by the early sixteenth century "books were bought and sold as freely … as loaves of bread".[50] This may be an exaggeration as the price of books, despite the fact that they were below those of manuscripts, remained much higher than bread, but the remark is valid for the change of pace. With the rapid expansion of printing in Europe, there was scarcely an important town in Italy, France, Germany or the Low Countries that did not have its own press since the fifteenth century. For a slightly later period, the same was true of Portugal, Spain and Poland. Only in England was the printing trade artificially confined by law to the city of London. Once famous printers such as Gutenberg, Fust and Schoeffer had perfected printing in their workshops in the city of Mainz, they had hoped to maintain a monopoly over the new technique. Yet too many inventors had for some years been seeking to learn the craft for it to remain the monopoly of a few experts.

According to Lucien Febvre there is a story that the King of France sent a spy to Mainz in 1458. The printers had a legal monopoly for ten years; yet, a Bible was printed in Strasbourg as early as 1459. A small group of apprentices actively broke any possible monopoly. With a great spirit of adventure and enterprise, not to mention personal risk, they left their masters' shops and traveled throughout Europe carrying their heavy equipment with them to instruct others in this new art. They led difficult nomadic lives. They stopped in a town and hoped for orders locally. What they sought was someone to provide capital so that they could establish themselves permanently. The prime factor in the spread of the printing press was the interest of certain influential men and institutions. Individual patrons would sometimes invest in the production of as many as a dozen books. Churchmen, particularly those interested in classical literature, took the lead in supporting the printing press. In 1466, Cardinal Torquemada, the prominent leader of the Holy Inquisition, invited a printer to Rome and entrusted him with the printing of *Meditationes*. Numerous monasteries also supported printers and invited them to their sites.[51]

By the close of the fifteenth century, about fifty years after printing had begun, 35,000 editions had been produced amounting to at least fifteen or twenty million books. In fifty years, no fewer than 236 towns had their own printing presses.[52] The printed book, cheaper but still collectible, became the first mass-produced object in history bought by European elites. The fact that people wished to take a book with them helped develop the growing success of a portable format, which also dates to the first half of the sixteenth century. The Elzeviers, famous printers, adopted the small format to keep their presses going. In addition to the clergy, to students, and to the upper classes, the bourgeoisie began to form their own private libraries. Famous painters such as Holbein were commissioned by Basel publishers to illustrate popular books for this merchant class such as the story of the Old and New Testament or the *Metamorphoses* of Ovid. Many new centers of book production developed during the life of Luther, during the early years of the Reformation. Publishing books in the vernacular languages rather than Latin was one of the consequences of Luther's doctrines. Trying to contain the powerful effects of the Reformation through printed books, the Kings of England intervened and stopped the trade in books between England and the continent.[53]

Censorship was an important element in the Renaissance book trade. For example, during the reign of Francis I the Paris University, the Sorbonne, went through several crises. The professors were theologians who participated in the religious debates of the time. First came the chaining of the books of William of Occam and other nominalists; chaining books to the walls of the libraries was a procedure routinely followed at the time so that the books could no longer be opened and taken from the shelves to be read. In the process of condemning Occam, scholasticism and its use of Aristotle was imposed as a doctrine in the university; however, there were several factions among the professors. Once Aristotle was imposed, the nominalist faction got the upper hand in 1481 and it was Aristotle's writings that were chained in the university library. The university was deeply divided and the quarrels were so intense that the Parliament of Paris, who had never had any power of censorship, had to intervene. In interfering in these quarrels, the Parliament of Paris modified the university's bylaws and took the authority of censorship in its own hands. This intervention tied the King, the Church, the city and the university in a power struggle over censorship. Just as the Reformation was about to divide all of Europe in 1522, and the Pope created a list of forbidden texts, the King of France had the upper hand over the Parliament of Paris and the Sorbonne. Royal censorship over knowledge was born; it effectively took away the power of the intellectual doctors of the Sorbonne over book production.[54] The rise of Protestantism changed the papacy's attitude towards books. The popularity of Martin Luther's writings led to the creation of the first catalogue of banned books in 1522, called the Index. A first formal version of the Index appeared in 1557–1559 and was published in 1563. Censorship would not cease to torment those striving for new knowledge and hoping for vernacular translations in a world still dominated by Latin learning. Forbidden books continued to have a black market and be collected by scholars.[55]

Beyond religious quarrels in Europe, the book was a powerful tool of propaganda. In their African and Asian territories, Portuguese traders quickly understood the importance of printing for religious propaganda purposes. There is much to be learned from the fact that while the first book printed in Russia was dated 1563, the first book in Constantinople 1727, and the first in Greece 1821, a printing press was imported into Abyssinia by the Portuguese as early as 1515. Portuguese presses were operating in Goa by 1557, in Macao by 1588, and in Nagasaki, Japan by 1590. The first exotic types to be cast in Europe were made in Lisbon in 1539 for the historian Juan de Barros, who intended to use them for books to teach children to read in Ethiopia, Persia and India. The King of Portugal made it a policy to send Portuguese books abroad. In 1490, when a Portuguese expedition was sent to the Congo, he not only sent books but also dispatched two German printers.[56] When the Portuguese arrived in China in 1513, they found a highly developed printing process that had been in place for centuries: xylography, a form of printing from woodcuts. The earliest dated printed book known is the *Diamond Sutra*, printed in China in 868 CE. However, scholars speculate that book printing may have occurred long before this date.

China was a country where scholars had a uniquely influential role. The most ancient written records indicate that the printed book was in existence in China as early as the Chang Dynasty (1765–1123 BC). Printing was done on fragments of bones and on the scales of tortoise shells. Some 2,500 different characters have been deciphered as the ancestors of the 800 characters used today. A book that we today would recognize as a book in its most ancient form was made of wooden or bamboo tablets inscribed vertically with a pointed stylus dipped in varnish. The book was bound and held together by leather thongs or silk cords. Confucius used this type of book to study the *i-Ching*. The most ancient of such Chinese books were excavated at the beginning of the twentieth century in the desert of central Asia. They are official documents relating to the Chinese garrisons guarding the silk route.[57] The arrival of European merchants and explorers in China, Africa and the Americas gave rise to a new secular literature that recorded the customs, traditions and the landscape they encountered.

Travel Accounts and Atlases

The late fifteenth century saw the rise of the travel account, which was very often a secular description of the world. Daphne Vanessa Taylor-Garcia explores the relationship between early colonial print culture and exploration of the Spanish and Portuguese "discoveries" of sea routes to southern Africa, the Americas and India.[58] The sixteenth century saw the printing of the first world atlas, *Theatrum Orbis Terrarum* (Theatre of the World). It was based on an early eight-leaved map printed by the same cartographer and geographer, Abraham Ortelius, considered the father of the first world map. The first modern atlas was printed in Antwerp in 1570 and consisted of fifty-three maps. It was not a completely accurate map of the world, for example South America had a very faulty outline, but it was soon corrected in the 1587 French edition of the atlas. In 1573 Ortelius published seventeen supplementary maps to the atlas. His atlas and the seventeen additional maps were popular collectors' items with extremely high prices. Although the first edition of Ortelius's atlas had Latin text on verso maps, later editions had texts in French and Dutch according to the audience for which they were intended; Latin remained the common language of academia. These popular or vernacular texts were aimed at affluent merchants, administrators and aristocrats, and were not only among the most expensive but also among the most popular of the sixteenth century.[59] The printing of the maps of renowned cartographer Abraham Ortelius was perhaps the clearest case of a tie between European exploration and the production of best-selling books. The long print runs of books, including this atlas of expensive maps, show that the book trade was guaranteed to produce a large profit over a period of time.[60] Books were among the first objects collected in large quantity, but rather than quench people's love for goods, their descriptions encouraged the quest for the exotic. Imagining far away riches played a large part in exploration and the quest for goods.

The New World Imagined

Imagining the world was as important as its real representation. In the 1480s, merchants from Bristol made a number of attempts to locate the "Island of

Brasil". The merchants of Bristol were not alone in imagining the riches of Brazil. In the middle of the sixteenth century, Brazil was reconstructed in the city of Rouen in France for King Henry II. The royal entry into the city of Rouen was an entry into the city of Brazil. Among the spectacles greeting him, the King found an entire Brazilian village complete with its "savage" residents. In Rouen's burg of Saint Sever, a neighborhood inhabited by wealthy cloth merchants, most of this imagery came from the real familiarity of the merchants of Normandy with Brazil. They had traded in Brazil wood well before this royal ceremony took place. Wood played a large role in this early exploration; Europe built cities and had deforested so rapidly that it needed to import wood by the fifteenth century. New World and Old World were often imagined as one in this early age of exploration when the Americas, yet to be named, were only seen as a route to the riches of India or Cathay.[61]

The most famous of all explorers, Christopher Columbus based some of his knowledge of the world on earlier travel accounts; a copy of Marco Polo's manuscript travels annotated by Columbus's hand showed him the way to gold and spices. It was in order to reach Marco Polo's Cathay that Columbus's proposal to reach the Indies by sailing westward received the support of the Spanish Crown that saw in it a promise of gaining over rival powers in the contest for the lucrative spice trade with Asia. Spices such as cinnamon, cassia, cardamom, ginger and turmeric were known and used in Asia; they had made their way to Europe since the Roman Empire. In 1492 the Spanish Crown gave funds to a Genoese pilot, Christopher Columbus, and made him the leader of Spain's first expedition to find a new route to India. The first European power that set out to explore the routes of the riches of India was Portugal. The spice that would form the basis of Portugal's wealth was black pepper; the other aspect of their trade, acquiring African slaves to send to the Americas, was prosperous for even longer. They started to finance ventures to start trading with the west coast of Africa as early as 1420 in search of gold. What was to be called the gold coast of Africa by the Portuguese would soon become the slave coast of Africa, as the trade for gold was replaced with the trade for human beings. The Portuguese empire grew when they "discovered" the Azores, Madeira and the Canaries by 1432. They reached Cape Verde by 1444 and by the 1460s they had established themselves in Sierra Leone and the Guinea coast in Africa. They held their monopoly on trade by creating the idea of licensing the sea and issuing taxes, the *cartazes*. All other ships had to pay for passage. In the fifteenth century, the value of gold was considered reliably fixed while the value of silver bullion fluctuated. The quest for gold with the hope to hoard it in one state's reserves was the incentive behind many voyages of exploration, most famously Christopher Columbus's. This hoarding, called bullionism, was a mercantile policy in Spain and Portugal, yet the fervent hope for the acquisition of silver and gold from the Americas was not an immediate success. The apparent failure of states and formal companies has hidden the success of the dispersed merchants acting in the Atlantic diaspora as the Portuguese nation. Individual merchants abroad created a vast and very successful network whose commercial success contrasted deeply with the decline of the Spanish economic system. The merchant houses that participated in this success were decentralized quasi-autonomous units.[62]

In quest of gold and silver, Portugal spearheaded exploration for new routes to Asia; Columbus's failure to discover a passage to the riches of the East would be erased by Vasco de Gama's arrival in India in 1497. Until then, the King of Portugal had relied on obtaining Sudanese gold via Arab middlemen in North Africa. John II of Portugal also funded the voyage of Bartolomeu Dias around the Cape of Good Hope in 1488.[63] The Portuguese kings, King John II and King Manuel, funded major expeditions to capitalize on Vasco de Gama's contacts with Indian merchants. He also hired Pedro Alvarez Cabral who ran off course, as Columbus had done before him, and accidentally "discovered" the west coast of Brazil. On 8 July 1497 Vasco de Gama led a fleet of four ships with a crew of 170 men from the capital port of Lisbon. The distance traveled in the journey around Africa to India and back was greater than around the equator.

Eight decades after Columbus, a now-forgotten Spanish explorer Miguel López de Legazpi (1502–1572) succeeded where Columbus had failed. He sailed west from Mexico to establish continual trade with China and started a new global circuit of silver that would dominate the next two centuries. In Manila, a city called Legazpi was founded. Silver mined from the Americas by Indian and African slaves was sent to China in return for silk for the European market. Manila became the first market where goods and people from every corner of the globe were connected in a single worldwide exchange. Surprisingly, royal edicts restricted the number of galleon ships allowed to travel to Manila. They set import quotas for Chinese goods and ordered the Spanish merchants to form a cartel to raise prices. Charles Mann has argued that if Columbus created a new world biologically, Legazpi and the Spanish empire he served as Governor General of the Spanish East Indies created a new world economically. Both Charles Mann and the historian Andre Gunder Frank argue that this exchange of silk for silver allowed the rise of Europe as the ruling economy of the world.[64]

Next to silk and silver in economic importance came the spices. Black pepper (*piper nigrum*) is native to India and sits with salt on most of the world's tables today, but it was a rare luxury good in the fifteenth century. The Portuguese would create pepper plantations outside of its native India, where it had been used as a spice since prehistoric times. After the medieval period where the Crusaders brought it back from the Levant markets, virtually all of the black pepper found in Europe, the Middle East and North Africa was imported exclusively by the Portuguese from India's Malabar region. By the sixteenth century, due to the Portuguese conquests, pepper was also being grown in Java, Sunda, Sumatra, Madagascar, Malaysia and elsewhere in Southeast Asia, although these areas traded mainly with China or used the pepper locally.[65] When the Portuguese reached India and brought their king exotic lavish gifts to obtain trade privileges, Portuguese success created intense commercial pressure to bypass the use of Ottoman middlemen for the purchase of luxury goods.[66]

The Portuguese aim to establish direct maritime trade and avoid the Ottomans was not successful. Even decades later, France was still adamant to establish close contacts with Ottoman merchants. The first formal French embassy consisted of twelve men sent to Constantinople, among them Guillaume Postel.[67] Guillaume Postel was thus sent away from Paris in 1536 in the suite of the first ambassador, Jean de la Forêt. He was not sent as a translator since he did not yet know any Turkish, but as someone who was to protect France's new commercial interests acquired through the concessions of 1535. The collection of books was the embassy's main mission for the French king. Postel's mission was to gather rare manuscripts for the royal library at Fontainebleau, which the king had opened to scholars and alchemists.[68]

An Alchemist's Promise

Science had a role in consumerism; it offered another quest for gold and silver. Medicine, religion and alchemy were important areas of book collecting. The tie between alchemy and consumption may seem surprising, but alchemists sold contractual promises to produce, jewels, gold, silver and even ripe fruit. Recently, several historians have done excellent work on the philosophical and spiritual aspects of alchemy. They have demonstrated that not only did European political elites view alchemy as possible, but as a central idea within their world view. Historians have been key to reevaluating alchemy's original marginality to Early Modern European culture and to appreciating its centrality in both scholarly and commercial culture. Tara E. Nummedal argues that to understand the relationship between alchemy and commerce, one must first grasp the practice of alchemy and its deep relationship to markets and to the world of goods.[69] She has found that both patrons and practitioners found a great deal of alchemical knowledge for sale in the sixteenth century. In bookstalls, novices could find literature by both Islamic and Christian practitioners of alchemy as well as by a modern alchemist such as Paracelsus (1493–1541). It may come as a shock to the modern reader that an educated elite could believe that an alchemist could make silver or gold out of mercury but Nummedal has found numerous contracts between alchemists and wealthy patrons in which a specific alchemist promised to produce a certain amount of silver and was paid regular wages in order to succeed. A well-known mint official and technical author by the name of Lazar Ercker wrote to a duke promoting himself and the potential profits his art could offer. Ercker described his alchemical skills by promising that by using a powder, he could bring low quality gold in a few days to the proper ducat high quality gold, which was worth twice as much. He promoted the efficiency of his process by highlighting that the silver byproduct of his process could be melted out of the powder again. Ercker emphasized the profits that his chemical process would generate for the duke. To support his claims, he cited his results after minting coins for a famous merchant from Nuremburg. Tara Nummedal uses Ercker's pledge to suggest the practical aspects of alchemy and its marketing. When alchemists did win the support of patrons, they set down their terms of employ in businesslike contracts. These legally binding documents stipulated in great detail the type of processes the alchemist was to carry out, the deadline for completion, as well as the patron's fees and the facilities and the materials provided. These contracts were often limited to the performance of a single specific process.

Alchemy had wider applications. The entire laundry list of practices is examined by Nummedal as it appears in a 1597 text. It seems to lump together medicine, metallurgy and the production of jewels. Practical alchemy was by no means limited to the production of gold and silver. A female alchemist by the name of Anna Zieglerin (1556–1575) extended alchemy not only to the generation of metals and gems, but to animals and vegetables. In a book she published for her patron in 1573, she described a method to obtain cherries and grapes that could be ripe in early winter. Zieglerin also recommended that women having trouble getting pregnant drink an alchemical mixture daily. Just as metals like gold could be used to cure humans, she advocated that babies, once born, should taste no mother's milk and should thrive on the same tincture that made noble metals out of base metals. This form of knowledge was considered productive knowledge as it was involved in the production of *things*. Important patrons were willing to pay for their skills.[70]

To understand the central role of alchemy, Nummedal asks why important princes devoted substantial resources to alchemical projects. She cites several historians who have convincingly argued that alchemy offered solutions to their political and religious problems. The alchemical view of nature posited a united, single, divine order that connected the natural and human worlds. As such alchemists sought not only the regeneration of metals but also the moral and spiritual rebirth of mankind through knowledge. The idea of a single divine order held particular promise as Europe was divided by the religious wars following the Reformation. There were, however, more practical concerns. The newly fashionable chemical drugs wanted by Paracelsus and his followers promised material medical cures in a world that still believed in Galenic medicine. As their doctors were still offering the cures offered by Galen of Pergamon (AD 129–c. 200/ c. 216) in Rome, such as purging and bleeding, few Renaissance princes could have turned down the pearls and gemstones some alchemists offered, let alone one of Zieglerin's miraculously ripe winter fruits.[71] Diet and nutrition were the basis of medicine. It was the legacy of a more frugal society, that of ancient Rome, but Renaissance princes were happy to delight in wonders such as ripe fruit in winter and alchemy's production of goods.

Some European princes saw clear economic reasons for the practice of alchemy, as they understood it as a solution to the financial and mining crises that hit Europe in the second half of the sixteenth century. New technology and financial investment had increased silver production in central Europe fivefold between 1460 and 1550. This growth leveled off in the second part of the sixteenth century as the balance shifted towards imported American silver. Silver imports to Europe increased more than thirty-fold in more than sixty years, surging from 86 metric tons in the 1530s to 1,118 in the 1570s, to 2,707 tons in the 1590s.[72] For several princes, practical alchemy was intimately tied to the pursuit of profits through mining. Alchemists assisted princes whose mined ore was difficult to smelt but they also promised either to multiply the existing metals mined or to turn these metals into better quality ones. This was primarily a utilitarian use of alchemy but one that had many patrons hoping for unusually spectacular results. Alchemists' participation in the world of commerce and their claims to produce goods did not go unnoticed. Critics of alchemy expressed doubts about the creation of the wealth it promised. Alchemists themselves were divided as the sixteenth century came to a close. The alchemical community was split between practitioners who believed that alchemy's objective should be the production of profit and those who pursued alchemy as a spiritual act with a potential of regeneration of the world itself. Some alchemists believed that their true purpose was to use the philosopher's stone to heal bodies "human, animal and metallic" of the worldly corruption that ensued after the fall of Adam and Eve.[73] Among those proponents of spiritual healing, it was believed that alchemy dealt with God's greatest secrets. This belief created sharp disapproval of those with a pursuit of profit and worldly goods.[74]

Cabinets of Curiosity

In the cultural world of sixteenth-century Europe, the intersection of art, nature, science and economics came together under the phenomenon of the cabinet of curiosities or as they were called in German, *Kunst-* and *Wunder-kammern*. These cabinets were used to display private collections but Mark A. Meadow has argued that they served many functions, such as pragmatic tools of economic statecraft, repositories of ready funds, sites of cultural production and practical laboratories for a variety of disciplines.[75] The extraordinarily wealthy families of Europe, usually merchant banking families such as the Fuggers, the Medici or the Welsers, played a key role in importing exotic materials to their own courts. One of the most famous collectors of rare objects was Hans Jacob Fugger (1516–75) who is argued to have played a key role in the conceptual formation of the *Wunderkammer*, or cabinets. Fugger's office in Antwerp was making contracts in 1548 to exchange 6,750 hundred-weight of brass rings against large shipments of ivory from Benin, in Africa; the ivory was to be crafted into fine objects. Max Fugger in the 1560s was active in procuring exotic gemstones, finished necklaces and other pieces of jewelry for Albrecht V and for King Phillip II of Spain. In the latter part of the sixteenth century, Antwerp was the key commercial town through which the house of Fugger imported monkeys, parrots, peacocks, wildcats, as well as orange trees, almond trees, rosemary bushes and other live plants. The other goods they collected through Antwerp were pearls, camphor, leopard skins, indigo, a variety of gemstones, and other precious goods. These last examples all fall under the category of *naturalia* and many were also kept in the collection of the Fuggers themselves. They not only supplied monarchs but also sent rare objects to merchant scholars such as Philipp Hainhofer who relied on them to obtain South American objects to create his own *Kunstkammern*. Mark Meadow argues that the question of how the Fuggers contributed to the procurement of exotica for these famous collections is not a trivial one. He argues that the Fuggers and their representatives were critical participants in the live histories of these objects. Their collecting brought them close to humanists, scholars trained at the finest universities of Europe as well as making them the intimates of dukes and kings. In the sixteenth century collecting was a communal activity. Princes, scholars, merchants and apothecaries assembled collections through a complex network of exchanges, gift giving and other forms of social networking. Lorain Datson and Ken Arnold have both stressed the importance of travel in relation to the formation of curiosity cabinets.[76] Datson has not only argued that the voyages of exploration and the newly discovered lands created a steady flow of exotica, but has also pointed to the fact that the formation of these cabinets of curiosities created occasion for travel across Europe. Inspecting them in Amsterdam, Oxford, Venice, Paris, Augsburg, Uppsala and Bologna created a group of peripatetic scholars. Mark Meadow adds the dimension of commercial trade to this argument.

Mark Meadow cites Hans Jacob Fugger as an excellent example of a single individual who brought together the world of the university, the courts and commerce. Fugger was himself a patron, a scholar and collector. During a financial reversal, he even worked as a librarian and procurer of books and rare objects to one of the very earliest collections, that of Albrecht V, elector of Bavaria. The organizational plan of Albrecht V's collection is the earliest known treatise on museum. Hans Jacob Fugger was also a historian, drafting a history of his own family and one of the Habsburgs in 1555. This form of genealogical history was itself a sort of collection, containing scores of portraits, images of places and monuments. At the time, collecting medals and medallions was also very significant. The earliest wonder cabinets were neither collections of art nor of curiosities, although they were present. But one should think of them as treasuries, as they contained gold and silver work, gems and jewelry, and religious reliquaries. Many of these objects could raise ready cash. To avoid the sale of certain objects, some collectors wrote stipulations making the objects inalienable property, never to be sold by their descendants; Albrecht V's two narwhal tusks are a great example. By and large, European collections continued to emphasize monetarily valuable objects, most of them acquired through mercantile houses such as the Fuggers. These objects moved in and out of the collections, both to generate cash and to cement relationships with other princes and scholars. They also were repositories for intellectual capital, functioning in a way not dissimilar to universities and their collections.[77] Perhaps one of the most famous of such collections is still housed today at the University of Bologna. It was assembled by a scholar named Ulisse Aldrovandi.

Ulisse Aldrovandi

The collection of rare manuscripts and books was not the only way that a desire for the exotic was satisfied. The possessors of unique and exotic objects became noted as authorities among an elite of collectors. Paula Findlen has argued that the early collector was "always in search of opportunities to gain new patrons and increase his visibility in the learned world, Ulisse Aldrovandi (1522–1605) briefly had the attention of all of Italy."[78] Aldrovandi was a naturalist and a cousin of the newly elected Pope, who immodestly proclaimed his museum to be the eighth world wonder.[79] His collection, which would become posthumously the museum of the University of Bologna, attracted humanists and scholars from all over the world. Much scholarship was devoted to describing and analyzing the exotic objects in Aldrovandi's collection.[80] The wonder of reading the exotic that Mary Campbell has described in her study on travel books was channeled ceremonially in visits to Aldrovandi's museum. Findlen describes that there even existed a proper code of conduct to his collection, detailing that the visitor had to exhibit gentlemanly behavior and abstain from having emotional and inappropriate reactions to wonder.[81] Before his death, Aldrovandi produced four hundred volumes of descriptive work dedicated in large part to the description of his own collection. As a Renaissance naturalist, Aldrovandi, like other early collectors of curiosities, had established the encyclopedia of nature itself as the ultimate goal of his collection.[82]

Encyclopedic aspirations to recover the science of Adam provided a common motivation for a number of Early Modern collections and philosophical projects. The idea that since Original Sin there was a fall from knowledge directly informed the methods of the new sciences. It has been suggested that the biblical narrative of the fall played a direct role in the development of Early Modern knowledge. In the early seventeenth century, Francis Bacon had famously observed in his *Novum Organum* that the human dominion over nature, which Adam had possessed last at the fall, could be restored in some measure by the sciences.[83]

John Tradescant the elder collected plants from Russia, the Levant, Algiers, France, Bermuda, the Caribbean and Southeast Asia for his collection. It is his son, John Tradescant the younger, who traveled to the New World and arrived in Virginia in 1637. Just like his father, he collected flowers, plants, shells and a rather famous Indian deerskin mantle believed to have belonged to Powhatan, the father of Pocahontas. Their collections also had rarities such as a mermaid's hand, a dragon's egg, feathers from the Phoenix's tail and a piece of the True Cross. Tradescant's Ark, as it came to be known, was a major cabinet of curiosity opened to the public for a small fee.[84] Elias Ashmole, scholar, astrologer, alchemist, antiquarian and officer of arms, became one of the most important collectors in Europe. Ashmole had a strong Baconian bent for collecting nature. His encounter with John Tradescant the younger around 1650 led to Elias Ashmole financing the publication of the catalogue *Musaeum Tradescantianum*. Tradescant the elder legally deeded his collection to Ashmole. In 1669, Ashmole received the Doctorate of Medicine from the University of Oxford. In 1677, he made a gift of the Tradescant collection to the university with the condition that a suitable home be built to house the collection and that it should be made available to the public.[85]

Wealthy Amateurs as Collectors

Paula Findlen argues that from the sixteenth to the seventeenth century, there were major changes as collecting changed from a professional pastime such as Aldrovandi's to a hobby often pursued by wealthy amateurs. Naturalists who spent their lives in study and description were replaced by prominent collectors who were part of a wealthy elite interested in displaying their wealth.[86] A new form of consumption marked rank among the wealthy. Elias Ashmole was one such wealthy collector. His close connections to power made him part of an important political elite.[87] The other major change between the world of Aldrovandi in the sixteenth century and the world of another famous collector Athanasius Kircher, whom Findlen calls the first scholar with a global reputation, was the transformation of collecting from a modest practice into a lavish and highly subsidized corporate activity. Both Aldrovandi, who had Pope Gregory XIII as a patron, and Athanasius Kircher, who was subsidized by Pope Alexander VII, were supported by funding from the Vatican. Yet Aldrovandi's correspondence with 760 scholars and his support from fellow Jesuits all over the globe might help explain his miraculously vast output as a scholar. Aldrovandi was more of a Renaissance Aristotelian while Kircher was more of a neo-Platonist. Nevertheless Aldrovandi's world of collecting was also linked to travel, exploration and his quest was for collecting a total encyclopedic knowledge of the world.[88]

In Bologna, Aldrovandi held approximately 20,000 objects and, according to Paula Findlen, the level of information he was seeking and the organization of his collection required the majority of his time. Findlen also notes his need for the acquisition of novel objects that were "in". Trends and fashions were important in the collecting world. She demonstrates that he clearly sought certain artifacts because he thought that they would be popular with the people visiting his collection.[89] Museums first appeared in the homes and courts of the elites of Italy and soon represented their owners and their power within society. Findlen argues that the more impressive the collection, the more social prestige the owner was granted. Botanical gardens, academic organizations, studiolos, and cabinets of curiosity were early types of museums for the collection of knowledge and a way for the powerful to collect the world. These new institutions of academic honor and wealthy display changed the dynamics of society. As Paula Findlen has argued, possessing nature and knowledge of the world was the new means to classify society itself.[90]

Many objects were visually presented and empirically described to counteract old textual myths while others, such as sirens and a unicorn's horn, were displayed to the public to keep ancient truths alive.[91] Botanical gardens collecting exotic flowers were living museums for a world of plants. The first European gardens appeared in Italy. The University of Pisa in 1543 was a precursor to Aldrovandi's large and rich collection of medicinal plants in Bologna. He amassed about 1,500 medicinal plants within a decade.[92] Just as plants arrived from Asia and the Americas to Europe's botanical gardens, Europe's powerful were collecting exotic animals in their private zoos. The arrival of a rare rhinoceros or a lone American moose did not disrupt Europe's ecological balance, while on the other hand the arrival of animals from Europe would transform the Americas. Some scholars have argued the European livestock was at the root of Europe's Empire a century later.[93]

The Transfer of Knowledge and Goods to the New World

By the sixteenth century maritime trade routes had become more important to European imports. The dominant navies were the Spanish and Portuguese because France had no navy of its own and it would take another half century for the English to defeat Spanish naval power during the Grand Armada of 1588. The sixteenth century was therefore a period of dominance for the Spanish and Portuguese in exploration and trade.

By Columbus's second voyage, livestock from the Old World had reached the New World. As early as 1518, a Spanish royal envoy to Saint-Domingue wrote a letter to Emperor Charles V about how livestock was thriving with cows giving birth to two calves and sometimes even three, instead of one. He mentioned that in Española there were already hogs, sheep, mares and further suggested sending Merino sheep. Antonio Barrera-Osorio wrote that the story of Spanish activities in the Atlantic World helps to explain the emergence of the imperial practices of science in the sixteenth and seventeenth centuries. He also explores the institutionalization of these new empirical practices in the *House of Trade*. The transformation of nature in the New World was not limited to adapting European plants and livestock. In 1534, Charles V ordered that experts be sent over to observe the new Spanish territories. The Spanish Crown, royal officials and ordinary artisans and merchants shared the hope of transforming the ecology of the new lands to make them economically and ecologically inhabitable for Europeans. The introduction of many plants such as saffron, pastel and mulberry trees for the cultivation of silk were among the many projects that changed the landscape. The mechanisms for collecting and disseminating knowledge about the new lands and the Atlantic Ocean were institutionalized at the *House of Trade* over a period of fifty years.[94]

The establishment of this chamber of knowledge facilitated exchanges between navigators, scholars, cosmographers and imperial agents. All the reports and information arriving from the New World prompted the Spanish Crown to establish the office of chief pilot for the purpose of bringing together "practice and theory". King Ferdinand appointed Amerigo Vespucci (1454–1512) as the first chief pilot of the *House of Trade* in 1508. He was in charge of drawing sea charts with the title of *Piloto Mayor*. The Americas were named after this first scientific professional who officially was engaged to organize knowledge of the New World. In the years to follow, many controversial debates took place between the cosmography professors and the instrument makers appointed by the Spanish Crown. As the American enterprise grew, the activities of those appointed to collect knowledge became more specialized. The House of Trade's chamber of knowledge became the institution to normalize and distribute knowledge and practices according to the political interest of the Spanish Crown.[95]

In sixteenth-century Spain, navigation and cartography became critical industries. Commerce with the Americas was at the basis of many new fortunes. Having a systematic representation of the world in a sea chart became a matter of crucial financial interest. Because Seville had become the center of the silver trade from the New World, it became the center of attention. A number of debates took place about the best navigation charts to the Indies with Seville as the destination. These debates took place in the House of Trade and led to the idea that the creation of a new pattern chart was needed. Royal support funded the creation of the *padrón real*, or royal pattern chart, which all charts used at sea were supposed to match. After many failed boundary talks with the Portuguese, Spain realized the inadequacy of the available navigation charts. The revision was entrusted to the younger son of Christopher Columbus, Hernando Colón, who was ordered to produce both a sea chart and a world map. As a cosmographer and bibliophile, Colón had long been involved in the conflicts involved with Spain's territorial claims in the Indies. After compiling information from more than 150 pilots, his attempts to make a new chart and a world map seemed to have been abandoned. The work seemed to have been taken over by the pilot major Sebastian Cabot, who worked for Spain. Cabot took over most of the cosmographical work in Seville. Eventually, a new group of cosmographers took over the project of the *padrón real*. In the 1540s, a chart approved by Suárez de Carbajal became the official royal pattern chart that was going to serve Spanish navigation. The debate between proponents of theory and pilots relying on observation did not cease. Most of the issues, however, were ignored by the Council of the Indies because the proponents of theory were able to gain the support of the Council and receive patronage.[96]

The Price Revolution: Theories on the Rise of Capitalism and Consumption

The Spanish Crown became the world's purveyor of silver through its galleons that carried it from New Spain to Europe and Asia. This new influx of precious metals in the world economy has given rise to a debate called the "Price Revolution". Silver bullion, together with silk, were the main commodities consumed during this period. In Europe, there occurred what has been called a price revolution in the sixteenth century when European prices expressed in grams of silver increased by more than 100 percent and in some other countries by more than 200 percent from the beginning of the sixteenth century to the middle of the seventeenth century and in some cases by more than 600 percent for that entire period.[97] The causes and consequences of these price increases have been intensely debated since Jean Bodin in the sixteenth century. In the 1920s, Earl J. Hamilton linked these price increases to the arrival of massive amounts of silver from the New World.[98] Equally important was, he argued, the redistribution of income in the hands of new social groups, which he believed played a key role in the rise of capitalism in Europe. Scholars of the Ottoman Empire have studied the price revolution of the sixteenth century within the Empire as a key element of Ottoman economic decline. This argument made by Ömer Lütfi Barkan pointed out that these price increases were imported into the Ottoman economy because of trade with Europe. He linked the decline of Ottoman economic strength to the rise of a European Atlantic silver economy of tremendous vitality and force.[99] The accepted theory was that capitalism was born in Europe during this price increase.

Another school of thought has attributed the rise in prices to growing populations. More recently, however, the debate has shifted from the increase in silver supplies to the change in the demand for silver and the increase in the velocity of its circulation to Asia via Europe in the sixteenth century. One contribution came from H. A. Miskimin who reasoned that an increase in population meant an increase in trade. These recent efforts shifted the focus from the supply of money to consumption. The demand for silver and not the supply of silver is seen as the basis for the Price Revolution. Earlier literature assumed that the demand for money or the velocity for circulation was constant or stable and that it could just safely be ignored. Fluctuations in demand, so familiar to us because of marketing, were often ignored in monetary theory. Despite Hamilton's contentions, the Price Revolution did not produce a social revolution in Europe as the main beneficiaries were landowners and the real victims were laborers who witnessed a decline in their standard of living. Manufacturers did not benefit from this rise in prices.[100]

The economic and price decline of the Ottoman Empire has also been revised. A recent study by Şevket Pamuk on prices between the sixteenth and twentieth centuries looked at the budget of the average urban consumer as well as the price of non-food items such as soap, wood, coal and nails by weight. He established a reliable price series, a first for the Middle East. His price index indicated that prices in Istanbul increased by approximately 500 percent from the end of the fifteenth to the end of the seventeenth century. Pamuk also argued that this price index needs to be examined in two distinct periods, one before the *Akçe* was debased in 1586 and one after monetary instability played havoc with prices in the Ottoman capital.[101] He also argued for the spread of local and regional markets and fairs both in the Balkans and in Anatolia to point to the commercialization and monetarization between urban and rural areas. This counters the established opinion that monetarization in the Ottoman Empire was simply for long distance trade. Pamuk concluded that neither Hamilton's contention that the Price Revolution was at the inception of the rise of capitalism in Europe nor Barkan's view that the Price Revolution was at the basis of Ottoman decline are acceptable. Pamuk shows that the volume of trade with Europe remained limited and that Ottoman manufacturers were not subject to European competition. Pamuk argues that if the Ottoman system faced severe fiscal and economic difficulties, it was not due to the impact of silver inflation per se nor to the Price Revolution in Europe. Ottoman imports from Europe were limited to some luxury goods.[102] He concentrates on the domestic economy of the Ottoman Empire.

The Ottomans and Sugar: A Precedent to Atlantic Slavery

As in most of the Islamic world, the Ottomans had the common practice of plantation slavery and produced sugar and madder on large estates. According to Halil İnalcik, slavery knew a steep decline in the Ottoman Empire during the sixteenth century when the *ciftlik-re'aya* system, land-owning peasant paying taxes, became the dominant agricultural system in the Ottoman Empire. It was not originally an Ottoman invention, but it was rather the re-establishment of an old system that had replaced slave labor as the major form of agricultural labor. İnalcik argues that the use of war captives in agriculture had a limited application by the reign of Sultan Suleyman I (1520–1566). During previous centuries of Ottoman conquest, a large number of captives were used for agricultural plantation slavery.[103]

The Ottoman conquest of Europe completely disrupted the international conditions of the slave trade in the Mediterranean, most of which had been under Genoese control. The slave traffic from the Balkans to Italy through Dubrovnik stopped after the Ottoman conquests of Istanbul (1453) and Caffa (1475) and the prohibition of traffic in Muslim slaves, mostly Turco-Tatars of the steppes north of the Black Sea. According to İnalcik, the slave trade between the Crimea and Egypt slowed down and changed its early character. The slave trade was first in commercial importance for the Black Sea and was a Genoese monopoly until the Ottomans imposed strict control of the straits. The new circumstances resulted in the ruin of the Genoese prosperity in the Black Sea, higher prices for slaves throughout the Mediterranean, and the replacement of Turco-Tatar slaves with Caucasian and Russian slaves. The slave trade did not cease, however; the new situation caused the prices to triple in Italy. The paradox is that this scarcity seems to have reinforced the anti-slavery feeling in Western Christendom and undermined slavery as an institution in sixteenth-century European discourse. The only exception in Europe was the great need for galley slaves who were provided mostly by European corsairs from the territories under Ottoman rule.[104] This anti-slavery discourse was amplified by the fact that many Europeans became captives and slaves themselves. In this period, the corsairs settled European captives mainly in North Africa after auctioning them on the local slave markets or sent them to the Ottoman capital. In her book *Captives,* Linda Colley has powerfully demonstrated that our view of an all powerful European Empire after 1715 blinds us to the vulnerability of Europe in the two and a half preceding centuries.[105]

Although slavery had existed since antiquity, the scale of what is now called Atlantic Slavery was far more global and the numbers much higher. Sugar was so labor intensive that first in Asia and later in the Americas it demanded a large labor force. Until well into the fifteenth century, once refined, the sugar cane cultivated in Egypt, India and China or on islands like Cyprus was sold to Europe on the Ottoman markets at high prices. The Spanish and Portuguese would not only become the world's purveyor of silver through their galleons, but distributed New World commodities such as tobacco, chocolate and sugar. Sugar became an American commodity through Atlantic slavery. Some have argued that the plantation system is at the root of Europe's modern consumer society and the source of its riches. Sugar produced in the Caribbean through free African labor was to become much cheaper than the one sold on the Ottoman markets.

Study Questions

1 What impact did Marco Polo's voyage to China have on European consumer expectations?
2 What are sumptuary laws? What role do they play in the history of consumption?
3 Why is standardization important to the growth of consumption? When were books and textiles standardized and how was it tied to the rise of the bank?
4 In what ways did collecting printed maps and travel accounts, exotic *naturalia*, represent a form of consumption?
5. How was alchemy, an early practice of science, tied to consumption?

Notes

1 Marco Polo, *The Travels of Marco Polo*, 3 Vols (New York: Dover Publications, 1903) Vol. 1, Book 1, 41.
2 Florin Curta "Merovingian and Carolingian gift giving" *Speculum 81, 3* (2006) 670–699, 670–673.
3 Marco Polo, *The Travels of Marco Polo*, trans. Ronald Latham (New York: Penguin, 1958), 138–141.
4 Lauren Arnold, *Princely Gifts and Papal Treasures: The Franciscan Mission to China and its Influence on the Art of the West, 1250–1350* (San Francisco: Desiderata Press, 1999), 32–36, 138.
5 Marcel Mauss, *The Gift: The Form and Reason for Exchange in Archaic Societies* (London: Routledge, 1900).

6 Arnold, *Princely Gifts and Papal Treasures*, 22.
7 Arnold, *Princely Gifts and Papal Treasures*, 22–26.
8 Arnold*, Princely Gifts and Papal Treasures*, 22–26.
9 Arnold, *Princely Gifts and Papal Treasures*, 9.
10 Arnold, *Princely Gifts and Papal Treasures*, 33.
11 Arnold, *Princely Gifts and Papal Treasures*, 36.
12 On this exchange, see Thomas Allsen, *Culture and Conquest in Mongol Eurasia* (Cambridge, UK; New York: Cambridge University Press, 2001).
13 Giorgio Riello and Peter McNeil, eds., *The Fashion History Reader: Global Perspectives* (Abingdon, Oxon; New York: Routledge, 2010).
14 Sir John Harold Clapham, Michael Moïssey Postan, and Edwin Ernest Rich, eds., *The Cambridge Economic History of Europe* (Cambridge: Cambridge University Press, 1941), 203–206.
15 Richard A. Goldthwaite, *The Economy of Renaissance Florence* (Baltimore: Johns Hopkins University Press, 2009), 265.
16 Goldthwaite, *The Economy of Renaissance Florence*, 265.
17 Goldthwaite, *The Economy of Renaissance Florence*, 267.
18 Goldthwaite, *The Economy of Renaissance Florence*, 275.
19 Goldthwaite, *The Economy of Renaissance Florence*, 314.
20 Goldthwaite, *The Economy of Renaissance Florence*, 288.
21 Luca Molà, *The Silk Industry of Renaissance Venice* (Baltimore: Johns Hopkins University Press, 2000), 96.
22 Goldthwaite, *The Economy of Renaissance Florence,* 265–292.
23 Giorgio Riello and Peter McNeil, "Fashion and Social Order: the Early Modern World" in Glenn Adamson and Sarah Teasley, eds *Global Design History*, (New York: Routledge, 2011), 85–93 and Patricia Allerston, "Clothing and Early Modern Venetian Society", in Giorgio Riello and Peter McNeil, eds., T*he Fasion History Reader: Global Perspectives* (Milton Park, Abingdon, Oxon; New York: Routledge, 2010), 93–111.
24 Catherine Kovesi Killerby, *Sumptuary Law in Italy 1200–1500* (Oxford: Clarendon Press; New York: Oxford University Press, 2002), 3.
25 *Articles for the execution of the Statutes of Apparel, and for the reformation of the outrageous excess thereof grown of late time within the realm, devised upon the Queen's Majesty's commandment, by advice of her Council, 6 May 1562* (Westminster, London) <http://elizabethan.org/sumptuary/ruffs-hose-swo rds.html>
26 Allen Hunt, "A Short History of Sumptuary Laws". In Riello and McNeil, *The Fashion History Reader*, 43–59.
27 Killerby, *Sumptuary Law*, 2–325.
28 Jean Baudrillard, *Système des Objets* (New York, London: Verso, 1996), 100.
29 Killerby, *Sumptuary Law*, 9.
30 Speros Vryonis, *Byzantium and Europe* (New York: Harcourt, Brace & World, 1967), 152.
31 Steven Runciman, *The Fall of Constantinople 1453* (Cambridge: Cambridge University Press, 1965), 79.
32 Lisa Jardine, *Worldly Goods: A New History of the Renaissance* (London: Macmillan, 1996), 39, 44–45.
33 Jardine, *Worldly Goods*, 73.
34 Çiğdem Kafescioğlu, *Constantinopolis/Istanbul: Cultural Encounter, Imperial Vision, and the Construction of the Ottoman Capital* (University Park, Pennsylvania: Pennsylvania State University Press, 2009), 179.
35 Ina Baghdiantz McCabe, *The Shah's Silk for Europe's Silver: The Eurasian Trade of the Julfa Armenians in Safavid Iran and India* (Atlanta, Georgia: Scholar's Press, 1999), see Introduction.
36 Jardine, *Worldly Goods*, 65–69.

37 Richard A. Goldthwaite, "The Medici Bank and the World of Florentine Capitalism", *Past & Present* 114 (Oxford University Press for the Past and Present Society, February 1987), 3–31.

38 Niall Ferguson, *The Ascent of Money: A Financial History of the World* (New York: Penguin Press, 2008), 44.

39 Ina Baghdiantz McCabe, *Orientalism in Early Modern France: Eurasian Trade, Exoticism and the Ancien Régime* (Oxford; New York: Berg, 2008), 37.

40 Josée Balagna Coustou, *Arabe et humanisme dans la France des derniers Valois* (Paris: Editions Maisonneuve et Larose, 1989), 44.

41 Baghdiantz McCabe, *Orientalism*, 38.

42 Jacob Strieder and Norman Scott Brien Gras, eds, *Jacob Fugger: Merchant and Banker of Augsburg, 1459–1525*, trans. Mildred H. Hartsough (Washington, D.C.: Beard Books, 2001), 151.

43 Jardine, *Worldly Goods*, 96.

44 Streider et al., *Jacob Fugger*, 154.

45 Lucien Febvre and Henri-Jean Martin, *The Coming of the Book: The Impact of Printing, 1450–1800* (London; New York: Verso, 1976), 219.

46 Jardine, *Worldly Goods*, 135–180.

47 Raymond De Roover, "New Facets on the Financing and Marketing of Early Printed Books" (*Bulletin of the Business Historical Society*, Vol. 27, No. 4, Dec., 1953), 222.

48 De Roover, "New Facets on the Financing and Marketing of Early Printed Books", 222–226.

49 Febvre and Martin, *The Coming of the Book*, 232.

50 Jardine, *Worldly Goods*,164.

51 Febvre and Martin, *The Coming of the Book*, 167–172.

52 Febvre and Martin, *The Coming of the Book*, 186.

53 Febvre and Martin, *The Coming of the Book*, 43, 98.

54 Baghdiantz McCabe, *Orientalism*, 24.

55 Jardine, *Worldly Goods*, 172–174.

56 Febvre and Martin, *The Coming of the Book*, 212.

57 Febvre and Martin, *The Coming of the Book*, 71.

58 Daphne Vanessa Taylor-Garcia, *The Emergence of Racial Schema in the Americas: Sexuality, Sociogeny, and Print Capital in the Sixteenth Century Atlantic* (Berkeley: University of California Press, 2008).

59 Marcel van den Broecke, *Ortelius' Theatrum Orbis Terrarum (1570–1641).* (Utrecht: Utrecht University, Royal Dutch Geographical Society, 2009).

60 Baghdiantz McCabe, *Orientalism*, 27.

61 Baghdiantz McCabe, *Orientalism*, 73.

62 Daviken Studnicki-Gizbert, *A Nation upon the Ocean Sea: Portugal's Atlantic Diaspora and the Crisis of the Spanish Empire, 1492–1640* (Oxford; New York: Oxford University Press, 2007), 92–94.

63 Jardine, *Worldly Goods*, 79.

64 Charles C. Mann, *1493, Uncovering the New World Columbus Created* (New York: Alfred A. Knopf, 2011), 23–25.

65 Andrew Dalby, *Dangerous Tastes: The Story of Spices* (Berkeley: University of California Press, 2002), 93.

66 Bailey W. Diffie and George D. Winius, "Europe and the World in the Age of Expansion" Book 1 *Foundations of the Portuguese Empire, 1415–1850* (Minnesota, University of Minnesota Press: 1977), 177.

67 Coustou, *Arabe et humanisme dans la France des derniers Valois*, 58–59.

68 Marion Leathers Kuntz, *Guillaume Postel, Prophet of the Restitution of All Things: His Life and Thought* (The Hague; Boston: Nijhoff; Hingham, MA: Kluwer Boston, 1981), 32–39.

69 Tara E. Nummedal, "Practical Alchemy and Commercial Exchange in the Holy Roman Empire" in Pamela H. Smith, Paula Findlen, eds., *Merchants & Marvels: Commerce, Science, and Art in Early Modern Europe* (New York; London: Routledge, 2002).

70 Nummedal, "Practical Alchemy and Commercial Exchange" in Smith and Findlen, eds., *Merchants & Marvels*, 204–205.

71 Nummedal, "Practical Alchemy and Commercial Exchange" in Smith and Findlen, eds., *Merchants & Marvels*, 205–208.

72 Richard Bonny, *The European Dynastic States, 1494–1660* (Oxford: Oxford University Press, 1991), 420 in Nummedal "Practical Alchemy and Commercial Exchange in the Holy Roman Empire" in Smith and Findlen, eds., *Merchants & Marvels*, 210.

73 Alexander Lauterwald, *Colloquium Philosophicum* [unfoliated, 16r-v] in Nummedal "Practical Alchemy and Commercial Exchange" in Smith and Findlen, eds., *Merchants & Marvels*, 214.

74 Nummedal "Practical Alchemy and Commercial Exchange" in Smith and Findlen, eds., *Merchants & Marvels*, 201–222.

75 Mark A. Meadow, "Merchants and Marvels: Hans Jacob Fugger and the Origins of the *Wunderkammer*" in Smith and Findlen, eds., *Merchants & Marvels*.

76 Meadow, "Merchants and Marvels" in Smith and Findlen, eds., *Merchants & Marvels*, 84.

77 Meadow, "Merchants and Marvels" in Smith and Findlen, eds., *Merchants & Marvels*, 182–200.

78 Paula Findlen, *Possessing Nature: Museums, Collecting, and Scientific Culture in Early Modern Italy* (Berkeley; Los Angeles; London: University of California Press, 1994), 22.

79 Findlen, *Possessing Nature*, 17–24.

80 Findlen, *Possessing Nature*, 26.

81 Findlen, *Possessing Nature*, 29.

82 Findlen, *Possessing Nature*, 35.

83 Peter Harrison, "Original Sin and the Problem of Knowledge in Early Modern Europe", *Journal of the History of Ideas* 63.2 (April 2002), 239–259.

84 Wolfram Koeppe, "Collecting for the Kunstkammer" in Heilbrunn Timeline of Art History (New York: The Metropolitan Museum of Art, 2000) http://www.metmuseum.org/toah/hd/kuns/hd_kuns.htm (October 2002)

85 Josten, C. H. ed, *Elias Ashmole (1617–1692). His Autobiographical and Historical Notes, his Correspondence, and Other Contemporary Sources Relating to his Life and Work* Vol. I, (Oxford: Clarendon Press, 1966).

86 Findlen, *Possessing Nature*, 43.

87 Michael Hunter, (September 2004; online edition May 2006) "Ashmole, Elias (1617–1692)", *Oxford Dictionary of National Biography* (London: Oxford University Press, 2004).

88 Findlen, *Possessing Nature*, 55.

89 Findlen, *Possessing Nature*, 67.

90 Findlen, *Possessing Nature*, 97–99.

91 Findlen, *Possessing Nature*, 209.

92 Findlen, *Possessing Nature*, 258.

93 Virginia DeJohn Anderson, *Creatures of Empire: How Domestic Animals Transformed Early America* (Oxford; New York: Oxford University Press, 2004).

94 Antonio Barrera-Osorio, "Empiricism in the Spanish Atlantic World" in James Delbourgo and Nicholas Dew, eds., *Science and Empire in the Atlantic World* (New York; London: Routledge, 2008).

95 Barrera-Osorio, "Empiricism in the Spanish Atlantic World".

96 Alison Sandman, "Mirroring the World: Sea Charts, Navigation, and Territorial Claims in Sixteenth-Century Spain" in Smith and Findlen, *Merchants & Marvels,* 83–108.

97 Şevket Pamuk, "The Price Revolution in the Ottoman Empire Reconsidered", *International Journal of Middle East Studies*, Vol. 33, No.1 (February 2001): 69–89, 69–70.

98 Earl J. Hamilton, *War and Prices in Spain, 1651–1800* (Cambridge, MA: Harvard University Press, 1947).

99 Ömer Lütfi Barkan, "The Price Revolution of the Sixteenth Century: A Turning Point in the Economic History of the Near East," trans. Justin McCarthy, *International Journal of Middle East* Studies 6 (1975): 3–28. As quoted in Şevket Pamuk, "The Price Revolution in the Ottoman Empire Reconsidered", *International Journal of Middle East Studies.*

100 Pamuk, "The Price Revolution in the Ottoman Empire Reconsidered", 73.

101 Pamuk, "The Price Revolution in the Ottoman Empire Reconsidered", 78.

102 Pamuk, "The Price Revolution in the Ottoman Empire Reconsidered", 85.

103 Halil İnalcik, "Servile Labor in the Ottoman Empire", A. Ascher, B. K. Kiraly, and T. Halasi-Kun, eds., *The Mutual Effects of the Islamic and Judeo-Christian Worlds: The East European Pattern* (Brooklyn, N.Y.: Brooklyn College, 1979), 25–52.

104 İnalcik, "Servile Labor in the Ottoman Empire", 27–28.

105 Linda Colley, *Captives: Britain, Empire and the World 1600–1850* (London: Pantheon, 2002).

Figure 2.1 'Punishment of Negroes' illustration from *Voyage Pittoresque et Historique au Bresil* (1835). © The Art Gallery Collection/Alamy.

2   American Gold

Sugar, Tobacco and Chocolate

A Broken Apothecary will make there a Topping Physician; A Barber's Prentice, a good Surgeon; a Bailiff's Follower, a passable Lawyer; and an English Knave, a very Honest Fellow.[1]

Sugar had been used as a luxury good since the Crusades; by the eighteenth century it became a commodity that would have the global importance of steel in the nineteenth century and of oil in the twentieth. Both the rich and poor left Europe to grow sugarcane in the New World and seek their fortune abroad. About 30,000 European indentured servants went to the Caribbean during the reign of Charles I (1629–49) and about as many left for North America.[2] Ned Ward, a Grub Street writer, was one of the many impoverished Englishmen seeking opportunities in the Caribbean. His description of Jamaica as a "sweating chaos" has become famous. Crossing the Atlantic permitted the breaking of rank and degree that were so prevalent in Europe. Ward not only criticized the men who broke their ranks to become physicians and lawyers without training but also the few women on the island. He wrote that they were "such who have been Scandalous in England to the utmost degree, either Transported by the State or led by their vicious inclinations".[3] Matthew Parker argues that the chance for such social transformation was the primary motive for many Europeans undergoing the dangerous adventure of emigration. If by the eighteenth century sugar had become an affordable commodity, it was due to the initiative of a few European men who grew rich while thousands of African and European men and women died as indentured servants or slaves in the difficult Caribbean climate.

Originally from New Guinea and grown in Egypt, Africa and Asia, sugarcane traveled west from Eurasia to the Americas. Initially refined and unrefined sugar made its way to Europe from India via Muslim trading routes. Ottoman sugar plantations were established in North Africa and the first slaves working in this labor-intensive industry came from Balkan Europe. The Arab expansion westward marked a turning point in Europe's use of sugar. One scholar claims that sugar did not reach Venice until 996 from where it was exported northward but this date is perhaps late. The Arabs were halted in their European expansion in Poitiers in 732; established in southern Europe, they knew the use of sugar well before that date. Some portions of the Mediterranean world fell to Islam after Spain had been conquered and where they went, Arabs brought with them sugar and the technology to produce it.[4] The role of sugar in medieval Mediterranean trade is well documented in Arabic and Italian sources and archeological records find early sugar mills throughout the Middle East and parts of North Africa.[5] Sugar consumption was therefore well established in both those regions before reaching European tables.

Sugarcane is a tropical and sub-tropical crop with a growing season that is in excess of twelve months, sometimes fifteen. It demands large amounts of water and labor. In the Mediterranean, the production of sugarcane was possible as far south as Marrakech and as far north as Valencia, Spain and Palermo, Sicily; the Arabs tested the potentiality of these newly conquered lands to their limits. Though some scholars have argued that slavery was not part of growing sugar under Arab rule, this is unfounded, as slavery played a crucial part in the Moroccan sugar industry as well as elsewhere. A slave revolt involving thousands of East African laborers took place in the Tigris-Euphrates Delta. Yet Sidney Mintz contends that slavery did grow more important in the Middle East because the European crusaders seized the sugar plantations of the eastern Mediterranean.[6]

The Portuguese had early plantation colonies worked by slaves in their Atlantic islands of Madeira and São Tomé before establishing plantations in the Americas. When in 1500 Pedro Álvares Cabral, leader of an expedition to India, stopped briefly on the Brazilian shore, a mass was celebrated. A Portuguese rivalry with the French and later the Dutch over Brazil and the much contested Caribbean was constant. In the Caribbean islands the English, French, Dutch and Spanish first planted tobacco, then cotton and indigo, but soon the most important crop was sugarcane. Once sugarcane was planted under Portuguese rule, Brazil would become the world's main producer of sugar.[7] Well before the New World sugar plantations and industries were established, there was competition between sugar plantations on Atlantic islands and Malta, Rhodes, Cyprus and Sicily, which were sugar producers. By 1580, the Sicilian sugar industry did little more than supply its domestic market and in Spain itself sugar production began to decline.[8] From the tiny island of Gomera in the Canaries, it was Columbus himself who transported cane seedlings to Hispaniola in his second voyage of 1493. His first wife had thrived in the sugar business and Columbus himself had traded sugar from Madeira to his native Genoa. Cane grew faster in the New World than anywhere else but the Spanish experiment with sugar was brief; if there had been 100 sugar mills on Spanish ruled Hispaniola, by 1600 there were 11. Most men, indentured servants from Europe, were dead by the time a first crop was ready for harvest.[9]

The Rise of Atlantic Slavery

Sugarcane and slavery have been closely associated since antiquity. Sugarcane was first grown in the New World on Spanish Saint-Domingue, where the first slaves arrived shortly after sugarcane. It was Spain that pioneered sugarcane, sugar making and African slave labor that shaped the plantation system in the Americas. Fernando Ortiz has argued that plantations were "the favored child of capitalism" while other historians disagree.[10] It is to the Spanish that the first sugar experiments belonged. Two planters started as early as 1505–1506 but Spain was not ready to support their ambitions. The only available milling techniques at that point were probably modeled on tenth-century Egyptian edge-water mill designs used to press olives. These devices were inefficient, but the main problem was the labor supply. The rapid destruction of the indigenous Taino of Saint-Domingue through disease had left too little manpower even for the gold mines, let alone for sugar. Christopher Columbus casually described the Taino as "innumerable, for I believe there to be millions upon millions of them".[11] Spanish sources give varying numbers but no matter what the original number might have been by 1514, twenty-two years after Columbus's first landing, when the Spanish government counted the Taino on Hispaniola, they found only 26,000 of them. Thirty-four years later, according to one Spanish resident of Hispaniola, fewer than 500 Taino remained alive. The destruction of the Taino plunged Saint-Domingue into poverty as the colonists had wiped out their own labor force mostly through disease. European livestock, new to the Americas, enabled the spread of many of these diseases.[12]

Over the course of four centuries, the international slave trade displaced thirteen million Africans from their homes and killed well over two million Africans. Sugar alone consumed over six million lives.[13] In 1441, a Portuguese captain decided to curry favor with Prince Henry of Portugal by capturing some natives for the first time.[14] The first African slaves were imported before 1503 and by 1509 enslaved Africans were being imported to work the royal mines on a regular basis. Others soon followed to power the new sugar industry. The surgeon Gonzalo de Vellosa took a first step towards creating an authentic sugar industry in the Caribbean in 1515, when he imported skilled sugar masters from the Canaries.[15] With these technicians, he imported a mill with two vertical rollers that could efficiently process sugarcane. One scholar has estimated that the mill could grind enough cane in one season to produce 125 tons of sugar a year if it was water-powered and perhaps a third of that if it was powered by animals. In the other greater Antilles – Cuba, Puerto Rico and Jamaica – Spanish settlers brought in sugarcane and the process for grinding, boiling and fabricating sugar and molasses from the extracted juice of the sugarcane as well as for distilling rum from molasses. Within only a century, the French and even more the British, with some competition from the Dutch at the onset, became the world's great sugar makers and exporters. Sidney Mintz wonders why the early phase of the Spanish sugar industry stagnated so swiftly. Perhaps the Spaniards' obsession with metallic riches or the flight of island colonists to the Mexican mainland could offer an explanation but Mintz does not consider them sufficient; he argues for consumption. He posits that the production of marketable commodities mattered more to their northern European rivals to meet the rising consumption of sugar in their domestic markets in western Europe. Sugar production grew steadily as more Westerners consumed sugar and as each consumer used it more heavily even while technological advances in grinding and refining remained minor.[16]

Sydney Mintz cites Fernandez-Armesto who wrote that the striking feature of the sugar industry in the Canaries was to use both free and enslaved labor and that this pioneering system resembled what would happen later in the British and French Caribbean plantations, on which enslaved and indentured laborers worked alongside each other.[17] The labor model used in the old world was the one practiced in the Caribbean and the Americas. The sugar industries of the Spanish and Portuguese Atlantic were characterized by slave labor whether in the Spanish Canaries or Portuguese São Tomé. In the Caribbean islands, most of the labor was initially done by European indentured servants. Studies of English ship rosters to Barbados in the 1630s show that 90 percent of the emigrants were male, between the ages of fifteen and twenty-four. They worked three to nine years with the promise of ten acres of land at the end of their servitude, though most died well before owning anything.[18]

Sugar as Political Power

Mintz argues that as sugar production in the Mediterranean waned, desire for consuming sugar waxed in Europe. There were intimate links between the early experiments of growing sugarcane by the Portuguese especially in São Tomé and commercial centers in northern Europe such as Antwerp. From the thirteenth century on, the refining cities for Europe were Antwerp followed by Bristol, Bordeaux and later London. Control of the final product moved into European hands but not the same Europeans who produced sugar overseas. No longer as precious as musk or pearls, the Portuguese shipped sugar to the courts of Europe via intermediary countries and their luxury traders. Mintz argues that to a surprising degree sugar figured in national policies and indicated influence over political futures. Sugar production in the colonies became an object of debate with early mercantilists such as Sir Joshua Child arguing that plantations in the colonies damaged "Mother-Kingdoms". The Governor of Jamaica, Sir Dalby Thomas, grasped the unfolding of what was to become the greatest market for foreign luxuries. He argued against mercantilists that the colonies themselves would be important markets for the consumption of luxury goods. Everything consumed in the West Indian colonies came from England. Even if there were no direct exchanges between England and its overseas holdings, there grew in effect several so-called "triangles of trade" that eventually worked for the long-term benefit of imperial enterprises. Even if trade was initially run by merchants rather than the state, European states would, through military control and taxation, reap the benefits of the global trade borne in the seventeenth century and perfected in the eighteenth.[19]

Dutch, British and French Consumption of Sugar

Many sugar traders grew rich through the new popularity of sweet dishes. The odd consequence of cheaper sugar from the Caribbean was that it was confined to fewer and fewer dishes at the end of the meal. This broke centuries old traditions of sweet and savory dishes where sugar was often used in main courses and there was no distinction between salty and sweet. The seventeenth century saw the invention of the "dessert course", a sweet dish that followed the other dishes of an elaborate meal. At first the English resisted what they saw as an "unnatural" French invention, but when in July 1666 Samuel Pepys (1633–1703) was served dessert in London he made no remarks as to this custom being either new or unusual as most of Europe knew of desserts by then.[20] Nevertheless he was used to his dishes all being served simultaneously and if they were served in succession, he called his dinner "in the French manner".[21]

Early English cookbooks such as the 1545 *A Propre new booke of Cokery* used as much as half of a pound of sugar for a traditional sweet savory dish, a recipe for *blanc mange* (*Bleaw manger*). A later seventeenth-century recipe for French *macarons* is simply sweet and calls for a half of a pound of sugar to a pound of fresh Jordan almonds. The proportion is much higher than the 1545 recipe for *blanc mange*, which used half a pound of sugar for a breast of capon, milk, cream, rice flour and rose water. Recipes for sweet dishes are much more common in seventeenth-century cookbooks than in earlier ones. During the sixteenth century a connection between elaborate manufactures of sweet edibles and the validation of social position remained clear.[22]

Despite the protests against desserts, it was not a total French novelty, especially at court. In England, Elizabethan feasts were followed by the banquet course consisting of sugar confections. Elizabeth I loved *marchpane*, marzipan made of almonds, sugar and dried and candied fruits. Her sugar habit gave her such bad teeth that they turned black with old age. In order not to show their white teeth, the ladies of the court blackened their own teeth to imitate their queen. John Nichols' history of Queen Elizabeth's journeys through Britain offers a vivid glimpse of the nature of the grand and spectacular feasts held by the rich aristocracy:

> Where the Queen paraded through a country town, almost every Pageant was a Pantheon; even the pastry cooks were expert mythologists: at dinner select transformations of Ovid's Metamorphoses were exhibited in confectionery and the splendid icing of an immense historic plumb-cake was embossed with a delicious basso-rilievo of the destruction of Troy.[23]

This splendid display highlighted the rank of the consumer through the price of sugar.

Early in the seventeenth century some powerful people in Britain became convinced that commodities such as sugar mattered much more than the goods that British trade had previously been concerned with. They argued fiercely for capital to be invested in developing sugar plantations. If the sixteenth century had been a century of Spanish and Portuguese domination, the seventeenth century saw the English and the Dutch become fierce competitors for trade. The English connection between sugar production and consumption at home was welded in the seventeenth century when the English acquired Barbados, Jamaica and other sugar islands. With an expansion of the African slave trade, England made inroads into the Portuguese domination of maritime trade. British success was largely built on a broader internal consumer market.[24] Once the Dutch became dominant in the spice trade and invigorated by gains in the East, they quickly decided to also exploit Portugal's weakness in the Americas by attempting to seize control of the sugar trade. However, they encountered British competition; the English would be the most successful in exporting American grown sugar to the rest of the world. According to Matthew Parker, by the 1690s, England was importing 23,000 tons of sugar a year, making it by far the most important commodity in the empire.[25]

Consumption in Europe was the basis of this fierce competition for the global sugar trade. The unloading, storing and selling of sugar was worth more than half of all the English imports from their colonies by the end of the seventeenth century. The trade was in the hands of a small number of English factors; in 1686 twenty-eight London merchants imported nearly half of all the products from the Caribbean. Benefits also went to the English Crown, which reaped £300,000 a year from sugar taxes by the mid 1670s. In London, banks, insurance companies and brokers all benefited from the trade with the number of sugar refineries growing to more than thirty by 1695.[26]

If in the early seventeenth century sugar remained a sign of ostentation both in France and England, in France it disappeared from the main cookbooks devoted to daily meals for the elite in the second part of the seventeenth century. Cheaper sugar gave rise to a new culinary art, confectionery, but confectionery was for the rich. The famous François Massialot, who ran Louis XIV's brother's kitchen, wrote a separate book on confections, which continued to be a sign of social prestige.[27] This period is better known for a revolutionary cookbook, La Varenne's *Le cuisinier françois* published in 1651. Criticized for its Arabic influence and its new emphasis on vegetables, it notably turned away from the heavy exotic spices traditionally used in Renaissance cooking. Just as cheaper sugar had disappeared from most dishes, spices that were now more available through the Dutch disappeared from French elite cooking. Seen as the beginnings of both a national French cuisine and of a tradition of *haute cuisine*, La Varenne's dishes are left naturally flavored, sugar and spice are gone from his recipes, but the new condiment here is the sauce.[28] Sauces would become the marker of *haute cuisine* in the French style, a style adopted by courts and elites across Europe within a short time. Perhaps this disappearance from main dishes was because sugar and spice, now much cheaper for Europeans, were no longer clear markers of class.

The main change in France and England by the end of the seventeenth century was that sugar consumption went beyond the courts. One commentator was at pains to explain how mere merchants could pick and choose sugar confections to serve at feasts as if they were the nobility of the land. Thomas Warton's *History of English Poetry* documented the growing importance of the feast as a form of symbolic validation of social power as early as the fifteenth century. He described a "curious" dish that was entirely made of sugar. While kings and archbishops were displaying magnificent sugar castles and mounted knights, the aspiring upper classes began to combine what was called "coarse paste" to mold men of war with marzipan guns as festive centerpieces for their tables. These pieces for display could keep indefinitely and were called "conceits in sugar-works".[29] Sidney Mintz has argued that as sugar spread downwards, it lost some of its power to distinguish the rank of those who consumed it.[30] The sugar trade was closely linked to both the slave trade and the trade of silver. Silver remained the main commodity of importance in the seventeenth century despite the rise of sugar on the global markets.

The Global Triangle Trade behind Cheaper Sugar

Silver, sugar and slaves were part of the same trade. Slaves for the sugar trade were provided by a new company, *The Royal Adventurers in Africa*, presided over by the King's own brother. The King's sister owned many shares as did the philosopher John Locke and the diarist Samuel Pepys. In 1663, this English company shipped 3,075 slaves to Barbados alone during seven months. The free labor of these new slaves was the underlying cause of falling sugar prices across Europe. Matthew Parker argues that of greatest importance was the effect it had on consumption of sugar in England. The retail prices for sugar slipped from 1.5 shillings a pound in the 1650s to 0.8 shillings by the 1680s. At this juncture, new consumers were created by the thousands. Annual per capita consumption in 1650 was barely a pound of sugar. At the end of the century, it was five pounds of sugar per person.[31] Sugar reached a level of affordability for confectionery for the merchant elite through the expansion of the plantation system and slave trade. Sydney Mintz has calculated that the increase in sugar production in the mid seventeenth century was so successful that the prices of sugar fell across Europe between 1645 and 1680 by a staggering 70 percent. In Amsterdam the price of sugar fell by one third between 1677 and 1687.[32]

At the very end of the seventeenth century, the Brazilian market was transformed by the discovery of large deposits of gold. Brazil had been the first in South America to develop sugar plantations and now was the first to experience a gold rush. Indian slaves were used to open gold mines but demand for African slaves increased as more and more gold was discovered. Hugh Thomas finds that mine owners made distinctions amongst different slaves and favored the captives from Guinea, who were judged to be stronger than those arriving from Angola. Slaves for Brazil's gold and sugar were directly carried across the South Atlantic from Angola, the Congo and possibly Mozambique, but many still came from the Gulf of Guinea. One estimate gives an overall figure of over 150,000 slaves carried to Brazil in the first ten years of the eighteenth century. Though the journeys of the slave trips were still organized with a stop in Lisbon, increasing numbers were now sent across the Atlantic directly by merchants based in Rio.[33] Brazil had three successful direct exports to Africa: sugar, molasses-dripped, third rate tobacco that was especially in demand in Benin, and the Brazil-made, strong, rough cane brandy called *gerebita* that was extraordinarily popular in Angola. By 1700, all the chartered international companies including the smaller Scandinavian companies set up to trade with Africa to carry slaves to the New World.[34]

By the seventeenth century, Africans were settled everywhere in the Spanish world. As many as six trading companies in Argentina were sending slaves to the silver mines in the town of Potosi. Enslaved miners in Potosi provided the bullion that was shipped through the Spanish galleon trade to China and to Manila in the Philippines.[35] Manila was an important trading center born in the conflict between the Spanish and powerful Chinese pirates; it had even been threatened by a dissident Chinese regime in Taiwan in the 1660s. Various blends of Spanish and Philippine fears and hatred ignited terrible massacres of the Manila Chinese in 1603, 1639 and 1662. In 1686, a royal order was issued in Madrid that all non-Christian Chinese were to be expelled from Manila. This created violence and confusion especially when the Chinese threatened with expulsion claimed to be creditors of the Spanish Crown from loans that helped pay the Spanish garrison.[36] In the wake of the massacres, Manila's Spanish government claimed jurisdiction over all the Philippine islands but in fact commanded only a few small garrisons and there was very little settlement. Economically, Manila was the meeting point for the two greatest economic phenomena of the seventeenth century: the stream of Spanish silver from the Latin American mines and the sophisticated Chinese manufactured goods that silver bought for Europe's consumption. North America's captains and pirates soon started importing Chinese goods directly, bypassing the English.[37] The main global trade remained Portuguese and Spanish because of their access to gold and silver.

Every year, several galleons crossed the Pacific from Acapulco to Manila bringing New World silver to buy Chinese silks, Indian cottons, china and other fine consumer goods that were in great demand. In Lima, even the slaves of the great households were said to wear liveries of Chinese silk. However, household slaves dressed in silk were the exception and most slaves worked on plantations. Manila depended on its Chinese population for more than this very important trade with China. Its very survival depended on Chinese financing.[38] Behind this global trade, often called the "triangle trade" because of the galleons stopping in Africa, was the slave trade.

The plantation system that made sugar cultivation and silver extraction possible was a very harsh reality. Very few slaves survived more than a short period of labor. According to Hugh Thomas, as early as the 1550s, the Kings of Congo and Ndongo were rivals to become the main suppliers of slaves to the Portuguese. Although Portugal was obliged to support the Congo, her economic interests were becoming aligned with the King of Ndongo.[39] Luanda soon became the headquarters for all operations south of Nigeria. By 1590, 300 Portuguese were settled in Luanda. With the relative peace established by the King of Congo there was nothing to prevent the slave trade from prospering and it soon became the economic mainstay of Angola and the Congo. A historian of Portuguese and African race relations, C. L. R. Boxer has argued that the slave trade was the reason why Angola did not become a colony in the sixteenth century. Colonial settlement was not the priority, buying slaves was. The main purpose of the Portuguese presence in Angola was to run ships for the slave trade to Brazil. The African coast had been divided into several zones of commercial exploitation. In these zones, the collection of royal taxes to Portugal was farmed out to individuals. The last quarter of the seventeenth century saw a great increase in the export of slaves from Africa. The best historian of the statistics on slavery, Philip Curtin, estimated that nearly 370,000 slaves were exported between 1650 and 1675 and 600,000 were taken into captivity and exported between 1675 and 1700.[40]

The slave trade caused political changes in Africa. Just as the medieval Arab trade in slavery had inspired new cities on the Niger River such as Timbuktu, the slave trade inspired policies and reforms that led to the increase of the number of slave warriors. The Bambara Kingdom founded about 1710 on the Niger River became "an enormous machine to produce slaves".[41] Most African slaves were sent to Brazil and the Caribbean.

The Transmission of Culinary Customs from Africa to the New World

The triangle trade played an instrumental role in global cultural and biological exchanges as people, plants and animals were moved across continents. The sweet potato played a seminal role in the slave trade, as the basic food fed to slaves while crossing the Atlantic. This was not monotonous the fare the people captured as slaves were accustomed to. Adding to the local agricultural riches, which will be discussed further, the Portuguese introduced several new European and West Indian crops to Africa. Portuguese imports to central Africa such as rice, oranges, coconuts, onions and cassava established themselves readily. This last crop, cassava, inspired an agricultural revolution in the seventeenth century, enabling the population to grow food crops to previously unattained levels. Hugh Thomas argues this new bounty indirectly made more candidates available for the Atlantic slave trade. American maize planted in Africa had similar consequences later.[42] Angola, Congo and Brazil were more and more linked in the years when Brazil was becoming Europe's most important sugar supplier, just as São Tomé had succeeded Madeira, the Canaries and other Mediterranean islands. It became a major destination for

African slaves. By 1600, Brazil had about 120 sugar mills and was among the richest European colonies.[43]

In the Caribbean and the Americas, food traditions mingled. James E. McWilliams' work on food is one of the rare works to study how African slaves brought African culture to the Americas, an important contribution that still demands further study for the Early Modern period. West African and native Caribbean agriculture and culinary traditions had developed in total isolation of each other for thousands of years. Sugar plantations and the middle passage brought them together. Culinary history is a story of adaptation but the involuntary migration of Africans to the Americas was an especially intense transition. The origins of West African cereal cultivation and livestock domestication went back tens of thousands of years. Central to this agriculture was the decision around 1500 BC to replace wild crops with cultivated wheat and barley in the savannah. Savannah farmers came to rely on a number of other cultivated crops including rice, cowpeas, sesame, okra, fluted pumpkins, gourds, calabashes and watermelons. These farmers practiced a combination of agricultural methods that outlasted Africa's colonization. There was also forest agriculture that started around 800 AD where hunters and fishermen augmented proteins with several new Southeast Asian crops that their savannah neighbors had first cultivated. Bananas, plantains, Asiatic yams, Asiatic rice, cocoyams (taro) and sugarcane came to West Africa via Madagascar. A plant that was central to African culture was the baobab tree; the bark was used to make rope, the sap was used to make medicine and its trunk was used to make coffins but it was even more important for food. Its leaves were used to thicken stews, a grainy meal was made from its pulp to incorporate into breads and its seeds provided cooking oil. Several seeds were ground, such as watermelon, pumpkin and squash seeds that were used as seasoning while baobab trees provided seeds for oil. Palm oil was also used. A market day in West Africa was a social and culinary feast as dishes were also served. A popular dish was *kilishi*, roasted meat basted in oil, herbs and spices.[44]

With the help of the native guinea yam and oil palm tree, these goods fueled agricultural development in the sixteenth century. Europeans and some freed slaves returning from Brazil began to introduce American crops to the African continent; a sampling of these new crops includes maize, cassava, peanuts, avocados, potatoes and pineapple, which transformed and broadened the West African diet. Africa developed an internal and international trade network as maize and cassava played a powerful role in weaving Africa into foreign markets. Maize became even more central to the African diet than cassava did. Two types of maize dominated, the flint or hard variety first came to Spain with Columbus and then worked its way to West Africa via Italy and Egypt. The soft variety of flour maize arrived on the African coast with the Portuguese. Contrary to older characterizations of Africa as being technologically backward, we now know that West African farmers were open to innovation and that they actively and strategically invented technologies supporting their particular needs. Iron making was especially popular in West

Africa because of the region's lack of bronze and copper. Through the production of handheld hoes, West Africa came to rival contemporary iron making techniques in Europe and the Middle East.[45]

The yam, with its origins in the Pacific islands, was grown in Africa for centuries as a main West African crop that became especially critical to the slaves' diet and cultural identity after the sixteenth century. Slaves mainly cultivated the yellow guinea yam and the cush-cush, mixing these yams with as many as six other varieties imported directly from West Africa to the West Indies. Aside from being a good source of starch, yams rotted slowly and could be cooked in many ways. Slaves produced and consumed enough yams that they were allotted "yam grounds" by their masters who allowed them to grow yams on fallow sugar fields. Back in Africa, the yam was so central to the diet that it was linguistically linked to the verb "to eat".[46]

On their journey to the Americas, enslaved Africans cramped and chained below deck had to choke down a cold mush of yams, cassava and rice. Some slave traders who expressed more concern for the health of their cargo might sometimes complement the mush with cod and shrimp. Many slaves refused to accept their new fate and threw themselves to the sharks. If one single event best signaled the onset of their impending fate, it was this dietary doom for West Africans used to rich meat stews and abundant fare. Upon landing in the West Indies, the food situation unexpectedly improved for the captives. The underlying reason behind this was anything but newfound respect for the African culture by the slave owners. Slaves and their food provisions initially comprised 30 to 40 percent of a plantation's expenditures. Sugar dominated the West Indies and was capital intensive so the planters continually sought ways to reduce capital costs. Accordingly, planters set aside garden plots and a few of the least desirable planting fields to grow a part of their subsistence living for themselves. That a plantation owner ceased to make provision should not be looked at as a positive aspect of slavery, but it benefited more than the masters. Slaves enjoyed a chance to apply familiar farming habits to New World soil. Many of the crops they grew were unfamiliar, but Caribbean food soon became a mixture of African and Native American foods.[47]

Caribbean Food

James E. McWilliams argues that while every native Caribbean culture, and there were hundreds, developed distinctive food habits they shared several common ones. Fishing dominated the culinary life of Caribbean natives, as almost all of their protein came from fish and shellfish. Caribbean communities invariably settled within a mile of the coast so the sea was the main source of Caribbean cuisine, supplemented heavily by cassava. A pink-ish cigar-shaped tuber indigenous to South America, cassava can reach about six feet. The root's chief advantage is its durability. It has to be prepared carefully; the root has to be soaked in water and heated gently to eliminate the poisonous prussic acid. Native American cooks prepared the white root in a variety of ways;

more often than not they made ground meal and turned this into flat cakes over a griddle. The prussic acid was used as an effective poison to stun fish and to preserve meat. Potatoes, tobacco, maize, beans, pumpkins, coco yams, squash, peppers and pineapples were growing in the Caribbean when African slaves arrived in the sixteenth century. One social habit that was common to all Caribbean natives and to the newly arrived Africans was that the job of cooking generally fell to women.[48] Men were too important as laborers in the fields; women also worked the fields, but were left to do the domestic chores.

Caribbean natives and West Africans negotiated a wide range of equipment practices and ingredients within the confines of a brutally oppressive existence. The course of change always followed the dictates of sugar and thus it was through importation rather than natural increase that the slave population in the Caribbean grew immensely through the seventeenth and eighteenth centuries. As the demography of the British West Indies changed to meet Europe's sweet tooth, the culinary practices of the islands became the exclusive domain of slaves who came to comprise up to 90 percent of the population on some British American islands. They made the agricultural and cooking decisions that shaped the region's overall culinary habits. Slaves pioneered food habits that a stubborn historical record has ignored. Nevertheless enough evidence survives to argue that the ingredients of a genuine American cuisine emerged through their efforts. The ingredients slaves combined had a substantial culinary influence not only on the islands but throughout British America.[49] In Dutch and British America, African slaves brought their expertise of keeping livestock in open pastures, a form of herding unknown to the Europeans who kept their cattle in enclosed spaces.[50] For their European masters this skill permitted the consumption of a familiar meat, beef, in the Americas.[51]

Plantation owners did not share the same diet as their laborers. If Europeans in the islands had known starvation in the 1630s no matter their rank, by the middle of the century several visitors described the well-laden tables of sugar masters, which easily competed with the best tables in Europe. Plantation owners seem to have made it a point to live like in Europe. A Frenchman Father Biet visited Drax House, a major planter's house in Barbados, and described being served spectacular food. He found nothing lacking in the meats; in one meal he describes being served suckling pigs, hens, chickens, turkey hens and mutton, all of this accompanied by wines from Madeira, Spain and France. The drinking was so heavy that he often turned down invitations because it was considered offensive not to stay and continue drinking. After such a repast, his hosts would have their slaves fill their tobacco pipes and bring a bowl of brandy in which they broke eggs. Starting with the host, guests drank to each other's health. This would go on for hours and Father Biet wrote, as did others before him, that it was a life of sybaritic torpor and drunken leisure for the wealthy on the islands.[52]

One of the most important markers of life on the Caribbean islands was heavy drinking no matter which social group you belonged to. A visitor to Barbados described the European settlers, both servants and masters, as "such great drunkards". Often the Europeans could not import wine and ale and drank "mobby", fermented from sweet potato, which reminded them of sweet wines from the Rhine. Another drink called "perino" was fermented from cassava; it must have been strong as the same visitor describes people passed out and sprawled by the side of the road, their toes being bitten off by land-crabs.[53] A byproduct of sugar distillation, rum was actually poisonous. It gave drinkers what was known as "Dry Belly-ache", agonizing stomach cramps. Only as late as 1676 was this severe cramping identified as lead poisoning. Not until the middle of the eighteenth century was distillation seen as the cause of the disease. The pipes used for distilling rum were lead pipes. Drinking contributed to a life expectancy for the Europeans in the West Indies that was as low as ten while in England it was thirty-five.[54]

American Commodities: The History of Tobacco and Chocolate

Whether it was growing tobacco, sugar or cotton to replace the exports to Europe from the Levant, the work on American plantations was grueling and the heat intense. This pattern of taking rare luxury goods from Asia and mass-producing them on American plantations through African slaves and indentured labor would be a pattern that dominated the next centuries. It would be the fate of Chinese oranges called *Portughal* in the Muslim world after the main producers of the fruit in Brazil, the Portuguese. New American products would also form European tastes. Tobacco did not do well on the islands but several colonial experiments would be devoted to cultivating it on the American continent. Chocolate and tobacco were deeply rooted in several Amerindian cultures and their consumption completely unknown to the Spanish and Portuguese upon their arrival. Through cross-cultural relationships, Europeans learned about the importance of the use of tobacco and chocolate, because many trading relationships between the Spanish and the indigenous populations were completed upon offering these two goods.

Michael and Sophie Coe believe, based on a slew of evidence, some linguistic, some archaeological, that the roots of chocolate go much further back to the great Olmec civilization, which preceded the Maya. The Olmec lived in the southern Gulf of Mexico between 1500 and 500 BC, and their influence extended to Guatemala, Honduras, Belize, Costa Rica and El Salvador. It was through Christopher Columbus during his fourth voyage in May 1504 that the Spanish encountered chocolate in Guanaja. This encounter was documented by Columbus's son Ferdinand. The conquistadors who followed them in Mesoamerica appreciated the cacao bean as currency but were at first baffled and repelled by chocolate in the form of a drink.[55] Yet among the Spanish fashions adopted by other European courts, chocolate drinking was a most elitist and expensive habit that was imitated by the European aristocracy. Marcy Norton marked the 1518 expedition of Juan Grijalva as the first recorded encounter with tobacco smoking.[56] Spanish observers left knowing that tobacco smoking was important in celebrations of diplomatic and peaceful allegiances. Hernán Cortés' conquest expedition against the Aztec Empire was famous for its violence and bringing Mexico under the rule of the King of Castille in the early sixteenth century. Yet Cortés made use of diplomacy in order to establish relations with the Aztecs and it is through these diplomatic relations that his men consumed chocolate during negotiations at the court of Moctezuma. It was apparent to Spanish witnesses that the consumption of chocolate was central to the elite in Mexico.

Marcy Norton has found that the first European representations of tobacco and chocolate that appeared in travel accounts about the New World did not correspond to the real experiences of the explorers and conquistadors that had witnessed their consumption. While the Spanish in Mexico might have been well immersed in the consumption of tobacco and chocolate like the locals, the colonial discourse in books portrayed these new goods as symbols of Amerindian otherness and evil in Spain. Tobacco, in particular, was used as a moral and ethical justification for the conquest of the Indies. In this discourse its use divided the Christians from the heathen and the civilized Spanish from the savage Amerindians.[57]

Many of these travel accounts, which included the first descriptions of tobacco and chocolate, were written by men who had never left Europe's shores; a most famous one was written by Peter Martyr D'Anghera who relied on a source written by a friar who had accompanied Columbus on his second voyage in the autumn of 1493 to what is today the Dominican Republic.[58] The description was of Saint-Domingue natives and Martyr framed his descriptions of the Indians by comparing all Amerindians with the pagans of antiquity. Martyr's imagination was captured by his description of *choba*, later identified as tobacco, used by shamans in the Dominican Republic to communicate with their idols. He described the many parts of Mexico reminiscent of an over-developed, sophisticated and antique Rome inhabited by decadent pagans. Martyr described chocolate in the context of the luxuries of Moctezuma's Aztec court, among them flowing gold and "1,500 garments of Gossampine cotton".[59] He reported that at Moctezuma's court, food and clothing could be classified according to rank and he referred to chocolate as the wine of kings and nobles. He qualified it as a "wonderful drink" composed of "certain almonds" exclusively the privilege of royalty.[60] Martyr also qualifies chocolate as "happie money" contrasting it with gold for it is not found underground but "groweth upon trees".[61] In his travel account, tobacco belonged to the simple savages of the Dominican Republic while chocolate belonged to the evolved Aztec civilization of Mexico.

Girolamo Benzoni thought chocolate to be a murky, sinister-looking beverage and in 1575 he wrote "it seemed more a drink for pigs than a drink for humanity".[62] Sophie Coe points out that new settlers had equally low opinions of the food eaten by Mesoamericans such as corn, turkey, avocados and tomatoes. They imported beef cattle, milk cows, sheep, goats, pigs and chickens from Europe and forced their native laborers to plant wheat, chickpeas and peach and orange trees. They also brought the novelty of sugar to

Mesoamerica and grew it on a vast plantation scale.[63] Few European observers understood the rigid class divisions of Aztec society and the fact that it had strict sumptuary laws. Chocolate had a long history before the Spanish arrived. One of the more sympathetic observers of Mesoamerican society was Fray Bartolomé de las Casas. Las Casas stated that chocolate was very substantial, cooling, tasty, agreeable and did not intoxicate. Indeed he seemed to be aware that chocolate was a drink for the elite and that the Aztecs held alcoholic beverages in contempt. An alcoholic drink made from agave, *octli* was a native wine that was forbidden to most people and drunkenness was punished by death. Nevertheless, *octli* drinking was allowed for the elderly and the elite. The Aztecs considered chocolate a desirable beverage, especially for the military. At banquets and ordinary meals for the elite, chocolate was never sipped nor drunk during the meal but was served at the end.[64] To these European writers, tobacco signified native depravity while cacao was seen positively. Cacao was compared to wine, served as a reminder of European nobility's decadence and excessive wine drinking, but was seen a marker of class.[65]

Marcy Norton has shown that both chocolate and sugar were initially used for their medicinal properties. Indigenous Mexica/Aztec medical views of cocoa are recorded in several sixteenth century documents, among them the famous *Codex of Barbarine Latin 241*, published in 1552 and a *Florentine Codex* published in 1590. They were compiled by Spanish priests and as previously argued, early texts contain pre-European views regarding the medical uses of chocolate. *Codex of Barbarine* is a Mexican herbal document that identified more than one hundred medical conditions and their cures. It also contains a passage that described how cocoa flowers were strewed to perfume the baths to reduce fatigue. The *Florentine Codex* published towards the end of the sixteenth century was compiled by the priest Bernadino Sahagún who arrived in New Spain in 1529. While many Catholic priests viewed these locals as savages, Sahagún held an opposing view and expressed a deep curiosity about Mexica/Aztec medical knowledge. The *Florentine Codex* contains some of the earliest known medical passages associated with chocolate. In one passage, he records that drinking large quantities of green cacao made consumers confused and deranged but regular consumption invigorated and refreshed. Chocolate was drunk to treat stomach and intestinal complaints by local inhabitants when combined with the liquid that came from the bark of the silk cotton tree *Castilla elastica*. Childhood diarrhea was treated with five cacao beans blended with the root of a plant we do not recognize today. In the decades that followed the Spanish conquests of the Americas, cacao was introduced as a beverage to the Spanish court. Within a century both culinary and medical uses of cacao spread to the Dutch Republic, France and England and the increased demand for chocolate led the French to establish the first Caribbean cocoa plantations. The history of Europe's consumption of chocolate is closely tied to consuming sugar.[66]

In 1535 the word "*tabaco*" first appeared in print in *La historia general de las Indias*. Its author, Gonzalo Fernández de Oviedo y Valdés, had a great personal stake in the colonial project and part of his motivation in writing it was to defend the Spanish conquistadors. Oviedo left Spain and arrived in America to participate in the conquest of Panama in 1514 and spent several years as a colonial official. He later settled in Saint-Domingue where he wrote his history of the Indies. Tobacco appeared in book five of his history, a book devoted – as he describes it – to the crimes, abominable customs and rites of the people of Hispaniola. He complained that the population, despite over forty years of being exposed to Christianity, refused his teachings. According to Marcy Norton, more than any object introduced in the *Historia general*, tobacco was the embodiment of the "bad" Indian. Oviedo's account of tobacco illustrates how Spanish notions of diabolism and witchcraft influenced their perception of tobacco. The closest herb to tobacco that they could find in Europe was henbane, which had long been associated with witchcraft and sorcery. In the second part of the *Historia general*, Oviedo made the devil a centerpiece of Indian rituals of smoking tobacco. Oviedo knew that some Christians used it, in particular those who suffered from *mal de bubas* (syphilis). Oviedo managed to portray tobacco negatively and wrote that the Indians used it amongst their other vices to become "insensed".[67]

Marcy Norton noted that Oviedo completely left out cacao from the *Historia general*, because it did not fit well into the negative colonial discourse dividing barbarian rituals from civilized manners.[68] Unlike his description of tobacco, Oviedo's treatment of chocolate waffled between clear declaration of cacao's otherness and its actual appropriation by Christians. He emphasized the Indians' passion for making cacao appear like blood by the addition of achiote. He wrote that this was a horrific thing, for it appeared as if they were drinking their own blood; the drinking of chocolate was a "disgusting view" for him, while the drinkers considered it the best thing in the world.[69] In many sources, it is written that the cacao pod was a symbolic term used in ritual for the human heart torn out in sacrifice. Eric Thompson suggested that this might have arisen because of the resemblance in shape but it may also be that both were repositories of precious liquids, blood and chocolate. In one spectacular ritual that took place annually in Tenochtitlan, the capital of the Aztecs, drinking cacao was directly related with heart extrication during sacrifice.[70] All of these descriptions are European. Nevertheless, despite these negatives, Oviedo recommended the use of cacao because one of his wounds was healed through applying cacao fat. This medicinal categorization of cacao was derived from knowledge transmitted by his own black slave. He also found it acceptable that an Italian companion during the expedition used cacao fat to fry fish and eggs to make an excellent meal. This was a European way of using a foreign substance, independent of Indian cultural forms, so that it became acceptable.[71]

The Indigenous Use of Tobacco in the Americas

All knowledge of tobacco in Europe was from travel accounts; they remain the main source of our knowledge about the consumption habits of the

Amerindians. Because of the lack of knowledge of the observers who left us these records, it is often difficult to distinguish myth from reality. The Christian lens of the observers completely deforms the descriptions that have reached us. There are very few ways to redress this, but some modern studies try to amend these early views. In *Tobacco Use by Native Americans* Joseph C. Winter highlighted the different uses of tobacco consumption amongst Native American tribes, including burning tobacco plants in hopes of a better harvest, applying it to wounds to stop bleeding and stimulating visions and sleep.[72]

The sacred and central nature of tobacco escaped most early writers. An important myth of the Cochiti Pueblo Native Americans centered on tobacco and its purifying features, which exemplifies the association of tobacco with beneficial properties.[73] Due to the cultural importance of tobacco, exposure to it began even before birth. A Mazatec shaman, for instance, would rub tobacco on a pregnant woman's belly to ward off sorcery while the Tzotzil Mayans would sometimes rub tobacco onto the lips of newborn babies.[74] Under the belief of a social contract between the mortals and immortals, Native Americans offered tobacco to gods and deities in return for the right to live on, and off of the earth. The extent to which the Native Americans lived off of the earth can be exemplified in the many substances out of which tobacco pipes were made: pottery, stone, bone, wood, reeds and even lobster claws.[75]

Although certain Native American societies used tobacco for religious and medicinal purposes, many groups abused the commodity to a hallucinatory degree. The Huichol Native Americans practiced tobacco shamanism, where the shamans used peyote and tobacco to induce hallucinations and catatonia to then communicate with their deities. Shamans continuously smoked tobacco for four days during ceremonial periods that may have also included the ingestion of alcohol, bat blood and turtle meat. Praying for the health of their community, connecting with the plants and animals of their surroundings, deducing the cause of death and talking to the deities were all achieved during these catatonic states induced by tobacco.[76] The consumption of tobacco had strong rituals in America that disappeared when it reached Europe. In European accounts only the most negative aspects of its consumption by Amerindians were highlighted.

One of the most negative descriptions was of human sacrifice. The Cult of Cihuacoatl was an Aztec priesthood dedicated to Cihuacoatl, a goddess who was represented in earthly form as tobacco and was thus honored and presented with prayers and human offerings. Fray Bernardino de Sahagún, in *General History of the Things of New Spain,* described several of their ceremonies, including the "Bathing Ceremony", which was held in honor of the war god and Cihuacoatl's son, Huitzilopochtli. Slaves and captives were forced to walk around local markets smoking tobacco and holding flowers before being bathed and further anointed with more tobacco. These slaves were then killed as human sacrifices, cooked and served over maize in honor of Huitzilopochtli.[77]

The constant description of intoxication and visions in European sources may surprise the reader today. It is important to note that the species of tobacco that Native Americans consumed was much higher in nicotine levels, up to 18 percent of nicotine. This high level of nicotine allowed shamans to enter trances, have hallucinations and become catatonic. Some shamans became color blind, paralyzed or died of an overdose. Through the European domestication of tobacco, nicotine levels have decreased to 1.5 percent of nicotine in the average commercial cigarette today.[78]

Tobacco Described in Europe

In 1535, the same year that *"tabaco"* first appeared in Oviedo's *La Historia general de las Indias*, the Frenchman Jacques Cartier also mentioned the use of tobacco in Canada. The use of tobacco in the Spanish territories in the south and in the French territories in the north points to a generalized use of tobacco in the Americas. Although the use of tobacco seemed generalized it was by no means a common ritual, as different groups have varied uses of tobacco and some have very deep spiritual ties to the plant. Between 1564 and 1700 a book about agriculture that contained large sections on tobacco was re-edited a hundred times. *Agriculture et maison rustique* was a work finished by the medical doctor Jean Liébault, a friend of Jean Nicot. Under the article *Nicotiane* in the 1570 edition, one reads that nicotine's origin is the name of the French ambassador to Portugal, Nicot, who brought tobacco to France via Portugal. There follows an enumeration of all the medical cures that Nicot applied to several illnesses in Portugal or in France.[79]

Other French authors André Thévet and Jean de Léry also wrote about tobacco in their travel descriptions. Thévet also had claims to discovering tobacco. Jean de Léry described the mores or customs of the Tupinambas and starts polemics with Thévet. Léry is the first to argue that the *pétun* of André Thévet is not the *nicotiane* of Jean Nicot; Thévet was disputing the fact that Jean Nicot had first brought tobacco to France. Before the French, many had mentioned tobacco such as Christopher Columbus, Amerigo Vespucci, and the companions of Cortés in Mexico but all of them were simply content to cite tobacco without much elaboration. The first French doctor to cite tobacco as a cure is Ambroise Paré in his *Oeuvres* printed in 1551.[80]

Spaniards started the cultivation of tobacco in the West Indies by AD 1531. By 1580, the Spanish in Cuba and Venezuela had cultivated the commodity while it took the Portuguese another twenty years to cultivate it in Brazil. Although many sources consider Oviedo's description of tobacco to be the first, other sources insist that the earliest European description of tobacco dates from 1554 by Rembert Dodoens in his *Cruydeboeck*. Soon after, in 1563 and 1565, tobacco appeared in other European herbals. By 1557, despite Nicot's claims, André Thévet took tobacco from Brazil to France and three years later it was taken to Portugal from Florida. China, Japan, and southern Africa received or were known to use tobacco around 1600.[81]

By the middle of the sixteenth century, tobacco appeared in European herbals but not under that name. Pietro Mattioli described tobacco as a new variety of *Hyoscyamus,* from the family of henbanes. In 1571 Nicolas Monardes, a doctor in the city of Seville, reported that in Seville black slaves smoked themselves into a stupefied trance.[82] He also noted, three years later, that even at the other end of the social spectrum, he saw gentlemen smoking in the Mesoamerican fashion. That same year, in 1574, the Dutch Matthias de l'Obel mentioned tobacco as being smoked by sailors who carried small tubes that they lit with fire, these were the first cigarettes.

Medical Discussions of Tobacco in Europe

A first trace of tobacco in Spanish written sources comes from an account of a visit made to Prince Philip by a group of Indians who also brought him a gift of cacao in 1554. Chocolate appeared nearly twenty years earlier in the sources, as part of a lawsuit.[83] Early mentions of chocolate were not elaborate. It is interesting to note that the first reference to cacao in print was in a work intended for European consumers, written by a female physician by the name of Oliva Sabuco de Nantes Barrera. Marcy Norton notes that, given women's specialization as producers of chocolate in Spain, it made perfect sense that a female physician would be responsible for cacao's inaugural appearance in print. In her 1588 *Colloquies on the nature of man,* she offered advice on health. Because of the law of similars, she believed that the brain-shaped cacao pod had the capacity to revitalize the brain. Again, for the same reason based on similitude, she counseled that breast-feeding women should eat foods with white marrow including hazelnuts, almonds, pine nuts and cacao. Male authors took great pleasure in deriding her views and proclaiming her ignorance.[84]

Both chocolate and tobacco were new substances in Europe and the objects of important medical debates. In his book, Monardes noted twenty different uses for tobacco and described the plant's effects in humoral terms. Humoral theories were the basis of medical knowledge. Based on Hippocratic methods developed in Greece, humoral theory holds that the human body is filled with four basic substances that are in perfect balance when a person is healthy. These substances are black bile, yellow bile, phlegm, and blood. All diseases are the result of an excess or deficit of one of these four humors or substances. Humors not only affected health, but also personality. This theory of substances in the body was closely related to a theory of elements in the world: earth, fire, water, and air. Earth was believed to be predominant in black bile, fire in yellow bile, water in phlegm, and all four elements were present in blood. The word humor in Greek is *chymos,* which means juice or sap. Each substance has qualities: blood is warm and moist, yellow bile is warm and dry, black bile is cold and dry, and phlegm is cold and moist. Just like these four humors, food also possessed these qualities of hot and cold, moistness and dryness. In early Greek medicine, nutrition affected the balance of the humors and could lead to a person becoming more melancholic with an excess of phlegm or more sanguine and angry if he or she had an excess of blood. New substances, such as chocolate, were objects of medical debate because it was difficult for European physicians to determine their humoral qualities.[85]

Monardes described tobacco's qualities as hot and dry to the second degree. He described tobacco's properties as providing heat that would dissolve any surplus of cold humors that caused congestion and discomfort in the head and chest. Marcy Norton notes that his classification was not based on a comparison with a similar plant, such as henbane, which was classified as cold. Strikingly Monardes' classification followed the Mesoamerican classification of tobacco as a hot substance.[86] If tobacco was at the heart of Monardes' 1571 book, his obsession was the question of whether the Europeans who embraced tobacco became pagan and potentially diabolical because they emulated idolaters. He had to contend with the legacy left by Oviedo's religious description of tobacco as diabolical. He had to employ a number of strategies to show enthusiasm for tobacco's therapeutic potential. His solution to encourage tobacco consumption was the following: while he described the rituals that had painted smoking tobacco as a diabolical rite, he distanced himself by making clear that tobacco, as a commodity, was innocent. He argued that it was the rites that were diabolical and not tobacco; that it was the devil that had shown the Indians the virtues of tobacco, but that tobacco itself did not cause demonical delusion. Tobacco, once consumed, caused a hallucinatory state wherein the devil was able to more easily penetrate vulnerable minds and then to implant demonic delusions. The devil was not the creator of tobacco, but its discoverer. Tobacco was still good, or at least neutral, so it was not the agent of demonic power – the power was the devil. In the sixteenth century, there was a growing debate among theologians that denied the devil's direct agency in the world. This allowed Monardes to participate in the debate. In Monardes' views, those who over-indulged in food or alcohol were made vulnerable and their imaginations allowed Satan to plant delusions in their minds. Monardes sought to sanitize tobacco by proving that the commodity could be used medically for a purpose that was not an Amerindian habit. He designated this medical consumption as civilized. Once again, this European usage is reminiscent of Oviedo's arguments for the positive medicinal and culinary use of cacao fat.[87]

Monardes gave descriptions of some of the healing aspects of tobacco as an aid during physical labor. He described the consumption of tobacco after the dancing and physical labor of black slaves as a way to calm their nerves and enter into deep sleep. He wrote that after smoking tobacco "thei remaine as dedde people",[88] but that their fatigue was gone when they awoke. Most striking was his description of the use of tobacco balls by Native Americans during travel.

> Then they use to travail by ways, where they find no water nor meat: They take a little ball of these, and they put it between the lower lip and the teethe, and they go chewing it all the time that they do travel and that which

they do chew, they do swallow it down, and in this sort they do journey, three or four days, without having need of meat, or drink, for they feel no hunger, dryness, nor weakness, nor travel does trouble them.[89]

Monardes is also one of the only sources that gives an explanation for the origin of the name of the plant: "The proper name of it amongst the Indians is Pecielt, for the name of Tabaco is geven to it of our Spanairdes, by reason of an Ilande that is named Tabaco."[90] In Europe, for a very long time, there was simply no common name for consuming tobacco. Only in the course of the seventeenth century did smoking become a commonly used term. Up to then, one spoke of drinking smoke and drinking tobacco. As late as 1658, a Jesuit preacher Jakob Balde titled his satire against smoking, *Dry Drunkenness.* The analogy with drinking was a conceptual aid for grasping a bewildering novelty. Tobacco's main active element, nicotine, had comparable effects to alcohol. Unlike chocolate, nicotine did not stimulate but dulled the nerves because it was a nerve toxin. A high dosage of nicotine consumed in the course of one day, or in one single dose is fatal.[91]

Several pamphlets were written in Europe against smoking, equating smoking with degeneracy, yet other pamphlets argued for the positive effects of tobacco. Unlike the Spanish, the French often wrote that tobacco was beneficial to one's health and Jean Nicot took it upon himself to personally popularize its use in Europe.[92] An eighteenth-century text echoes previous French ones by stating that

There is nothing better for contemplation than tobacco smoking, for here straying thoughts are recollected, this being most beneficial for students, in that while smoking they can grow accustomed to pondering everything well. Often enough one's faculties are divided, so that it is impossible to reason correctly over some difficult matter; among tobacco smokers, on the other hand, thoughts are collected.[93]

Tobacco can be considered the first global American drug commodity. It spread across the world with great speed. Its use was very varied and cultural differences affected its consumption. The first groups to use tobacco in Europe were soldiers and sailors in the ports of Lisbon, Genoa and Naples. Once the English set up plantations in Virginia, they would become the main distributors of tobacco. Despite the fact that the French, like Jean Nicot, did a lot to introduce it to Europe, they were not importers. The use of tobacco was introduced through commercial contacts, such as when English merchants brought it to Russia in 1560. The Portuguese and Dutch merchants introduced it to Africa and Asia. Smoking was common in Sierra Leone as early as 1607 while southern Africa was exposed to tobacco with the foundation of the Cape Colony in 1652. In Asia, the Portuguese introduced tobacco to Iran and to the Ottoman Empire. It spread from Iran to Central Asia. Japan also learned how to smoke tobacco directly from Portuguese merchants and sailors. Scholars guess that tobacco spread to Korea and Manchuria rather late with the Japanese occupation, while it was introduced directly to China by the Portuguese in Macao.[94]

It has been argued that the popularization of tobacco followed an ambiguous trajectory on the two opposite sides of the social spectrum. Sailors and soldiers spread tobacco among the working people while Europe's royal houses helped to popularize it among the elite. Tobacco briefly came to be called *Catherinaire* because the French Queen Catherine of Medici used the plant as snuff to cure her headaches. The papal nuntius in Lisbon introduced the tobacco seeds to the Vatican where it grew in the gardens and acquired the name of *herba santa* or sacred herb. As such, it became associated with religious circles and a form of consumption closer to Amerindian views of tobacco. Italian clergy did not smoke tobacco but used it in the form of snuff as had Catherine of Medici and the courtiers of Louis XIV. The French were in fact instrumental in introducing tobacco to the rest of Europe. French Protestants (the Huguenots) seemed to have taken it with them from France to many other countries, including Germany. Pipe smoking was disdained by the elite in most of Europe except the Dutch; it has been argued that Holland was an exception, as tobacco was smoked by all classes.[95] As the first republic in the world, this egalitarianism in the consumption of an exotic good demonstrates the lack of demarcation between classes.

In May 1683, the Spanish Crown agreed that the monopoly on tobacco would no longer be leased, but directly administered by the state. Marcy Norton argues that the Castilian tobacco monopoly had a great role in European state formation. The experiment of the direct administration of the monopoly of tobacco by the state did not last and the Crown reverted to contracting private arrangements. It had been argued that the leasing arrangements of the tobacco monopoly in the seventeenth century were the building blocks that made the emergence of the powerful Spanish state possible. The fiscalization of tobacco by the state affected its cultural meaning and made legal the status of tobacco as a vice and as the first "mass luxury" commodity.[96] State monopoly led the consumers and producers of tobacco to associate the state with the consumption of tobacco; the state became the guarantor of tobacco supplies and legitimized its existence. Norton argues that this state monopoly challenges the accepted narrative of modern consumption, which is that dominant political discourse from the state disdained luxury until the eighteenth century. Studying tobacco consumption confirms the existence not only of certain forms of mass consumption before the eighteenth century, but also the existence of the blessing of a luxury good via state sponsored propaganda.

The Consumption of Tobacco by the Dutch

The Spanish predominance in the tobacco trade and other goods was countered in the early seventeenth century by Dutch and English competition. The Dutch East India Company, founded in 1602, and the English East India

Company, founded two years earlier in 1600, soon followed by West India companies for the trade of the Americas, successfully challenged the Spanish and Portuguese monopoly granted by the Pope on long-distance trade. In 1592 during the war with Spain, the English captured a large Portuguese carrack in the Azores that held 900 tons of merchandise from India and China. Its worth was estimated at half a million English pounds.[97] The possibility of accessing this kind of wealth from Asia was at the inception of these new maritime companies. The Dutch inaugurated the first republic in the world, the New Republic of the Seven United Provinces, which needed a steady source of income after its independence from the Spanish. Through independence, the Dutch had lost their most profitable trade partners, the Portuguese, now enemies. Seizing ships was part of commercial war. In 1603, three ships of the new Dutch East India Company seized the *Santa Catharina*, a Portuguese carrack that doubled the initial capital of the new-chartered company. The Portuguese demanded the return of their cargo from their now estranged trading partners. This conflict led to the publication of Hugo Grotius' *The Free Sea* (*Mare Liberum*) in 1609. Grotius argued that the sea was free international territory; this was of course against Portuguese interest as their main wealth came from taxing the sea. The Dutch eventually managed to break the Portuguese monopoly on the spice trade and by 1619 they conquered Jayakarta, renaming it Batavia. Goa, a Portuguese city in India, and Batavia, now a Dutch center, fought over the monopoly of the spice trade for the next twenty years. The outcome of the Dutch-Portuguese war would be the conquest of Malacca in 1641, Ceylon in 1658, and the Malabar coast in 1663. Pepper and spices had made the Portuguese rich, now the Dutch rose to dominate and eventually monopolize the spice market.[98]

The Dutch East India Company was granted a government charter that gave it the right to a monopoly of the spice trade in Asia. A government charter to the armed ships of the Dutch Company gave its directors both the right and the power to colonize any territories it desired to enslave the indigenous population for cultivation and harvest to reach its commercial quotas. This meant that the Company could wage full-scale warfare on indigenous people. The Dutch committed genocide on the island of Banda. They massacred any populations who would not cooperate with their demands for the production of cloves, nutmeg and pepper. In the American Dutch colonies of the Chesapeake, the Dutch were also involved in the tobacco trade. The fortunes of the Dutch Golden Age came from its spice islands and from other colonies. Thanks to this global maritime trade, the Dutch Republic became Europe's center for banking and commercial activity and a scientific hub. It developed a relatively large middle class not only at home but in its extensive colonial holdings in the East and West Indies. Many among them were not merchants but scholars deeply engaged in learning from Dutch colonial holdings and the new goods they produced.[99] Tobacco consumption by the Dutch has an unusual history in two ways. First it would be produced domestically, and second this American product would be mixed with the exotic spices imported from Asia by the Dutch to produce perfumed tobaccos, which still make Holland famous today.

Johann Neander's book *Tabacologia* written in 1622 records the prevalent Dutch belief that tobacco held curative and preventive properties for a wide range of diseases. It was widely consumed in the Dutch Republic and beyond. Within Dutch society, the consumption of spices was not confined to food. As Simon Schama has argued, the Dutch did to their colonial goods what they did with exotic Ming china and oriental carpets; they domesticated both the exoticism of spices and tobacco. Dutch tobacco processors were keen to promote both of these colonial products by saturating and mixing the cut and spun tobacco leaf with a variety of spices. Not all of them were exotic; the spices included citron, anisette, thyme, saffron, lavender, dill, nutmeg, coriander, vinegar, brown beer, mace, fennel, rosemary and even prunes. The most competitive of the Dutch tobacconists would go to great lengths to guard the secrecy of the mixes they used to patent their blends. It was unclear as to whether or not tobacco was considered a drug, a food or even a poison. A succession of humanist doctors and botanists lauded tobacco for its miraculous qualities as a panacea capable of soothing toothaches as well as curing worms. It became acceptable as a social habit for pleasure.[100]

Simon Schama demonstrates that there were important economic interests engaged in the Dutch tobacco industry. The Dutch West India Company that traded with North America was the chief importer of tobacco to the Netherlands. It soon had competition from a domestic Dutch tobacco industry that grew a leaf that was coarser than its Virginia counterpart. By 1675, around five to six million pounds of tobacco were being exported annually by the Dutch. The Dutch West India Company did not see domestic tobacco as competition, rather it complemented its own imports from Brazil, Venezuela, Virginia and Maryland with domestic Dutch tobacco. To complete the picture, there were the pipe makers in Amsterdam and other Dutch cities; pipe factories employed some 15,000–16,000 workers. As good Calvinisits, the Dutch should have deplored the growing and sale of tobacco and the manufacturing of pipes but there were ample economic reasons for the Republic to turn a blind eye.

There was certainly negative talk in churches against alcohol and tobacco as the devil's food but what the churches failed to stigmatize was their consumption. Smoking and drinking were thought of as socially innocuous. As in China, the use of pipes and tobacco could actually confer honor and status in the Netherlands. In Dutch feasts as well as in the wigwam of the Indians, there were literally pipes of peace smoked in the group. The Dutch might not have been the first users of tobacco in Europe, but they were its first connoisseurs and started making luxurious implements tied to its use. Tobacco boxes and pipes made of sumptuous materials helped integrate tobacco into the "home life" of the country.[101] A commonplace observation at home and abroad was that "a Hollander without a pipe is a national impossibility, akin to a town without a house, a stage without actors, a spring without flowers".[102] Dutch grown tobacco was never enough to satisfy European demand. The plantation system and the systematic exploitation of the New World to bring in tobacco, sugar, furs and other goods had unwanted impacts on the Americas and the Caribbean.

The Consumption of American Commodities in China

Timothy Brook's study shows that tobacco became part of Chinese daily culture by the end of the seventeenth century. The year 1644 was one of great turmoil in China as the Manchu Qing conquered the Chinese and became the last dynasty of emperors to rule China. Under the new Qing Dynasty (1644–1911) tobacco was called "golden thread smoke" and "lovesick grass", the latter referring to the desire for smoking. An ostentatious use of tobacco became the hallmark of the fashionable rich. Men boasted of their inability to eat, converse and even think without a lighted pipe. Men and women both smoked; women carried special silk tobacco purses and smoked with extra long pipes. Some of these pipes were so long and ostentatious that they had to be carried around by servants. Aristocratic women slept with their heads on special blocks so that attendants could do their hair and makeup while they were unconscious between waking and the first tobacco of the day. Timothy Brook found the tale of these elite sleeping smokers in Chen Cong's *Yancau pu* (tobacco manual), a collection of tobacco-related poetry. Tobacco was also embraced beyond the elite by Ming soldiers. A Chinese physician wrote that most units of soldiers were attacked by malaria except for a single unit that was spared. In his opinion they were in perfect health because they smoked tobacco. As a child in the 1630s, writer Wang Pu had never heard of the use of tobacco. As an adult, "customs suddenly changed and all the people, even boys not four feet tall, were smoking".[103]

Tobacco was not the only American plant that China embraced. At the time, China was home to roughly a quarter of the world's population so food crops were of tremendous importance. The Song, Yuan, Ming and Qing dynasties understood the political vulnerability caused by famine and the necessity of maintaining China's agricultural base through imperial control. In China, water management was so important to agriculture that European thinkers such as Karl Marx and Max Weber considered it the most important institution in Chinese society. Most sinologists today do not believe in this absolute despotic imperial rule that was based on this idea of water control and think of Chinese society as a diverse one. Yet no sinologist today would dispute that China had a relative paucity of land suitable to grow rice and wheat, which demanded large quantities of water. To China, the Columbian exchange was very important and no society was quicker to adopt American food plants than the Chinese. As Alfred W. Cosby has remarked in *The Columbian Exchange*, sweet potatoes, maize (corn), peanuts, tobacco, chili peppers, pineapple, cashew and manioc (cassava) arrived in Fujian via the Spanish and Portuguese galleon trade, in Guangdong via Portuguese ships and in Korea via Japan. Today China is the world's biggest producer of sweet potato. This new American crop spread through the province of Fujian before the fall of the Ming Dynasty in 1644.[104] The new plants needed less water and therefore were adopted and accepted with great enthusiasm.

Like many new plants coming to a society, they were first adopted under duress. The turmoil under the Qing created a mass of refugees. Coastal people flooded into the mountains of Fujian and Guangdong. Landless and poor, the Hakki refugees were mocked as shack people who rented land so high that it was no use to farmers. Neither rice nor wheat would grow on soil so thin and so dry. They turned to American crops such as corn, sweet potato and tobacco because corn could thrive and grow quickly, maturing in far less time than wheat, rice or millet. Brought in by the Portuguese, it was called "wrapped green" or "jade rice". Sweet potato could grow where even corn could not. The Qing actively promoted a westward movement; much as the United States had later encouraged its citizens to move west, the Chinese were convinced that settling space was essential. For almost two thousand years, China's population had grown slowly but this changed after the violent Qing takeover. From the arrival of American crops at the beginning of the new dynasty to the end of the eighteenth century, China's population soared.[105]

China as a Participant in Global Consumption

Bin Wong has argued that China was a very important participant in the global long-distance trade during Early Modern times yet historians continue to look at China's economy by looking at what *didn't* happen to China. The argument is often that China did not follow any European path of economic development. Studies of Chinese economic practices between 1500 and 1900 usually proceed in one of two ways. The first explanation is that the Chinese imperial state obstructs progress to protect its power, a model known as Oriental despotism and one that was favored by Karl Marx and Marxists for a long time. The second explanation is to look at imperialism that warps economic exchanges to serve European interests. In the first despotic model, the emperor is sometimes replaced by feudal power holders anxious to defend their elite positions. What unites almost all assessments of economic change in late imperial China is an agreement that China possessed all the ingredients for continued economic change. The Marxist analysts look for villains that blocked what would have been a natural development towards capitalism. Another way of approaching what didn't happen in China is to find social explanations by finding a key that the Chinese lacked. The most famous of such analysis remains Max Weber's contrast of the Protestant ethics with religious beliefs in other parts of the world. The argument that Protestantism was conducive to the development of capitalism has been criticized in several ways: first, Catholic Europe also achieved economic development and consumerism and second, the argument of religion leading to capitalism has also been made for China. Yu Ying-shih has demonstrated how concerns in sixteenth and seventeenth century Confucianism paralleled the rise of a distinctive commercial culture, a merchant point of view, as trade expanded in importance.[106]

China had a long tradition of seeing its agricultural production as central to its economic health. In Europe, the elaboration of banking and marketing institutions made possible increasingly sophisticated patterns of exchange, a division of labor and a specialization in production. Yet these new developments rested upon a very fragile base: Europe's agriculture. Harvest conditions determined the annual fluctuation in food prices and heavily influenced the cost of manufacturing. Harvest shortfalls triggered cyclical declines in industry as well as agriculture. This cycle made famous by Ernest Labrousse marked the rhythm of Europe's economy from the fifteenth century on. Both the economy and the population of Europe grew in the Early Modern period but slowly and not without cycles of expansion and contraction. The seventeenth century is often seen as a century of "general crisis" due to economic, social and political difficulties. At a time when Europe was engaged in very successful long distance trade, the cycle of famines and population decline continued at home. Bin Wong has argued that contrary to the view that China's economy was stagnant, one can witness Smithian dynamics across much of China between the sixteenth and nineteenth centuries, with an increase in cash cropping, handicrafts and trade. Most famous are the expanding cotton and silk industries of the lower Yangtze region near Shanghai, industries that joined rice and other cash crops to create China's richest region. Other cash crops and handicrafts such as cotton, indigo, tobacco, pottery and paper emerged in these provinces. The development of product markets provides the clearest indication of commercialization in China between 1500 and 1900.[107]

Regional economies in China, the equivalent in many cases to national economies in Europe, experienced great cycles of expansion. Sixteenth-century expansion was most important in the lower Yangzi, on the southern coast, and in south China. New groups of merchants organized expanded patterns of exchange between market towns and the countryside. Nevertheless, these realities were not known in the eighteenth century to Adam Smith. Based on his writings European economists Ricardo and Malthus, shared his belief that economic growth was limited in China. All three argued that subsistence cost and wages were dynamically linked through the economic determination of demographic rates. In Adam Smith's view, high wages permitted the survival of children and as more children survived, population growth drove wages down.[108] He also held that profit levels and interest rates fell in wealthy countries when opportunities to multiply riches had been witnessed.[109] Working with this same framework, Ricardo anticipated the exhaustion of natural resources in China, while Malthus feared the multiplication of China's population beyond its resources.

Adam Smith, Ricardo and Malthus all lived in a world where agriculture remained the dominant sector of the economy.[110] Their ideas and much scholarship produced since them have created the idea of a great divergence between Europe and China. This idea of a great divergence is thoroughly addressed by a new school of thought; Kenneth Pomeranz exposed the great divergence as a fallacy, as we will explore in a later chapter, as he examines the eighteenth century and consumption in China.[111] His argument counters the idea that the rise of consumption was a Western phenomenon. Others have argued that the Early Modern period was also a period of consumption growth for the Ottoman Empire, which grew so much in economic and military strength that it reached the walls of Vienna in 1683. The famous Ottoman markets through which Eurasian trade flowed were not yet overshadowed by the maritime trade of the European chartered companies. While the Portuguese and Spanish ruled the seas, the Ottoman markets remained important centers of trade.[112] Despite famines and poor harvests the European elite remained avid consumers of novel commodities and imports. Imports of "oriental" goods to Europe were carried both by sea and by land. Dutch and English ships first used porcelain as ballast, until Europe's elite began to collect it. A taste for the exotic marked the seventeenth century, as will become clear: further, whether objects were American or came from China, it mattered little to their description; they were all considered "Indian". Two Asian imports that would change European consumption very profoundly were tea and coffee, which were not described as "Indian"; their origins, their properties and effects would be even more debated than American chocolate and tobacco. European consumers were profoundly transformed by the use of new exotic goods. Yet, nothing matched the transformations that European settlement brought to the New World.

Study Questions

1 How was sugar cultivation related to the expansion of European trade and settlement from the sixteenth century onward? How did this cultivation change patterns of African settlement in the world?
2 How did sugar cultivation and distribution change European cuisine?
3 In what ways did African food influence American and Caribbean diets?
4 In what ways did Christians in Europe and the New World reconcile their consumption of drug foods (e.g. tobacco and chocolate) with the religious debate about them?
5 Where did American commodities fit in the consumer economy of China in the late Ming period? What does this tell us about conventional hypotheses regarding Chinese consumption?

Notes

1 Ned Ward. As cited in Matthew Parker, *The Sugar Barons: Family, Corruption, Empire, and War in the West Indies* (New York: Walker & Co., 2011), 5.
2 Parker, *The Sugar Barons*, 25.
3 Parker, *The Sugar Barons*, 4.

4 Sidney W. Mintz, *Sweetness and Power: The Place of Sugar in Modern History* (New York, NY: Viking, 1985), 24–32

5 Katherine Strange Burke, "A Note on Archaeological Evidence for Sugar Production in the Middle Islamic Periods in Bilād al-Shām" *Mamluk Studies Review* 8/2 (University of Chicago, 2012): 109–118.

6 Mintz, *Sweetness and Power*, 24–32.

7 Parker, *The Sugar Barons*, 11.

8 Mintz, *Sweetness and Power*, 24–32.

9 Parker, *The Sugar Barons*, 10–11.

10 Mintz, *Sweetness and Power*, 32.

11 Charles C. Mann, *1493, Uncovering the New World Columbus Created* (New York: Alfred A. Knopf, 2011), 11.

12 Mann, *1493*, 79.

13 Elizabeth Abbott, *Sugar: A Bittersweet History* (London; New York: Duckworth Overlook, 2009), 77.

14 Abbott, *Sugar: A Bittersweet History*, 18.

15 Mintz, *Sweetness and Power*, 33.

16 Mintz, *Sweetness and Power*, 36.

17 Mintz, *Sweetness and Power*, 24–32.

18 Parker, *The Sugar Barons*, 27.

19 Mintz, *Sweetness and Power*, 41–44.

20 Brian Cowan, "New Worlds, New Tastes" in Paul Freedman ed, *Food: The History of Taste* (Berkeley: University of California Press, 2007), 220.

21 Cowan, *Food: The History of Taste*, 205.

22 Mintz, *Sweetness and Power*, 64–90.

23 British Library Board "1500s Food" Last accessed February 21, 2012. http://www.bl.uk/learning/langlit/booksforcooks/1500s/1500sfoods.html

24 Mintz, *Sweetness and Power*, 61.

25 Parker, *The Sugar Barons*, 126–127.

26 Parker, *The Sugar Barons*, 126–127.

27 François Massialot, *Nouvelle instruction pour les confitures, les liqueurs, et les fruits : avec la maniere de bien ordonner un dessert, & tout le reste qui est du devoir des maîtres d'hôtels, sommeliers, confiseurs, & autres officiers de bouche: suite du cuisinier roïal & bourgeois: egalement utile dans les familles, pour sçavoir ce qu'on sert de plus à la mode dans les repas, & en d'autres occasions. Seconde édition, revûë, corrigée, & beaucoup augmentée* (Paris: Chez Charles de Sercy, 1698).

28 Cowan, *Food: The History of Taste*, 224–225.

29 Mintz, *Sweetness and Power*, 92.

30 Mintz, *Sweetness and Power*, 92–94.

31 Parker, *The Sugar Barons*, 126.

32 Mintz, *Sweetness and Power*, 160.

33 Hugh Thomas, *The Slave Trade* (New York, NY: Touchstone Books, 1999), 220–221.

34 John Thornton, *Africa and Africans in the Making of the Atlantic World, 1400–1800* (Cambridge; New York: Cambridge University Press, 1998).

35 Mann, *1493*, 304.

36 John E. Wills, *1688: A Global History* (New York: Norton, 2001) 29–30.

37 Caroline Frank, *Objectifying China, Imagining America: Chinese Commodities in Early America* (Chicago: University of Chicago Press, 2011), 12–13.

38 Wills, *A Global History*, 29.

39 Thomas, *The Slave Trade*, 130–133.

40 Thomas, *The Slave Trade*, 226.

41 Thomas, *The Slave Trade*, 227.

42 Thomas, *The Slave Trade*, 133.

43 Thomas, *The Slave Trade*, 135.
44 James E. McWilliams, *A Revolution in Eating: How the Quest for Food Shaped America* (New York: Columbia University Press, 2005), 34.
45 McWilliams, *A Revolution in Eating*, 31–32.
46 McWilliams, *A Revolution in Eating*, 40.
47 McWilliams, *A Revolution in Eating*, 36–38.
48 McWilliams, *A Revolution in Eating*, 36–38.
49 McWilliams, *A Revolution in Eating*, 43–44.
50 McWilliams, *A Revolution in Eating*, 150.
51 McWilliams, *A Revolution in Eating*, 115–118.
52 Parker, *The Sugar Barons*, 83.
53 Parker, *The Sugar Barons*, 29.
54 Parker, *The Sugar Barons*, 84.
55 Sophie D. Coe and Michael D. Coe, *The True History of Chocolate* (New York: Thames and Hudson, 2007), 109–110.
56 Marcy Norton, *Sacred Gifts, Profane Pleasures: A History of Tobacco and Chocolate in the Atlantic World* (Ithaca and London: Cornell University Press, 2008), 50.
57 Norton, *Sacred Gifts, Profane Pleasures*, 52–53.
58 Norton, *Sacred Gifts, Profane Pleasures*, 53.
59 Norton, *Sacred Gifts, Profane Pleasures*, 54.
60 Norton, *Sacred Gifts, Profane Pleasures*, 54.
61 Norton, *Sacred Gifts, Profane Pleasures*, 55.
62 Coe and Coe, *The True History of Chocolate*, 111.
63 Coe and Coe, *The True History of Chocolate*, 112.
64 Coe and Coe, *The True History of Chocolate*, 74–96.
65 Norton, *Sacred Gifts, Profane Pleasures*, 55.
66 Louis E. Grivetti, "Medicinal Chocolate in New Spain, Western Europe and North America" in *Chocolate: History, Culture and Heritage*, trans. Louis E. Grivetti and Howard-Yana Shapiro (Hoboken, NJ: Wiley, 2009), 67–89, 68–69.
67 Gonzalo Fernández de Oviedo y Valdés, *La historia general de las Indias* (Seville, 1535) Book V, Chapter 2, "De los tabacos o ahumadas que los in dios acostumbran en esta isla Española, e la manera de las camas en que duermen. Usaban los indios desta isla, entre otros sus vicios, uno muy malo, que es tomar unas ahumadas, que ellos llaman tabaco, para salir de sentido. Mas, porque de suso se dijo que cuando algún principal o cacique cae por el tabaco, que lo echan en la cama, si él lo manda así hacer, bien es que se diga qué camas tienen los indios en esta isla Española, a la cual cama llaman hamaca".
68 Norton, *Sacred Gifts, Profane Pleasures*, 55–59.
69 Norton, *Sacred Gifts, Profane Pleasures*, 59.
70 Coe and Coe, *The True History of Chocolate*, 103–104.
71 Norton, *Sacred Gifts, Profane Pleasures*, 60.
72 Joseph C. Winter, ed., *Tobacco Use by Native Americans: Sacred Smoke and Silent Killer* (Norman: University of Oklahoma Press, 2000), 39–44.
73 Winter, *Tobacco Use by Native Americans*, 44.
74 Winter, *Tobacco Use by Native Americans*, 54.
75 Winter, *Tobacco Use by Native Americans*, 72–73.
76 Winter, *Tobacco Use by Native Americans*, 276–281.
77 Winter, *Tobacco Use by Native Americans*, 298–300.
78 Winter, *Tobacco Use by Native Americans*, 307.
79 Marc and Muriel Vigié, *L'herve à Nicot: Amateurs de tabac, fermiers généraux et contrebandiers sous l'Ancien Régime* (Paris: Fayard, 1989), 26.
80 Marc and Muriel Vigié, *L'herve à Nicot*, 16–25.
81 Winter, *Tobacco Use by Native Americans*, 186.

82 Nicolas Monardes, *Segunda parte del libro des las cosas que se traen de nuestras Indias Occidentales, que sirven al uso de la medicina; do se trata del tabaco, y de la sassafras, y del carlo sancto, y de otras muchas yervas y plantas, simientes, y licores que agora nuevamente han venido de aqulellas partes, de grandes virtudes y maravillosos effectos* (Seville: Alonso Escrivano, 1571).

83 Norton, *Sacred Gifts, Profane Pleasures*, 102–103.

84 Norton, *Sacred Gifts, Profane Pleasures*, 105–115.

85 Norton, *Sacred Gifts, Profane Pleasures*, 105–115.

86 Norton, *Sacred Gifts, Profane Pleasures*, 117.

87 Norton, *Sacred Gifts, Profane Pleasures*, 120.

88 Nicholas Monardes, *Joyfull Newes out of the Newe Founde Worlde wherein is declared the rare and singuler vertues of diverse and sundrie hearbes, trees, oyles, plantes, and stones, with their applications, aswell for phisicke as chirurgerie, the daied beyng well applied bryngeth suche present remedie for all deseases, as maie seme altogether incredible: notwithstanding by practize founde out, to bee true: also the portrature of the saied hearbes, very aptly discribed* (1577) trans. John Frampton, 2 vols. (London: Constable and Co. Ltd; New York: Alfred A. Knopf, 1925) Vol. 1 "Of the Tobaco, and of his great vertue", 75–98, 87.

89 Nicolas Monardes, *Joyfull Newes out of the Newe Founde Worlde*, trans. Frampton (London, 1577). The original text: "When thei use to travaile by waies, where thei finde no water nor meate: Thei take a little baule of these, and thei put it bewtwene the lower lippe and the teethe, and thei goe chewyng it all the tyme that thei doe travail, and that which thei doe chewe, thei doew swallowe it doune, and in this sorte thei dooe journey, three or fower daies, without havyng neede of meate, or drinke, for thei feele no hiunger, drieth, nor weaknesses, nor travaile, doeth trouble them." 90.

90 Monardes, *Joyfull Newes out of the Newe Founde Worlde*, trans. John Frampton (London, 1577), 75–76.

91 Wolfgang Schivelbusch, *Tastes and Paradise: A Social History of Spices, Stimulants, and Intoxicants*, trans. David Jacobson (New York: Pantheon Books, 1992), 97.

92 Jean Baudry, *Jean Nicot* (Lyon: La Manufacture, 1988).

93 Schivelbusch, *Tastes and Paradise*, 107.

94 Rudi Matthee, "Exotic Substances: The Introduction and Global Spread of Tobacco, Coffee, Cocoa, Tea, and Distilled Liquor, Sixteenth to Eighteenth Centuries" in Roy Porter and Mikuláš Teich, eds., *Drugs and Narcotics in History* (Cambridge, UK: Cambridge University Press, 1995), 26.

95 Rudi Matthee, "Exotic Substances", 40.

96 Norton, *Sacred Gifts, Profane Pleasures*, 228.

97 Rogério Miguel Puga, "The Presence of the 'Portugals' in Macau and Japan", in Richard Hakluyt, *Navigations, Bulletin of Portuguese/Japanese Studies*, Vol. 5 (Lisbon, Portugal: Universidade Nova de Lisboa, December 2002), 81–116.

98 Kristof Glamann, *Dutch-Asiatic Trade, 1620–1740* (Copenhagen: Danish Science Press, 1958).

99 Harold J. Cook, *Matters of Exchange: Commerce, Medicine, and Science in the Dutch Golden Age* (New Haven: Yale University Press; 2008), 3.

100 Simon Schama, *The Embarrassment of Riches: An Interpretation of Dutch Culture in the Golden Age* (Berkeley; Los Angeles; London: University of California Press, 1988), 196–199.

101 Schama, *The Embarrassment of Riches*, 194–198.

102 G. D. J. Schotel quoted in Schama, *The Embarrassment of Riches*, 198.

103 Timothy Brook, "Smoking in Imperial China", S. Gilman and X. Zhou, eds., *Smoke: A Global History of Smoking.* (London Reaktion Books, 2004), as quoted in Charles C. Mann, *1493*, 84–91, 164–165.

104 Mann, *1493*, 168–169.

105 Mann, *1493*, 173–175.
106 R. Bin Wong, *China Transformed: Historical Change and the Limits of European Experience* (Ithaca and London: Cornell University Press, 1997), 14–15.
107 Bin Wong, *China Transformed*, 18–20.
108 Adam Smith, *An Inquiry into the Nature and Causes of the Wealth of Nations* (New York: Random House, 1937), 64–86.
109 Smith, *The Wealth of Nations*, 87–98.
110 Bin Wong, *China Transformed*, 22.
111 Kenneth Pomeranz. *The Great Divergence: China, Europe and the Making of the Modern World Economy* (New Jersey: Princeton University Press, 2000).
112 Halil İnalcik and Donald Quataert, eds., *An Economic and Social History of the Ottoman Empire*, 1300–1916 (New York, NY: Cambridge University Press, 1994).

Figure 3.1 Quaker tobacco plantation in Barbados in the seventeenth century. © Pictorial Press Ltd/Alamy.

3 Consuming the New World
Settlements and Transformation

> Furs, silks and fine cottons, stimulants – tea, coffee, sugar, rum, gin, tobacco and
> spices of all kinds – scrimshaw and curios for cabinets, travel books and atlases,
> topazes, feathers, [were] orientalizing and Americanizing changes in clothing
> and ornament: these things did not simply 'improve the quality of life' in the
> metropole, they altered it, and altered the people who wore, ate, owned, con-
> templated, and changed their moods with them. 'You are what you eat', and
> Europe was cannibalizing the places and peoples that eventually made up its
> empires.[1]

Mary Blaine Campbell summarized the deep transformation in European
customs and food ways by the phrase "you are what you eat". In the Early
Modern period, Europe obtained from its colonies some of what it had
acquired previously in small quantities and at high prices. Other products
were new to Europeans. Sugar and spices from the East came to Europe with
the Crusades. Coveted and highly prized, they were seen as belonging to lands
close to paradise. Medieval and Renaissance food was heavily spiced on the
tables of the European elite with the only difficulty being price. If Europe
cannibalized the world, as Mary Campbell contends, the views it held about
new commodities were key to their cultural integration in Europe. Columbus's
voyage was unsuccessful in reaching the luxuries of Asia but brought the largest
unintentional biological exchange in the history of mankind. Famously called
the Columbian Exchange by historian Alfred Crosby, the exchange's impact
on the world – both Old and New – continues to this day. The exchange had
consequences that none of Europe's theologians, medical doctors or thinkers
could have imagined. Fixed on the idea of Creation, Europeans had to ask
the very important question: why did they not know what they were encountering? After 1492, European explorers faced unknown plants and animals.
Sensitive to the economic importance of the luxuriant vegetation they
encountered, Europeans collected samples of the new goods and thus Spanish
galleons brought coconuts, maize, potatoes and chillies back to Seville together
with silver and gold. The encounter between Europeans and this new world of
food transformed their culinary habits, but did so extremely slowly. Unlike the
Chinese, Europeans did not adopt these New World foods with ease. Their

resistance to several New World foods was extraordinary. It took Europeans several centuries to culturally integrate foods they viewed as low in the hierarchy of foods they had culturally constructed.[2]

Ranking Foods: The Original Food Pyramid, Air, Water, Sky

Although initially viewed negatively, chocolate was encountered at the court of American potentates, therefore it was adopted by European courts, but potatoes and tomatoes, mere vegetables, were slow to become part of Europe's diet. Once they became part of the European diet, the result was a hybrid cuisine that eventually would be seen as Europe's own national cuisine.[3] Is it possible to imagine southern Italian dishes without tomatoes, German and Belgian dishes without potatoes, or Spanish cuisine without *pimenton*? Yet these New World vegetables had difficulty being accepted in the culinary culture of Europe. Only one American food import had immediate success: Europe's aristocratic tables immediately accepted the turkey.[4] While even chocolate had some negative views associated with it, this New World bird did not. Feudal Europe reserved the hunt to landowners. The aristocracy had the privilege of owning and hunting all the animals on their lands. The most prized foods were birds. Alen J. Grieco has discovered that food was classified according to its origins and placed in a large hierarchical chain between heaven and earth. The world was thought of as organized by God's will, therefore the closer to heaven a plant or animal was, the higher its cultural value. Vegetables and animals were part of this great "chain of being", which comprised the four main elements: water encircling earth, air encircling water, and fire encircling air. Vegetables belonged to the earth element and were inferior to fish, which being water creatures were in turn inferior to birds. Pigs, cows and sheep walked the earth and were inferior to birds. They were still found on aristocratic tables because Galen considered meat the most nutritious and best of foods for the human body. Birds were the preferred food in aristocratic circles, not only because they were abundantly hunted, but also because they were highest in the Christian hierarchy of foods. They lived the closest to heaven as they were in the element of air.[5] Most aristocratic feasts comprised over a dozen different birds, the most prized being the peacock. American turkey was culturally prized and familiar in this cultural hierarchy. When the turkey arrived in Europe, it was much larger than most game birds, yet turkey could be easily understood as a high food that was proper for the table of the elites. It was compared to a large chicken and to a peacock. When encountering new animals or vegetables, Europeans compared them to the ones they had known in their own environment.[6]

The turkey remains a Christmas delicacy in France, England and many European countries. On his first voyage, Christopher Columbus observed the turkey, which he described as a very fat chicken with feathers that looked like wool. During Cortés' conquest of Mexico in 1519, he observed a number of domesticated turkeys. In Spanish writing it was very quickly called an "India hen", and in Latin it was given the name *Gallopavo*. This scientific name underlines the law of similars used by European observers to describe an unknown animal, *Gallo* for chicken and *Pavo* for peacock. It was quickly accepted on the best tables in Spain and in France. A study of the evolution of the price of turkey can determine its appearance as an aristocratic bird and later its diffusion on other tables. In 1538 a turkey was worth eight times the price of a chicken. In 1711 it only cost twice as much as a chicken. Beyond a cultural explanation how can one explain this single rapid culinary integration of an American food in practical terms? Domesticated turkeys could integrate perfectly into the long tradition of other domesticated birds such as geese, chickens, ducks and peacocks. Even though it didn't fly very much, the turkey as a bird belonged to the sky in the hierarchy of food and thus was an elite food in European views. Some cases were less clear; ducks from the New World, whom observers saw as living exclusively on water, created classification problems that caused debates because of the Catholic Church's calendar.[7]

Of the 365 days of the year, there were 150 days of fasting and abstinence in the Catholic calendar when meat was forbidden except for the ill or elderly. The ducks observed in the New World created problems as they were seen as water animals. Because on Fridays during Lent fish was customary, it was acceptable to eat animal food coming from the element of water. Since the Vatican accepted the duck as belonging to water in the sixteenth century, it was possible to eat New World duck. The division between sky, water, and earth was considered more important than the duck belonging to the category of birds. Other New World products also created problems. Long discussions took place about the drinking of chocolate before Mass. It was customary to fast before Mass, but in the seventeenth century even ecclesiastics began to drink chocolate in the morning because chocolate escaped traditional classification. Despite the many fast days when any meat was prohibited, vegetables were not an important part of the European diet until the end of the sixteenth century. As they belonged to earth in the hierarchy of foods, vegetables were considered inferior foods. Within the inner classification of fruits and vegetables, there was also a hierarchy of origin, which placed mushrooms at the very bottom because they grew on putrefied earth. Just above mushrooms were any bulbs growing underground such as onions, shallots, leeks, and garlic. That bulbs were habitually eaten by the peasantry did not endear them to the rest of the population. Above bulbs were root vegetables, such as carrots and turnips, followed by salad greens and spinach whose leaves touched the earth directly, and then plants that had a stem, such as mint or cabbage. Right above were any fruit or berry-bearing bushes and then on top of the hierarchy were fruit-bearing trees that were higher in the sky. If this hierarchy of foods was not based on Galenic medicine, the unpopularity of fruits and vegetables was also in great part due to Galen's medical ideas.[8]

Raw vegetables and fruits were considered detrimental to digestion and dangerous for the consumer. Once cooked much of the danger became innocuous because of heat but the use of wine with fruits and vegetables was seen as a must to help add to the heat of digestion. Fruits were considered too humid and cold; eating foods too cold and humid led to melancholy as it disturbed the balance of the four humors in the body. In this chain, the most ignoble was the lowly mushroom because it was considered putrid. Bodily harm was done by raw foods through what Galenic medicine called "corruption" or "putrefaction" in the stomach.[9] In a world where even familiar vegetables were considered dangerous, new vegetables were very difficult to integrate culturally. By the seventeenth century Galen's medical ideas about diet slowly disappeared. He had recommended that if should one have to eat fruit, one should preferably eat it cooked, or if it were raw, it should be at the beginning of the meal and preferably always accompanied with wine to help digestion. By the end of the seventeenth century, fruits would be consumed as dessert at the end of the meal.[10] Breaking old traditions would slowly permit the integration of what was to become one of the most important vegetables on the European table: the potato.

The Potato: A History of Food and Famine

The Spanish encountered the potato in the Andes. The sixteenth-century Spanish explorers who first observed the potato in today's Peru, Bolivia, Colombia and Ecuador compared the unfamiliar tuber food crop to the truffles they knew in Europe.[11] Because of this, the potato was called *tartifle* in French, the white truffle. The German name *kartoffel* reveals the same law of similitudes for naming after the truffle. Like many new vegetables, such as the tomato, potatoes were first cultivated for curiosity alone by botanists and collectors. The fact that it was an underground plant put it low on the hierarchy and gave it a rather sordid reputation: the other analogy drawn was with the mandragore, commonly associated with witchcraft.[12] The first potato from Colombia probably reached Spain around 1570. From there the potato spread to the collectors of botanical curiosities, and through their gardens it spread to farmers in Italy, the Low Countries, and England. There was probably a second introduction by Sir Francis Drake, who recorded an encounter with the potato off the Chilean coast in 1578. British and Irish sources and Folklore credit Sir Francis Drake, Sir Walter Raleigh or even his employee Thomas Harriot for introducing the potato to England and Ireland. Given that his return voyage took two years, it is probably no more than folklore because the tuber could not have survived the length of the journey. The botanist Clusius received the first tubers known to be cultivated in a garden in 1588 and he is still credited with introducing the plant to his fellow plant collectors in Germany, Austria, France and Flanders. The first botanical description of the potato dates to 1597 in John Gerard's *The Herball*. Potatoes spread across Italy and Spain with a hospital in Seville leaving us the first record of a large purchase of potatoes in 1573. By 1650 potatoes were a field crop in Flanders and in the Netherlands. They arrived as a food of famine and war. Because the tubers could be kept underground, they were less subject to looting and burning by marauding armies than wheat and other cereals. A war in Germany unintentionally provided the catalyst for introducing the potato to France. In the eighteenth century a French pharmacist by the name of A. A. Parmentier was a German prisoner of war who had been forced to survive on a diet of potatoes. When he returned to Paris, he championed the potato as an anti-famine food at a time when the French King had become responsible for the supply of bread in Paris. Marie Antoinette paraded with potato flowers in her hair, while King Louis XVI wore them on his coat. Nevertheless widespread potato consumption in France had to wait for the next century. The French were bread eaters, it was considered central and indispensable, and because potatoes could not be made into bread, the potato's popularity was not immediate. European writers credit the potato with the virtual elimination of famine by the early nineteenth century because it yields more calories per acre than any other food. No less an authority than Adam Smith, in *An Inquiry into the Nature and Causes of the Wealth of Nations*, estimated that the land allocated to potatoes yielded three times the nutrient value of land planted with wheat, so that more people could be maintained by the same acreage of land. But Smith seemed to reserve the potato to consumption by chairmen, porters and coal heavers in London, or to the unfortunate women who had to live by prostitution. Admittedly, the tuber did not seem to rank high in Adam Smith's food hierarchy.[13]

The potato was a famine food adopted by Northern Europe. Other food substitutes were found in warmer climates. In the sixteenth century Olivier de Serres had gone as far as to argue that different foods suited the stomachs of different classes so while the nobles and the bourgeoisie could only digest white bread, white wine and white meat from birds or fish, he relegated dark bread, red wine and the "coarse meats" such as beef to manual workers. Some of these ideas about a class-based diet persisted well into the twentieth century.[14] Massimo Montanari has argued that many new foods were only accepted because of famine and necessity, when bread was impossible to obtain. Corn or maize, so prized by the Native Americans, also became food for the poor; the peasantry of northern Italy planted it to escape taxes because land-lords had not yet inventoried the new food crop. Eventually peasants in the region became dependent on it, developing *pellagra* because of a lack of niacin in their diets. Unlike Native Americans they did not use lime to plant maize in Europe; only lime made niacin nutritionally available. Even high foods could change status within the European diet. In the same category as maize, Montanari argues for the late spread of pasta made with durum wheat in the diet of southern Italy's urban poor. In the 1630s there was a food crisis in Naples because of overpopulation and because the city's Spanish rulers did not make enough provisions for the population. Technological inventions such as the kneading machine and the mechanical press made it possible to produce pasta from durum wheat, a new variety, coarser and more nutritious. "Suddenly pasta took on a central role in the diet of the urban poor, and in the eighteenth century the Neapolitans took the title of 'macaroni eaters' away from the Sicilians. Pasta and cheese replaced the traditional pair of meat and cabbage."[15] Previously made with wheat, not durum wheat, pasta was considered food for the elite; in the middle of the sixteenth century it was still three times the price of bread and was served during aristocratic feasts as lasagne and ravioli. Thanks to pasta made from durum wheat, the urban poor in southern Italy did not experience the diseases that came with dependence on maize or potatoes alone as the north had.[16] Not until 1830 was pasta dressed with tomato sauce.[17] Considered poisonous for a very long time, the tomato was one of the last New World foods to penetrate the European diet.

When European settlers were heading for the New World, famines and food shortages were endemic in Europe. Seventeenth-century France, despite the glory of Versailles under Louis XIV, knew some of the worst famines in its history under his reign. The first attempts to establish price control and good distribution were made by Louis XIV, but these measures failed and until the eighteenth century it was the municipality that was in charge of food control. Even Paris, which had a market that was provisioned on a national scale for its population of 450,000, knew severe food shortages. In all the large urban markets of Europe, such as Paris and London, animals were marched alive into the city and butchered close to the market place. In Paris salt water fish arrived from Dieppe for Friday within twenty hours. Fresh water fish were kept alive in tanks and boats while farmed fish already existed on a large scale in ponds for carp and pike. The price of fish was determined by its freshness. In the days before refrigeration the smell of food could become overpowering on warm days. Perishable foods such as herbs, fruits and vegetables also had to be grown close to the market place. Salted fish and meat played a large role in this market economy. Pickled herring and salted cod were very important all over Europe.[18] The population of Paris grew to 600,000 by 1780 and the city's population devoured 206 million pounds of bread, 70,000 cows, 120,000 veal calves, 350,000 sheep, 78 million eggs, 3,175,000 pounds of fresh butter, 2,700,000 pounds of salted butter, 6,500,000 pounds of white and brown sugar, 6,000,000 liters of all kinds of oil, 2,500,000 pounds of coffee, and 650,000 hectoliters of ordinary wine annually.[19] Fish, birds and many other foods are missing from this list because the historical record of market foods is incomplete. Butchering animals close to the time of their consumption was the rule. When ships left for the Americas they took provisions of fresh meat on board, and just as for the city market there was only one solution: keeping animals alive until the last minute. The animals were boarded alive and their arrival in the New World had tremendous consequences, as livestock carried with it some of Europe's worst diseases.

Europeans in the New World: Death through Disease and Plantation Slavery

On the impact of these diseases Charles C. Mann has written that:

> from Bristol to Boston to Beijing people became part of an international culture of tobacco. Virginia played a small but important part in creating

this worldwide phenomenon. From today's perspective though, *N. tobacum* in the end was less important in itself than a magnet that pulled many other non-human creatures directly and indirectly across the Atlantic, of which the most important were surely two minute, multi-faceted immigrants, *Plasmodium vivax* and *Plasmodium falciparum.*[20]

He is referring to malaria, a disease that played a devastating role in American life. It is well known that Europeans brought smallpox, influenza, hepatitis, measles, encephalitis, pneumonia, bacterial tuberculosis, diphtheria, cholera, typhus, scarlet fever, bacterial meningitis and other diseases that made the conquest of the Americas a possibility.[21] Many of these diseases were carried by European livestock, but one had a smaller host: malaria was carried by mosquitoes.

Researchers generally agree that human malaria also did not exist in the Americas before 1492. Malaria played a huge role in the past along with another mosquito-borne disease, yellow fever. It turned the Americas upside down. Just as tobacco brought malaria to Virginia, sugarcane brought the disease to the Caribbean and Latin America along with its companion yellow fever. Both diseases killed European workers and African slaves in the tobacco and sugar plantations.[22] Growing these newly global commodities was linked to the global spread of diseases, many carried by livestock. David Hackett Fischer has demonstrated that about 60 percent of the first wave of English immigrants to the New World came from nine English counties; these were England's plasmodium belts. Of the one hundred plus colonists who began Jamestown in Virginia, the birthplaces of fifty-nine are known and thirty-seven of them were born in malaria-ridden English counties. The symptoms of malaria can take a long time to manifest themselves, therefore future colonists could board the ships without any symptoms, land in the tobacco plantation, and then be struck by the chills and fevers of malaria.[23]

Plantations in the New World initially depended on European indentured servants who got the price of the passage against indentured work for four, seven or even nine years on a tobacco or sugar plantation. High European mortality rates had a long lasting impact.[24]

Charles C. Mann argues that the ecological introduction of diseases shaped all global economic exchanges. Famous economists Daron Acemoglu, Simon Johnson, and James A. Robinson have argued that up to this day the places where European colonists could not survive remain much poorer than the places that European settlers found healthy. They argue that the reason for this is that the conquering Europeans established different institutions in diseased zones that these economists call "extractive states", such as the ghastly Belgian Congo described in Joseph Conrad's *Heart of Darkness*. In this form of state, a tiny group of Europeans condemned a mass of chained slaves to forced labor for Europe's consumption of local commodities, whether it was to grow sugar, tobacco or later build railroads or grow rubber. In this view, captive Africans were the human wing of the Columbian exchange. The economists have argued that this exchange had political consequences that continue to endure to this day. The places where European colonists could not survive remain much poorer than places where Europeans thrived. In extractive states Europeans had little interest in building any of the institutions necessary to maintain complex societies such as schools, highways, sewers or hospitals. According to their analysis, history suggests that industrialization cannot occur without "both investments from a large number of people who were not previously part of the ruling elite and the emergence of new entrepreneurs".[25] This form of exploitation and slavery, essentially the consumption of human beings for Europe's consumption of commodities, was well accepted because of beliefs held by the Church that non-Christians did not have souls.

Consuming the New World

Views about the pagans of the "rest of the world" were transmitted by books. Some Europeans who set out for the New World and formed a new American elite were well read and literate. Reading about the world was a form of desire for conquest, a way of consuming the world. Mary Blaine Campbell has argued that the imagined New World itself was an object of consumption for Europeans. She quotes Christopher Columbus writing a letter to Queen Isabella about a new earth, another paradise, even a new "Heaven".[26] In many ways, the New World would become an object of desire. She points out that the most obvious case of sixteenth-century travel literature that successfully mixed the business of colonialism with pleasure is the account of Thomas Hariot. It includes an inventory of Virginian "commodities" (including Algonquin peoples and their customs) illustrated by Governor White. After graduating from Oxford, Hariot sailed to the Americas in the expedition that was funded by Sir Walter Raleigh. He translated and learned the Algonquian language. His description of the New World became a part of a famous series of travel accounts on the Americas.[27]

Hariot's description was published by Theodore de Bry as the first volume of *America*, a series of illustrated travel accounts in the New World, the first in a series called *Grands Voyages* (1590–1634). Mary Campbell argues that these travel accounts as well as those by the Frenchmen Thévet and Jean de Léry and the Spaniard Fernandez de Oviedo were commodities themselves, offered for sale all over Europe and regularly translated and illustrated. She argues that both Thévet and Léry exploit the chapters of "manners and customs" for providing erotic and narcissistic pleasure to the reader. The dissemination of first-hand information about the Americas evolved from the very start, the work of professional writers who collected and re-cast in their own words the journals, letters and reports of early explorers such as Columbus, Vespucci, Cartier, Magellan and so on.[28] In Hariot's work, the illustration by White included many watercolors of plants, animals, birds, fish and insects, but when de Bry published the book, he used none of them though they might have served to illustrate the information on the edible, marketable and consumable flora and fauna of Virginia. De Bry chose only ethnographic pictures and erased Hariot's and White's concern with natural history.[29]

The scientific societies of colonized territories generally absorbed natural history into data for the more immediate use of commercial gain. Nature as a resource was transformed into product, and this included colonized people. It is not surprising that the Algonquians were mainly described in terms of their potential for transformation into Christian subjects and into laborers on tobacco plantations and in silver mines. Yet Campbell notes that even in the resulting ethnography published by de Bry, the concern remains focused on raw materials and the watercolors by White that are used in de Bry's volume serve to illustrate a discussion of "commodities". The most reliable kind of data, these watercolors represent tools, weapons, jewelry, clothing, agriculture and cuisine. White's watercolors were clearly informational, for example they showed an American man and woman squatting at dinner. An engraving shows the couple sitting more like Europeans at a picnic table. Campbell analyzes this as a form of colonial discourse that she calls "coloniology" and its transformation bias: Indians would soon learn to sit like Europeans. In the illustrations, they were shown already playing with European dolls and rubbing their bodies with European Bibles. The result of these distortions and omissions was exoticism.[30]

For commercial reasons, Campbell argues, de Bry struck a balance between the erotic appeal of these half naked bodies that set off their ornamentation as exotic but avoided the unfamiliar, such as the squatting position. Although these are visual documents of early ethnography, commercial motives and eroticized representation go hand in hand with the economic interest that underwrote this field of work. The naked vulnerability to European disease is not mentioned in Hariot's captions. They emphasized the wholesomeness of the environment, the moderation of Algonquin eating habits, and their longevity and freedom from sickness. Hariot also points out that the colonists were unusually healthy during their stay in Virginia, and despite the death rate, highlighting European invulnerability as God's will in this new land. He also depicted the diseases that killed the Algonquin population as "God's providential scourging of the Algonquians with plague".[31] Campbell argues that the text and its visual illustrations reinforce each other in their objectification of Algonquin life. Hariot's description of the Algonquin existed in the same "thoughtless, passive, ahistorical moment as do the plants and minerals of part 1 and 2" of his travel narrative, much like his description of the area's other commodities.[32] Hariot's and Thévet's descriptions were useful to commerce but also to the birth of science. Francis Bacon was soon to make explicit the tie between empire and empirical knowledge in his *New Atlantis*.[33] Much like the *House of Trade* in Spain had gathered empirical descriptions to advance knowledge, descriptions of the New World would serve European "curiosity" and bring about a desire for collecting the exotic. Mary Campbell also argues that the New World was eaten up. Campbell argues that the ethnographic discourse of Thomas Hariot included the mute discourse of commodities as a grammar of fashion, that fashion was a form of time as well as a theatre of display. She argues that it was exploration, colonization and the print revolution that were key to the rise of fashion.[34]

Fur as a Consumer Good: France in the New World

Among the most prized American commodities, fur was key in European clothing. In seventeenth-century Europe, consumer demand for beaver was immense because beaver fur served to make warm waterproof coats and most importantly fur and brimmed felt hats. The French fur trade in the New World was tied to this European demand for warm waterproof pelts, but it was not established easily. Seventy-five years after the territory was first explored by Jacques Cartier, as a representative of the French King, Samuel Champlain declared Quebec to be a French Territory in 1608. Champlain brought the missionary monks of St Francis of Assisi (Récollets) to Quebec in 1615. Inspired by the Catholic Counter-Reformation in France, these Jesuits were trained like soldiers and planned to convert the native peoples at all cost. To achieve this goal a large number of the American native inhabitants of Quebec had to be "Gallicized". Conversion to Catholicism meant assimilation and would add more subjects under the French crown at little expense.[35] Without the collaboration of the local Hurons and Montagnais there would be no fur trade as they purveyed the settlers with furs. Because for the French conversion was part of the colonizing effort, this made French presence more difficult for the natives. The English and the Dutch did not have the same agenda; they concentrated on trading fur and lumber.

The French population in New France grew slowly, 28 people in the summer of 1608 to 20,896 inhabitants at the death of Louis XIV in 1716. During this period the city of Quebec grew from 28 to 2,574 inhabitants. A 1666 census finds 1,407 inhabitants in the city of Quebec. This very slow demographic growth of the colony was understandable in light of the political and economic constraints. For half a century New France and Quebec belonged to private business enterprises that watched over their economic interests, even though the region was run by viceroys. The main trade of this settlement remained fur despite efforts to ship lumber. For the Native Americans who provided the furs, the presence of a large European population was not desirable, as a large sedentary European population reduced the number of fur-bearing animals.[36]

To get closer to the consignments of furs they could buy from the natives, the French spread out from Quebec and established the posts of Trois-Rivières and Montréal in 1634 and 1642, respectively. This had a disastrous effect on the Huron population of the region, which in 1648–1650 was destroyed by European diseases and attacks by the Iroquois, who now had Anglo-Dutch weapons. In 1660 there were rumors that 1,200 Iroquois were about to attack Quebec. Even though the attack never happened, France initiated a policy of sending one hundred workers and soldiers annually. In light of this, it is not difficult to imagine why the private company in charge of the colony, the *Compagnie des Cent Associés*, failed to fulfill its obligations and the King himself, Louis XIV, decided to take charge of New France directly in 1663. In 1665, there was a first dispatch of 1,200 men, the first real troops sent to New France. Most of the regiment, however, went back to France three years later. In Louis XIV's reign, nearly 6,000 people, mostly craftsmen, civil servants, unmarried women, and soldiers, were sent from France and settled in the region. Women, called *les filles du roi*, were to marry the settlers upon their arrival in order to discourage Frenchmen from going native. While in the first half of the seventeenth century the population of Quebec consisted of single males employed by private companies in the fur trade, the city's demographics underwent a major change after the King of France took over administration in the 1660s. Quebec's society became more diverse. The censuses of 1666 and 1681 cited thirty-five to forty-five professions. Despite diverse occupations, nearly all of the settlers were French and French remained the main language. Nevertheless, the French feudal castes were not generally transplanted to New France. Social classes certainly existed, but it was possible for the people of Quebec to move up the social ladder based on their degree of initiative and wealth.[37]

Although it had been chiefly the poor who had immigrated to Quebec, once it became a military and administrative center, Quebec attracted both aristocrats and gentlemen. The civil posts of administration and justice were entrusted to the nobility, as were the posts of treasurer and controller of the navy. The King's officers and police were part of an urban middle class that was given privileges that exempted them from performing *corvée*, forced labor, and they aspired to become part of the nobility. Artisans and professionals represented one-third of the working people of Quebec in 1681. The lack of masterships and guilds facilitated the growth of trades. The fur trade still constituted the main economic activity in New France and made up most of the export goods leaving for France. As a royal colony, New France was handed over by the King in 1664 to the new *Compagnie des Indes* for a period of ten years, but Louis XIV retained control over New France after 1674.[38]

Jean Talon was the *intendant* who ruled Canada from 1665 to 1672. Talon hoped to undertake a systematic exploitation of New France while executing Jean-Baptiste Colbert's economic policies by attempting to make Canada self-sufficient. He promoted Canadian agriculture, commerce and industry with a view to revitalize the West Indies in the event that France fell short of supplies. In spite of this form of mercantilism that was advocated by the French authorities, who hoped to make the colonies providers of raw materials for France, Quebec bustled with activity without much control from France. Small industries were established by the new *intendant* Talon. In spite of a sawmill installed by Talon, the lumber trade remained limited because of a shortage of ships. The manufacture of beer never really flourished because the French Canadians preferred to drink wine and strong spirits just as they had in France. Talon's brewery was capable of producing 4,000 barrels per year but it closed its doors shortly after the departure of the *intendant*. Most importantly, Talon successfully established tanneries in order to manufacture shoes.[39] The aim was to provide shoes not only to the settlers but for every Frenchman and woman. Hides and furs remained the main trade after Talon's departure.

The close dependence of the survival of the French colony on the fur trade was evident in the problems that appeared once French territory was expanded and there was a large increase in the supply of furs. The success of the military activities against the Iroquois and the increase in the supply of fur that could be shipped to France occasioned a rapid fall in prices, which brought serious financial problems to the *Compagnie des Indes Occidentales*. In 1670, the prices of furs had fallen from fourteen *livres* to four *livres* per pound of fur. On the other hand, expenditure in the colony on fortification and war had increased rapidly. By 1674 the company had accumulated a debt of 3,523,000 *livres* and as a result, it went bankrupt and was dissolved. To prevent further decline in prices, it was planned to place the fur trade under control and fix prices. The King took control of the fur trade, which was then sold as a monopoly to Nicholas Oudiette in 1675 for 350,000 *livres*. He was obliged to fix prices and to accept beaver furs at four *livres* ten *sols* per pound and to sell in France at no more than ten *livres*. The sale of surplus beaver in Holland and other markets reduced the price and prejudiced the position of Oudiette. Since beaver was purchased by weight, the thick skins and lighter furs of the poorer grades were sold more cheaply than the light skin and thick furs of the *castor gras*. Together with fraudulent practices such as keeping beaver skins in water or damp cellars to increase weight, the European market bankrupted Oudiette. He wrote to the King with a plea for a revision of prices and a compromise was reached in 1677; the classification of beaver skins were changed, with furs carefully prepared for trade in Russia, where they were in great demand. But the chief issue of value was a question of controlling supply. As long as supply outdid demand, the prices for fur would plummet. Despite Russia's consumption of beaver the French still had a deficit.[40]

New prices and trade regulations were scarcely more effective in limiting supply and the monopoly that was given by the King to Oudiette was losing money. Continual price adjustments and regulations for control created further difficulties, especially after 1700. At the turn of the century there was a decline in the consumption of beaver for the manufacture of beaver hats. In 1696 it was estimated that the cost of manufacturing a beaver hat was fourteen *livres* and ten *sols*. Roughly one-third of the final sales price of a hat was profit, one-third was the price of raw materials, and the remainder went for labor and manufacturing. The decline of hat sales was due to the high percentage of the cost of raw materials to the total cost of the hat. Foreign markets were also inadequate in absorbing the increasing fur surplus that followed the decline in consumption on French domestic markets. Beaver, which usually arrived in the autumn in France, was usually sold the following spring, a portion to the hat makers in France, a portion to Russia and a portion to Germany for the manufacture of sleeves and furs.[41]

In 1700, Russia explored Alaska in order to provide its own fur supply, further damaging French prospects of prosperity. They competed for the hat trade, as beaver was used in two ways: fur was used for winter coats and hats, but its underbelly fur was used for felt. Large brimmed felt hats were fashionable in seventeenth-century Europe. Native Americans were key to the fur trade and conflicts between the English and the French, which involved many native groups, were detrimental to the provisions they could bring. Larger European settlements and wars contributed to a lack of supply that reversed the precarious situation of over-supply. Harold Innis has argued that the population of beavers decreased dramatically even before the European rivalry at the turn of the eighteenth century. European livestock also changed the nature of North America's landscape, and nowhere was this more acute than in areas where Europeans established plantations and pasture.[42]

The Use of European Livestock in the Making of Empire

Plantations were disruptive to the native landscape. For Virginia and Carolina, tobacco was what sugar was to the Caribbean. Initially, Virginia had relied on white European indentured servants for labor on the tobacco fields. After 1619, Africans began to arrive from the Caribbean even though slavery was not yet institutionalized in North America. Africans arriving in small numbers from the Caribbean in 1619 met with a very low number of white settlers and a majority of Native Americans.[43] Europeans arriving in North America were perplexed by the unusual close ties between animals and Native Americans. The Narragansett's unusual treatment of crows, birds that English villagers destroyed with abandon because of the way they devoured grain in their fields, was a surprise. Narragansett parents stationed their children to keep an eye on the planting fields and chase crows away. Roger Williams, an English observer, called the children "little watch houses". He learned that this respect stemmed from a belief that the crow brought them the first Indian grain of corn. Other birds, ducks, geese, swans, pigeons and cormorants were hunted and eaten but the crows had a special link to the origins of horticulture.[44]

The use of pasture has been well documented as instrumental to the legalization of ownership of land by Europeans arriving in New England by Virginia DeJohn Anderson.[45] Owning animals or land, as it was understood in England, was a foreign concept to Native Americans. The colonists found it impossible to replicate English practices of herding and fencing. Even in closely built homes in New England the animals constantly wandered off. The Indians also tried many strategies in attempts to accommodate, eliminate or finally accumulate these animals. The herding of cattle in the new landscape of North America was accomplished by Africans who were used to open spaces. Bills of sale and wills in Carolina and Virginia have left us records of the importance of African slaves for keeping track of cattle on large expanses of land while riding horseback late into the night and corralling the animals into cow pens. In Carolina, in 1674, a settler remarked that "cattell" began to be plentiful. In 1682, a planter named Thomas Ash wrote "not six or seven years past the country was almost destitute of cows, hogs, and sheep and now they have many thousand head".[46] These animals were new to the Americas. West African slaves fully understood the challenges of grazing cattle in large pastures. They had exceptional herding skills that European settlers lacked because of their enclosed pastures. The colonies' new masters were, as a result, finally eating the beef they were accustomed to in England. While Africans herded recently imported European domestic animals, Native Americans hunted and helped the new European settlers enter the fur trade. They had ample experience catching deer, fox, and other animals that the Carolinians traded. When the English showed up in the 1580s on Roanoke Island, Native Americans viewed them as just another tribe with whom to do business.[47]

Information on the consumption of Native Americans has only reached us through European observers. English observers commented on attire worn by the natives made of the skins of bears and wolves and on headdresses made with feathers and claws as ornamentation. William Wood reported that during the winter Massachusetts native men donned fur mantles made of bear skins, moose and beaver skins sewed together, as well as otter and raccoon skins, which could all be worn at once. Colonists expressed total amazement at the profusion of animal-shaped ink decorations on their skin. The faces of Massachusetts Indians, William Wood declared, bore portraitures of beasts such as bear, deer, moose and wolves. These ink tattoos were a novelty that surprised the English who were fascinated that whole bodies, legs, thighs, arms and faces were covered with images of fowl, fish and beast. These designs bore special significance for those who wore them but few colonists went beyond mere observation. Because of their lack of knowledge of the hierarchy in these native societies, it is difficult to reconstruct the meanings Indians actually attached to these images or to analyze the importance of their clothing. European observers came up with distorted interpretations that bore a suspicious resemblance to the symbolic association between virtues and certain animals found in European heraldry.[48]

Many of these animals depicted were commonly identified with *manitou* and shamanistic spirits. Pohatan shamans, for instance, donned ceremonial garb that included a mantle fashioned from feathers and weasel skins. They wore a crown made from a dozen, sixteen or more snakeskins stuffed with moss to give them a lifelike appearance. In both the Chesapeake and New England, Indians exhibited a distinct fondness for using animal parts and whole animals as ornaments. An astonished William Strachey encountered Pohatan men who sported whole animals, such as a dead rat tied by its tail, as part of their attire. He saw other natives embellish their pierced ears with legs of eagles and hawks or sometimes bear or raccoon claws. Even more striking, Strachey reported, was a spectacle of a Pohatan man wearing a small live yellow and green snake in his pierced ear. The wearer allowed the snake to coil around the neck and even to kiss his lips. Massachusetts Indians, unlike the Pohatan, preferred animal images on jewelry to real creatures. Native people were observed with pendants resembling birds, beasts, and fishes carved out of bone, shell and stone.[49]

Virginia DeJohn Anderson points out that views held by the Europeans that animals were property were very different from those held by the Native Americans who saw life with animals as a negotiated relationship. To their surprise, nowhere in the New World did colonists see the type of domesticated creature they took for granted in England and the Netherlands.[50]

The colonists viewed this lack of domestication as proof of the savageness of the natives. This stemmed, however, from the nature of the fauna of the Americas. The Americas had very few large animal species capable of being domesticated. The two possibilities, indigenous horses and camels, had become extinct from over hunting or climate change in 11,000 BC. Various Indian groups grew to depend on bison and caribou meat but did so by exploiting the animals' predictable migrations. The two large animals consumed by the Eastern Algonquians, deer and bears, were not suitable candidates. Creatures that can be domesticated are generally social animals whose group behavior demonstrates a dominance hierarchy. This social structure allows humans to substitute themselves with the leaders of the herd. Indians in Central and South America domesticated llamas, turkeys and other birds. Before the English arrived, Eastern Algonquians were familiar with only two types of tamed beasts, dogs and hawks, which they kept around their houses to chase small birds. The Algonquian populations around the eastern seaboard of North America enjoyed a varied diet of wild and cultivated plants along with abundant game and fish. Native dogs performed important functions that English observers failed to notice. Indian dogs earned their keep by scavenging, ridding villages of food scraps and reducing the presence of vermin. Indian dogs did not bark, so the Europeans did not think of them as domesticated. Because we only have European sources and their possible misconceptions, the precise nature of Native American relationships with domesticated hawks and dogs is difficult to discern.[51]

Although colonists defined domesticated animals as property, Indians did not have an equivalent conceptual category for living animals. Native peoples granted individual property rights only to a hunter over an animal once it was killed. Several incidents document this difficult encounter over property rights. This implied that cattle owned by Europeans could be hunted as long as the proper rituals for this peculiar animal were discovered and followed by the natives. This led to one of the most complicated series of incidents between the native population and English settlers.[52]

Hunting practices were different. In Europe, vivid demonstrations of human dominion over animals characterized hunting practices that were reserved strictly for royal and aristocratic circles. Gentlemen (and sometimes high born women) aimed arrows or spears at deer while on horseback. Elizabeth I occasionally bestowed mercy on a fleeing stag by prohibiting further pursuit, much as she might have pardoned a criminal. Many hunts culminated in an unmistakable dominion with the severed head of a deer presented to the most eminent member of the group, with its nose touched to the ground as a sign of submission. English hunting practices reinforced the dominion of some people over others, as aristocratic hunters commanded retinues of men barred from hunting whose jobs included controlling the hounds and driving game out of the woods.[53] Most of the vocabulary for the hunt remained from French, which was the court language at many European courts, another sign that this sport was for the high born alone.[54]

Through social rituals during the hunt and in the feast that followed, each participant was reminded of his or her proper place in Early Modern European society. In contrast, Indian men acquired prestige through demonstration of hunting prowess but the activity was open to all males. Gentlemen in Europe vigorously promoted their monopoly on game through laws and severe punishments for poachers. The law set stringent property qualifications for hunters that only a minority of Englishmen could meet: an annual income of at least forty pounds and ownership of goods worth a minimum of two hundred pounds. These laws thoroughly demonstrated how hunting privileges and property were tied together. Indian peoples, on the other hand, only recognized a hunter's right to his killed prey. In England the hunt reserved to the wealthy was defined as a recreation and not a subsistence activity. On the other hand, Indian peoples hunted according to their subsistence needs.[55] A feast described by Jean Louis Flandrin gives a list of game hunted for the aristocratic table in England. The feast was of dizzying quantity and diversity. Even if we forget the large quantities of fish, venison and other meat, and count the birds alone the count consisted of: 400 swans, 2,000 geese, 1,000 capons, 104 peacocks, 400 plovers, 1,200 quail, 24,000 rees, 400 wild ducks and teal, 204 cranes, 2,000 chickens, 4,000 pigeons, 204 bitterns, 400 herons, 200 pheasants, 500 partridges, 400 woodcock, 100 curlews and 1,000 egrets. While there are domestic birds such as chicken on this list most of these birds were hunted, along with the 500 deer that were served with other large quantities of fish and meat to the 2,500 guests of this fifteenth-century feast in England.[56]

Virginia DeJohn Anderson argues that armed with their notions of hierarchy and property, the newly arrived English settlers were eager to demonstrate the exercise of their dominion over a new American setting that they were beginning to define as their own. Efforts to categorize animals according to their uses initialized the process of appropriation for the colonists. Schemes to domesticate New World creatures came from the firm conviction that animals could be made into private property, though few of these designs ever succeeded.[57] Virginia DeJohn Anderson has argued that the upshot of their efforts was the formulation of a different imperial vision from Spain's, one that unwittingly assigned livestock as instrumental in England's overseas expansion. The English looked at Roman legal theory to justify their imperial ambitions. The concept of *res nullius*, which held that empty things including land remained common property until they were put to use, would be the instrument of their conquest. Proponents of colonization argued that the discovery of these empty lands conferred similar rights to a nation. Accordingly, the English depicted America as a boundless space open to anyone willing to make good use of it through labor. Farming, because it required the instrument of labor and capital, clearly established legitimate claims. It conformed to England's long-standing agrarian tradition and also enjoyed the stamp of divine approval according to the Church of England. Agriculture had originated with the Lord's instruction to Adam and Eve. England's empire would be an agricultural one populated by colonists and their livestock. Colonists who envisioned cattle grazing where deer and foxes once ranged imagined themselves replacing the peripatetic Indians. The insistence that Indians only lightly touched the land became the mainstay of England's justification of colonization.[58]

Paradoxically in North America, wolf and bear populations may have surged as a result of the colonists' introduction of a new food supply. According to the colonists, adult cattle, horses and even pigs could hold their own against wolves but younger animals were easy prey. Colonial officials responded by offering bounties to anyone who would help rid the land of predators. In the Chesapeake, at least at first, the colonists themselves turned out to be equally voracious predators. Starving Jamestown settlers declared open season on what was supposed to be Virginia's breeding stock. For years, regular infusion of imported animals augmented livestock numbers. In New England, the colonies' livestock population became self-sustaining long before its human population did. William Wood cited livestock numbers to scold Massachusetts's detractors that called it impoverished in 1644. He wrote that there was no place where there were 4,000 souls, 1,500 heads of cattle, 4,000 goats and swine that could qualify as poor.[59]

The traditional view that English expansion in North America depended on the plantation system still holds. Land, considered empty by the colonists, was divided into units under private ownership. The system started in Virginia and spread to the New England colonies. The crops grown on these plantations were labor-intensive cash crops. Tobacco, sugarcane and cotton were grown by both men and women. The British sent convicts as indentured servants to the colonies but this never satisfied the demand for labor. The slave trade and the arrival of Africans would make cash crops an economic success. The proceeds of the trade would help the wealthy settlers who owned slaves live as in Europe.

An Empire of Dutch "Indian" Goods

The Dutch Atlantic Empire in the Americas was much smaller in size and shorter in duration than that of the British or the Spanish. How much smaller or shorter is now the subject of a new debate among scholars. Nevertheless, it has been argued that the Atlantic trade was much more important to the Dutch Republic than its more visible Asian trade and that New Amsterdam (New York) was a more common destination for the Dutch than their outposts in the East Indies. New Amsterdam's population of 2,000–3,500 inhabitants in

1655 grew to 9,000 in 1664 just before the Dutch colony was renamed New York by the victorious British. Despite the 4,000 Dutch immigrants who arrived between those dates, the Dutch North American enterprise remains marginal in the Dutch cultural imagination about its Empire compared with their long lasting East Indian holdings.[60] Dutch trading posts in the Americas precede its more famous Asian endeavors; whereas the first post was established in present day Indonesia in 1600, Dutch traders had established posts in Guyana and the Amazon as early as 1590. In 1609, Henry Hudson sailed along the northeast coast of America with the goal of reaching Asia. Like other Dutch explorers before him, he was seeking a northern trade route to India, China and Japan in order to avoid the Portuguese and Spanish who were now controlling the known trade routes. Hudson was commissioned by the *Dutch East Indian Company* (VOC), founded in 1602 for trade with Asia; his mission to find a new route to Asia, referred to as the "Indies" failed. The *Dutch West India Company* (GWIC) was founded for trade in the Americas two decades after the VOC, in 1621.[61] Because of its policy of settlement, by 1624, a colony of New Netherlands was successfully founded and a substantial Atlantic trade with the Dutch Republic was initiated. Although forty to fifty soldiers were on each of its ships for defensive reasons (piracy and hijacking were common on the seas), unlike the VOC, the West India Company did not have the right to deploy troops.[62]

The seventeenth century has been called the Golden Age for the Netherlands. The central position of Antwerp in Flanders in the world of trade was soon challenged by Dutch success in Asia and the New Netherlands in the Americas. When the Dutch gained independence in 1585 from the Habsburgs and became the first republic in the world, they established the preeminence of the port of Amsterdam over Antwerp not only by successfully capturing Spanish and Portuguese ships but also by fighting the Spanish. The Dutch revolt against Spanish rule had split the Netherlands in half, with a southern part (today's Belgium) with the city of Antwerp, remaining Catholic and under Habsburg rule. After returning to the Netherlands, Henry Hudson gave a report to the VOC. After Hudson's report two more covert expeditions to find a route to China were sent to what is now the state of New York. These reports stimulated emigration.[63]

If the VOC began its career by seizing a Portuguese carrack with Asian luxury goods in 1602, over two decades later the Dutch West India Company (GWIC) successfully seized the Spanish silver fleet that was carrying silver from Spanish colonies to Spain in 1628. The ambitious privateering for the two Dutch companies was at first the most profitable employment for Dutch men; since they were commissioned to capture ships by the Company it was not considered piracy. To make this activity legal, Hugo Grotius wrote a famous treatise on the freedom of the seas called *The Free Sea*, published in 1609, which argued that the sea was a free zone, although in that period the Iberian Empire considered it its own territory. Grotius's work is still the basis of international maritime law today.[64]

Very early in the history of the Dutch Republic, international trade became a truly global enterprise that financed the Republic's administrators at home. Dutch holdings in Asia became consolidated with the founding of Batavia in Java, which became the administrative center of the VOC. That the round trip between Batavia and Amsterdam took eighteen months should not mask the fact that Batavia became the VOC's political heart.[65] In the early part of the seventeenth century, however, Dutch settlers left not for Batavia, where a few VOC employed men were stationed without spouses, but for New York. Women were often sent by trade companies or even by the French King to form colonies and European settlement. Dutch women did not leave for Batavia because the merchants of the VOC were initially not allowed to marry during the early part of its commercial activities in Asia. This rule changed but initially celibacy as a requirement made Dutch Asian trading colonies in Asia. This rule was different from what was to become the New Netherlands in the West. Family was key to establishing colonies in North America. The New Netherlands area where Dutch families settled included New Amsterdam (New York after 1664) and parts of four present-day states: New York, Connecticut, Delaware and New Jersey.[66]

The Collection of Margrieta Van Varick

In seventeenth century Dutch New York, virtually all female Dutch New Yorkers were married. The independence and capabilities of these Dutch women were exceptional and have attracted some scholarly attention. Losing a husband occurred frequently and left widows to fend for themselves. Most women were primarily occupied with raising children and domestic work. What set Dutch women apart from their peers were personal histories that could be traced back to some experience with Dutch settlements across the globe. They were often well traveled and had known some hardship. Joyce D. Goodfriend has argued that Dutch women subscribed to an ideal of female competence that lacked a counterpart in other cultures whether they were single, married or widowed. In the Dutch Republic and its holdings, women enjoyed a great deal of latitude in the marketplace and in the courts as a result of both Dutch custom and law.[67] Daughters in New Netherlands' households were given lessons in business as a matter of course. Joyce D. Goodfriend gives several examples of husbands who not only encouraged but expected their wives to engage in overseas commerce. Such was the case of Jeremias van Rensselaer who even took up brewing for the sake of his wife's interest in running a business. When he died, his wife Maria – beyond her own brewing business – assumed total responsibility for four sons and two daughters all under the age of eleven, as well as for running the large family estate on the Hudson River, including keeping accounts and managing tenants. She also engaged in the fur trade as her husband had done. These independent women were nonetheless often confronted with legal impediments to a full participation in the marketplace and in the courtrooms of New York. They often had to rely on male relatives to protect their rights. Joyce D. Goodfriend's work on Dutch women in New York puts into perspective the life of one of its most studied widows, Margrieta van Varick, a Dutch New Yorker who has recently been the object of an exhibition.[68]

Margrieta van Varick was a widow and a successful textile merchant who died in 1695 leaving an extensive collection of global, exotic goods. The New York Historical Society's library holds the nineteen-page inventory of both her household and her textile shop. The inventory lists 2,000 goods acquired from around the world such as a teapot, tankard, caster, cup, astrolabe, bowl, porringer and trunk.[69] Only 11 out of the 2,000 goods in the collection are described as "East Indian silver" in the inventory listings, a label that is questioned by Marybeth de Filippis' thesis in which she argues for a much larger number of objects from around the world.

Margrieta van Varick's collection from around the globe is now scattered once again around the world, although the objects are not back in their places of origin. Her collection boasts fascinating objects from Asia, including a celadon Chinese ewer (c. 1400) with seventeenth-century Ottoman silver-gilt mounts now located at the Topkapi Saray Museum in Istanbul. Another is a silver tobacco box from Dutch Batavia engraved with the town mark for Batavia held at the Gemeentemuseum in The Hague. The Victoria and Albert Museum in London houses one of her covered beakers, which dates from mid-seventeenth century Mughal India; the Hermitage Museum in St Petersburg now owns a northern Indian gold plate with enamel dating to the seventeenth century. A page from the illuminated manuscript *Khamseh* of Nizami (Herat, Persia, 1524–1525) is now held at the Metropolitan Museum of Art in New York. A cotton tent hanging from early eighteenth-century Burhanpur, India, stenciled and hand-block printed resides at a museum in Mumbai. There is a Chinese silver teapot marked with the London hallmarks for 1682 located at the Peabody Essex Museum in Massachusetts. Where these objects initially came from, where they were collected and where they have ended up today constitute a clear map of how the consumption of luxury objects and political power go hand-in-hand in history. Colonial patterns are clear: the objects from the Dutch colonies are in Holland, save for a cotton tent hanging, the objects from India are in England. Patterns of collecting from well-funded museums dictate the rest of the itinerary: the Metropolitan Museum of Art for the *Khamsa* from Iran, and the Peabody Essex Museum, which specializes in the China Trade, for the Chinese teapot.[70]

"India" was a general term used by the Dutch, the English and the French for their overseas factories.[71] Van Varick's "East Indian silver" has been questioned because none of the eleven pieces have been located and identifying any piece under this label would be difficult for many reasons. Firstly, most silver was sold via dealers, erasing most traces of origin. Additionally, most seventeenth-century silver that originated from the "East" did not have hallmarks. Most often silversmiths in Europe who bought the piece would stamp it with their own hallmark after purchase. The most common "East

Indian silver" objects were also called "VOC silver" because they were made for VOC employees in Batavia, home to the VOC East headquarters. Workshops held such a varied demographic of workers (European, Indian, Ceylonese) that the "VOC silver" resembled Chinese and Islamic goods. Hallmarking regulations put in place in 1667 were updated and more readily enforced after 1730. Despite this regulation, free Indonesian, Chinese, Muslim, and Mestizo silversmiths only had to hallmark their silver objects if they converted to Christianity.[72]

Her collection reflected her cosmopolitan past. When Margrieta was orphaned at age eighteen, she moved in 1667 from Amsterdam to Malacca, Malaysia, to live with her uncle, Abraham Burgers. There, her uncle and both of her two future husbands all worked for the VOC. After her first husband, Egbert van Duins, passed away, Margrieta went back to the Dutch Republic and settled down with her second husband, Rudolphus van Varick, a minister of the Dutch Reformed Church. They eventually crossed the Atlantic and moved to Flatbush (Brooklyn). The scholar Marybeth de Filippis demonstrates that the majority of the van Varick silver was obtained through her husbands' and uncle's involvement in the luxury trade of the VOC. These van Varick silver objects could have been from Malaysia, Indonesia, Mughal India, Persia, Turkey, Ceylon or China. Due to the fact that New Yorkers completed the inventory of the collection, they probably used the label "East Indian" for all these different types of silver originating from the East. By the seventeenth century, many of the aforementioned locations produced silver that featured common Islamic and Eastern motifs. The fusion of design styles across cultures made it more complex for anyone to differentiate the exact origin of the silver. In fact, certain Eastern motifs can be found in colonial American silver in the seventeenth and early eighteenth centuries such as the "cut-card banding" seen on New York tankards. The same leaf banding can be found in sixteenth-century Islamic architecture and seventeenth-century Mughal silver.[73] Margrieta's collection may be extraordinary for this early period but it is far from unique in North America a few decades later. Exotic goods and "Indian" style goods, were avidly collected by English and Dutch settlers in New York, Boston, Philadelphia and elsewhere. These new Americans shared Europe's taste for collecting objects in the "Indian" style, otherwise known as *chinoiserie*.

Pirates on the Free Sea

In the seventeenth century, collecting Chinese or East Indian objects was important to the wealthy new elites of Salem, Boston, New York and Philadelphia. The Anglo-Americans along the Atlantic seaboard were implicated in the East Indies trade. At the end of the seventeenth century in New York over 30 percent of the surveyed estates held Chinese porcelain, as did 10 percent of households in Newport, Salem. By the end of the second decade of the eighteenth century, the ownership of Chinese objects had spread beyond mansions and manor walls. Chinaware was found beyond Dutch cupboards in almost all sectors of Northern colonial society. In her book *Objectifying China,* Caroline Frank studies the material evidence offered by Chinese porcelain, tea and lacquer in an interdisciplinary way, in order to "read" Chinese commodities for their meaning. There is unanimous consensus among decorative art scholars that there was ignorance of the Chinese significance of the decorations of these collected objects. Some had branded this as a form of illiteracy that gave way to references such as "India china" and "India tea", neither of which came from India.[74] This is a rather harsh judgment, as it has been clearly argued elsewhere that this was a generalized view across Europe.[75]

The English East India Company (EEIC), formed in 1600, considered that it had the monopoly of trade on these "Indian" goods. In its American colonies, any trader that participated in the trade on these "Indian" goods did so illegally. Caroline Frank describes how, in 1689, New York's governor Jacob Leisler outfitted one of the first Indian Ocean voyages from North America. It was one of his first responses to his newly usurped position. He sent a ship overseas in search of fabulous exotic goods. Leisler's ship was a captured French *prize* that was renamed the *Jacob.* After a stop in Rhode Island, the *Jacob* sailed to Madagascar, India and the Red Sea before returning to New York in April 1693. The details of the *Jacob's* voyage were told by a crewmember named Samuel Burgess. In London the Acts of Trade legally labeled American traders in the Indian Ocean as "pirates". Burgess, who spent most of the three-year voyage in Madagascar, does relate being part of the taking of three ships in the Red Sea. The East India Company had also sent letters to London complaining about attacks committed against Mughal vessels. Like many English ships, the American vessel *Jacob* may have targeted more Asian vessels than European ones, although the *Jacob's* commission was to raid ships from France only. The *Jacob* also seems to have had some experience fighting North African pirates, typically called "turks" in the documents of the time. A decade earlier, Leisler, his sons and nine crewmembers had been taken captive by Algerian raiders in a small vessel or *pinke.* Leisler had to personally pay 2,280 pounds in ransom for himself and his crew to be spared from forced conversion to Islam and/or slavery. Leisler, like many American mariners, shared prejudices against Asians and was not averse to raiding "infidels". Whatever the *Jacob* had managed to accomplish before her return in 1693 (the record is unclear), her sailors had returned very wealthy men, each claiming about 1,800 Spanish silver dollars and a bulk cargo of East India goods.[76]

Caroline Frank in a section entitled "Regulating Irrepressible American Consumers" shows that the American attempts to link directly with Asian trade to satisfy the demand for "Indian" objects was a threat to England's colonial hold over North America. Shortly after taking power in New York in 1698, a new English governor, Richard Coote, Earl of the Bellomont, wrote anxiously about the trade carried out by the previous governor with Madagascar. He pointed out that the trade his predecessor enjoyed was illegal. This "India" trade had been carried out without the consent of the Lords of Trade in London. Frank argues that few issues were as significant to the dignity of the English crown, and even more so to the powerbase of the Parliament, than the East India trade. Statutes issued by King William and his Parliaments a few months later formally reinstated the English East India Company's monopoly, closing the Indian Ocean to direct American trade for three quarters of a century. This reinstatement points clearly to the importance of the illicit trade. While direct trade was taking place, Americans often did not sail farther than the coast of India or Madagascar, but this did not hinder their access to Chinese goods. This was the case for most English ships as well. By the time the North American colonies had entered the Indian Ocean trade in the late seventeenth century, there was a long established and extremely sophisticated exchange of goods with objects produced all over Asia circulating in many locations. All of these objects were labeled as coming from the "East Indies", and this geographic confusion continued well until the end of the nineteenth century. Once direct trade was closed because of the British monopoly, historians have argued that Chinese ceramics and furniture became honorary British objects. American consumers carried little consciousness about their cultural provenance.[77] The American consumer, Caroline Frank argues, saw possessing these objects as a form of participation in honorary Britishness.

At the time when the statutes were issued by the British King, American-born Adolph Philipse still had an outstanding order for porcelain and lacquer from China. Frank writes that we do not know if the young Philipse ever managed to sneak in his desired Chinese luxuries but that his estate inventory taken fifty years later contained an enormous holding of china porcelain as well as lacquered furniture. These luxury objects and furnishings were spread out over several Hudson properties. There are also other significant inventories in the 1690s from the estates of two sea captains who sailed to the Indian Ocean and who had worked for Philipse's father. Frank notes that they lived to reap the fruits of their "private adventures" in the East Indies and escaped the gallows. Indeed, "adventure" was the label under which captains could keep some of these goods for their own profits. Private trade was always responsible for the highest quality Asian luxury goods on the Dutch and English markets.[78]

Many governors had close relationships with sea captains and privateers and took their share through extortion or gifts. They gained much from the return of ships once they hit American harbors, but Governor Bellomont was unlike his predecessors as he banned these goods and confiscated everything. By 1699, he was aggressively pursuing the colonial "pirates" and their sumptuous treasures.[79] Frank contends that the "Red Seamen", or pirates as the English officials and the governor now labeled them, were so successfully vilified that they became completely marginalized in American history. She notes that in his witch-hunt for East Indian goods, Bellomont searched within the intimate spaces of colonial homes and the very bodies of American suspects for evidence of any East India contacts and objects. The zealous governor searched the homes of Jonathan Selleck of Connecticut, of Duncan Campbell and Andrew Knott of Boston and of Thomas Paine and ran searches in a large number of New York homes. Perhaps the most famous sea captain he victimized was a very wealthy Dutch New Yorker later known as Captain Kidd.[80]

After successfully privateering for the English, Captain Kidd returned to New York in 1699. The wealthy sea captain seemed unaware of Bellomont's rapacity. He sent Lady Bellomont a Chinese lacquered box containing four jewels. As Caroline Frank puts it, Bellomont raised his nose where other governors had given in to temptation. She contends that, just as in many witch panics, Bellomont's paranoia surrounding East Indian goods stemmed from elite male power brokers who feared evil and temptation buried deep within "societies most intimate or female realms".[81] Not only the seamen but the exotic objects themselves were seen as evil in New York. However, the independent-minded Quaker governor in Pennsylvania has been called a steady friend of the Red Seamen. Governor William Markham settled down in Philadelphia and even accepted a marriage proposal for his daughter from Red Seaman James Brown. The governor staunchly defended Brown and other pirates when they claimed that they did not know that they were on piratical voyages.[82]

Captain Kidd did not realize that while he was away from New York the political climate had been transformed by Governor Bellomont, who not only refused Captain Kidd's *chinoiserie* gift but made sure to subject him to searches and imprisonment. At the time of the capture, Kidd was working as a privateer for some English lords who kept their anonymity. When Kidd returned to New York to defend himself against charges of piracy for capturing *Quedagh* and another ship, he had abandoned *Quedagh Merchant* on an island (called *Mona* in Kidd's time) because he knew its Indian make would be terribly conspicuous and give away his return to his hometown of New York. He was a wanted man, and the EEIC had urged the English government to punish Kidd; English ships were on the lookout for him as a pirate.[83]

Captain Kidd was put on trial specifically for the capture of the *Quedagh Merchant*. The ship had two French passes and he was a privateer paid to seize them. The details about the departure of the ship are clear on the second French pass used by the ship, now kept in the English archives.[84] As a privateer for the English, Captain Kidd was entirely within his rights. When he arrived in New York, Captain Kidd was still in possession of two French passes to justify his capture of the *Quedagh*. Kidd felt that both of these captures were legal, as the ship had a French pass, and following his commission by his lords could be considered an enemy ship, yet word spread quickly that Captain Kidd was a pirate. His passes disappeared, although they are in the archives now.[85]

Both pirates and privateers such as Captain Kidd brought in lots of coveted fashionable goods that are difficult to find in records or archives. This illicit trade was very important to collectors and merchants and was a large part of the market for goods. Like Europeans, the Americans were looking for the exotic to stay fashionable. Whether it was Margrieta van Varick's collection of objects or Captain Kidd's loot for the British lords who betrayed him, these exotic goods were part of a new early globalization where consumer desire traveled from Madagascar to London or to Boston and New York.

Was Contact with the New World Tied to the Birth of Fashion?

Mary Blaine Campbell argues that exploration and exploitation was tied to the birth of fashion in Europe. She writes "Furs, silks and fine cottons, stimulants – tea, coffee, sugar, rum, gin, tobacco and spices of all kinds – scrimshaw and curios for cabinets, travel books and atlases, topazes, feathers, [were] orientalizing and Americanizing changes in clothing and ornament".[86] If one looks at what was consumed as food and clothing in Early Modern Europe this transformation truly holds. Most historians of fashion have their own theories about the birth of fashion and few refer to this transformation. There is ample disagreement so it is important to examine the different opinions not only about when fashion was born, but what it was.

There are many debates about the birth of fashion in Europe. Sarah Grace Heller, after looking at the many different origins given by scholars, has concluded, "Fashion is a Phoenix constantly dying and reincarnating itself".[87] It is a graceful way to escape a thorny problem. Giorgio Riello has argued for fashion's inception in the fourteenth century in the Italian city-states after contact with Oriental sartorial splendor and textiles.[88] Well before him, Paul Post had also argued for the fourteenth century as a starting point for fashion based on a new strong gender differentiation, as male clothing became figure hugging at the court of Burgundy. Post argued for the birth of male fashion based on the jerkins worn under armor.[89] On the other hand, Joan DeJean has argued that fashion was born during the reign of Louis XIV in the 1660s.[90] The growing significance attached to fashion and society resulted, in both cases, in the increased consumption of fabrics, precious stones and furs, much of it imported. Giorgio Riello's argument is strengthened by the general increase in economic prosperity in the Italian city-states, during which improvements in textile technology strengthened the social position of artisans, of the textile guilds and of prosperous merchants. As argued previously, the wealth of several wealthy textile merchants led to political power and to the blossoming of a courtly life. The best-known examples are the Medici of Florence. This new consumption was made possible by a thriving trade between the Italian cities and Asian markets as well as between other European centers of wool production in the north. Flanders provided wool and clothing ranging in quality from the plainest to the finest. Expensive materials such as silk, damask, baldachin and atlas were brought in from Italy via the Orient. Important dyes such as indigo, saffron and scarlet were imported by the Italians from the Ottoman markets.[91]

Before the American fur trade was taken over by the French, Dutch and English, Russia and Scandinavia provided furs, expensive sable and ermine among them, via the trade of the Hanseatic League. These close ties with the towns and trade with the Orient proved particularly important for the Burgundian court under Charles the Bold (1433–1477), who was responsible for the extreme refinement and stylization of fashion in his domains. This court is where, Paul Post argues, fashion was first born in Europe. Charles' privilege was to determine the colors worn at court to denote his territorial claims and social superiority. Many historians argue that his initiatives made the Burgundian court a model for other European courts.[92] The most widely accepted argument for the birth of fashion remains Charles' court of Burgundy. This is Paul Post's early twentieth-century study on male dress, in which he demonstrates that what can be considered male modern dress appears around 1350 in France.[93] None of these changes – because fashion is understood as change – are the equivalent of what we understand as fashion today, a mass consumption of constantly changing industrial clothing. The argument is for change and sartorial splendor. All these theories have something in common: the desire for novelty and the exotic and rare.

Sarah Grace Heller points out that there are a number of problems with accepting the fourteenth-century date. Post's study is purely visual and does not account for desire for novelty or address the issue of consumption.[94] The study of fashion has taken a more interdisciplinary approach that no longer considers form and style in isolation, but views fashion as the socio-cultural dress practices of various historical actors. While costume history assumed a chronological continuity of form and style, it has become clear that there is constant discontinuity and sudden changes.[95] The history of clothing can follow an independent course in the historical process. The concept of *mode* was used for clothing as early as the fifteenth century but the term spread in the seventeenth century. A French dictionary published by Antoine Furetière in 1690 defined the word *mode* as custom; clothing is only referred to in the context of court dress, and it was only mentioned in third place. The increasing discussion of courtly dress in almanacs and calendars resulted in the word *mode* acquiring a specific reference. As a cultural phenomenon that is characterized by constant change and consumption, fashion has been often regarded as a phenomenon of Western modernity. Contradicting a long held position that fashion was a Western phenomenon, new scholarship has proven that non-Western societies have displayed similar evolution and changes in clothing habits.[96] Nevertheless, Mary Blaine Campbell is right in arguing that fashion's rise is tied to Europe's contacts with the "rest of the world" in the sixteenth and seventeenth centuries.[97] Europe witnessed accelerated changes in fashion and consumption due to increased Eurasian trade and the age of exploration.[98]

Yet it was not the arrival of new exotic goods alone, but the rise of wealthy merchants that precipitated the transformations that led to the birth of fashion. The broadening of European contacts with the "discovery" of the Americas and the intensification of trade with Asia was at the inception of a major social transformation that was key to the acceleration of European fashion. The rise of the powerful new social group of international merchants created a new urban merchant class in Spain, Portugal, France, England and the Netherlands. These traders imported exotic commodities to Europe that were previously unavailable. If indigo from Baghdad and saffron from India as well as Egyptian cotton had been known to Europeans in the medieval period, they were now widely available. Gabriele Mentges argues that in the sixteenth century European nobility began to experience increasing competition from the urban merchant class, which used clothing as a means of displaying its enhanced social status and new political power. This new middle class deliberately contravened all the sumptuary laws put in place to safeguard the prestige of the nobility. Gabriele Mentges argues that the richly illustrated costume book of Matthäus Schwarz (1496–1564), the chief bookkeeper of the wealthy Fugger trading company, provides evidence of clothing practices for the merchant class. This is a clothing biography that describes a luxurious wardrobe with precious metals and dyes. It testifies to the importance of mercantile networks and their impact on the availability of such expensive commodities. Mentges argues that a central trend of the period was the homogenization of the fashions of the urban elites and the increased social stratification of clothing.[99]

Nevertheless she argues that even in this context courts reclaimed their central position to the crafting of fashion; that if Italian fashion served as the model for most European courts until the middle of the fifteenth century, its influence was increasingly replaced by the fashions of dominant courts. Due to the dominant position of Spain under Charles V, Castilian Spanish fashions enjoyed influence over other European courts until about 1620. Hilary Davidson argues that this widespread influence was due not only to power but to style. Strict geometric forms subjugated the body to the elaborate etiquette of the court. With Europe torn between the Catholic and the Protestant faith, Spain became the defender of Catholic faith, with Felipe II's personal devotion as a beacon. His austere tastes – he was usually clad in unadorned black as was his sister Juana of Portugal – was to represent "Spanishness". Color was usually confined to white for collars and to glimpses of pink, red and sometimes green all turned inward in rows to emphasize the clothing's strict linear shape. Women's farthingales (*verdugado*), the hooped conical skirts, were known in other courts as Spanish farthingales; this garment's bell shape epitomized the European female's silhouette in the sixteenth century.[100]

If the color black is usually ascribed to Spanish fashion, Mentges provides an example of how a common fashion culture can emerge despite political and religious differences. The color black was accepted by the Reformation, but it was also the color of Spain's Counter-Reformation. Black, as an element of so-called Dutch Protestant fashion, was accepted in England, Germany and Scandinavia and even worn by the Quakers of North America. Mentges argues for a common culture among these different countries based on ethical views that prized bodily discipline. The color black came to symbolize respectability and decency both in Catholic and Protestant circles. Beyond the elite, it became the central norm of the new merchant class.[101]

It would be a mistake to assume that black was ubiquitous in Spain; sixteenth-century trade between the Iberian peninsula and India introduced the nobility to the printed and embroidered textiles produced in Asia.[102] Beverly Lemire follows the impact of these Asian cottons across Europe and finds that their impact went far beyond the elite.[103] When East Indian cottons arrived in Europe, England and Spain, the Dutch and the French would adopt them readily. These imports came in diverse assortments and Lemire shows that this fashion affected both consumers with pounds and those with pennies to spend. Initially in the middle of the seventeenth century robes of Indian floral cotton were worn by the elite on retiring and rising, but the general movement of fashion away from restrictive garb spread them among the middling ranks. Lemire finds their popularity spreading well beyond the middle class. Distribution of East India products began with auctions in London and Amsterdam, which were the first step in a vast distribution network of shopkeepers great and small, linked in turn with armies of peddlers.[104] Outside the metropolis, shopkeepers supplied muslin and calico to their rural customers, then legions of peddlers linked urban outlets with rural buyers. Lemire argues that this network took copious amounts of exotic goods to towns, villages and rural communities, and that there was plenty of cheap striped and plain muslin and calico in the inventory of shops in the provinces.

At a time when voyages of exploration brought flowering plants and shrubs to the wealthy and exotic gardens and cut flowers were in vogue, these Indian floral cottons brought decorative material unlike anything previously seen. Silk and brocades were long available to the elite, but these floral calicos, chintzes and muslins were made in many qualities and sold at different prices. She concludes that these novel commodities were prized by both the wealthy and "folks with just pennies to spare".[105] If a more widespread consumption is taken into account, and the study of fashion is no longer a visual study of costumes, then perhaps this more generalized desire for Indian fabrics and their local imitations in seventeenth-century Europe could speak of the birth of fashion as we see it in the modern sense, a change that goes beyond the elite. Lemire's study is mostly of the seventeenth and eighteenth centuries. Although one cannot firmly argue that it did not exist in certain cities, that form of consumption beyond the elite has not yet been traced for earlier periods. Another argument is made for the seventeenth century as the century of the birth of European fashion in Paris, France. Joan DeJean and Jennifer Jones both argue for fashion's beginnings in the second half of the seventeenth century in the court of France. The dominance of Spain in European court fashion would be consciously and openly challenged by Louis XIV (1641– 1715). After the 1670s it would be the French court that would set *la mode* for all of Europe.[106]

Study Questions

1 What philosophical, scientific, and religious discourses complicated Europeans' adoption of various foods from the New World? What exigencies facilitated their adoption?
2 How did the plantation system and African slavery facilitate the consumption of drug foods in both the New World and Europe?
3 What impact did the different views about animals and hunting held by Europeans and Native Americans have on colonizing the New World?
4 What role did newly settled Dutch women play in trade and consumption in the New World?
5 How did smuggled trade in *chinoiserie* impact American separatism from Great Britain?
6 How did Spanish settlers in the New World use fashion to express loyalties alternative to the Spanish monarchy? How did Spaniards use fashion to reinforce their authority in the New World?

Notes

1 Mary Blaine Campbell, *Wonder and Science: Imagining Worlds in Early Modern Europe* (Ithaca; London: Cornell University Press, 1999), 226–227.
2 Florent Quellier, *La Table des Français: Une Histoire Culturelle (XV-début XIX siècle)* (Rennes: Presses Universitaires de Rennes, 2007), 191–208.
3 Alfred Crosby, *The Columbian Exchange: The Biological Consequences of 1492* (Westport CT: Greenwood Press, 1972).
4 Quellier, *La Table des Français*, 197.
5 Alen J. Grieco, "Les plantes, les regimes vegetariens et la melancolie a la fin du Moyen Age et au debut de la Renaissance italienne" in Alen J. Grieco, Odile Redon, and Tomasi Lucia Tongiorgi, *Le monde végétal (XII-XVII siècles): savoirs et usages sociaux* (Saint-Denis: Presses universitaires de Vincennes, 1993), 11–29.
6 Quellier, *La Table des Français*, 174.
7 Quellier, *La Table des Français*, 197.
8 Quellier, *La Table des Français*, 175.
9 Quellier, *La Table des Français*, 175–177.
10 Quellier, *La Table des Français*, 175.
11 Ellen Messar, "Potatoes (White)" in Kenneth F. Kiple and Kriemhild Conee Ornelas eds., *The Cambridge World History of Food, Volume I* (Cambridge: Cambridge University Press, 2000) 187–201.
12 Quellier, *La Table des Français*, 202.
13 Ellen Messar "Potatoes (White)" in *The Cambridge World History of Food, Volume I*, 191–192.
14 Quellier *La Table des Français*, 183.
15 Massimo Montanari, *The Culture of Food*, Carl Ipsen, trans. (Oxford, UK; Cambridge, MA, USA: Blackwell, 1994), 143.
16 Montanari, *The Culture of Food*, 144.
17 Montanari, *The Culture of Food*, 144.
18 Florent Quellier, *La Table des Français*, 151–159.
19 Established by Lavoisier in 1791 and cited by Quellier, *La Table des Français*, 152.
20 Charles C. Mann, *1493, Uncovering the New World Columbus Created* (New York: Alfred A. Knopf, 2011), 75.

21 Mann, *1493*, 14.
22 Mann, *1493*, 75–77.
23 Mann, *1493*, 85.
24 Mann, *1493*, 79.
25 Mann, *1493*, 112–113.
26 Campbell, *Wonder and Science*, 9.
27 Campbell, *Wonder and Science*, 52–55.
28 Campbell, *Wonder and Science*, 30.
29 Campbell, *Wonder and Science*, 55.
30 Campbell, *Wonder and Science*, 27, 54–57.
31 Campbell, *Wonder and Science*, 61.
32 Campbell, *Wonder and Science*, 63.
33 Campbell, *Wonder and Science*, 62.
34 Campbell, *Wonder and Science*, 227.
35 James C. Kelly and Barbara Clark Smith, *Jamestown, Quebec, Santa Fe: Three North American Beginnings* (New York: Smithsonian Books, 2007), 103.
36 Kelly and Smith, *Jamestown, Quebec, Santa Fe*, 96–98.
37 Kelly and Smith, *Jamestown, Quebec, Santa Fe*, 103–107.
38 Kelly and Smith, *Jamestown, Quebec, Santa Fe*, 107–112.
39 Kelly and Smith, *Jamestown, Quebec, Santa Fe*, 115–116.
40 Harold Innis, *The Fur Trade in Canada* (Toronto: University of Toronto Press, 2001), 63–81.
41 Innis, *The Fur Trade in Canada*, 63–68.
42 Innis, *The Fur Trade in Canada*, 69–83.
43 James E. McWilliams, *A Revolution in Eating: How the Quest for Food Shaped America* (New York: Columbia University Press, 2005), 138–139.
44 Virginia DeJohn Anderson, *Creatures of Empire: How Domestic Animals Transformed Early America* (Oxford; New York: Oxford University Press, 2004), 22.
45 Anderson, *Creatures of Empire*, 78.
46 McWilliams, *A Revolution in Eating*, 136.
47 McWilliams, *A Revolution in Eating*, 137.
48 Anderson, *Creatures of Empire*, 23–24.
49 Anderson, *Creatures of Empire*, 25
50 Anderson, *Creatures of Empire*, 32–33.
51 Anderson, *Creatures of Empire*, 34–36.
52 Anderson, *Creatures of Empire*, 35–42.
53 Anderson, *Creatures of Empire*, 59.
54 William Perry, *Martin Hunting Law and Ritual in Medieval English Literature* (D.S. Brewer: Cambridge, 2006).
55 Anderson, *Creatures of Empire*, 62.
56 Flandrin, "Distinction through Taste", in Philippe Ariès and Georges Duby, eds., *A History of Private Life* (Cambridge, MA: Belknap Press of Harvard University Press, 1987–1991), Vol. III, 281.
57 Anderson, *Creatures of Empire*, 71.
58 Anderson, *Creatures of Empire*, 78–79.
59 Anderson, *Creatures of Empire*, 103–104.
60 Benjamin Schmidt, *Innocence Abroad: The Dutch Imagination and the New World, 1570–1670* (Cambridge: Cambridge University Press, 2001).
61 Wim Klooster, "An Overview of Dutch Trade with the Americas, 1600–1800", in Johannes Postma and Victor Enthoven, eds., *Riches from Atlantic Commerce: Dutch Transatlantic Trade and Shipping, 1585–1817* (Leiden: Brill Academic Publishers, 2003), 368–84 and Victor Enthoven, "An Assessment of Dutch Transatlantic Commerce, 1585–1817," in ibid., 385–445; Benjamin Schmidt, "The Dutch Atlantic From Provincialism to Globalism," in Jack P. Greene and

Philip D. Morgan, eds., *Atlantic History: A Critical Appraisal* (Oxford; New York: Oxford University Press, 2009), 163–187.

62 Deborah L. Krohn, Peter N. Miller, and Marybeth de Filippis, *Dutch New York between East and West: The World of Margrieta van Varick* (New York: Bard Graduate Center, Decorative Arts, Design History, Material Culture: New-York Historical Society; New Haven: Yale University Press, 2009), 13–22.

63 Krohn, Miller, and de Filippis, *Dutch New York between East and West*, 13.

64 Hugo Grotius, *Mare Liberum* (Leiden, 1609).

65 Klooster, "An Overview of Dutch Trade with the Americas, 1600–1800", 368–384; Victor Enthoven, "An Assessment of Dutch Transatlantic Commerce, 1585–1817", 385–445; Schmidt, "The Dutch Atlantic From Provincialism to Globalism", 163–187.

66 Krohn, Miller, and de Filippis, *Dutch New York between East and West*, 13–22.

67 Krohn, Miller, and de Filippis, *Dutch New York between East and West*, 71.

68 Krohn, Miller, and de Filippis, *Dutch New York between East and West*, 25–39.

69 A collaboration between the Bard Graduate Center and the New York Historical Society, the exhibition *Dutch New York between East and West: The World of Margrieta van Varick* was on display from September 2009 to January 2010 at the Bard Graduate Center.

70 Marybeth de Filippis, "Margrieta van Varick's East Indian Goods", *The Magazine Antiques* (September 2009), accessed October 24 2012, http://www.themagazi neantiques.com/articles/margrieta-van-varicks-east-indian-goods-a-possible-influe nce-on-colonial-american-silver/

71 Ina Baghdiantz McCabe, *Orientalism in Early Modern France: Eurasian Trade, Exoticism and the Ancien Régime* (Oxford; New York: Berg, 2008), 1–11.

72 De Filippis, "Margrieta van Varick's East Indian Goods", *The Magazine Antiques,* 2.

73 Krohn, Miller, and de Filippis, *Dutch New York between East and West*, 316.

74 Caroline Frank, *Objectifying China, Imagining America: Chinese Commodities in Early America* (Chicago: University of Chicago Press, 2011), 12–13.

75 Baghdiantz McCabe, *Orientalism*, 1–11.

76 Frank, *Objectifying China*, 35–37.

77 Frank, *Objectifying China*, 44–45.

78 Frank, *Objectifying China*, 45

79 Frank, *Objectifying China*, 47.

80 Frank, *Objectifying China*, 47–49.

81 Frank, *Objectifying China*, 49.

82 Frank, *Objectifying China*, 50.

83 The best book on Kidd remains Robert C. Ritchie, *Captain Kidd and the War Against the Pirates* (Cambridge, MA, 1986). Ritchie based his work on serious documentation, but only one source affirms *Quedagh* was burnt until nothing remained of it, so the claim of its discovery has to be double-checked as well; Ritchie 164–66. See the seventeenth-century *Journal of Nathaniel Cary* who reported that the *QM* burned for six hours on June 9, PRO 5/860, folios 372–3.

84 A copy of the French passport signed by Martin is in the Public Record Office and has been published as an image many times without the archival number. It should be correctly cited as: PRO CO 5/860 folios 161–2.

85 Robert C. Ritchie devotes the last two chapters of his book to the trial and it remains the best account of it.

86 Campbell, *Wonder and Science*, 226.

87 Sarah Grace Heller, *Fashion in Medieval France* (Cambridge; Rochester, NY: Brewer, 2007), 59.

88 Giorgio Riello and Peter McNeil, eds., *The Fashion History Reader: Global Perspectives* (Milton Park, Abingdon, Oxon; New York: Routledge, 2010), 40–41.

89 Riello and McNeil, *The Fashion History Reader*, 40–41.

90 Joan DeJean, *The Essence of Style: How the French Invented High Fashion, Fine Food, Chic Cafés, Style, Sophistication and Glamour* (New York: Free Press, 2005).
91 Gabriele Mentges, "European Fashion (1450–1950)" *European History Online (EGO)* (Mainz: Institute of European History (IEG), 2011), 4–5.
92 Mentges, "European Fashion (1450–1950)", 4.
93 Sarah Grace Heller, "Birth of Fashion" in Giorgio Riello and Peter McNeil, eds., *The Fashion History Reader: Global Perspectives* (Abingdon, Oxon; New York: Routledge, 2010), 27.
94 Heller, "Birth of Fashion", *The Fashion History Reader,* 29.
95 Mentges, "European Fashion (1450–1950)", 6.
96 Most new studies on the Early Modern period concern China.
97 Campbell, *Wonder and Science*, 226.
98 Mentges, "European Fashion (1450–1950)", 3–6.
99 Mentges, "European Fashion (1450–1950)", 5.
100 Hilary Davidson, "Fashion in the Spanish Court" in Giorgio Riello and Peter McNeil, eds., *The Fashion History Reader: Global Perspectives* (Abingdon, Oxon; New York: Routledge, 2010), 169.
101 Mentges, "European Fashion (1450–1950)", 6–7.
102 Beverly Lemire, "Fashioning Cottons: Asian Trade, Domestic Industry and Consumer Demand, 1660–1780" in Giorgio Riello and Peter McNeil, eds., *The Fashion History Reader: Global Perspectives* (Abingdon, Oxon; New York: Routledge, 2010), 195.
103 Beverly Lemire, "Domesticating the Exotic: Floral Culture in the East India Calico Trade with England, c. 1600–1800", in *Textile: A Journal of Cloth and Culture, I/I (2003)*: 65–85.
104 K. N. Chaudhuri, *The Trading World of Asia and the English East India Company 1660–1760* (Cambridge; New York: Cambridge University Press, 1978), 131–4. As cited in Lemire, "Fashioning Cottons" *The Fashion History Reader,* 197.
105 Lemire, "Fashioning Cottons", *The Fashion History Reader,* 198–201.
106 DeJean. *The Essence of Style*, 4.

Figure 4.1 Advertisement for London Coffee (c. 1700). © Getty Images.

4 Domesticating the Exotic

A Fashion for Coffee, Tea and Porcelain

The smell of the mire is horrible. Paris is a dreadful place. The streets smell so badly that you cannot go out. The extreme heat is causing large quantities of meat and fish to rot in them, and this, coupled to the multitude of people … in the street, produces a smell so detestable that it cannot be endured.[1]

Seventeenth-century Paris created fashion, *haute couture* and *haute cuisine*, but chamber pots were emptied into its narrow streets. The opinions of the German-born Duchesse d'Orléans cited above were often negative when it came to the food and manners of France, but her description of Paris can be confirmed through other observers. That Paris was a stinky and rather poor market town did not preclude it from becoming Europe's capital of "taste". If Joan DeJean has argued that modern shopping was born in Paris and that fashion was born at the court of its king, then none of it could have happened without a profound change in views held by the Parisian elite. The Duchesse d'Orléans, quoted above, married to Louis XIV's younger brother, is most quoted when she writes against the French court's love of exotic chocolate and coffee. She strongly expressed her own preference for beer-soup in the face of these new beverages. In doing so she was discussing taste, a most fashionable and new way to express opinion. Indeed, Jean Louis Flandrin, the foremost historian of food, has found that a real revolution took place in Paris during the second half of the seventeenth century. The concept of "taste" became prominent in daily discourse. Since the Middle Ages, food had been tied to the dietetics of Galenic medical thinking and to its influence on health and on the humors of the body, not to taste. If this traditional discourse did not entirely disappear, it was superseded in every domain by a new one, individual judgment; the taste of the consumer. Whether in the arts, in clothing, in literature or at the table, it was for the consumer to discern whether things were in good or bad taste. Flandrin writes of the birth of the concept of "*l'homme de goût*" or "the man of taste" who judges what is beautiful or ugly, good or bad, in painting, in furniture, in manners and especially on his plate. Cooks discussed the harmony of tastes in dishes, neglecting the classifications made by doctors about the nature of food. Previously classified as hot or cold, dry or humid based on Galenic medicine, foods were assembled to be balanced for digestion. These hygienic precautions slowly disappeared to leave a discourse about the way the tastes of different foods harmonized to make a successful and succulent dish judged for its flavor.[2] It can be safely argued that without this transformation there would not have been a novel *haute cuisine* or *haute couture*.

French Merchants' Influence on Fashion

It is debated whether a new form of consumption based on taste was generated by the bourgeoisie or by the court. The works of Joan DeJean and Jennifer Jones both argue for the leadership not only of the French court, but for the King's conscious initiatives. The demands of the luxury market played a large role in expanding foreign trade: Jacques Savary de Brûlons wrote that the commerce of the guild of the mercers was responsible for expanding French trade to the Indies. Carolyn Sargentson has documented that it was the mercers who were successfully retailing oriental goods on the domestic markets. Consumer demand drove the need for overseas trade. In Jacques Savary de Brûlons' wake, and from his views in his famous *Dictionnaire universel de commerce* published in 1723, it can be argued that merchants, the mercers, were in no small part responsible for the rise of the consumption of luxury goods and fashion in this period.[3] Published eight years after the King's death, most of this dictionary's information concerns Louis XIV's long reign. Carolyn Sargentson has studied the guild of the mercers closely. Some mercers could have acted as wholesalers of porcelain as some were wealthy enough to buy porcelain in bulk from the East India Company. Mercers could alter imported goods for the French market; they mounted porcelain in gold and silver. The guild of mercers in Paris was responsible for the sale of oriental goods to the wealthy bourgeoisie and the aristocracy through their shops. Many women kept the stores, especially those selling silk hose and ribbons, and there were also many widows as owners of inventories. These were family owned businesses. The storefronts often carried orientalist names such as *La Pagode d'or, la Perle d'Orient* and *Au Grand Turc*. The mercers of Paris also changed imports to adapt them to the "taste" of their customers. They had the right to modify furniture and goods and the most important are some examples of commissions of Japanese porcelains adapted through metal decoration to suit the French taste.[4]

The role of these Parisian merchants seems to successfully counter Norbert Elias' argument that the court solely drove fashions and demand. Carolyn Sargentson's work on the mercers of Paris demonstrates the same reality. Nevertheless, if the bourgeois-versus-aristocratic origins of modern consumption is a debate classic, it may be a false one in France, as the lines between a wealthy bourgeois, such as Colbert and his descendants, and the aristocracy in France had been slowly blurred since Richelieu (1585–1642).[5] It is clear that Louis XIV did expand on some of the habits of collecting and domesticating that were prevalent in France since Henry IV and in some cases Francis I, giving credence to an earlier rise of the consumption of luxury goods during the Renaissance in France. By the turn of the eighteenth century, Louis XIV was carrying 15,000 carats of diamonds on his daywear; he even wore diamonds on the buckles of his shoes and garters. Above and beyond the debates about when the consumption of luxury goods began in France, there is no question that the French court's affection for oriental luxury goods – from diamonds and flowers to expensive textiles, porcelain and Arabian horses – was at its height under Louis XIV.[6]

The International Influence of French Fashion Trends

The court leadership is still upheld by several scholars. If Louis XIV conquered new territories, his power was not simply territorial. Joan DeJean has argued that Louis' real empire was conquering most of Europe's elites through *coiffeurs* and cooks and that France's cultural impact was far more important than its territorial conquests. The French King adopted a strong red color to counter Spain's black. DeJean has shown that although Louis XIV's own preoccupation was with court dress, his influence would go well beyond the court, through the first fashion magazine created by his historiographer and via pamphlets and fashion dolls dressed in French style traveling through France and the world.[7] Jennifer Jones has shown how the French King elaborated a very confining corseted silk *grand habit* for the women of his court in 1670 at a time when looser clothing styles and robes were taking over in Europe. Saint Simon wrote "Whether pregnant, ill, less than six weeks after delivery, and whatever the ferocity of the weather, they had to be in the grand habit".[8] Earlier in 1664 he had created a vest for men to mark privilege, which was bestowed only on those courtiers who had the right to his proximity; the warrant coats, *justecorps à brevet*, were made with blue silk lined with scarlet, embroidered with silver and gold thread.[9]

Louis XIV would take great care in constructing his own image and ceremonial appearance in which the commodities bought through the trade with India and Asia would be key.[10] He bought an unparalleled diamond collection from Jean-Baptiste Tavernier, who had brought them from his travels in Golconda, India. In 1668 Tavernier sold the King a huge diamond. Tavernier called its extraordinary color violet. It weighed 112 3/16-carats. Louis XIV acquired it along with fourteen other large diamonds and several smaller ones. For ceremonies, Louis wore the large diamond cut and reset by Sieur Pitau, the court jeweler, now a 67 1/8-carat stone. In the French royal inventories, the diamond was described as an intense steely blue and the stone became known as the "Blue Diamond of the Crown"; later it became famous as the Hope Diamond.[11] Eurasian trade was key to the luxury that was coveted at court and by the aristocracy. Beyond the court, a wealthy merchant class was thriving; lighting and shopping made Paris a center for high-end consumption. Joan DeJean writes "In the 1660s, Paris began a reign over luxury

living that still endures three and half centuries later", for the first time customers stepped inside Parisian shops to make purchases.[12] DeJean argues that
it was because the French administration, Louis XIV in particular, understood
marketing that fashion and shopping in the modern sense were born.[13]

While diamonds from India were avidly collected at court and candles
glittered in the mirrors, most of the French remained poor. This was the
century of Versailles, when French fashions ruled most courts and one's imagination often only sees the glitter of diamonds and silks in the tall mirrors of
the palace of Versailles. Descriptions of Paris in the same era depict it as
smelly, dirty and mostly poor; the people of France were not the ones dressed
in silk and diamonds, sipping chocolate or smoking tobacco. The new
American goods were for the elite alone. If it was in the seventeenth century
that exotic commodities such as sugar, chocolate, tea, coffee and tobacco
became consumed on a global scale geographically, their consumption was
confined to the elites of many European societies. For most inhabitants of
Paris these were yet unreachable new luxuries. Beyond Europe this was also a
reality: the new drug foods from the New World and from Asia, such as
coffee and tea, belonged to the elite alone. France still bought most of its
Asian luxuries from its competitors the Dutch, as its own empire in the New
World provided only one luxury good, furs. Furs would never be conceived of
as French, but one exotic good would come to represent French identity in
the eighteenth century. Coffee drinking in the morning and after meals
became a French habit by the eighteenth century, despite resistance from
some high court figures such as the Duchesse d'Orléans and her preference
for beer soup. The evolution of coffee drinking was slow and met with other
forms of resistance from both doctors and merchants avid to protect French
wine as a French drink and as a major French import to the rest of Europe.

From Ethiopia to Europe: Coffee's Spread

The first European to notice coffee was a natural philosopher from Augsburg,
Leonhard Rauwolf (d. 1569). He was part of a large network of botanists
with whom he exchanged letters and seeds of new plants.[14] The first descriptions
of coffee came from travelers with an intellectual interest in the Ottoman
Empire or Persia. Many seventeenth-century sources about coffee are Dutch,
French and English travel accounts. Antoine Galland, a famous orientalist
and translator, claimed that one of the first to serve coffee in France, in the
first half of the seventeenth century, was the traveler Jean de Thévenot.[15] Jean
de Thévenot, who encountered coffee drinking in Constantinople, introduced
his friends to this exotic drug. Antoine Galland also pointed out that it was
the Armenians who spread its usage throughout Paris. There were already
several cafés in Paris in 1699 when Antoine Galland was translating the ideas
held about coffee in the Ottoman Empire from an Arabic manuscript: a work
by Abd al-Qadir al-Jaziri (c. 1558) who traced the history, usage and controversies of *qahwa* (coffee) in the Islamic world where it was first used. Arab

views on coffee became widely quoted in Europe. Al-Jaziri credited one Sheikh Jamal-al-Din al-Dhabhani (d. 1470–71), *mufti* of Aden, as the pioneer who first made and drank a cup of coffee (c. 1454). Its usefulness in driving away sleep made it a religious drink in Sufi circles and its all night ritual of worship. Europe's knowledge of coffee, which was largely based on Galland's French translation of the origins and medical properties of coffee culled from Al-Jaziri's Arabic manuscript. In the realm of the arts, however, coffee was clearly associated with the Ottomans alone. The most blatant of all identifications of coffee with the Ottomans is a much reproduced engraving in Philippe Sylvestre Dufour's *Traitez nouveaux & curieux du café, du thé et du chocolat. Ouvrage également necessaire aux medecins, & à tous ceux qui aiment leur santé*.[16] The properties of coffee were considered new knowledge even before Galland's translation of 1699. Serious work had been published on coffee by French physicians, notably Philippe Sylvestre Dufour's in 1671 and 1684,[17] and Nicolas de Blegny's in 1687.[18]

Coffeehouses had been well established for over a century in Cairo, Istanbul and Isfahan. The diffusion of coffee in the Ottoman Empire was chiefly a consequence of the Ottoman conquest of the Mamluk state of Egypt in 1516, where the first coffeehouse was opened. Ethiopia could not fulfill the new demand for coffee in the Ottoman Empire so Yemen, later the largest exporter of coffee, began to supply this market in the 1540s.[19] Coffee drinking was common in the Islamic world well before the 1670s when the new *cafés* were opened in Paris, where they opened a new sphere of sociability beyond the tavern, which was exclusively male and not upper class.[20]

Much repeated in books is the first prohibition against coffee according to Al-Jaziri. It took place in 1511 in the town of Mecca. Stories of opposition to coffee in the Ottoman Empire have made their way in many histories of coffee.[21] The Mamluk pasha Khair Beg was depicted as the principal opponent to coffee. He was the inspector of markets in Mecca and the arbiter of morals, a combination of being head of consumer affairs and head of the vice squad. Troubled by the riots in coffeehouses, the authorities banned coffee across the Empire, but to assert that coffee itself was contrary to Islam, it had to be actually proven harmful. One Friday, Khair Beg brought a large vessel of coffee and set it in the middle of a group of doctors; coffee itself was now on trial. Muslim clerics from several sects discussed the issue with doctors. The faction wanting to ban coffee won and the pilgrims and the Meccans were forbidden to drink coffee, albeit for a short time.[22]

In the Islamic world, where its drinking originated, the last prohibition against coffee itself, rather than against gatherings around coffee, was issued during the Hajj of 1544 by the Ottoman Sultan. According to Al-Jaziri, the jurists of Mecca acted out of sheer fanaticism (*t'assub*) when they banned coffee.[23] Coffee was important during *ramadan* and despite some individual arrests of consumers, its usage could not be prohibited. Ralph Hattox finds that there is pattern to the bans on coffee: none of them were successful for very long.[24] There were separate coffeehouses for the rich and poor in all the main cities, such as Baghdad, Istanbul, Isfahan, Mecca and Cairo.[25] Hattox rightly implies that the Islamic debates about coffee have been misrepresented in European writings on coffee as a sign of Muslim fanaticism or reluctance to innovate and as "haughtily and righteously preaching against even the most innocent of earthly pleasure".[26] A century later the same debates were to arrive in London and Paris and bring medical controversies about coffee with them. Ideas held by Arab physicians entered Europe via translations and travel accounts.

Coffee's Arrival in Europe Met with Medical Debates

In seventeenth-century France, natural history, medicine, commerce and the economic state of the nation were closely linked in the writings on exotic plants. Royal commissions for the study of the subject of coffee were rare. Only one of Louis XIV's personal physicians, Monsieur Nicolas de Blègny (1652–1722) wrote a treatise on coffee at the King's request. Most works on coffee were written by independent merchants and scholars.[27] Treatises on the exotic new beverages of tea, coffee and chocolate were commissioned by private individuals both for their commercial and scientific value. Like many historical transformations, the birth of the French café as a major institution and the French habit of coffee drinking happened without much conscious planning. Discourse from the court, the guilds, café owners and consumers offer a complex view of its early history. They help to reconstruct how the taste for coffee was acquired and shed light on the social agency of what was considered to be an Ottoman beverage. Coffee drinking affected elements as diverse as receiving habits in the domestic sphere, the transformation of the public sphere by the *café*, medical knowledge and drugs. As Braudel wrote so pertinently, certain minute events that are barely marked in time and space became part of the structures of everyday life.[28]

Seventeenth-century physicians wrote entire dissertations about the properties of the new drug at the Sorbonne and at the University of Montpellier.[29] Paradoxically, these learned tomes were the most popular, as they were summarized and became public reading. Because medical controversies about drinking coffee were so hotly debated at universities in Montpellier and Paris they made news in pamphlets and gazettes.[30] Views about coffee and health changed dramatically and gave way to some interesting debates that hid their initial political underpinnings. Scientific knowledge of coffee in Europe culled from Arabic sources was important before use of the beverage became familiar. The Arabic belief that the consumption of coffee caused leprosy did not find its way in the medical discourse that arose in France, but impotence, lust, headaches and its diuretic effect were among the many properties debated about coffee's influence on the body.

The controversy over drugs was one that continued for many decades. Coffee was seen as a potent drug. The debates around coffee in France were at the center of some of the discussion about the digestive system. In England,

Francis Bacon's new scientific interest in coffee is better known, as is the contention that coffee had helped Harvey discover blood circulation.[31] The fierceness of the debate in France continued well into the middle of the eighteenth century; one of the earliest participants in the debates was Claude Colomb.[32] As a doctor he was sure that coffee was not of a cold nature but a hot one, and that it would burn as it had a dry nature. His views were not unique, as some Arab doctors had argued this in Mecca. His opinions were not confined to academic debates. After his public defense on 27 February 1679 in City Hall, coffee was banned and publicly burned by the city of Marseilles.[33]

Colomb argued that coffee disturbed the balance of the humors through excessive consumption. That Colomb's dissertation was defended in City Hall, the domain of the Provost of the merchants of the city of Marseilles, is extremely telling of Colomb's sponsorship by local merchants who did not control the import of coffee. Wine was a major French export to the rest of Europe and beyond and was part of Marseilles' brisk business. The merchants of Marseilles had even sent Colbert petitions to ban the commerce of the Armenians and Jews from the Levant from the port of Marseilles. Among other goods that irked the Marseillais, were silk and cotton cloth and to a lesser degree coffee; the Armenians were the chief importers of these exotic goods at this date.[34] The merchants of Marseilles demanded that a tax of 20 percent be levied on all merchandise brought into the port on foreign ships or on all foreign cargo carried on a French ship. Several Europeans had written about tea, notably the Dutch. It was brought to France as early as 1636 by the Dutch. Decades later the famous cooking manual *Le Nouveau Cuisinier Royal et Bourgeois* stated that tea was less common than coffee because it was not as cheap.[35] Coffee became France's favorite exotic drink, cheek to cheek with wine, France's national drink. This success was sponsored at a later date by Louis XIV himself when the King raised money for his wars on the sale of coffee and publicized that it was better for one's health than wine.[36]

Imitating the Orient's Coffee-drinking Habits

In Audigier's 1692 treatise *La maison bien reglée* there is information about the very early arrival of coffee to Paris.[37] Audigier was a master of ceremonies, to the countess of Soissons and later to Colbert the Minister of France. He went to Italy in the 1660s to learn about making the new beverages of tea, coffee and chocolate. He hoped to open the first shop serving exotic beverages. He applied to get permission to open an Italian-style establishment to serve coffee and many other beverages but his application was fraught with bureaucratic difficulties. According to Audigier, his failure was due to a political *contretemps*: his request had been supported by a lady who had fallen out of favor. Meanwhile, Armenians were importing bales of coffee beans into France for decades but not finding much of a market for it. According to

Audigier's own work a *"levantine"* attempted to sell coffee beans as early as 1643 in a covered passage that existed between the Rue Saint Jacques and the Petit Pont. Cardinal Mazarin (1602–1661) brought his own coffee maker from Italy. It is often thought that the Ottoman ambassador's visit to Paris brought the fashion of coffee drinking to the elites in 1669. Yet coffee was already brewed in France; not only was it served in court to Mazarin, it was more widely known beyond the court at least three years before the Ottoman ambassador arrived, as a 1666 poem attests. In this trite poem, the poet complains of a headache and fears the usual bloodletting, the galenic *saignée*; instead the poet preferred the drug, coffee, "kave".[38]

The cultural-functionalist tradition among historians of consumerism assumes that taste follows discourse or a dominant ideology, a *mentalité*. This sometimes leaves out how a *mentalité* was forged in the first place; orientalists and travelers participated in forging this *mentalité* as authorities on the "Orient", sometimes well before coffee became a generally known beverage. The study of coffee in Paris suggests a complex relationship between taste, fashion, politics, commerce and discourse. Here it is argued that a taste for coffee was constructed simultaneously on several levels to refute the vertical "trickle-down model" popularized by Norbert Elias: at court by the ambassador, in cafés by the middle class and even through street merchants. Norbert Elias was a sociologist who argued that the court of France had a civilizing effect on the French elite; his trickle-down theory places the King at the center as a model for all to imitate. Elias' helpful model of social analysis argued that habits were adopted in the imitation of the court by the powerful and then by the bourgeoisie. This is a standard explanation for the spread of fashion and manners. In acquiring this etiquette, which was key to rising in the hierarchy, imitation and restraint were crucial. Elias wrote specifically with the French court in mind, as under Louis XIV it was the most powerful court in Europe and it became an arbiter of taste and fashion.[39] The King was at the center of this system like the sun was the center of the planetary system.[40] What Elias argued for the process of civilization only holds true for one level of the diffusion of coffee: in court through the Turkish ambassador. Yet what is clear in the history of *cafés* is that the taste for coffee appeared in several groups of society simultaneously. The taste for the beverage was spread by an Ottoman ambassador at court, also by the Armenians who served coffee to the aristocracy and to the bourgeoisie in the first *cafés*, then also almost at the same time by a Greek street vendor, Candiot, who served coffee from a pot on his back as la Roque tells us.[41] Once coffee was successful in Paris, Louis XIV directly attempted to use the new fashion of coffee drinking for his own political advantage to raise funds for his European wars, which impeded the spread of coffee drinking. The hope to promote coffee backfired, but the court followed him. It is apparent from a *courtisane*'s correspondence, Madame de Sévigné's, that her negative views on coffee changed after the sponsorship of the King. She saw it as poison in one letter and as healthy in another.[42]

Armenians and the First Cafés in Paris

Few footnotes in the voluminous history of trade have had such revolutionary and global socio-economic consequences as the introduction of cafés to Europe. The role of the Armenian diaspora in the spread of new products in Europe is not well known. The role of the Jews in chocolate is a little better known than that of the Armenians in the coffee trade, but both deserve to be highlighted due to their role as ideal agents of cross-cultural exchange. While the Armenians were specialists in Eurasian cross-cultural trade and played a considerable role in popularizing coffee, their role was not unique. The Sephardic Jews played a role in importing and spreading the usage of American chocolate in Europe via their Atlantic trade, especially in the Dutch Republic, where they took refuge after being expelled from Spain and Portugal in 1492.[43] The Sephardic Jews were introduced to chocolate in Portugal and Spain and they carried it further north with them. Just as coffee was becoming better known, by the end of the seventeenth century, American chocolate became widely consumed as a drink in European courts. These two major trade diaspora, the Armenians and the Jews, are only recently being well studied to expose their important role in world trade.[44] Their role as outsiders establishing themselves in a craft in France or the Dutch Republic was not impeded by the guilds until later when the guilds caught up with the new unregulated products and took over the profit and distribution of these exotic goods.

Jean de la Roque names five Armenians as the pioneering force in spreading coffee drinking in Paris. Thanks to la Roque's careful survey of the first *maison de café* opened in Marseilles and Paris, the name of each café owner is recorded. It is fascinating that in orientalist fashion, de la Roque's treatise on coffee had an Ottoman model. De la Roque proudly stated that his survey of the *maisons de café* was in imitation of a Turkish historian who had surveyed the first *maison de café* in Constantinople. He recorded the names of the first men who opened these public places in Paris for the sake of history.[45] Jean de la Roque recorded that in the year 1672 an Armenian named Pascal who arrived via Marseilles opened a café first in the *rue du Louvre* and then at the *quai de l'Ecole*.[46] Previously he had served coffee at a major fair held annually in Paris. His *maison de coava* was by some accounts a replica of the ones in Constantinople, decorated with Turkish trappings where black slave boys carried silver trays of coffee among the public sitting in the 140 booths set up annually at the fair of St. Germain.[47] Several cafés owned by Armenians were successful. Audiger was angered by the success of the Armenians as late as 1692. Two cafés opened by Armenians were not far from where Procopio initially opened his coffeehouse, the third café to open in Paris. Over the two centuries that it operated, the Procope became a literary café and a center for political discussions that allegedly attracted the likes of Voltaire and Rousseau in the eighteenth century.[48] Most importantly, Procopio Cotelli's establishment was where the sale of coffee as a beverage first fell under guild rule.

Because of the guild records making it the first legal café, it is considered to be the first café in Paris.

A rare work published in 1700 gives a description of what was consumed in Parisian coffeehouses and when. It states that the usual time Parisians went to the *café* was when returning from different kinds of venues, most commonly after church in the morning. Two friends gave in to some excess after they decided to go to the café after hearing a sermon in church: "they entered at the Armenians' where they ordered liqueurs and biscuits, as few limit themselves to just drinking a cup of coffee, which is often the excuse for excess." Clearly the author was pointing out that the Armenian cafés served more than coffee and that he believed that coffee was an excuse for "even greater excess".[49] So much for coffee displacing liquors. There were many more cafés in Paris by 1716 and the three hundred that Jean de la Roque cited were no longer Armenian establishments. There was, however, an oriental, not to say orientalist, style to these establishments. Jean de la Roque wrote that the frequenting of cafés was initiated by the upper class (*gens de qualité*) and that within these cafés one found the most magnificent objects the Orient could offer; the gold and silver spent there was nothing compared to the rare Chinese porcelains and furniture that decorated them.[50]

A New Oriental Garb for Café Patrons

Coffee drinking brought new fashions to Europe that came from the Ottoman Empire. Contacts with the Ottoman world were visible in sartorial details from an early period that pre-dated coffee drinking. Luxury goods were cosmopolitan almost by definition. Bursa silks and fine Ankara mohair clothes found customers in sixteenth-century Poland as well as later among the electors of Saxony. On the other hand, Venetian silks were bought by members of the Ottoman upper class that favored luxuries from Venice as late as the seventeenth century when wealthy Europeans were switching to French fashions. If French fashion was influenced by Ottoman fashion, certain textile workshops in France produced specifically with Ottoman customers in mind. Louise Mackie's article demonstrates that Venetian products so closely resembled genuine Ottoman silks that only technical experts could tell them apart.[51] While this was a product of intercultural exchange, the successful mimicry of the Venetian manufacturers made this exchange invisible. An Ottoman sultan who wore Venetian silk that imitated Ottoman patterns was, for all intents and purposes, clothed in authentic Ottoman silk. The situation was more complicated when it came to other imitations of Ottoman fashions in Europe, studied by Charlotte Jirousek. She successfully argued that the imitation of the powerful Ottoman court and its clothing was part and parcel of royal culture during the English Renaissance.[52] The influence of Oriental fabrics and designs had been very important in Europe since the Renaissance but it was clearer in the seventeenth and eighteenth centuries.

Thomas Kaiser has shown that in the eighteenth century the French aristocracy delighted in posing as Turks, in Ottoman costume.[53] It was true for the seventeenth century; the carrousels and masquerades at the French court were occasions for the court to pose in Oriental disguise at key moments such as the birth of the dauphin.[54] Oriental dress was far more sumptuous than French court dress, especially the *khalat*, the robes of honor received by merchants such as the Huguenot Jean-Baptiste Tavernier in Iran, with its splendid silks. Charlotte Jirousek studied the influence of Ottoman and Persian fashions on European dress.[55] She describes that wearing many layers of silks or cotton always had been a characteristic of Ottoman ceremonial or festive dress as a sign of wealth and status, and that layering several coats of different length was particularly characteristic of Turkish dress. The layers signified luxurious dress and brought modesty and bulk. Layering, she argues, became a feature of style in Europe in the late seventeenth century. Most important perhaps is the influence of what was called the "Persian vest" on the modern male suit. The Persian vest was imposed by Louis XIV's cousin, Charles II, in England. After the plague and fire of London in 1665–1666 destroyed most of the city, it was widely felt that the licentiousness of the court, which included French court dress, had brought down God's wrath on England.

> Charles did announce a reform, which was to be a 'vest' … .a term usually associated with eastern garments, and therefore presumably improper attire for a Christian gentleman. In the new ensemble proposed by the King, the exotic vest was to be worn buttoned over the shirt as a more modest covering to that controversial inner garment, but under the coat that had come into fashion, with both being the same length. The entire ensemble was to be made in one fabric, in a sober solid color. A neck cloth, or cravat, was added to the ensemble; an item purported to have been introduced from the costume of Croatian soldiers. The vest soon became a fancier fabric, however. Thus all the components of the modern suit came together.[56]

Beyond the vest, the Oriental outer coat for layering was also an influence. In an illustration showing a coffee shop, there is a representation of a masked *Arlequin* putting his arms through what was called an "Armenian coat" by the seventeenth-century engraver.[57]In Parisian cafés both the owners and the servers wore long coats. This was not so much an Armenian overcoat as some called it, but the general top layer worn throughout Mughal India, the Ottoman Empire and Persia. Parisian Armenian coffee shop owners wore them. The overcoat would become a form of robe for men called the banyan or *banian*.[58] Regarding the popularity of the *banian*, Jirousek notes that diarist Samuel Pepys borrowed Indian gowns and posed for a portrait in one, as well as visiting Sir Phillip Howard dressed "in a gown and turban like a Turk". These gowns were widely imitated by English tailors. There is also a mention of a rare collection of Chinese "vests" admired by John Evelyn.[59] For women the *mantua* was a fashion that came via Italy as the name indicates, and later became the French word *manteau* for coat. It was a new fashion in the 1680s and remained popular until the 1750s. Instead of the traditional short French bodice with a big *décolleté* and skirt cut separately and sewn at the waist, the *mantua* hung straight in one piece from the shoulders, covering them, and had a long train. The train was often looped back or tucked back to show the layering of clothing underneath. It was worn over everything else and draped over a contrasting petticoat and a stomacher creating layers as in oriental dress.[60]

Accessories for drinking coffee and tea soon followed the fashion for these beverages. The oldest known surviving English coffee pot modeled on its Ottoman predecessor was made in silver and is now in the Victoria and Albert Museum in London and was probably made in 1681. Modeled on the simple conical Ottoman ibrik with a handle covered in leather and a long spout, it is engraved with a coat of arms. Later coffeepots kept in this collection show considerable change and refinements in decoration. Both coffee and tea were expensive commodities and more luxurious sets of vessels came into demand for domestic use. The dishes used for coffee drinking in England were similar to those employed in the Levant. Coffee was consumed in small ceramic drinking bowls called *finians*. Some more elegant forms of *finians* came with a matching flat dish underneath, a precursor to the saucer. The Levant Company imported small quantities of Turkish Iznik wares for the luxury market in London. Some of these dishes were kept in cabinets of curiosity. The Dutch East India Company started regular shipments of Chinese porcelains in 1624. Among these shipments were small drinking vessels known as teacups but they were often used for drinking spirits, wines and eventually tea and coffee. Home roasting was done using a frying pan over a smoky fire. Early coffee making was developed using equipment available in every kitchen.[61] It is unclear how much coffee was brewed at home. Most of the records we have are about public coffeehouses.

Coffee's Medical Classification upon Arrival in England

The coffeehouse was to have immense success in England. According to Brian Cowan the first ones were in Orientalist fashion, making coffee's origins clear. In 1600, the clergyman William Biddulph sent a letter from Aleppo containing the first reference to coffee in the English language. In England, as in France, interest in exotic cultures and goods came from the need to reliably observe nature and was very much part of the birth of modern science. Francis Bacon's vision of a comprehensive natural history is well known and travel writing was an important source of data for his collection. Many exotic drugs and commodities were classified together in his work such as coffee, bethel roots, leaves, tobacco and opium, which were all "medicines that condense and relieve the spirits".[62] John Parkinsons' *Theatrum Botanicum* (1640) was the first English herbal to include the coffee plant in an entry on "the Turkes berry drinke".[63] One of the debates in the Royal Society's meetings was coffee as an exotic drug and the question of the possible harmful side effects it could cause. To resolve the issue, Dr. Harpur, an English physician residing in Aleppo, was asked by the fellows of the Society to verify the effects of coffee from his observations of the Turks. The question was whether the over consumption of coffee could lead to apoplectic fits or paralysis. In the early seventeenth century, coffee berries were considered to be rarities worthy of the society's collection. The English never obtained a live plant and the explanation was that the Arabs were as careful at guarding their coffee plants as the Dutch were of their nutmegs.[64]

The biggest problem faced by new exotic drugs in English society was that they were associated with the licentious sexuality described in travel accounts. Unlike coffee, a number of drugs new to Europeans were linked to licentious oriental habits. Among these, the use of marijuana or "bang" was associated by several travel accounts with prostitutes, soldiers and slaves. Robert Hooke was curious about marijuana's putative abilities to stimulate the appetite and treated the royal society to a short discourse on the drug. The indiscriminate culture of curiosity prevalent in England allowed the investigation of all sorts of drugs, medicines and even poisons newly obtained from the West Indies. Some of the extremely curious even took to experimenting with these drugs themselves. Coffee, chocolate and tea became profitable commodities in their own right and were assimilated with relative ease into wider British society unlike betel nuts, marijuana, datura and opium.[65]

In 1659 there was a translation made into English from a short Arabic manuscript. Doctor Edward Pockoke's (1604–1691) translation, *The Nature of the drink Kahue, or Coffee … Described by an Arab Phisitian* was a short extract from a sixteenth-century Arabic work by an author who specialists have identified as Da'ud ibn Umar al-Antaki.[66] This English translation was only a fragment of a manuscript that held the distinction of being among the first texts to be printed in Arabic. The extract in Arabic was first printed in Oxford in 1659 by Henri Hall using Oxford's first Arabic type. The work aroused the interest of the scientifically curious some years after a coffeehouse had been opened in Oxford by a Jew named Jacob.[67] Clearly the discourse about coffee preceded the first public coffeehouse in England. Much of the debate about coffee followed the medical debates in the Arab world just as the reputation of chocolate was based mostly on Mesoamerican views. The Spanish had brought with them chocolate's reputation as a stimulant and an aphrodisiac. Chocolate never reached the popularity of coffee in seventeenth-century England perhaps due to this reputation of promoting sensuality and carnal desires. Coffee's reputation of sobriety, especially in dissipating the effects of alcohol, was key to its acceptance.[68]

English Coffeehouses as Centers of Commerce

It has been argued that a fall in prices helped the spread of coffee drinking. Jan de Vries observed a rise in real wages and a decrease in the price of exotic imports in England and northwestern Europe in the late seventeenth century that created a favorable demand for the enormous new consumption of tobacco, sugar, cacao and tea.[69] Jordan Goodman has also offered the profit-seeking motivations and the mercantile bent of the European colonizers of the New World as an explanation for the expansion of the trade in drug foods.[70] But Goodman and other historians have moved beyond these functionalist explanations to look at the factor of taste and fashion in the spread of these new commodities. The idea of social emulation or the "trickle-down theories" of Thorstein Veblen and Norbert Elias do not deny the importance of these previous arguments. They take into account taste, fashion and social emulation to achieve social power, rather than profit seeking or imperial expansion. In some theories discussed in the introduction of this book, taste is recognized as a symbolic marker of social status and the pace of fashionable change is thought to be set by social elites.

Coffeehouses in England became centers of business transactions, commercial contracts and financial speculation. The founding of the Levant Company in 1585 was dedicated to the advancement of English trade with the Ottoman Empire. It was during its fourth voyage in the spring of 1609 that the merchants of the Levant Company encountered the coffee markets of Yemen. In 1618 and 1619, the Company made a number of supplications to the Ottoman Governor of Mocha for the privilege of a trading factory in the port. From the 1620s through the 1650s the East India Company took an active interest in supplying coffee to markets in Persia and the Indian subcontinent where coffeehouses were well established. The Company sent the first coffee samples to England as early as 1629 but this was several decades before a coffeehouse opened anywhere.[71]

It is recorded in John Evelyn's memoirs that the first coffeehouse opened in England in 1650. Evelyn found the coffeehouse a deplorable place "where gentlemen sit, and spend much of their time; drinking a muddy kind of *Beverage*".[72] Early English coffeehouses were centers for news culture as they were in France. Brian W. Cowan argued that because England's *virtuosi* were interested in the exotic and they were curious collectors, they became the chief proponents of coffee consumption in coffeehouses. It was not an accident that the first coffeehouse in Britain was established in Oxford by a Jewish entrepreneur named Jacob. Oxford was an important early center for the creation of a distinctive coffeehouse culture. In 1656 Arthur Tillyard joined the coffee trade and began to sell coffee in his house next to All Souls College. Early coffeehouse virtuosi joined him. The new coffeehouse saw a peculiar conjunction of Orientalist scholarship at the university and a vibrant new scientific community in the town of Oxford.[73]

In May 1663, a commission survey found that there were eighty-two keepers of coffeehouses in the city of London. The "coffee man" became a focus of considerable curiosity as it was a new trade. Some successful coffeehouse keepers used their Levantine origins in the manner of Pasqua Rosée, a Greek servant brought to England by his merchant employer. Rosée was an accountant, translator, agent and valet. Coffee men were often the subjects of satire; the best known is *The Maidens Complaint Against Coffee* (1663), which states that not only do coffeehouses keep their men from their homes, but that the drying effect of coffee makes men impotent. This was perhaps because there were few trades that could offer such high profits in so short a time.[74] Rosée's coffeehouse mainly attracted merchants in the Levant Company and intellectuals. As more coffeehouses opened, the relative open house of coffee-house learning made it vulnerable to criticism. It was accused of debasing learning through its association with vulgarity and dilettantism. Coffeehouses were compared to a school without a master. A pamphlet held that you may become a scholar for the mere spending of a penny. This was just one of the ongoing debates about the role of the coffeehouse.[75]

According to Cowan, not everyone approved of the Orientalism of the coffeehouse, which consciously constructed a Turkish aura. All the refutations against coffee and coffeehouses in England denied that drinking coffee was simply consumption. They did not view drinking as an innocent thing divorced from its cultural origins. One of the earliest anti-coffeehouses pamphlets ful-minated: "Like Apes, the English imitate all other people in their ridiculous Fashions. As Slaves, they submit to the Customes even of Turky and India … With the Barbarous Indian he smoaks Tobacco. With the Turk he drinks Coffee."[76]

Nevertheless, English coffeehouses soon established themselves as important centers of commerce. The best-known example is Lloyd's Coffeehouse, fore-runner to the famous insurance firm Lloyd's of London. Garraway's and Jonathan's coffeehouses in Exchange Alley are often remembered for their role in the financial revolution of the 1690s as forbearers of the stock exchange. Coffeehouses were also auction houses for prized ships, bulk goods, draperies and whale oil as well as books and artwork. The coffeehouse brought the collectors out of their cabinets of curiosity and into the public sphere in con-tact with a wider group of people. The auction became an established aspect of sociality in the coffeehouse. Brian Cowan gives the example of Robert Hooke visiting as many as four auctions in a day. John Evelyn criticized the popular auctions as the "sad dispersions of many noble libraries and cabi-nets".[77] John Evelyn nevertheless applauded the efforts of Samuel Pepys to build his own collection of curiosities out of these sales. Clearly the coffee-house had so many social functions that it was the center of a transformed sociability.[78] In these coffeehouse auctions there were separate accommoda-tions for prospective female purchasers; women became most prominent at art auctions.[79] Jean de la Roque makes clear that Le Procope in Paris was open to ladies and that it was frequented by the elite.[80] There seems to be no such equivalent in London.

The Crown's Fear of the Politically Charged Coffeehouse

For Steven Pincus and C. John Sommerville, the coffeehouse signaled a break with the elitist politics of the first half of the seventeenth century. It forged the way for a more inclusive and more secular political culture. Margaret Jacob's reading of Jürgen Habermas' theory on the public sphere and the role of the coffeehouse within it is celebratory. She has argued that it set the scene for the emergence of modern democratic society in the West.[81] When the monarchy was restored in England, Charles II discussed the possibility of suppressing the coffeehouse. He argued that the politics discussed in coffeehouses had helped the monarch regain his throne. He proposed banning coffeehouses by royal proclamation but was cautioned against this. Rather than ban, Charles II decided to chastise what he considered seditious discourse. This instigated much venting of criticism at the regime. Steven Pincus has shown how the influence of high-church royalists provided the necessary power to push through a proclamation suppressing coffeehouses. The King declared that after January 10, 1676 it would be forbidden to sell any coffee, chocolate, sherbet or tea. Resistance to the King's uncompromising ban was immediate.[82] Brian Cowan has found that skeptics were quick to doubt the effect of the ban.[83] Business continued more or less as usual. Coffeehouses with powerful patrons fared well while those with less powerful patrons could not escape the royal wrath.[84]

The court was not alone in its fear of coffeehouse politics, as even members of Parliament looked at this new popular interest in the affairs of state with some apprehension. In September 1681, in a need for control, the Court of London Aldermen ordered an investigation into the qualifications of all persons keeping coffeehouses in the city. Patrons of some notoriously seditious coffeehouses such as The Amsterdam or Richard's (Dick's) were interrogated and were encouraged to inform on their friends.[85] In this climate of fear, few could escape suspicion. When King James II ascended to the throne, he was no less suspicious of coffeehouses than his elder brother had been. A number of royal proclamations were issued against voicing criticism of the Crown or spreading "false news". The coffeehouses did not cause King James' demise, they outlasted him.[86]

Lion, Tigers and Women, Oh My! Coffeehouse Happenings

The coffeehouse had strayed far from its exotic beginnings. Early in the century, extraordinary animals had been on exhibition in coffeehouses. An Asian elephant had been brought to London in 1675 and a rhinoceros had arrived in 1684. Collectors such as Pepys and Evelyn went to see fairs and auctions in coffeehouses for the curiosities that they offered but they were uncomfortable mixing in a nasty crowd of commoners. As collectors they did not accept the displays offered in the coffeehouses without any criticism and considered them of a much lower rank than the displays offered in the curiosity cabinets of their esteemed wealthy fellows. The literary critic Dennis Todd has argued that the English fascination with these bizarre and exotic spectacles in coffeehouses was provoked by the blurring of boundaries between social identities. At the heart of this was the experience of monstrosity. Although human monstrosities had been on display in fairs since the mid sixteenth century, there was novelty in the form of spectacles offered in the seventeenth century. Not everyone approved of the Orientalism of the early coffeehouse, but by the end of the seventeenth century many traces of this Orientalism were gone and the coffeehouse had found a very wide public.

Gentlewomen going to a coffeehouse were an exception and not a rule. Women who had specific business to attend to might have been comfortable in such a setting. An important exception was in the case of auctions held by the coffeehouses, particularly when there was a sale of artworks when ladies were welcome. Ladies were actively invited in the coffeehouse for the sale but this remained a special event. Brian Cowan argues that if there were no separate spheres for men and women in Post-Restoration London, neither was there a gender-neutral social world. Women were found in coffeehouses as proprietors. More than 20 percent of coffeehouse keepers in 1692–1693 were women. These working women had the title of "coffee women" but the term was not entirely an honorable one. Often coffeehouse women were associated, most of the time unfairly, with prostitution. Moral censorship against coffeehouses never went out of business and the fact that they were kept by women was one more excuse to attack the coffeehouse. Cowan concludes that one cannot see the rise of an unfettered and unproblematic public sphere due to the coffeehouse. Public social life and even more so public politics were problematic in Early Modern Britain.[87]

Tea and Coffee's Consumption by the Dutch

Anne E. C. McCants has challenged the view held by many historians that tea and coffee were luxury goods reserved for the elite until the nineteenth century, at least in the Dutch Republic. Maxine Berg has made the same argument for the consumption of these colonial goods well beyond the elite in eighteenth-century England.[88] In her article "Porcelain for the Poor: The Material Culture of Tea and Coffee in Eighteenth Century Amsterdam", McCants studies, through reading after-death inventories, the widespread existence of cups, saucers and pots in middle class and even poor households in Amsterdam. Thanks to the importation of enormous amounts of cheap porcelain from Asia by the VOC, and the imitation of these Chinese wares by the Dutch in Delft, McCants traces the transformation of material life brought about by the consumption of the new hot beverages of tea and coffee.[89] Looking through the documents she does find that in the seventeenth century only the wealthy owned pots or cups and saucers, but concludes that by the middle of the eighteenth century they were owned both by the middle class and the poor in Amsterdam. This clearly points to the well-established consumption of tea and coffee in the Dutch city by many classes, including the poor. However, as McCants points out herself, the evidence does not yield any numbers for how much coffee, tea or sugar was consumed. Her study also successfully challenges the long held idea that porcelain was only collected as a luxury by the wealthy. As the largest importers of porcelain in the world, the Dutch could sell porcelain cheaply as well as imitate it at an even lower cost. Porcelain was far more accessible to the "lower sorts" than the other imports from Asia, such as silk and cotton textiles.[90] Not only did the Dutch have a commercial advantage in the Asian trade over the rest of Europe, but they could grow coffee in their colonies.

If coffee consumption was popular in Paris, London and Amsterdam, Dutch were the only Europeans who managed to grow the coffee bush. The Dutch governor in Malabar (India) sent a Yemeni or Arabica coffee (*Coffea arabica*) seedling to the Dutch governor of Batavia in 1696. The first seedlings failed due to flooding in Batavia so a second shipment of seedlings was sent in 1699. The plants grew in Java and in 1711 the first plants were sent from Java to a hothouse in Amsterdam by the Dutch East India Company. After winning a war against the Dutch, Louis XIV demanded as a trophy one of the few rare coffee bushes that had survived in an Amsterdam hothouse. In 1714, a five-foot tall plant was formally presented to Louis XIV at the Chateau de Marly. It arrived caged under glass and kept under the guard of the "Hollander, who has the Tree under his Care, and was come from Marly to the Garden-Royal, with the Servants of Monsieur, the chief Physician".[91] Transferred immediately to one of the glass hothouses of the *Jardin du Roi*, the plant was received by several scientists invited by Antoine de Jussieu, the new director of the royal gardens. The French hoped to be able to grow coffee bushes from its seedlings.[92]

The coffee bush was a scientific curiosity. Since the sixteenth century, as wave after wave of strange flora arrived in Europe, botanists struggled to fit the unfamiliar species into the plant families they had inherited from Pliny. To facilitate these projects, botanical gardens were established at the medical faculties of Padua and Pisa in the 1540s. The University of Montpellier followed suit in 1598, Oxford in 1621 and Paris in 1640. The *Jardin du Roi* under Louis XIV was an experimental garden where the newly arrived coffee bush was guarded and observed day and night. Through the intervention of Colbert, Louis XIV had also helped create many nurseries for exotic flowers, including the tulip. His rivals, the Dutch, had perfected the cultivation of the bulb in the seventeenth century and competition for trade, science and the arts remained a rule. It is in a Dutch garden in the seventeenth century that an observer first saw the tea shrub: a merchant from Dantzig, a distinguished botanist, Jacob Breyn, reports seeing a tea shrub in his description of the plants of Holland printed in 1689.[93] The Dutch remained the chief importers of tea to France in this early period, and probably as a consequence, tea did not become immediately fashionable at the French court.

The Origins and Spread of Tea

French doctors rivaled the Dutch in their writings about tea, but once again the Dutch had the upper hand. We owe to the Dutch the first scientific description of tea; a doctor residing in Batavia, Jacob Bontius, gave the first accurate description of the tree shrub in 1631 although it was published at a later date in the Netherlands. He admitted never having seen the shrub and owes the description to another Dutchman who had lived some years in Japan.[94]

Importing tea from China was perhaps not as central to the Dutch trade in the seventeenth century as spices were, but tea became a fashionable drink in high society in The Hague. The Dutch introduced the new drink to Germany, where a handful of tealeaves could cost as much as fifteen gold coins in pharmacies. In France, tea was made sporadically fashionable by Cardinal Mazarin, chief minister to Louis XIII, who drank it for medicinal purposes.[95] The medical properties of tea were described by the Dutch; a doctor by the name of Tulipus wrote about its properties in 1641.[96] The first English advertisement for tea appeared on September 6, 1658 at which date it was sold only in small quantities in England due to its high price. In 1660, Samuel Pepys wrote in his diary that he sent for a cup of tea, a China drink that he had never drunk before. In 1660, the coffeehouse had become an English institution but tea was not common.[97] In competition with the Dutch, Charles I had hoped to open English trade with China so ships went to Macao as early as 1637. But several further attempts after his reign failed until the allegiance of a famous Chinese pirate, Xoxinga, let the English Company enter the trade in 1677 in areas he controlled, Formosa and Amoy. In the first phases of this direct commerce, tea did not have the importance it would have in eighteenth-century England. English botanists were collecting exotic new plants from China, among them ferns, flowers and tea.[98] There is a very famous apocryphal story that comes from Engelbert Kaempfer's *History of Japan* (1727). The austere Bodhidharma once fell asleep during his meditation. When he awoke full of sorrow the next morning for having broken his vow, he cut off both of his eyebrows and threw them to the ground. He returned the next day to the same place only to behold that out of his eyebrows grew two beautiful tea shrubs. He ate some of the leaves and was filled with a new joy to pursue his divine meditation. This tale about the Buddha is one of the most familiar stories about the origins of tea.[99]

A Brief History of Tea in China

According to Victor Mair and Erling Ho the earliest known reference to boiling tea appears in "The Contract for a Youth" written by the noted imperial panegyrist Wang Bao in 59 BC[100] In China, there is an apocryphal story according to which the mythical Shennog (r. 2737–2698 BC), China's second emperor and first agriculturalist, set out to taste a hundred different plants. Some seventy-two of these plants (seventy-two being a magic number throughout Eurasia) made him very ill but only one cured him of these illnesses: the tea plant. In the second century AD China was divided into three kingdoms (Shu, Wei and Wu); during these centuries of upheaval, the knowledge, consumption and cultivation of tea spread downstream through the Yangtze River. The main social drink in China was alcohol, indispensable at both ancestral rituals and feasts. The Chinese drank rice beers and rice wines.[101]

Herbal remedies fulfilled the needs of the common people; as such, tea was adopted by the Taoists who disseminated the custom of its consumption with propaganda about tea's curative properties. Tealeaves were steamed, pounded and patted into cakes that were then baked, pierced, strung together and sealed before they were brewed and drunk.[102] Buddhist monks also spread the use of tea in their wanderings. While tea was readily adopted by Buddhists, it encountered some resistance in northern China. The nomadic rulers of northern China had adopted Chinese language, dress, and customs under the Han but this policy did not stretch to food and drink. The nomadic Tabgatch rulers routinely mocked Han Chinese for their effete fare. The Han ate lily soup, crab spawn, lotus root, frogs, turtles, and drank tea while the Tabgatch lived on mutton and mare's milk. The nomads who ruled northern China still scoffed at tea, an insipid infusion, much preferring *kumiss*, fermented horse milk, to tea.[103]

If tea is seen as Chinese because of early usage, and was seen as a mark of Chinese habits to the nomadic tribes, the origin of tea is believed to be in the Himalayas. The global story of tea, how it spread to China and was consumed elsewhere, covers the extraordinary success of the tea plant stemming from its earliest origins. In order to survive in the hothouse of the eastern Himalayas, the most plant-rich eco-system in the world, the tea plant had to attract animals and birds to spread its seed. Because of tea's anti-bacterial and antiseptic properties, monkeys who ate tealeaves would be healthier, fatter and more likely to survive because tea killed the bacteria in their mouths and stomachs. About 40 percent of the tea leaf's weight is taken up by tannins (phenolics), the most powerful natural anti-bacterial whose antiseptic properties were only discovered in the nineteenth century. Joseph Lister, among others, used tea to make operations safer and help sterilize hospitals. Moreover, even if the tea plant is susceptible to parasites, fungi and rust, its resistance to disease is remarkable and unlike coffee or the potato vine, no serious disease has ever devastated the tea industry. It was monkeys who first spread tea through the Assam, Burma and West China jungles. Then the tea plant spread to a large portion of East Asia, which held half the population of the world and transformed the culture, esthetics, craft and society of India, Mongolia, Manchuria, China and Japan. In China it was part of the flowering of civilization.[104]

It was under the Tang dynasty that *The Classic of Tea* was written in 7,000 terse characters by Lu Yu. It is a compendium on tea including its origins, the tools and utensils needed in manufacturing and preparation, what water to use, how to boil the water, references to tea in Chinese history, tea cultivation, which utensils could be dispensed with if absolutely necessary and, last but not least, instructions on how to copy his book on four or six silk scrolls and hang them on the wall. As tea spread throughout the land, Lu Yu's instructions were revered and Lu Yu was elevated to the status of a demi-god especially among tea merchants and pottery makers. Among the twenty-four tea utensils listed in *The Classic of Tea* was a water strainer, a device brought to China from Buddhist monks who used it to avoid the accidental killing of any creatures in their drinking water. In the late Tang period, Lu Yu's *The Classic of Tea* was followed by several other works that offered insights into the hyper-ecstatic universe of connoisseurs. Zhang Youxin's *A Record of Water for Decocting Tea* provides a list of the twenty best water sources in China for making tea.[105]

Mair and Hoh describe how tea became an imperial product, its cultivation and sale controlled by the Emperor. In 977, as a result of what was called the "Little Ice Age", the Emperor's tea estates froze and were officially moved from Guzhu to the southeastern province of Fujian.[106] The Song Dynasty (960–1127) is remembered as a period of plenty. In this period Chinese cookery evolved into a *cuisine* complete with three regional cuisines, still recognizable today: Northern, Southern and Sichuanese. In agriculture, advances in irrigation and the introduction of a new rice variety from Vietnam helped fuel a surge in the country's population from fifty to one hundred million and gave peasants time and energy to cultivate cash crops such as sugar, cotton and tea. During this period, paper money came into widespread use and commercial centers flourished.[107]

Under the Tang Dynasty (618–907), ground tea had been boiled with a pinch of salt in an iron pot. Under the Song, the iron pot was replaced with a porcelain ewer with a lid and slender spout used to boil the water. The cakes of tea were crushed in a silk bag, ground into powder, sifted and placed directly in tea bowls. The boiling water was poured on the tea powder, then beaten into a rich froth with bamboo whisks. Under the Song, there were tea competitions called *doucha* to see who could whisk the tea into the thickest and most enduring froth. It became a fashionable entertainment among scholars, poets and officials. The *doucha* ushered in a new fashion for teaware. The most celebrated ware was purple black bowls with "hare's fur" streaks. Throughout the Song Dynasty, tea consumption continued to expand and by the twelfth century, one-third of the country's prefectures were growing tea. Tea farmers had to pay an annual tax and were forced to sell their tea to the government at a fixed low price. Tea was the Emperor's monopoly.[108]

In China, tea is considered to have important health properties. Green, or even semi-fermented tea, is considered better for one's health than black fermented tea. The list of benefits is long, but eliminating thirst and fatigue, clarity of mind and longevity are the most repeated in the literature. There are more specific benefits, among them digestion, creating more blood flow, chasing the effects of alcohol. It was and is highly regarded as a digestive for its ability to dissolve fat and counter poison. It was used against joint pain, to counter anemia, against wrinkles and tooth decay.[109] In China, there were teahouses that served tea and also food to both local and traveling customers.

Teahouses have a history going back to the thirteenth century and are still places of great importance for the general public. Like cafés in Turkey, France and Great Britain, they have played a large part in the political life of the Chinese.[110] Teahouses were found in villages, towns, cities, and also in the countryside, especially at scenic spots such as springs or ancient shrines. Mostly they were social places where customers stayed long hours discussing business or social matters. The usual patrons were men. The teahouse often served them more wine than tea to accompany noodle dishes, light food and snacks. Storytelling, poetry and even sexual services were part of some teahouse cultures. The culture of the teahouse as a community center was so strong in Schezuan that people from other regions had nicknamed the Schezuanese "tea house loafers".[111]

The teahouse rose in popularity in the nineteenth century. In the twentieth century a famous Chinese play, *Tea House*, was written by Lao She (1899– 1966) to tell the history of the teahouse from the beginning of the Qing dynasty to the 1950s. A famous teahouse named Lao She was built in Peking in his honor. After the middle of the twentieth century, the teahouse was transformed by political changes in Maoist China and its egalitarian views. It has been argued that there is a similarity between the function of teahouses in historical Chengdu at the turn of the twentieth century and teahouses in today's Quanzhou where some are luxurious, expensive and restricted to the new wealthy elites of post-communist China just as they were at the turn of the twentieth century. In historical Chengdu, class division was strict, so while some teahouses in back alleys served inexpensive meals and tea, the elite went to luxurious ones. Socializing in teahouses was strictly class-based before the communist era. None of the mingling present in early coffeehouses occurred in the Chinese teahouse. Today a larger group of new Chinese consumers participate in the elite version of the teahouse and the pursuit of high-quality tea. The quality of leisure and sociability in the teahouse has deep historical roots that maintain it as a central social institution.[112]

Tradition and Consumerism in Japan

When a delegation of four young converted Samurai came to Rome from Japan in 1585, they were presented to the Pope by the Jesuits. The Roman hosts witnessed the four Samurai preparing and drinking their tea but mistook it for hot water. The beverage amazed them as much as seeing them pick up ivory sticks to eat their food.[113] In 1607, the Dutch East India Company brought one of the earliest recorded shipments of tea to a European nation from Macau. Two years later, the Dutch purchased tea in the Japanese port of Hirado. The British, in competition with the Dutch, entered the tea trade and in 1613 set up a factory in Hirado. Japanese monks studying in China brought the custom of whisked tea back to Japan where it became enshrined in the Japanese tea ceremony *chanoyu*. Two of the most famous Japanese Buddhist monks were Siachō and Kūkai who traveled to China as part of an official embassy in the summer of 802. At Saichō's farewell party in 805, tea was served instead of rice beer and upon his return to Japan, Saichō planted the tea seeds he had brought with him at the foot of the Hiei Mountain and took tea to the capital of Kyoto.[114]

In the seventeenth century, Edo was the most important city in Japan. It was a great city of consumers, although not a center of fine craft production compared with the old capital of Kyoto. Literary, cultural and fashion trends tended to start in Kyoto and Osaka and then reach Edo in vulgarized forms. Edo was at least the equal of London or Paris as a center of pleasure seeking and the quest for social respectability through conspicuous consumption.[115] The rulers of Edo wanted everyone in his or her proper rank but the city's order had been disrupted by the 1657 fires, which destroyed the central structures in Edo castle, 160 daimyo residences, 350 shrines and temples, 750 residential areas and 50,000 merchant and artisan homes. The reconstruction of Edo was heavily regulated. Edo swarmed with samurai, housemen, bannermen and retainers of the daimyo (great lords who were vassals of the shogun) and was littered with commoners with newfound wealth. This group had leisure time on their hands and much money to spend. The lumber merchants, for example, were among the richest inhabitants of Edo. The daimyo spent great sums of money on performances of *nô* dance, dramas and also built magnificent landscaped gardens and held elaborate ceremonies. For those of a lower station, there were *kabuki* playhouses in at least three districts of the city. In Edo in the 1680s, kabuki plays presented contemporary political dramas with all the names of the participants changed but clearly recognized by the public. The shogun who presided in Edo castle in the latter part of the seventeenth century was Tokugawa Tsunayoshi, nicknamed the dog shogun.[116]

The year 1688 was the first of the new year period designated as *genroku*, which has become a byword among historians for the emergence of an urban, consumer-oriented culture. In this era, the shogun and his followers celebrated the arts of peace. However, peace, luxury and lectures about compassion could not stop cultural habits. In 1701, in Edo castle, a daimyo drew his sword on a rude official. He was immediately ordered to commit suicide for doing so. Two years later, forty-seven of this daimyo's samurai broke into the Edo mansion of the rude official who had provoked their lord and killed him. In turn, all forty-seven of them were condemned to commit suicide but the tale of the loyalty of the forty-seven samurai was widely retold and helped preserve the spirit of the warring samurai even through the long centuries of peace. Japan was now internally a collection of pacified, well-organized and competitive ministries. It faced the external world as a single highly unified polity. No other political system in the world engaged in such thorough monitoring and control of its foreign trade. The Dutch, for example, had to send an embassy every year to pay homage to the shogun but otherwise they were largely confined to Deshima, an artificial island off Japan. Prostitutes were allowed to come to serve them, interpreters came to learn their language, and Japanese artists must have been in contact with them as they left us a few vivid pictures of the Dutch on Deshima.[117] Here, just as in China, travelers noticed the social importance of the teahouse. It is from a Dutchman in Japan that Bontius got the first description of the tea shrub. In this early period the exports to Europe from Asia were not centered on tea as they would be in the eighteenth century. The most prized export from Japan and China was porcelain.

Porcelain Cups and Tea Accessories

Paul Butel records that according to Alexander of Rhodes, the Dutch who brought tea to Paris made a huge profit on it; they sold it for 30 livres a pound, about six times the price they paid for it in Canton. As late as February 26, 1706, when tea was expensive and much rarer than coffee, the Duchesse d'Orléans wrote that tea was necessary to Protestant ministers as well as to Catholic priests because tea brought chastity.[118] The fashion for tea was slowly on the rise; Madame de Sévigné, often a slave to court fashion, wrote in 1684 that she drank as many as forty cups a day because it was good for restoring vision. The porcelain cups she used were a prized novelty. Lacquered boxes and porcelain had the highest value in the eyes of contemporary consumers.[119] Tea and coffee porcelain cups and porcelain or silver teapots were rarely collected in France during her time. Even in the middle of the eighteenth century, parochial records and wills indicate that only the very rich owned cups and even fewer households owned teapots in Paris. In the richest district of Paris, Saint Eustache, ten out of sixty households owned a teapot; in the districts of Saint Germain and Saint Etiennne du Mont that number was one out of seventy-five households and five out of sixty respectively. Numbers increased for the eighteenth century. A member of parliament in Bordeaux owned eight teapots in 1789, when Anglomania was the fashion in France; he was made fun of by Madame de Genlis who wrote that because he drank tea twice a day he thought he had the same merits as Newton and Locke. By then in France tea was considered an English fashion. All kinds of accessories were made for tea, especially in England. Goldsmiths made scissors, tongs, sieves and many utensils that were used to serve the cakes and sandwiches that came to accompany teatime in England.[120]

The first great merchant to sell tea in England was Thomas Galway, who offered it at his coffeehouse in London in 1657. In the 1660s, tea was retailing for between six and ten pounds per pound in the city of London. The year 1660 was an auspicious one for the tea trade after the Restoration of Charles II who had become very partial to tea drinking during his exile in France as a guest of Louis XIV. It is believed, however, that he had acquired this taste from his own wife, the Portuguese Catherine de Braganza, who was an avid tea drinker. The English East India Company was its sole importer and imports rose from 40,000 pounds in 1699 to an annual average of 240,000 pounds by 1708 and to nearly a million pounds by the mid 1720s.[121] In England the smuggling of tea took on huge proportions. Armed bands would attack customhouses to steal the tea that was seized from illegal importers.[122] Taxation on tea was also one of the chief reasons for this smuggling. In the 1780s taxes went as high as 106 percent. In reality there were enormous quantities of tea that circulated illegally and were not submitted to taxation. Some of this tea, called *rubbish tea*, was falsified with the addition of other leaves. Ferns were a popular addition as were rose leaves.[123] One significant aspect of past tea drinking in England was the increased demand for sugar, the annual consumption of which rose from four pounds per capita in 1700 to ten pounds per capita in 1748. If drinking tea in the 1600s was an aristocratic pastime, a century later provisions of tea and sugar were even part of some servants' terms of employment.[124]

Initially, the fine porcelain used by socially well-born hostesses came only from China. China was brought by ships that carried Chinese silk and tea initially as ballast. So much ballast was required that merchants could strike a very hard bargain with Chinese porcelain manufacturers. Porcelain was very expensive in the 1600s and was collected by the aristocracy. By 1712 fine porcelain had become ridiculously cheap. A 216-piece dinner service cost a mere five pounds and ten shillings.[125] The habit of tea consumption and the chinaware that was part of afternoon tea stimulated the British pottery industry. The famous Josiah Wedgewood would soon develop his jasperware, which fetched very high prices.[126] Unlike in England and the Dutch Republic, in France, before the eighteenth century, collecting porcelain was the domain of the very wealthy. The Duc d'Orléans, brother of Louis XIV, was one of Europe's best-known collectors of Chinese ware. The blue and white pattern of Chinese porcelain was so highly prized that Louis XIV decided to build a porcelain palace to honor his favorite mistress.

Imitating Chinese Porcelain in the French Capital

Few buildings have left as many legends behind them as the fleeting *Trianon de Porcelaine,* the orientalist structure that was meant to be a Chinese-styled building, although it did not look anything like a Chinese structure. It preceded any building in the *chinoiserie* style by half a century. In 1663 Louis XIV acquired the hamlet of Trianon and razed it to the ground, including the church of Sainte Marie, in order to enlarge the gardens of Versailles. Dedicated to Madame de Montespan as early as 1670, the building was started by Louis Le Vau. The walls were covered in blue and white "Chinese-style" ceramic tiles, leading the building to be called the Porcelain Trianon. The gardens of the Trianon, rich with the scent of oriental bulbs and tuberose, appeared by magic one spring – or so claim the verses of the poet Félibien.[127]

Andrew Zega and Bernd H. Dams have their own reading of the imperial meaning of the Trianon and closely tie the building itself to France's commercial ambitions. They wrote that the pavilion's "naïve Orientalism" was a metaphorical claim to the riches of the East. They see the list of exotic luxury goods brought to Europe by the Dutch as interchangeable with the material used for the Trianon, foremost among them silks, porcelain and flowers.[128] They argue that this was the King's manifesto to supersede Dutch trade and overthrow the Dutch.

Even Jean Baptiste Colbert's systematic organization of the nursery gardens and *pépinières* to avoid buying flowers from the Dutch was ephemeral. By Louis XV's reign, the King was buying rare hyacinths, all the rage in the eighteenth century, from Dutch nurseries in Haarlem.[129] Dutch trade to France, although strictly forbidden, prevailed and was dominated by porcelain more than ever. Dutch tiles and porcelain, in imitation of their Chinese antecedents, were invading French markets. Louis XIV's wars against the Dutch provinces had disastrous economic results in France and brought impoverishment rather than the fabled riches of the East. The Dutch continued to enjoy their "Golden Age", and the upper hand for Asian trade.[130] The roof of the Trianon and its decoration with large Chinese porcelain vases was the most visible part of this French "folly". Well before other monarchs and aristocrats built follies, as orientalist buildings were often called. The palace was destroyed in 1687. The enormous vases of the roof exposed to the elements were the chief reason for the Chinese palace's extravagant maintenance costs. It was to be replaced by the Marble Trianon, which can still be visited in Versailles. Inside porcelain objects, tiles and *trompe l'oeil* porcelain were used in profusion. Ten large mirrors finished in oriental style lacquer work, called *lachine*, or *lachininage,* reflected the extreme luxury of the interiors. An abundance of Chinese silk brocade completed the orientalist theme. Andrew Zega and Bernd H. Dams argue that the building's *chinoiserie*, a baroque riot of blue and white, owed a great debt to the Dutch who had diffused oriental objects and fashions in Europe, chief among them porcelain.[131]

To make matters worse, Delft, the famous new Dutch manufacture, was making Dutch copies of Chinese porcelain that were flooding the French market and enriching the Dutch. As early as 1664 Colbert decided to create the royal manufacture of Saint Cloud, in the same year as he inaugurated the French East India Company to trade in India. In France the first soft-paste porcelains were made around 1677, although systematic production was not started until the 1690s. During the nineties, the English scientist Martin Lister visited Saint Cloud where he exclaimed that he could not distinguish between the porcelain made in France and the finest chinaware. Colbert's edict creating Saint Cloud gives us an idea of how important it was for things manufactured in France to actually look Chinese. The word used by Colbert for imitation is a very strong one in French *"contre-façon"*, which implies exact imitation: Saint Cloud ware was to be passed off as Chinese porcelain. Similar to the trajectory of coffee – which remained viewed and sold as oriental long after it was Caribbean – even when porcelain was no longer from China, it posed as Chinese to maintain its market value. Saint Cloud was called a *"manufacture de faience"*. In 1673 a patent was also issued for *faience* to Edme Poterat's family in Rouen.[132] Later on the manufacturers of hard-paste porcelain, Vincennes, Sèvres and Meissen, also produced pseudo-Chinese wares, often sold as Chinese or Japanese on the French markets.[133]

From fakes and imitations, there was also a transitional style where French porcelain was made in the *chinoiserie* style, without posing as Chinese. One of the most fascinating processes to follow is the gradual transformation in the representation of the same goods a century later. Louis XV's mistress, Madame de Pompadour, dictated taste through her many commissions directly to manufacturers and to importers. In the 1760s Sèvres ware was looking very French and no longer Chinese despite all its *chinoiserie*. The *chinoiserie* was now pure décor in the five pieces made for the bedroom of the Marquise de Pompadour, a great patron of the manufacture of Sèvres. After 1789 Sèvres lost much of is *chinoiserie* style decoration altogether. The demand for exotic imports and their imitations remained high among the aristocracy and the wealthy bourgeoisie of Paris until the French Revolution disrupted the order of taste as well as society.[134]

Study Questions

1   Through what social channels was coffee consumption adopted as a practice in France? Did this happen within one class or among multiple classes?

2   How did coffee come to be considered a French product and coffee consumption come to be considered a French practice?

3   What role did tea play in the growing maritime trade between Europe and East Asia?

4   How did the cultural meaning of tea consumption change in both China and Japan in the eighteenth and nineteenth centuries?

5   What does the production and consumption of porcelain tell us about the relationship between the indigenous and the exotic in European consumption?

Notes

1   From the correspondence of the Duchess of Orléans (October 9, 1694; date also given as August 25, 1718). As quoted in Norbert Elias, *The Civilizing Process: Sociogenetic and Psychogenetic Investigations*, trans. Edmund Jephcott (Malden, MA; Oxford, England; Victoria, Australia: Blackwell Publishing, 2000), 112.

2   Jean-Louis Flandrin and Massimo Montanari, eds., *Histoire de l'alimentation* (Paris: Fayard, 1996), 564–565.

3   Jacques Savary des Brûlons, *Dictionnaire universel de commerce: d'histoire naturelle, & des arts & métiers* (Paris: Estienne et fils, 1723).

4   Carolyn Sargentson, *Merchants and Luxury Markets: The Marchands Merciers of Eighteenth-century Paris* (Malibu, CA: Victoria and Albert Museum in association with the J. Paul Getty Museum, 1996), 62–86.

5   For debates about consumption and luxury in France see chapter 10 of Sargentson, *Merchants and Luxury Markets*. Werner Sombart, *Le bourgeois: contribution à l'histoire morale et intellectuelle de l'homme économique moderne*, Dr. S. Jankélévitch, trans, (Paris: Payot, 1926) and Sombart, *Luxury and Capitalism* (Ann Arbor: University of Michigan Press, 1967).

6 Ina Baghdiantz McCabe, *Orientalism in Early Modern France: Eurasian Trade, Exoticism and the Ancien Régime* (Oxford; New York: Berg, 2008), 256.

7 For how fashion was spread, see chapter 3 in Joan DeJean, *The Essence of Style: How the French Invented High Fashion, Fine Food, Chic Cafés, Style, Sophistication and Glamour* (New York: Free Press, 2005).

8 Louis de Rouvroy, duc de Saint-Simon, *Mémoires*, ed. Yves Coirault (Paris: Gallimard, 1984): t.3: 112. As cited in Jennifer Jones, "Clothing and the Courtier" in Giorgio Riello and Peter McNeil, eds., *The Fashion History Reader: Global Perspectives* (Abingdon, Oxon; New York: Routledge, 2010), 168. Also see Jennifer Jones, *Sexing la Mode: Gender, Fashion and Commercial Culture in Old Regime France* (Oxford; New York: Berg, 2004).

9 Jennifer Jones, "Clothing and the Courtier", *The Fashion History Reader,* 167.

10 Baghdiantz McCabe, *Orientalism*, 257–261.

11 The diamond after changing hands many times is held at the Smithsonian museum. Accessed July 6, 2013. http://www.si.edu/Encyclopedia_SI/nmnh/hope.html.

12 DeJean, *The Essence of Style*, 4.

13 DeJean, *The Essence of Style*, 4, 12.

14 Markman Ellis, *The Coffee-house: A Cultural Study* (London: Phoenix, 2005), 16–20.

15 Jean de Thévenot, *Relation d'un voyage fait au Levant* (Paris: L. Billaine, 1665–1684).

16 It was reprinted from Lyon: Jean Girin & B. Riviere, 1685. The earlier treatise is: Philippe Sylvestre Dufour, *De l'usage du caphé, du thé, et du chocolat* (Lyon, 1671).

17 A work now attributed to Jacob Spon.

18 See the preface of a 1992 reprint of Antoine Galland's translation. Antoine Galland, *De l'origine et du progés du café* (Caen: 1699; Reprint, Paris: L'écrivain voyageur, 1992).

19 Michel Tuchscherer, "Coffee in the Red Sea Area from the sixteenth to the nineteenth century," in Gervase Clarence-Smith and Steven Topik, eds., *The Global Coffee Economy in Africa, Asia and Latin America, 1500–1989* (New York: Cambridge University Press, 2003), 51–52.

20 For a discussion of civil society and the coffeehouse in Istanbul and Isfahan see: Saïd Anjomand, "Coffeehouses, Guilds & Oriental Despotism: Government & Civil Society in late 17th–early 18th Century Istanbul and Isfahan, and as seen from Paris & London", *European Journal of Sociology* 45, no.1 (2004) : 23–42.

21 Bibiothèque nationale Ms. arabe no. 4590 al-Jaziri, 'Abd al-Qadir ibn Muhammad al Ansari al Hanbali 'Umdat al al-sawfa fi hill al-qawha'.

22 This is all faithfully translated in Galland, *De l'origine et du progrès du café* (1992), 42–43.

23 Ralph Hattox, *Coffee and Coffeehouses: The Origins of a Social Beverage in the Medieval Near East* (Seattle: University of Washington Press, 1985), 42–43.

24 Hattox, *Coffee and Coffeehouses*, 40.

25 Hattox, *Coffee and Coffeehouses*, chapter three.

26 Hattox, *Coffee and Coffeehouses*, 5.

27 Nicolas de Blègny, *Le bon usage du thé du caffé et du chocolat pour La préservation & pour La guérison des maladies* (Paris: Estienne Michallet, 1687). Also a Lyon edition in the same year.

28 Fernand Braudel, *Civilization materielle, économie et capitalisme: XVe-XVIIIe siècle* (Paris: A. Colin, 1979), 13.

29 One such work on the properties of coffee: François Aignan, *Le preste médecin ou Discours physique sur l'etablissement de la Medecine. Avec un traité du caffé & du thé de France selon le système d'Hippocrate* (Paris: chez Laurent D'Houry, 1696).

30 Sabine Coron and Bibliothèque de l'Arsenal Staff, *Livres en bouche: cinq siècles d'art culinaire français, du quatorzième au dix-huitième siècle* (Paris:

BNF, Hermann, 2001). This volume lists a few titles but does not contain a study of them as the books were part of an exhibit.

31 Bennett Alan Weinberg and Bonnie K. Bealer, *The World of Caffeine: The Science and Culture of the World's Most Popular Drug* (London, Routledge, 2002), 108–110.

32 Weinberg and Bealer, *The World of Caffeine*, 105.

33 Claude Colomb, *Question de médecine proposée par Messieurs Castillons et Foque, docteurs de la faculté d'Aix, à Monsieur Colomb, pour son agrégation au collège des médecins de Marseille, sur lesquelles on doit disputer le 27 février 1679 dans la salle de la Maison de Ville*. Dissertation (Marseille, 1679).

34 For a protectionist taxation of 20 percent on foreign merchants see: Gaston Rambert, *Histoire du Commerce de Marseille Publié par la chambre de commerce de Marseille en sept Tomes* (Paris: Plon, 1953–57). This long work is a thorough study of the archives of the Chamber of Commerce of Marseilles. There are some as well at the archives of the Ministère de la Marine in Paris.

35 Paul Butel, *Histoire du Thé* (Paris: Presses Universitaires de France, 1997), 48–56.

36 Baghdiantz McCabe, *Orientalism*, 190–194.

37 François Audigier, *La Maison réglée, et l'art de diriger maison d'un grand seigneur & autres, tant à la Ville qu'à la Campagne, & le devoir de tous les Officiers, & autres Domestiques en général. Avec la Véritable Méthode de faire toutes sortes d'Essences, d'Eaux de Liqueurs, fortes & rafraîchissantes, à la mode d'Italie. Ouvrage utile et nécessaire à toutes sortes de personnes de qualité, gentilshommes de Province, étrangers, bourgeois, officiers de grandes maisons, limonadiers & autres marchands de liqueurs.* (Paris 1692 or counterfeit of same edition, Amsterdam: Paul Marret, 1697), 166.

38 *La muse de Cour*, 2 Dec. 1666, 28th week, 228.

> Ce mot Kave vous surprend! [The word Kave surprises you!]
> C'est une liqueur arabesque. [It's an Arab liquor.]
> Ou bien si vous voulez turquesque [Or better, Turkish if you like]
> Quand dans le Levant chacun en prend. [When in the Levant everyone takes it.]
> On s'en sert en Afrique, on s'en sert en Asie, [They serve it in Africa and Asia,]
> Elle a passé dans l'Italie, [It passed into Italy,]
> En Hollande et chez les Anglois [Into Holland and England]
> Où on la trouve fort utile, [Where one finds it more useful,]
> Et des Arméniens qui sont en cette ville [And some of the Armenians in this city]
> L'apportent encore au François

39 Norbert Elias, *La société de cour* (Paris: Flammarion, 1993), see especially Chapter III, *L'etiquette et la logique du prestige*, 63–115.

40 Elias, *La société de cour*, Chapter IV.

41 Jean de la Roque, *A voyage to Arabia Felix (1708–1710); and, A Journey from Mocha to Muab (1711–13); and, A Narrative Concerning Coffee; and, An Historical Treatise Concerning Coffee* (Cambridge; New York: Oleander, 2004), 353.

42 Baghdiantz McCabe, *Orientalism*, 194–197.

43 For comparisons of these two trading diasporas see Chapter 1 by Jonathan Israel and Chapter 2 by Ina Baghdiantz McCabe in Ina Baghdiantz McCabe, Gelina Harlaftis and Ionna Minoglu, eds., *Diaspora and Entrepreneurial Networks 1600–2000* (Oxford: Berg, 2005).

44 On the Sephardic Jews there are several important books by Jonathan Irvine Israel; the most recent one is: *Diasporas Within a Diaspora: Jews, Crypto-Jews, and the World of Maritime Empires 1540–1740*, Brill's Series in Jewish Studies (Boston: Brill, 2002), 30. My own work on the Armenians, *The Shah's Silk for Europe's Silver: The Eurasian Silk trade of the Julfan Armenians in Safavid Iran*

and India (1590–1750), University of Pennsylvania's Series in Armenian Texts and Studies (Atlanta, Georgia: Scholar's Press, 1999).

45 De la Roque, *A Voyage to Arabla Felix,* 323.

46 De la Roque, *A Voyage to Arabia Felix*, 319. "Finally, one has arrived in this city. Pascal, Armenian in origin, the one who thought to sell coffee publicly in 1672 at the fair of St. Germain, then installed himself in a small shop on Quai de l'Ecole where he sold coffee for 2 sous 6 deniers a cup."

47 Weinberg and Bealer, *The World of Caffeine*, 71–73. De la Roque did not give this account of Pascal's booth.

48 Voltaire denied going there or to any other cafés.

49 *Le porte-feuille galant, ouvrage mêlé de prose et de vers. Avec plusieurs questions sérieuses et galantes* (Paris: Jean Moreau, 1700), 3. "Ils entrèrent donc chez les Arméniens, où ils demandèrent des liqueurs et des biscuits; car peu de gens se bornent à une prise de caffé, qui n'est souvent que le pretexte d'un plus grand excez [sic]".

50 De la Roque, *A Voyage to Arabia Felix,* 382.

51 Louise W. Mackie, "Ottoman kaftans with an Italian identity", in Suraiya Faroqhi and Christoph K. Neumann, eds, *Ottoman Costumes: From Textile to Identity* (Istanbul, Turkey: EREN Press, 2004), 219–229.

52 Suraiya Faroqhi, "Introduction, or Why and How One Might Want to Study Ottoman Clothes" in Faroqhi and Neumann, eds., *Ottoman Costumes: From Textile to Identity*, 15–48.

53 Thomas Kaiser, "The Evil Empire? The Debate on Turkish Despotism in Eighteenth-Century French Political Culture," *The Journal of Modern History* 72, no. 1, New Work on the Old Regime and the French Revolution: A Special Issue in Honor of François Furet (Mar., 2000), 6–34.

54 Baghdiantz McCabe, *Orientalism*, Chapter nine.

55 Charlotte Jirousek, "Ottoman Influences in Western Dress" in Faroqhi and Neumann, *Ottoman Costumes*, 231–251.

56 John Evelyn, *Diary*, E. S. Beer, ed., Vol 3 (Oxford, 1955), 465 and n.1, cited in Jirousek, "Ottoman Influences in Western Dress," in Faroqhi and Neumann, *Ottoman Costumes*, 231–251. The analysis is Jirousek's.

57 See illustration in DeJean, *The Essence of Style*, figure 12.2, 240.

58 See in Richard Martin and Harold Koda a Banyan owned by the Metropolitan Museum of Art: Banyan, ca. 1735. English, Brown figured silk faille, Purchase, Irene Lewisohn Bequest, 1981 (1981.208.2).

59 Samuel Pepys, *Diary*, Robert Latham and William Matthews, eds., (London: Bell & Hyman, 1970), VII 373; John Evelyn, *Diary*, Vol. 3, 460, cited in Jirousek, "Ottoman Influences in Western Dress," in *Ottoman Costumes*, 231–251.

60 Jirousek, "Ottoman Influences in Western Dress" in *Ottoman Costumes,* 231–251.

61 Ellis, *The Coffee-house*, 127–130.

62 Brian William Cowan, *The Social Life of Coffee: The Emergence of the British Coffeehouse* (New Haven CT: Yale University Press, 2005), 5, 21.

63 Cowan, *The Social Life of Coffee*, 21.

64 Cowan, *The Social Life of Coffee*, 27–28.

65 Cowan, *The Social Life of Coffee*, 38–41

66 Edward Pocoke, *The Nature of the Drink Kahue, or Coffee, and the Berry of which it is made, Described by an Arab Phisitian* (Oxford: Henry Hall, 1659).

67 G. J. Toomer, *Eastern Wisdom and Learning: The Study of Arabic in Seventeenth Century England* (Oxford: Clarendon Press, 1996), 166 and n. 86.

68 Cowan, *The Social Life of Coffee*, 43.

69 Jan de Vries, "The Limits of Globalization in the Early Modern World", *The Economic History Review*, 63, 3 (2010): 710–733. De Vries, "The Economic Crisis of the Seventeenth Century after Fifty Years", *Journal of Interdisciplinary History* 40 (2009), 151–194.

70 Jordan Goodman, Paul E. Lovejoy and Andrew Sherratt., eds., *Consuming Habits: Global and Historical Perspectives on how Cultures Define Drugs,* second edition. (London; New York: Routledge, 2007).

71 Cowan, *The Social Life of Coffee,* 58–90.

72 Ellis, *The Coffee-house: A Cultural Study,* 39.

73 Cowan, *The Social Life of Coffee,* 90–91.

74 Ellis, *The Coffee-house,* 106–209, 27.

75 Cowan, *The Social Life of Coffee,* 100.

76 As quoted in Cowan, *The Social Life of Coffee,* 132.

77 Cowan, *The Social Life of Coffee,* 143.

78 Cowan, *The Social Life of Coffee,* 144–145.

79 Cowan, *The Social Life of Coffee,* 161.

80 De la Roque, *A Voyage to Arabia Felix,* 320 and 382.

81 Margaret C. Jacob, "Mental Landscape of the Public Sphere: A European Perspective" ECS 28:1 (Fall 1994) in Cowan, *The Social Life of Coffee,* 96.

82 Steven Pincus, "Coffee Politicians Does Create: Coffeehouses and Restoration Political Culture" *Journal of Modern History 67* (December 1995), 828–29 as quoted in Cowan, *The Social Life of Coffee.*

83 Cowan, *The Social Life of Coffee,* 187.

84 Cowan, *The Social Life of Coffee,* 199.

85 Cowan, *The Social Life of Coffee,* 204.

86 Cowan, *The Social Life of Coffee,* 211.

87 Cowan, *The Social Life of Coffee,* 248–256.

88 Anne E. C. McCants, "Porcelain for the Poor: the Material Culture of Tea and Coffee in Eighteenth Century Amsterdam" in Paula Findlen, ed., *Early Modern Things* (New York: Routledge, 2012).

89 McCants, "Porcelain for the Poor" in Paula Findlen, ed., *Early Modern Things,* 317.

90 McCants, "Porcelain for the Poor" in Paula Findlen, ed., *Early Modern Things,* 339.

91 De la Roque, *A Voyage to Arabia Felix,* 370.

92 Jean de la Roque, *Voyage de l'Arabie heureuse: par l'Ocean oriental, & le détroit de la mer Rouge, fait par les françois pour la premiere fois, dans les années 1708, 1709 & 1710; avec la relation particuliere d'un voyage fait du port de Moka à la cour du roi d'Yemen, dans la seconde expedition des années 1711, 1712 & 1713; un memoire concernant l'arbre & le fruit du café, dressé sur les observations de ceux qui ont fait ce dernier voyage; et un traité historique de l'origine & du progrès du café, tant dans l'Asie que dans l'Europe; de son introduction en France, & de l'établissement de son usage à Paris* (Paris: A. Cailleau, 1716), 399.

93 Emil Bretschneider, *History of European Botanical Discoveries in China* (Hamburg: SEVERUS Verlag, 2011), 26.

94 Bretschneider, *History of European Botanical Discoveries in China,* 25.

95 Victor H. Mair and Erling Hoh, *The True History of Tea* (London; New York: Thames & Hudson, 2009), 167–169.

96 Bretschneider, *History of European Botanical Discoveries in China,* 26.

97 Sophie D. Coe and Michael D. Coe, *The True History of Chocolate* (New York: Thames and Hudson, 2007), 167–168.

98 Bretschneider, *History of European Botanical Discoveries in China,* 29–31.

99 Mair and Hoh, *The True History of Tea,* 37.

100 Mair and Hoh, *The True History of Tea,* 30.

101 Mair and Hoh, *The True History of Tea,* 34.

102 Mair and Hoh, *The True History of Tea,* 35.

103 Mair and Hoh, *The True History of Tea,* 31–39.

104 Alan Macfarlane and Iris Macfarlane, *Green Gold: The Empire of Tea* (London: Ebury, 2003), chapter 14.

105 Mair and Hoh, *The True History of Tea,* 48–49.

106 Mair and Hoh, *The True History of Tea*, 57.
107 Mair and Hoh, *The True History of Tea*, 59
108 Mair and Hoh, *The True History of Tea*, 62–63
109 Frederick J. Simoons, *Food in China: A Cultural and Historical Inquiry* (Boca Raton: CRC Press, 1991), 447.
110 Maguelonne Toussaint-Samat, *A History of Food* (Chichester, West Sussex, UK; Malden, MA: Wiley-Blackwell, 2009), 536.
111 Simoons, *Food in China: A Cultural and Historical Inquiry*, 445.
112 Unn Malfrid H. Rolandsen, *Leisure and Power in Urban China: Everyday Life in a Chinese City* (Abingdon, Oxon; New York, NY: Routledge, 2001), 45–46.
113 Coe and Coe, *The True History of Chocolate*, 166.
114 Mair and Hoh, *The True History of Tea*, 43–44.
115 John E. Wills, *1688: A Global History* (New York: Norton, 2001), 150.
116 Wills, *1688: A Global History*, 150–155.
117 Wills, *1688: A Global History*, 155.
118 Butel, *Histoire du Thé*, 48 –58.
119 Butel, *Histoire du Thé*, 56–57.
120 Butel, *Histoire du Thé*, 90.
121 Toby Musgrave, *An Empire of Plants: People and Plants that Changed the World* (London: Cassell; New York: Sterling Publishing Co., 2000), 108–109.
122 Butel, *Histoire du Thé*, 96.
123 Butel, *Histoire du Thé*, 94.
124 Musgrave, *An Empire of Plants*, 109.
125 Musgrave, *An Empire of Plants*, 112.
126 Musgrave, *An Empire of Plants*, 112–113.
127 André Félibien, *Les Divertissements de Versailles, donnés au retour de la conquête de la Franche-Comté en 1674* (Paris: Imprimerie Royale, 1676).
128 Andrew Zega and Bernd H. Dams, *Palaces of the Sun King: Versailles, Trianon, Marly: The Châteaux of Louis XIV* (New York: Rizzoli, 2002), 102–103.
129 Elizabeth Hyde, *Cultivated Power: Flowers, Culture, and Politics in the Reign of Louis XIV* (Philadelphia: University of Pennsylvania Press, 2005), 201.
130 Zega and Dams, *Palaces of the Sun King: Versailles, Trianon, Marly: The Châteaux of Louis XIV*, 100.
131 For some examples see: Ingelore Menzhausen, *Early Meissen Porcelain in Dresden* (New York: Thames and Hudson, 1990). Ulrich Pietsch, *China, Japan, Meissen: The Dresden Porcelain Collection*, trans. Ulrich Boltz (Munich: Deutscher Kunstverlag, 2006).
132 Baghdiantz McCabe, *Orientalism*, 220–221.
133 Sargentson, *Merchants and Luxury Markets*, 75.
134 Baghdiantz McCabe, *Orientalism*, 219–220.

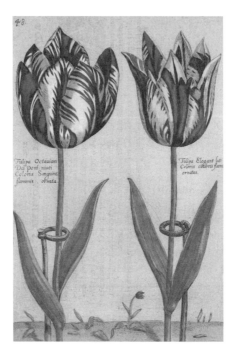

Figure 5.1 Tulipa Octaviani del pont, and Tulipa Elegant, from 'Hortus Floridus', published 1614–15, Passe, Crispin I de (c. 1565–1637). © Private Collection/ The Stapleton Collection/The Bridgeman Art Library.

5   Treasures from the East

Tulips and the Fashion for Asia's Luxury Goods

> Of late, 'tis true, quite sick of Rome and Greece
> We fetch our models from the wise Chinese
> European artists are too cool and chaste
> For Mand'rin is the only man of taste ... [1]

Europe's taste for *chinoiserie* is associated with the eighteenth century, when this poem *On Taste* was written as a tribute to Chinese style, which did away with lines and symmetry. Nevertheless, another eighteenth-century writer Daniel Defoe asserted that English taste for Chinese porcelain dated to the latter part of the seventeenth century. He pinpoints the marriage of Queen Mary II to the Dutch Prince William of Orange as the origin for this trend.[2] Global trade first took serious hold as European merchants established trading bases throughout Asia, they capitalized on the European demand for Asian luxury goods. They partook and profited from a long established intra-Asian trade in silk, deerskin and porcelain. Chinese traders, while not circumnavigating the globe to carry goods to Europe's markets, had monopolized the middleman market especially in the Indian Ocean. During this period, major European factories were established that later became colonies: the Spanish took the Philippines, the Portuguese Macau, and the Dutch Java (in modern-day Indonesia). Asian luxury goods were carried by European companies to consumers who had developed a taste for *chinoiserie*.

Historians such as Maxine Berg, who studied the taste for luxury in England, have attributed the taste for things Chinese to the Dutch.[3] The Dutch and the English are traditionally seen as rivals for the overseas trade of exotic commodities and Asian luxury goods. Recently, the vast cultural exchange that took place between England and the Dutch Republic has been well studied. In *Going Dutch*, Lisa Jardine describes how two countries that regularly declared themselves sworn enemies and rivals on the seas merged administrations and institutions by 1700. The *Glorious Revolution*, also called the Revolution of 1688, started with the overthrow of King James II of England (James VII of Scotland and James II of Ireland) by a union of the English Parliament with a foreign prince, the Dutch stadtholder William III of Orange-Nassau (William of Orange). William's successful invasion of England with a

Dutch fleet and army led to his accession of the English throne as William III of England with his wife Mary II of England. William of Orange's reign as King of Ireland began in 1689, shortly after his dramatic arrival.[4] "From the very start the Dutch fleet achieved its key strategic aim, creating an unforgettable spectacle, inducing a feeling of shock and awe in onlookers on either shore."[5] Jardine writes that the iconic image of the Dutch *sortie* into the English Channel was commemorated in countless images still to be found today in both England and contemporary Holland. The Dutch "invasion" was watched by crowds gathered on the cliff tops on the south of England.

In what Jardine calls "the Invasion that Never was", the cultural exchanges were the lesser noted consequences of the Dutch army's successful march towards London.[6] She demonstrates that garden design transformed itself and became ever more ambitious to match the aspirations of the new Dutch elite. Exotic plants, fruits and vegetables from the new Dutch colonies that had been sought after in the Dutch Republic were now sought after in London. In her description of Dyrham Park, she notes that even 300 years after the original owner's death, one can see fine Dutch landscapes and perspective paintings on the wall. There are also many pieces of blue and white Delft *faïence* everywhere, including very large pagoda-like pyramid vases designed for the display of tulips. The owner of this mansion was William Blathwayt, known as William and Mary's "imperial fixer".[7] He was known for his successful administration of the far-flung American colonies and the Caribbean islands. Jardine asserts that his salary could not have maintained his magnificent lifestyle and that he was systematically extracting money from his "clients".[8] Dutch and English governors in the colonies had a habit of accepting gifts, including imported exotic objects.

William Blathwayt's magnificent pagoda vases for tulips were Dutch Delft *faïence* and were a relatively awkward imitation of Chinese porcelain. His mansion is proof that *chinoiserie* had spread beyond courts into the houses of the powerful elites of England in the seventeenth century. Daniel Marot (1661–1720), a Huguenot engraver and designer, fled the court of Louis XIV and spread French styles; according to Madeleine Jarry it is through the published designs of Marot that *chinoiserie* spread well beyond the courts in the Dutch Republic and later England.[9] He published some of his designs by 1700 and the late baroque style he favored became loosely known in England as the "William and Mary" style. In the Netherlands, Marot was employed by the Stadtholder who later became William III of England; he designed interiors in the palace of Het Loo, which was built from 1684 onwards and has been called the "Dutch Versailles". The taste for *chinoiserie* extended far beyond the English and Dutch elites into the homes of the elite colonists overseen by William Blathwayt. Scholars argue that the collection of exotic objects reflects Europe's will to conquer the world. Anne Goldgar argues that such objects demonstrate a desire to conquer nature. To underline this trend she examines a flower: the tulip.[10]

Another Way to Collect: Consuming Nature

Paradoxically, even collecting a flower such as the tulip has been compared to collecting textiles and objects. Anne Goldgar cites Huygens in 1647 as saying that the painted flower rendered the real one a shadow.[11] Lorraine Daston and Katherine Park have argued that the opposition between the forces of nature and art remained crucial in the seventeenth century even as natural philosophy was just beginning to attempt to change the relationship between art and nature. With the strengthening view in the Renaissance that an artist's work was akin to that of the creating God, the view that art surpassed nature became more and more influential.[12] Dutch floral still-lives make this clear. The desire to idealize flowers in paint to improve on nature was a powerful impulse for seventeenth-century artists. Despite this tradition of challenging God and nature, botanists and gardeners continued to maintain that art could do nothing to imitate the beauty of a real flower. In the seventeenth century, there was a pleasure in blurring the boundaries between art and nature that can be seen in the objects collected by the elite. Many natural objects were turned into *artificialiai* by etching, carving or gilding coconuts, ostrich eggs, ivory and nautilus shells. Nautilus shells in particular were turned into luxurious beakers, reindeer antlers were made into candelabra and coconuts were carved with biblical scenes.[13]

Given the reigning debates on art and nature, the question of the authorship of tulip varieties was an important one during the period. Who actually created the tulip was alluded to in many works in gardening. Many gardeners writing on the alteration of tulips focused on the choice of seed and how the great attraction of the tulip was its unpredictability. It was hoped that in choosing the seed, one could produce superior tulips. The theory that tulips changed color because of disease led to experimentation in using weakened flowers that were made to fall sick. The purpose of the experiment was to understand and make them become better marked by colors the next year. In many Dutch paintings the association of tulips and luxury is evident. The names given to tulips are also reminiscent of patterned cloths, carpets and polished stone with beds of tulips often being compared to tapestries. While it was natural for an expensive flower such as the tulip to be compared to such goods, it was not an idle comparison. It becomes clear in Clusius' work that the petals of the tulips were thought to actually resemble silk, satin or velvet. Carolus Clusius (1526–1609), a Flemish botanist and physician, became famous for his scholarship but is remembered for his observations on tulips "breaking" their colors. The flamed and feathered varieties of tulips were the most prized among collectors. One Dutch gardening book goes as far as recommending that the chosen seeds be satin-like in order to obtain the effect of elegant cloth. The luster of tulips, if it did not come from shiny silk, was also said to resemble enamel work or vermeil. The other favorite comparison of the tulip was with polished stones such as marble or agate.[14]

Goldgar looks at tulip names in both Dutch and French and finds many comparisons to precious cloth and stones. She argues that the place of tulips is reminiscent in aesthetic comparisons to Dutch paintings of the period and that the resemblance of tulips to art had important implications. The flower fell into the category of connoisseurship and collecting while also becoming the object of criticism and discussion. Many scholars and connoisseurs formed a network to exchange the flower as well as a network of sociability around the tulip. Breeders in the Netherlands and in Paris were looking for the best flower; the first were the few *curieux,* many of them scholars and collectors.[15] The tulip was soon going to leave the hands of collectors to enter the market place.

The Tulip's Holy Beginnings

The tulip reached the United Provinces in 1570. Native to central Asia, the tulip originated from an area where China and Russia meet the Afghan borders. Wild tulips were usually blood red and survived harsh winters and dry summers.[16] The earliest known cultivation of tulips was in 1050 in Persia in the gardens of Isfahan and Baghdad.[17] In Persian poetry, tulips are a symbol of perfection, eternity and beauty. The thirteenth-century palace of the Seljuks contains tiles with tulips depicted on them. But it was the Ottoman sultans who were largely responsible for tulip cultivation and the importance of tulips.[18] The tulip was regarded as the holiest of flowers, a flower of God because of its name; in Arabic script, the letters which make up *lale,* the Turkish word for "tulip", are the same as those that form "Allah". Mehmed the Conqueror built the Topkapi palace and ordered sixty private gardens, all lush with streams of water, birds, fruit trees and tulips.[19] Before the tulip was introduced to Europe, it was a favorite of the Ottomans and was reconfigured on textiles, vases, tiles, royal armor, prayer rugs for brides, saddles and religious tokens.[20] In 1574 Suleyman's son ordered 50,000 tulip bulbs planted for the Ottoman imperial garden.

The tulip craze grew to such heights in the Ottoman capital that it gave its name to a whole period, the Tulip Period or the Tulip Era (1718–1730). The Tulip Period saw a flowering of the arts, culture and architecture. The Ottoman Empire was the stage for an anti-tulip rebellion. As tulip prices began to rise in the last decades of the seventeenth century and peaked in 1726–1727, there was a revolt as the high price of bulbs demonstrated the state's power to regulate the economy by increasing the price of tulip bulbs. Petitions were written to denounce the practice of flower sellers who were perceived as taking advantage of the elite.[21] Yet when one speaks of tulipmania today, people rarely think of the Ottoman Empire as its center: instead they think of Amsterdam a century earlier.

In 1562, tulip bulbs were found in a package of fabric sent from Istanbul to Antwerp. Mike Dash remarks how the recipient of the bulbs cooked and ate some of them while planting the rest in his garden. As the tulips flowered the next year, the Flemish merchant sought out the advice of businessman Joris Rye to help him understand their importance. Joris Rye did not know what the flowers were but he replanted them and wrote to his circle of friends including Clusius who was a notable botanist of the time and considered one of the fathers of modern botany.[22] His system of classifying plants according to their characteristics was furthered by Carl Linnæus in the eighteenth century. By the time he moved to the small Dutch town of Leiden, Clusius had a tulip collection that he had gathered while working for the Emperor in Vienna. Clusius' flowers soon attracted attention from gardeners, horticulturists, and merchants. Although his garden was guarded at night, the tulip thefts from his garden and gifts he made to other scholars are largely responsible for the spreading of tulip variants across the United Provinces.[23]

Used during the wedding of Louis XIII in 1615 to adorn the Queen's cleavage, the tulip set a fashion trend that spread to the rest of France after peaking at the French court. The newly independent Dutch were connoisseurs of the tulip, a flower that belonged to the new ruling class of the Republic.[24] Antwerp, where the tulip arrived, was the main port of northern Europe. After the Spanish blockade of Antwerp during the war that led to Dutch independence, the economy of Antwerp and its port were ravaged. Many merchants left Antwerp and other centers in the southern Netherlands with their capital and knowledge of trade, for the towns of the Dutch Republic.[25]

The Tulip: The First Financial Bubble

Simon Schama has argued that only a deeply bourgeois culture could possibly have selected the humble tulip rather than emeralds or Arabian stallions as a speculative trophy. They were exotic and rare at first, but it was precisely at the point where their rarity seemed capable of domestication for a mass market that the potential for runaway demand could be realized. The key was the reproducibility of an exotic object. Unlike Ming porcelain and Turkish rugs – that had been copied and manufactured in Europe as Delft blue ware and Flemish carpets yet remained approximations and bad copies – the tulip could be reproduced. An important luxury originating in central Asia could be domesticated and become Dutch. Tulips were critiqued by Calvinist preachers who saw the tulip as yet another dangerous addition to the lengthy catalogue of vanities that were subverting the godly Dutch Republic. Despite this criticism, the fervor for tulips took hold of Dutch society. Florists had their own professional interests in experimenting with unusual hues, petal shapes and sizes and created a huge range of variety destined to attract not only the wealthy connoisseur but thousands of small buyers.[26]

There were four phases in the extraordinary story of the tulip: the first phase of the connoisseurs and scholars, the second of professionals and growers, then the mass invasion of speculators, and finally the intervention of regulators to stop the speculation. By the early 1620s, tulips were established as the unrivaled flower of fashion throughout northern France, the

Netherlands and the western parts of Germany. In a world conscious of hierarchy, it was not long before an informal system of classification arranged varieties according to rank from the most noble to the most common. Superior ranking was often given to flamboyance and subtlety of color; it was the flamed and irregularly striped varieties that were most admired. These were grouped into three aristocratic estates according to the dominant hue: the roses, the violets and the *bizarden*. At the very head of this nobility were the imperial rarities, the *Semper Augustus* (red flames on white) and its attempted clone, the *Parem Augustus*. The next level included the viceroys but in the democratic Netherlands, titles such as general or admiral were preferred. One owner had a dozen *Semper Augustus*, which cost 1,200 florins a piece, but he would not part with them. He realized he cornered the market while speculation was high. Prices for the *Semper Augustus* were on the rise: in 1625, as much as 2,000 and 3,000 florins was offered but the owner could not make up his mind to sell. These high prices were very unusual before the 1630s, when the prices for tulips rose sharply.[27]

For many merchants 1,000 florins represented a substantial sum, but the accounts of a *bloemist* in the flower trade could be far more substantial. In 1644 the account of one *bloemist* at the Exchange Bank had a balance of f. 162,757 and showed payments of 2,530 to Guillelmo Bartholotti.[28] One of the richest men involved in the tulip business, Guillelmo Bartholotti van de Heuvel was an important merchant from the port of Antwerp, the main port of trade with Asia before the rise of Amsterdam. Dash clarifies that the income of a middle class merchant was between f. 10,000 and 30,000 a year. This newfound wealth was invested in the arts, culture and country estates and marks a period of prosperity for the Dutch. This period of wealth has been called the Golden Age for the Dutch because of a prosperous maritime trade, a new stock market and a love of collecting. Around 1635, the first professional gardener started to make a net profit from the entrance into the exotic tulip industry. As early as 1633, a house in the town of Hoorn was sold for three tulips; this transaction marked the height of the price of the bulbs and the beginning of the utilization of bulbs as a form of currency. The increase in the number of people entering the tulip business was followed by an increase in the price of bulbs and another surge of investors until the cycle reached its peak in December 1636 and January 1637.[29] Some flowers could double in price within days, the most valuable flower *Semper Augustus* had risen sharply from 5,500 guilders for one bulb in 1633 to 10,000 in the first month of 1637.[30] Dash clarifies that this sum was enough to clothe, feed and house a whole Dutch family for several decades. A few bulbs fetched as much as 6,000 florins each at the height of the mania. Tracts of land, houses, fine furniture and silver and gold vessels were all commonly traded against bulbs. Small growers had to go to elaborate lengths to protect their investments day and night. One horticulturalist in north Holland rigged up a trip wire in his garden attached to an alarm bell to alert him if intruders entered his garden.[31]

In her book on tulipmania, Anne Goldgar warns that stereotypes about the tulip fever that seized the Dutch should be dismissed. She writes that the prices of the specific tulips were briefly high but that many bulbs did not increase in value. She also warns that tulipmania did not destroy the Dutch economy and that it was not simply a financial crisis but a social and cultural one.[32] Even though the Dutch were very successful in overseas trade, they had undergone a recession lasting for most of the 1620s following aggression by the Spanish, who had ruled the Dutch before their independence in 1585. The Dutch economy was experiencing a new boom in the 1630s. The tulip craze happened during a time when the bubonic plague ravaged Europe between 1633 and 1637 and some authors think that this attitude of fatalism and desperation was what led to wild speculation on tulips.[33] Purchases used to be dependent on the flower's seasons but there was a revolution in the way flowers were sold. Flowers were kept in the ground and the buyer only had a piece of paper to prove his purchase. This period dominated by promissory notes was called "trading in the wind". It characterized the peak of tulipmania because individuals could buy and sell flowers without possessing them yet. This was the first appearance of the futures market and it has been called the first financial bubble in history. Anne Goldgar has argued that tulipmania was part of a new culture of risk. Sometimes it was even tied to speculations on life expectancy. An *Admiral Hazes* bulb was sold for f. 1000 in 1636; the seller agreed that if any of his five children died in the year to come, the bulb was the buyer's free.[34]

Dutch promissory notes that regulated the future trading started to measure the flowers by weight to keep track of them. They used *azen* or aces as units so tulips could be traded in units or shares of tulips. The lack of regulation and the increasing complexity over price destabilized the foundation of the tulip market. Many Dutch merchants became incredibly wealthy as tulip dealers. The only problem was that they could not get their hands on their money because it lay buried in the ground in the form of bulbs.[35] This was not just a matter of gaining wealth from tulips, but the construction of a hierarchy of expertise in commerce and natural history. The trade was swiftly organized, with commercial companies and a board to oversee them called the *collegie*, which held the ultimate authority over all transactions. Goldgar argued that communities found themselves at a loss when an assessment of values was thrown in doubt. Tulipmania highlighted the fact that value was a social construct. The shock of tulipmania went well beyond the tulip: a whole network of values was thrown into doubt for the very first time.[36]

The speculation in tulip bulbs always existed at the margins of Dutch economic life. It was not part of the strictly regulated stock exchange, or *beurs,* which had opened for business in 1610. Only permitted between the hours of noon and two, trading had to be packed into these two hours, so the daily ruckus and frenzy that erupted next to the big clock in the tower that struck midday was promptly ended when the clock struck two. Hundreds of traders were licensed to deal on the stock exchange. By 1636, at least 360 different commodities were traded on the Amsterdam exchange; however, tulips were not one of them. The colleges of tulip growers and dealers who sold tulip bulbs met in the back rooms of Dutch inns, often late at night in smoke-filled rooms. It was the larger and more reputable inns that were able to offer the private room required for the tulip trade. Many of the elaborate customs developed in the tulip trade were deliberately modeled on stock exchange methods, a practice that heightened the florists' sense of self-importance. Bulbs were put up for sale by auction. The tulips that were sold by tavern traders were rarely, if ever, of the superb fine varieties that obsessed collectors and wealthy dealers. These second-class flowers were known as "rags" or "common goods" and were sold not by the ace, but rather in baskets that were weighed out in the half-pound. In florist slang, they were often called "pound goods". Goldgar finds no records of tulip buyers at the bottom of urban society and argues that on the whole most buyers were just a level below the regents, or office-holders in Dutch towns' governments. This elite is also absent from the list of buyers.[37]

The tulip was a part of the culture of curiosity and collecting that marked this period in Europe. Many Dutch towns had benefitted from the fall of Antwerp as a center of culture and commerce. Besides Amsterdam, Middleburg was an important commercial center where an Antwerp merchant by the name of Baltharar de Moucheron had moved after his travels to find a new route to China. A specialist in the Caribbean trade, he set up his company in Middleburg. With the trade of exotica and curiosities that dominated his imports, he brought the curiosity culture of Antwerp further north. Among his imports were flowers. Travelers and commercial companies had brought many rare bulbs to European gardens: dogtooth violets, auricula, double narcissi, lilies, crocuses and many others. The doctors and apothecaries who were waiting for ships to arrive with the rare bulbs in the 1590s in Middleburg were all from Antwerp or southern Flanders.[38] The tulip was not simply an object of desire for florists, doctors or collectors; it became a swift business that maintained a certain specific etiquette. The tulip trade was full of dropped hints and veiled illusions because nobody was to openly offer a tulip for sale. A first method used called "with the boards" was a way of bidding at the auction. Wood back slates were given to both the buyer and seller. The florist who wished to buy would jot down the price he was prepared to pay on his slate but would choose a sum below the actual value of the bulb. The seller would name his own price, usually one that was exorbitantly high. The two bids would then be passed to intermediaries nominated by the buyer and seller and the compromised prices would then be scrawled on the slates and the boards would be passed back to the *florists*. At this point, both buyer and seller had the option of accepting or rejecting the arbitration. The buyer was expected to pay a commission on the purchase price if he accepted. If the deal was refused, it was signaled by rubbing the price off the slate. There was another system, called "in het ootje" meaning "in the little o", which refers to the diagram that the secretary of the college would draw to keep track of the bidding. In this system, it was the secretary who kept track of the bids by noting the highest offer in thousands in the top semicircle, in hundreds in the bottom part, and in units underneath the line that went through the circle.[39]

The Sharp Fall of the Tulip

The hundreds of novice florists that flocked to the tulip trade in the winter of 1636 generally began by dealing in pound goods. As remarkable as the tulip's history has been up to this point, it was in the months of December 1636 and January 1637 that the tulip trade turned into tulipmania. Sadly there is no eyewitness account as to what went on in the tulip colleges during the winter of 1636. However, there is a work by an author who had detailed knowledge of the tavern colleges in the form of three pamphlets.[40] Anne Goldgar argues that the tulip trade can be regarded as reckless gambling, bets on cows or any of the fancies that engrossed gaming Dutchmen.[41]

The last week of January and first of February 1637 marks the absolute acme of the tulip craze. In the pamphlets and songs of February and March, the crash is constantly portrayed as death. The plague raging in Amsterdam made this analogy a reality for the victims of the tulip trade.[42] At an auction to raise funds for the Orphans of Wouter Winkel, one individual purchased 21,000 guilders' worth of tulips, which was equivalent to two large houses in Amsterdam at the time.[43] Other exuberant examples noted by Dash include a mill that sold for a single tulip, a 30,000 franc brewery that sold for a single bulb and a bride's dowry that consisted of a single tulip.[44] The astonishing prices that were being asked for bulbs had even reached the cheaper bulbs sold as pound goods. Collectors would not touch them and most college florists were not interested in cultivating them. By early February, the wild trade in these second-class tulips made even devoted tulip maniacs uneasily aware that things were out of control. Anne Goldgar writes that the "why" remains unclear, though perhaps buyers feared the high prices were outrageous and could not be sustained.[45] Here and there, florists sold their holdings in a hurry and declined to reinvest their profits in more bulbs. In the tavern colleges across Holland, rival traders heard news of this and wondered if the sellers knew something that they did not. On February 3, 1637, the tulip trade burst.[46] A seller in Haarlem college started off at a fair price, yet nobody wanted to take his offer. He was met with total silence. Desperately, auctioneers offered bulbs for a third time, dropping prices. In a very short time, all the assumptions about the value of tulips had suddenly been shattered.

It took a few days for the panic to spread. The complete collapse of the tulip trade took around three months. A tulip worth 5,000 guilders before the crash was sold for only fifty guilders. The rapid increase of bulbs on the market was one of the causes of the crash because the higher prices rose, the fewer buyers there were for the amount of tulips that were to be purchased at those high prices. The high prices drove out everyone but the wealthy. The wealthy were connoisseurs who quickly deemed the cheaper bulbs as worthless. One of the greatest problems of the crash was that buyers had already made agreements even though the tulips were in the ground waiting to bloom. They were now worthless. They were contractually theirs and they were forced to pay the large sums that they had agreed on before the crash. "By valuing tulips over God, or indeed by valuing tulips over gold, *floristen* were showing a deplorable laxity of judgment", wrote Ann Goldgar, about the moment when the Dutch awoke to face their huge debts over the transitory flower.[47]

The largest bulb growers from all over the country decided to meet on February 23 to figure out how to diminish the financial effects of the crash. A compromise was made that all purchases before November 30 had to be paid but that any made after that date could be erased with a compensation fee of 10 percent of the sale price. The growers from Amsterdam refused to sign this agreement. The problem had to go to a higher authority. In April, the court of Holland admitted that it did not understand the mania completely and did not want to deal with the mess of angry buyers and sellers. The court decided to leave the problem to local towns.[48]

Effects of Tulipmania

To the Dutch humanists, the tulipmania had violated all their most sacred tenets: moderation, prudence and discretion. It had upset everything decent in Dutch life that believed in the proper relation between labor and reward; all had been fatally undermined by the wickedness of speculation. Many pamphlets were printed scorning tulipmania. The most famous of all, "Flora's car of fools" emphasizes the fool's hat; three of her attendants wear jester costumes festooned with the flowers while the fool's cap appears again on the flag at the back of the car. Nothing was more suitable for a satire on this trade than the "wind car". The print belongs to the tradition of the Antwerp *ommegang*, with its triumphal processions of vices and virtues. The tulipmania was represented through a form of graphic journalism that the Dutch were very fond of. It laid the ground for political prints and satires for the next generation. The obvious allusions in these prints would have been very clear to the Dutch who could read these emblems and symbols very much like a news gazette. When, in the 1730s, a similar craze for hyacinths took over for a while, the old tulip satires were reprinted for a new generation of speculators to warn them of the folly and corruption ahead.[49]

Merchants were long familiar with various means to hedge the risk of commerce. In fifteenth-century Venice, traders worked with bills of exchange to make sure to receive a collateral or personal bond to cover for counterparty risk. In the sixteenth century, Antwerp merchants were the first to take out insurance to cover the risk involved in bottomry loans that were only repaid upon a ship's safe arrival. These, and other techniques to minimize risk, had certainly spread to Amsterdam by the beginning of the seventeenth century. But Gelderblom and Jonker argue that we cannot tell whether stock traders in Amsterdam used them. Although evidence for self regulating, or forward and futures trading, in shares appears scant before 1650, we do possess a well documented example of how such a system of financing emerged in the commodity sector in the tulip trade before tulipmania gripped the Dutch countryside in 1636 and 1637. The tulip trade was based on, and is usually portrayed as, a form of speculative excess encouraged by taverns. However, Gelderblom and Jonker argue that there is a sober truth behind the drunken dealings of the tulip trade. On entering the inn, customers had to introduce themselves to the bookkeeper who then gave them a slate with their name for the purpose of bidding. The tulip trading clubs and their methods, as described above, proved very effective in smoothing transactions, which can make one conclude that the clubs acted as moderators of speculation and consumption, rather than as its drivers. This was the birth of derivatives. The aftermath of tulipmania demonstrates how widely the fundamentals of derivative trading had spread.[50]

When the court of Holland even refused to hear litigations issuing from the tulip sales, they judged them to be "bets" under Roman law and not transactions. It was left to individual city councils to clean up the mess after the bubble burst in February 1637.[51] Most local towns, after having mediated conversations decided to leave the issue to the individuals. This mediation, however, demonstrates that by the 1630s, city councils were sufficiently familiar with derivative trading to understand the core of the problem. The official adjustment by local authorities tarred all tulip transactions with the same brush, transforming all future transactions to be completed in two options. In the absence of firm documentary evidence, we can only surmise that these arrangements were copied from the Amsterdam securities market, where brokers presumably pioneered these new financial methods – which we consider novel – during the first quarter of the seventeenth century.[52]

Dutch Simplicity in Lifestyle and Art

Although the seventeenth century is considered a Golden Age for the Dutch when Amsterdam became the financial capital of Europe, most of the Dutch had a sober lifestyle. "Most portraits of wealthy seventeenth-century Dutch family members are formal, sober depictions of men and women in dark clothing, against a neutral background. Simple in pose and setting, they communicate moderation, restraint, calm and decorum."[53] The Dutch fetish for cleanliness is well known. Visitors would be required to wear slippers over their outdoor shoes to keep out dirt. Most Dutch interiors were sparsely decorated. An artisan house might boast a table, a simple cupboard, and perhaps a few chairs because it was expensive to acquire a bed. The cheapest varieties were called cupboard beds because they were set into a wall to help retain warmth. Often they were so small that they required their occupants to sleep in a sitting position. Only the members of the merchant class could afford a free-standing bed, which cost around a hundred guilders. Two national characteristics in the egalitarian United Provinces, the first republic in Europe, were the extraordinary beliefs in social mobility and in political equality. This was one of the main incentives for many to try their luck in the bulb trade. In their clothing, as in their furnishings, the Dutch were modest and conservative. This was not entirely due to their Calvinist faith, but to the remnants of Spanish court fashions.[54] Yet it is an error to make generalizations about Dutch fashion.

One cannot think of the Dutch as a Protestant Republic despite the prominence of Amsterdam. The Dutch distinguish between two major cultural subdivisions, and the southern part of the Netherlands was largely Catholic. The most important distinction was made between the *Randstad* (Rim City) and non-Randstad cultures. Randstad culture is urban, located in the provinces of North Holland, South Holland and Utrecht – it is mostly Protestant but many minorities also took refuge in Dutch cities. *Marranos,* Jews from Spain and Portugal, and Protestant merchants from the Spanish-ruled southern Netherlands (especially Antwerp) sought refuge in the Dutch Republic's cities in the sixteenth and seventeenth centuries. The non-Randstad culture corresponds to the historical divide between the predominantly Protestant north and the Catholic south, separated by the Rhine River.

Rembrandt often asked his Jewish neighbors in Amsterdam to model for his biblical scene paintings. A contrast between subjects painted by Jan Vermeer in Delft, a city south of the Rhine, and portraits made by famous portrait painters in the north in Haarlem shows distinct differences in dress. Jan Vermeer is the best known painter of Dutch domestic life today, yet was almost forgotten until 1866 when the art critic Thoré Burger published an essay attributing sixty-six pictures to him (only thirty-four paintings are firmly attributed to him today). Converted to Catholicism through marriage, like his father he ran an inn that was a center for art sales and in 1653 was elected dean of the Saint Luke guild of painters.[55] Vermeer mostly painted within Delft, and his fame never reached beyond his Catholic surroundings. His brilliant colors, especially his yellows and blues, mostly highlighted by folds in textiles worn by his subjects, are one of the reasons he is admired today. These vivid colors are not found on the habits worn by subjects painted in the northern, mostly Protestant towns of Haarlem or Amsterdam. A painting of the wealthy governors of the guild of St. Luke made in Haarlem in 1675 shows them wearing black robes.[56] Even portraits of wealthy women such as the portrait of Sophia Trip, wife of the merchant Balthasar Coymans, depicted her in a sober black dress topped by a lace collar.[57] She was the daughter of a major international merchant who handled trade all the way to Japan. Both portraits are by Bartholomeus van der Helst, who was the son of an innkeeper just like Vermeer. He became the main portraitist of the Amsterdam wealthy. All three painters were tied to inns that functioned as auction houses for paintings and other art objects. Rembrandt and Vermeer were collectors, sellers and buyers of artwork; through their inns as auction houses, their lives were marked by the business culture around them. The Dutch were avid consumers of culture. Today the curators of the Rijksmuseum in Amsterdam estimate that several million paintings were produced over the course of the seventeenth century for a population of about five million. According to them, it was the demand of the Dutch middle class that drove this market. English visitors were astonished to find the houses of Dutch farmers full of paintings.[58] Paintings, especially still lifes, were a major item of consumption and graced the wall of wealthy houses.[59] Van der Helst was a contemporary of Rembrandt and much influenced by him. His large group portrait, *Banquet of the Amsterdam Civic Guard in Celebration of the Peace of Münster*, was painted in 1648. Most of the men depicted in this celebration are wearing somber colors, black and gray predominantly followed by light browns. This contrasted greatly with the vivid colors worn by French notables, as we will demonstrate further below.

Simon Schama has wondered whether the Dutch, compared with other commercial cultures and in particular non-Calvinist cultures such as Venice and Antwerp, behaved differently in their consumption patterns. Based on the rhetoric about European parsimony, they may well seem to figure below the Calvinists of Geneva but above the Venetians, yet he argues that this is to mistake rhetoric for reality. For all the polemics against worldliness and luxury, there seems to be no reason to assume that the core group of Dutch society, from the elite down to the bottom, showed any special propensity to avoid consumption in favor of savings and investment. There were some Dutch writers who were not shy about celebrating the Republic as a consumer's paradise.[60] The walls of Dutch houses were covered with paintings. It was common for burgher (middle-class) families to own works of art. Most art historians have correctly surmised that low-life scenes and maid servant pictures seem to have been the cheapest while portraits were the most expensive, as might be expected. Compared with kitchen utensils and small furnishings, it was personal clothing that was the most expensive investment, but not the highest expenditure in the budget. It was not uncommon, for example, for a housewife to own thirty or more bonnets. Starched linen was the staple fabric of the Dutch. Twelve or even fourteen sets of bed linen for two or three beds, many napkins and handkerchiefs, were not unusual. The evidence of Amsterdam inventories suggests that around two-thirds of investments went to movable assets in domestic goods and furnishings and only a third went to clothing. For many among the Dutch, the display of status and fortune was expressed primarily in home comforts and not by the clothing they wore.[61] In neighboring France, clothing was a much clearer marker of status. The early part of the sixteenth century was still dominated by the dark colors favored by the Spanish court although the reign of Louis XIV was going to transform all that. Flamboyant color was going to become the mark of the *Ancien Régime* in France. In turn French fashions would eclipse Spanish fashions in the courts of Europe and Europe's aristocracy would begin to mimic French ways.[62]

To Each his Own Rank: Fashion and Sumptuary Laws

Social distinction through clothing and ornament was fundamental to a society of orders at the time of its formation. When, at the beginning of the seventeenth century, it was said that one should dress "in one's guise", it was meant that one should dress according to one's social condition. The sumptuary laws in most of Europe were there to prevent anyone from straying too far from their station. A magistrate who dressed like a nobleman broke the norms; in fact, he disguised himself and dressed wrongly. Parliament regularly fulminated against this at the end of the sixteenth century. In France, each order had its own badge: the clergy had the tonsure, the nobility had the sword and administrators had robes, long ones for the law and short ones for finance. As Daniel Roche has demonstrated, within the magistrates there were three hierarchies of distinction: form, fabric and color. Material provided a further means of distinction as sumptuary laws made a clear hierarchy of textiles. For example, in the chambers of recounts, the presidents alone enjoyed the right to lustrous silk velvet while only the *maîtres* and the King's men wore brilliant satins. Magistrates had the right to wear gowns of scarlet lined with flecks of ermine. In the King's council, the chancellor dressed in a long gown of crimson velvet, the counselors in long gowns of violet and the controllers and intendants of finance wore short gowns of the same color as the secretaries of state. Yet, the secretaries of state had the right to a long mantle while the secretaries wore short backed gowns and the ushers wore simple habits. A sumptuary order was thus clearly visible at the very heart of the kingdom but it was gradually eroded. There were many factors producing confusion. The domestic servants of the aristocracy are a case in point; the livery was to be in the colors of the house they served to affirm the powers of their masters. In practice, however, they exploited their reflected glory to behave insolently, acquiring the clothing habits of their masters and even transmitting them to others in town and country. The exchange of clothes between master and servant became a theme of seventeenth-century literature and theatre. While traditional dress valorized adhesion and social cohesion, innovation permitted diversity and free choice. Fashion, "that goddess of appearances", became the principal motor for change.[63]

In the first part of the seventeenth century, from Louis XIV's boyhood to his apogee in 1660, aristocrats took liberties to become the leaders of high fashion, the most famous of them being the Minister of Finance, Nicolas Fouquet. The arbitrary reign of tastes that decreed the cravat, a knee revealed by a boot or a lavish profusion of linens, went unbridled except by attempts to control this proliferation through sumptuary laws or a proclamation by the court of a model of male and female dress. Suddenly, in 1660, the young Louis XIV took charge of fashion single handedly like everything else. Fashion became part of his plan for political absolutism.[64] As Jennifer Jones has shown, in 1664, Louis XIV had officially created a French court dress. He created a *justecorps à brevet*, which was a brocade outer vest, light blue on the outside, lined with scarlet and embroidered with gold and silver. This short vest guaranteed the wearer court privileges, such as following the King in Saint Germain or Versailles. The vest became hereditary. The elaboration of a female court dress was also something he controlled. His minister Colbert hoped to support the French silk industry through new court fashions.[65]

The dress of the nobility had its place within an important luxury economy on which it had considerable impact through the manufacturing of cloth and the new commercialization of high fashion through imitation. Conspicuous consumption permitted social differentiation through the constant competition for rank and prestige that Louis XIV had initiated. Norbert Elias' theories on the civilizing effect of the court were based on Louis XIV's court.[66] His theories about self-affirmation through imitation, and hence considerable expenditure that constantly grew, were nowhere more apparent than among the courtiers of Louis XIV. Their clothing demonstrates the social mechanisms of court society in action. From Louis XIV to Louis XVI, from brilliant favorites to the frivolous young Queen Marie Antoinette, the speed of court fashions created tensions and disequilibria at the very heart of French politics.[67]

Marketing within the Fashion Industry

While people have always dressed fashionably, the marketing industry behind fashion was born in 1670s Paris.[68] Giorgio Riello and other scholars have successfully argued that fashion was born in fourteenth-century Italian cities, but the pace created at Louis' court and the industry attached to it led other scholars to believe that the birth of modern fashion happened in France under the leadership of Louis XIV. The King was at the center of creating new fashion that the *couturières* had to follow, but the fashion would not have reached across geographical and social boundaries without court propaganda.[69]

Joan DeJean points out that Jean Donneau de Visé created the first fashion magazine in history. Entitled *Le Mecure galant* (Galant Mercury), it was first published in 1672 and covered the social scene at court, news of arts and letters, of trends, decoration and style. De Visé was the King's historiographer and the first newsman to report on the fashion scene. From the start, *Le Mecure galant* reached out to one audience that had never been specifically targeted: women. It was not aimed at the court women or those in the capital of Paris because they could observe the trends for themselves; rather, it was aimed at women stuck in the provinces who dreamt of becoming as chic as the *parisiennes*. Donneau de Visé had several new concepts, one of them being fashion seasons. He argued that it was not only necessary to change one's clothing when the weather changed, but also the minute one noticed other women dressing in the same manner. Donneau de Visé's fashion seasons became more powerful at court than the weather. Before it was warm enough, fashionistas started parading around in new spring fashions. He also argued that there were colors to each season. The fall of 1678 was tinted in shades of grey, mouse grey and pearly grey, but absolutely not the linen grey he had featured the summer before. All these changes meant increased revenues for the textile industry, whether it was master dye craftsmen or weavers. The wheels of color turned so quickly that many hues didn't even last the entire season.[70]

Accessories also began to be reinvented on a seasonal basis under Donneau de Visé's pen. In 1679, *Le Mercure* ruled that narrow ribbons would reign over the summer fashions. Nicolas de Blégny, the court's physician, before he wrote on coffee, had written an insider guide to Paris in which he recorded the best shopping addresses. He informed consumers on such things as to where the best ribbons could be found. Fashions became crazes for exotic goods. Donneau de Visé announced the availability of fabulous hand-painted stockings with charming figures all the way from China. He also intimated that ladies who wore these patterned stockings must show off their legs: otherwise it would be useless to wear them.[71] Luxury depended on highly labor-intensive detailing such as embroidery, lace and ribbons.

Siamese Frenzy

Sometimes the fashion season was dominated by a special event. After the visit of the Siamese delegation to Paris in the winter of 1687, Parisian ladies were dressed à la Anna and the King of Siam, in a striped fabric known as Siamese cloth. This was in honor of the Siamese embassy when exotic visitors were the center of fashion in the French capital. For the French treasury and Louis XIV's ever-vigilant Minister Colbert, luxurious fashions were a boon as long as fabrics, stocking, lace and ribbons were made in France. When French designers started trends based on exotic imports, making money against the national textile industry, it was a different proposition.[72] French curiosity about the Siamese visitors was so high that Dirk Van der Cruysse tells us that Donneau de Visé, the director of *Le Mercure*, produced a "Siamese frenzy", with over 2,000 pages about the visitors.[73] There were several French accounts of the Siamese visit and three entire volumes of the news gazette *Mercure de France* that were exclusively devoted to the exotic dress, mores and moods of the Siamese visitors in France.[74] At least five almanacs – a new tool of propaganda for the court – were also printed to commemorate the event with images. This propaganda literature, controlled by the court, was so well circulated that it sparked Parisians' interest in Siamese fashions, some promptly adopted by the aristocracy. The Siamese, on the other hand, were awed by the luxury in France and were busy recording it. Kosapan, the ambassador, wrote an entire page describing his French bed in intricate detail. He described its height, its width and the curtains of luxurious crimson silk, the gold tassels and the precious wood.[75]

One French technical feat fascinated the Siamese visitors. France had recently stolen the secret of making large mirrors from Venice. The 1682 inauguration of the mirrors at Versailles was described in *Le Mercure galant* as "a dazzling mass of riches and lights, duplicated a thousand times over in just as many mirrors, creating views more brilliant than fire and where a thousand things more sparkling came into play. Add to that the splendor that was the court's finery and the gleam of their precious jewelry."[76] The gems imported from Asia were certainly more familiar to the Siamese embassy than the mirrors reflecting the gems. The enormous new mirrors at Versailles were, save for woolens, one of the rare items manufactured in Europe that were of any interest on Asia's markets. The *galérie des glaces* was new and dazzling to all visitors at Versailles. On the occasion of the embassy, the Siamese ambassador was given a large mirror as a gift. It was a promotional gift as the King hoped that the Siamese would purchase French mirrors. Indeed the Siamese put in an order to purchase thousands of them.[77]

The many items that were included in the order were diverse. The 160 French cannons were predictable, as were telescopes, glasses and clocks, but more interesting were a list of luxuries: a number of ceremonial velvet and gold masks for the beloved elephants of the palace, elephant harnesses made of red cloth lined with leather decorated with copper stars, 2,000 crystal ornaments to serve as ornaments on two animals, a male and female elephant. The ambassadors also ordered two globes, one terrestrial and one celestial, with inscriptions giving the correct information transcribed in Siamese letters, which must have been a feat for French artisans. Seven very large rugs came from the rug manufacture of the Savonnerie. The rugs were often the best diplomatic gift offered by France; the Siamese order was proof that the manufacture established by Louis XIII to make carpets "*à la façon de Turquie*" in 1627 had gained international reputation as a French luxury. The largest order was for the manufacture of mirrors established by Colbert at Saint Gobain; it received an order for 4,264 mirrors.[78] This was a first. Traditionally luxuries traveled to France and were not exported from France. European courts and grandees were avid collectors and consumers of Asian goods, creating a very imbalanced trade situation. Versailles itself was a display of luxury. Louis had amassed the best gemstone collection in Europe.[79] With the 1686 Siamese Embassy came several important gifts that would further contribute to the palace's oriental splendor: gold, tortoiseshells, fabrics, carpets, over 1,500 pieces of porcelain and many pieces of lacquer furniture.[80]

Parisians waited in the streets for hours in order to catch a glimpse of the Siamese visitors, but the Siamese were very busy; the *Mercure* reported that every evening they locked themselves in to record everything they saw in Paris.[81] Nevertheless, despite its luxury, the French court, in its images of itself, seemed intent on depicting its consumption as more austere than it really was. Engravings depicted Louis XIV's court as indifferent to the temptations of exotic gems and oriental luxuries. In most of the engravings that depicted Versailles, none of the luxury described above is visible. During the latter part of Louis XIV's reign, the King's austere Catholic views would become dominant.

The conflicting views held about luxury in the late seventeenth century were central to such a double discourse. Views about luxury were fast changing but still deeply marked by the negative attitude of the Catholic Church.

The Reformation added its own views, tying luxury to corruption. The positive views of opulence put forth by the gazettes speak of a new desire for unrestrained consumption and show at Versailles, a feature that was a turning point in Louis XIV's image building.[82] By the end of his reign, Paris had a worldwide reputation for luxury, not only for the grand scale of consumption at Versailles, but also for the luxury goods in Parisian shops and markets. Joan DeJean argued and demonstrated that the consumption of luxury itself was invented during Louis XIV's reign.[83]

The First Idolized French Model: The Fashion Doll

Sumptuary legislation controlled the consumption of luxury goods and largely restricted them to the nobility until the laws were repealed by Louis XV (r. 1715–1774). Despite the fact that the laws were broken, gems, silk and gold were still identified with the nobility, and as such were markers of class. There was good reason to depict oneself as frugal, as there was a long tradition of negative views about luxury in France. The construction of Versailles itself is enough to demonstrate the King's love of luxury, but to appear ostentatious was another issue. Many of these debates about luxury, consumption and production in France were older and stemmed from views about the New World, Habsburg gold, colonization and French trade with Asia. The consumption of luxury goods was the concern of successive governments who dealt with sumptuary laws and of philosophers concerned about theory. A trade policy since the end of fifteenth century, mercantilism was an old, zero-sum view of an economy meant to protect France against foreign imports and to conserve bullion.[84] The negative discourse on luxury was present since ancient and medieval times within the Church, but the debate over luxury and its consumption became a roaring debate a century later in the years preceding the French Revolution.[85] Selling luxury would protect France's economy.

Joan DeJean has argued that the newly invented fashion plate began selling more than actual clothing; it advertised the French aristocratic way of life. Fashion plates were confirming and marketing the notion that France and the French had a monopoly on style, sophistication and luxury.[86] The fashion doll was the first marketing device that targeted an international customer base. In the late 1670s, designers sent Donneau de Visé small mannequins decked out in the latest styles. Jean Bérain, the court designer, sketched the dolls as the basis for the illustrations used for *Le Mercure galant* as fashion plates. It was soon realized that these tiny models could be sent to shops around the world to show off the season's fashion. The arrival of the doll from Paris was anxiously awaited and an event covered in contemporary newspapers. Many early fashion dolls were mostly made of wood and sometimes had human hair so that they could also do double duty to advertise the latest hairdos fashionable in Paris. Fashion dolls made long journeys, arriving in shops in Boston and New York where they could be viewed for a fixed sum. These viewings highlight the dolls' limitations as a marketing tool. In fact it was fashion engravings or plates that circulated most widely, for DeJean has argued that by the 1680s the equivalent of *Vogue* or *Elle* was already in place.[87]

Fashion and power went hand in hand. Paris fashions were international; many courts wore French fashion by the late seventeenth century, just as they had worn Spanish fashions in the sixteenth. The English court was a case in point. Ribbons and huge wigs popularized by the French court reigned supreme. Louis XIII, also known as Louis the Bald, starting wearing wigs to cover up his thinning hair. However, it is not until the reign of Louis XIV that wearing wigs became a fashion statement among the rich and powerful. Initially, these new, very high wigs were a French fashion. Louis XIV's cousin, Charles II, who took a ten-year refuge in France after being exiled from England, brought the wig fashion to England with him once he was restored to the English throne. Under Louis XIV and Charles II, wigs were often worn in their natural colors. The habit of powdering wigs was popularized in France after the 1690s.[88] Powdering wigs was considered an aesthetic but also a hygienic measure.

Textiles: Hygiene and Comfort

The seventeenth century saw radical changes in the notion of cleanliness. As Jean-Louis Flandrin has argued, the individual place setting and individual utensils replace the less hygienic common bowl and drinking vessel.[89] Scholars have proposed that linens acquired an intrinsic connection with the new culture of cleanliness in Early Modern Europe. This concept of cleanliness was based on textiles touching the body rather than on bathing or on ablutions on the body. Physical comfort was related firstly to undergarments touching the body and from there to the bed where white linen sheets, nightcaps and nightgowns were seen as necessary for health and comfort among the elite. The hygienic and sanitary connotation of linen made it the most popular textile both for clothing and domestic use well into the late eighteenth century. The replacement of woolen hangings with linen provided a dramatic drop in the bugs and vermin that had for centuries infested beds, pillows, bolsters and bed curtains. It has been argued by Giorgio Riello that linen's identification with cleanliness was shifted from the intimacy of the bed into the realm of polite social interaction as napkins and tablecloths became omnipresent. They conveyed notions of wealth and established precise gender relationships in the management of the household. Gender relationships in seventeenth-century Dutch households were mediated through the symbolic and practical function of linen chests as textiles functioned as spatial markers of status. Women, as the key holders of the chest, controlled the right of access to the textile treasures within the chest. Despite the fact that these were centuries of war and famines, historians have suggested a rise in the physical presence of textiles in the seventeenth and eighteenth centuries in European households.[90]

The long history of achieving comfort has been central in explaining the use of textiles, especially upholstery, in the material life of the home. The division between domestic and clothing textiles became more marked in the Early Modern period. Textiles were key to European interiors. The use of wood in Japan or China allowed for better-insulated and lighter spaces. The tents used by wealthy elites in India were admired for their rich colors and designs. Fernand Braudel has underlined the different ways in which material culture was understood at the opposite ends of Eurasia. In Europe, rather than being in competition, textiles and furnishings went hand in hand.[91] The bed, which was the bedrock of the house, was the most prized piece of furniture but also the most important space for textile use and display. Several layers of textiles, including quilts, coverlets, sheets and pillows completed the bed. Heavy bed curtains provided protection from the cold and refuge for intimacy. The bed was central to the lives of the poor and rich alike. Beds were bequeathed to loyal servants or given as charitable gifts to hospitals and institutions. It was not uncommon for French households to invest 20 to 40 percent of their wealth in a bed. In North America, Adrienne Hood (cited in Riello) studied the role of textiles in creating and consuming the wealth of prosperous households in late seventeenth century Pennsylvania. She calculated that a family of six would need about forty-five yards of cloth a year just to replace a minimal amount of worn fabric.[92]

During the seventeenth century, especially in northwestern Europe, it was not uncommon to replace traditional linen tablecloths with more sophisticated, fashionable and expensive Turkish rugs. Middle class Parisian consumers preferred Auvergne tapestries. At the top of the social ladder, the very rich could afford Flemish tapestries. Wallpaper and wood paneling were also new options that transcended textiles and were possible thanks to new standards of warmth and lower humidity in interiors. The strong French tradition of textile wall decoration also meant a new engagement with exotic textiles such as velvets, *brocatelles*, *siamois*, silk moiré and printed cottons. Louis XIV's admiration for the Emperor of China was only the beginning of a taste for Chinese fashions that would dominate the next century. Louis corresponded with the Emperor of China. Beyond the court, the display of the exotic was used to pursue strategies of social, cultural and economic advancement.[93]

Chinese Fashion and Technology

In the seventeenth century, China remained closed to foreigners despite the arrival of the Portuguese at the end of the sixteenth century. In 1601, the Jesuit missionary Matteo Ricci received permission to go to the capital, Beijing. He presented the Emperor with a harpsichord, a map of the world and two ornate mechanical clocks that chimed. He presented himself to Emperor Wanli's court as a scientist specialized in astronomy, geography, geometry and arithmetic. His entrance at court was not as a missionary, but as a representative of the new technical advances made in Europe. His aim was

Christianization but he had prepared his entrance at court very carefully. Jonathan Spence writes that no Westerner had ever come near to attaining Ricci's level of knowledge of Chinese culture and society. He realized that in order to convince the Chinese to convert to Christianity, he had to demonstrate the superiority of Western culture. In pursuit of this goal, he produced a global map with commentary in Chinese in order to demonstrate the high level of astronomy and geography that had been attained in his country of origin. He also wrote a now famous manual on memory theory to show his Chinese hosts how the West organized knowledge. With the help of highly educated Chinese collaborators, he also translated the opening chapters of Euclid's geometry.[94]

According to Spence, Ricci left a long description of China that was mostly very favorable; he made very few criticisms of the Chinese in his lengthy manuscript. For the development of science, he argued that China had fallen behind simply because it failed to develop to its full potential. Just like his predecessors Galeote Pereira, Gaspar da Cruz and Mendes Pinto in their descriptions of the Chinese, Ricci had only one harsh criticism of Chinese society. He asserted that Chinese men were drawn to homosexual practices and gave as evidence the elaborately dressed male prostitutes visible on the streets of Beijing. Ricci estimated that there were 40,000 female prostitutes in the capital. Like the travel account of da Cruz, Ricci's view of prostitution in China was rather benign and gave him room to argue that one should pray for their salvation.[95] Most strikingly he was so obsessed by demonstrating European science that he never noticed the strength of Chinese technology.

A Manual of Chinese Technology

Chinese technology was quite advanced but very different from what European observers expected. There exists a manual on Chinese technology in the seventeenth century written in 1637 by one of the last public officials in the Ming Dynasty. It is an exceptional treatise on the history of traditional Chinese technology, but it is by no means unique. Its Chinese title translates as "The Creations of Nature and Man". It is by far one of the most complete of such manuals because it is of encyclopedic range. It covers all of the industrial techniques of its time, including agriculture, textiles, mining, metalwork, chemical engineering and the manufacture of weapons and boats. In it one can find details of what was cultivated as grains, what was used as clothing materials and details on ceramics. It is invaluable for many details: dyes, salt, ceramics, casting bells and cooking pots, paper, vermilion and ink. It also describes different pearls and gems that can help the reader reconstitute what was valuable among the elite. It also contains a description of minting: "for the convenience of the people, copper is minted into coins and circulated. On one side are inscribed characters indicating it is 'currency' of a given Dynasty, and the affairs concerning copper money are administered by a bureau in the Board of Works".[96] The manual goes on to say that the disadvantage of coins was that they could easily be minted illegally, which was harmful to the people and therefore, in all parts of the empire, circulation of the coins was frequently stopped. It goes on to describe the proportions of copper to zinc, the process of minting and the different kinds of coins, such as tin, iron and silver. The manual is richly illustrated by 150 woodcuts that demonstrate the techniques that are described. The chapter on sugar describes the whole process from the planting of sugarcane, the varieties of sugarcane planted and the manufacture of sugar in China. The making of white sugar is elaborately described and the percentage of the total sucrose is given as well as what remains in the solution as molasses. The manual states that to make rock sugar, the "Western sugar", one has to have the addition of albumen followed by skimming off the floating scum of the egg whites. When the correct temperature was reached, the sugar was split with blue-green bamboo, cut into bits, thrown back into the syrup and left overnight. The sugar then naturally crystallized into "rocks". There were five grades of white sugar, the best was "Rock Mountain" followed by "Clustered Branch", then "Glossy Jar" and "Small Grain". The lowest grade was called "Sandy Bottom". There follows an elaborate description of animal-shaped candy. Sugar was used to make lions, elephants and dolls.[97] This was done with the use of cold molds and hot syrup. The manual states that this was called "feast candy" and was used at banquets. Chapter five is devoted to salt. It describes the different sources of salt in China: sea salt, lake salt, well salt, powdered salt from soil and red rock salt. Rock salt was freely obtainable by scraping and was sold without refining. Salt was a state-controlled business and the manual states that the operators of the salt wells in Szechuan and Yunan managed to avoid paying the salt tax by covering up the wells.[98] The very detailed chapter on clothing materials opens with the statement:

> Master Sung observes that, man being the highest of all forms of life on earth his five senses and the numerous organs are all completely present and should be preserved. Members of the aristocracy are clothed in flowing robes decorated with patterns of magnificent mountain dragons and they are the rulers of the country. Those of lowly stations would be dressed in hempen jackets and cotton garments to protect themselves from the cold in winter and cover their nakedness in summer in order to distinguished themselves from the birds and the beasts. Therefore, nature has provided the materials for clothing.[99]

The manual states that beauty and plainness, as well as the high and low status of man in the world, are provided by nature. Next to explanations such as all materials are derived from vegetables, animals and insects, one finds a more legendary tone. It is asserted that the loom was first invented by a divine maiden who brought this skill to mankind. The chapter continues with an elaborate and precise description of the weaving of silk as well as the rearing, care and feeding of silkworms. There is a description of diseases, pests and of the sorting of the cocoons. Every step of the process is illustrated by a woodcut. The most striking is a woodcut of mature silkworms spinning cocoons on large bamboo screens. The dragon robes destined for the Imperial palace were woven in specific factories in Suzhou and Hangzhou. The manual states that two highly skilled artisans manipulate the "draw board" in accordance with a prepared figure design of the shape of the woven dragon which consistently changes after every few inches of weave. The design was the result of the collective effort of all the government establishments and never the work of an individual designer. For the Emperor, the silk was dyed yellow before weaving. "It is not possible to know the minute details involved in the weaving of these robes".[100]

A Brief History of Chinese Fashion

Despite the fact that many well-known scholars, among them Fernand Braudel, have argued for the "Asiatic mode of production", which implies that China did not embrace change, and therefore did not embrace fashion, there is ample evidence that China had dynamic commercial markets. A new school of scholarship has argued that the Chinese elite participated in consumption and followed trends in fashion. As Kenneth Pomeranz and other scholars have demonstrated, fashion is by no means solely a European phenomenon, even if it is culturally different.[101]

Clothing is among the main indices of the dynamic economic life of the urban centers of southern China. In the early seventeenth century, Gu Qiyuan (1565–1628) wrote about women's fashions in Nanjing. He wrote that while they used to change every ten years in the past, there was now a change in clothing trends every three or four years with a new style appearing regularly. The urban center of Suzhou at this time was playing a role similar to that of Paris in Europe, setting the tone for novel and extravagant styles of clothing. By 1614 black hats and clothes of white cotton had been replaced by colored clothing and changing fashions. Gu Qiyuan's commentary was on the rhythm of consumption and not on expenditure, but it gives serious grounds for arguing for changing fashions in late Ming China. In this period there was much talk of "outrageous dress" because of a proliferation of disturbing novel fashions in the urban centers of the lower Yangtze valley.[102]

Usually a discussion of Chinese fashion concentrates on the dragon robes and on museum pieces that belonged to the imperial palace.[103] There is ample proof of policy establishing fashion changes well beyond the palace during the Ming dynasty. As the Ming came to power in the fourteenth century, they decided to rid the empire of the barbarian costume of the Yuan era. This meant abandoning the tunics favored by the Mongols and returning to what was considered the Chinese style of the Tang dynasty (618–907). This return to the ideal of Chinese clothing was close to impossible because many descendants of the Mongol invaders were still part of the population of China.

Despite this policy, there were three different manifestations of fashion during the Ming dynasty that were exotic rather than Chinese. The first was horse-hair skirts from Korea and the second a military-style tunic inspired by the nomad warriors of the north. Both were part of new male fashions that developed first in the capital and then spread beyond it. The third trend appeared by the late fifteenth century, when local weavers had mastered the art of weaving horsehair garments, and in order to do so were stealing the tails of horses owned by officials.

In the sixteenth century, the military-style tunic evolved into the commonly worn *yesa*, which was worn with a pleated skirt and became the most popular way to dress for wealthy men in the sixteenth century. In the course of the sixteenth century, the *yesa* displaced two other styles of tunic and became the mark of all the grandees. Whether or not integrated with an upper garment, a flared, gathered or sometimes pleated skirt became a common look in male clothing.[104] Officials wore the biretta, scholars wore the square hat, but Gu Qiyuan writes that for hats there was something new every month. He cites the Han cap, the Jin cap and the Tang cap as examples. Illustrations of these hats are included in his treatise. The hat was an important element of the male wardrobe in China and a sign of social status. Nevertheless, it was not the only sign of ostentation. Expensive Tang style satins and Song style brocades became all the rage. Antonia Finnane argues that these "new and strange" styles flourished in the period known for its social climbing. For China she refers to Thorstein Veblen and Georg Simmel who have both argued that social emulation was the driving force behind fashion. Sumptuary regulations restricted the use of certain fabrics and types of adornment, but they were flouted with impunity by both merchant and common families in the commercial economy of the sixteenth and seventeenth centuries.[105]

Prostitutes and courtesans were probably the models for the paintings of women that have left us some images for the clothing worn in the Ming and Qing dynasties. These illustrations, along with artifacts from tombs and textual references, point to a number of styles in late Ming women's dress. They show the classic short jacket (*ru*) worn with a skirt and short overskirt. Skirts were also worn with a long jacket called *ao* or the open-sided gown, the *bigia*. A long over-jacket, called *pifeng*, was one of the most common. Historically, the most important development in women's dress during the Ming dynasty is the prevalence of long upper garments at the expense of the short jacket.[106] The sleeves of the *pifeng* changed until they were extended, going well over the fingertips, and the trend for gradually descending hems threatened to cover skirts completely. The *pifeng* came very close to looking like a man's tunic and created anxieties among the officials who attempted to reverse this trend in the sixteenth century. In order to attempt to eradicate a possible confusion between male and female, the Minister of Rites in Nanjing attempted to reverse the trend with a decree.

Craig Clunas, in his book *Superfluous Things*, describes the degree of high sophistication reached by the Ming cultural market. He sees it as a powerful expression of Pierre Bourdieu's ideas about "distinction", a way for fashion to express the role of rank and maintain socio-cultural hierarchies.[107] Clunas analyzes the language of elite writers and the types of Ming discourse there was about objects in a number of sources. For example, a manual regularly calls things *shiyang*, literally "the pattern of the day", clearly meaning fashionable. Affirming rank through consumption became perhaps even more important as distinction between menial men and women and those of free status, among scholars, merchants, and peasants, rich and poor became increasingly blurred as the economy commercialized. Ever-greater numbers of families aspired to genteel status, educating their sons, investing in land, collecting *objets d'art*, and accumulating women.[108] Although this was not a new change, it was a reality that became more prevalent in seventeenth-century Ming China as commercialization accelerated. Generalizations about the movement of prices in the Ming period are hard to make, but they have been used by socio-economic historians in the Braudelian tradition to produce a rough chart. Rice was twice as expensive in the decade 1641–1650 than 100 years earlier. There was a steep rise in the price of foodstuffs in general and other necessities, but a decline in the price of non-essential goods. China was experiencing a "price revolution" every bit as dramatic as Europe.[109] If the theory holds then it was experiencing a strong consumer culture with fashions to show for it.

One of the luxury items consumed that had the greatest differentiation in quality was silk textiles. The impression that silk textiles were relatively expensive and made in very different qualities is borne out by the prices quoted in the late Ming novel of *nouveau riche* life, *The Golden Lotus*. Written somewhere between 1582 and 1596, the material it contains on prices can be crosschecked with data in other sources. The novel goes into areas of consumption that Clunas writes "we would like to know much more about".[110] Traces of prices for material culture are not abundant. For example, the Japanese scholar Isobe Akira has found three references to the cost of books in the late sixteenth and early seventeenth centuries. Clunas writes that if we attempt to say something about the "commodity context" of Ming luxuries, we are even more bereft of hard information. He points to the fact that there is clearly reluctance in the sources to discuss prices in any detail. He finds implicit and explicit distaste for the notion of speaking openly of a work of art as a commodity. Clunas finds a studied vagueness of language used to cloud the fact of trade in prestigious items. Nevertheless, he argues that this unwillingness to articulate the workings of the market does not contradict the existence of a vigorous market and of a variety of transactions in which objects and works of art could be acquired and sold. Works of art could be sold individually or as complete family collections. At the end of the fifteenth century, two eunuchs paid the immense purchase price of 40,000 ounces of silver for the collection of Mu Zong, descendant of a Ming general, ruler of the province of Yunnan. The share of one of these eunuchs, who of course had no progeny, passed to a nephew, himself also probably a eunuch, and then to his younger brother before being broken up piecemeal at the end of the sixteenth century. Inheritance was an important method of transfer, but it was also known for sales to take place within a family.[111]

Pawnshops acted as places where *objets d'art* could be acquired and some specialized in very high value goods. Antique stores can be seen in some seventeenth century woodcut illustrations, exposed to the street similar to establishments selling textiles, medicines or grain.[112] Shops were closely associated with dwellings, even those of the grandest sort. In *Jin ping mei*, perhaps the most famous novel of the seventeenth century, the main character's silk shop and pawnshop are in the front of residential premises. In the same source, in the 1640s a grand secretary is recorded as having installed a jewelry shop in the street frontage of his Beijing mansion. Clunas quips that is not so much this fact that is worthy of note, but the scandal that the shop was used as a front for the reception of bribes. Luxury shops and businesses associated with the antiques trade were clustered in the famous Zhuanzhu Lane in Suzhou. Yet shops catering to the elite could just as well be situated outside the city walls in scenic spots. There was a parade of shops specializing in luxury ceramics, including *Yixing* teapots, a couple of miles outside the city of Wuxi. Periodic markets offered antiques mixed with contemporary luxuries such as silk textiles and decorated writing paper together with imported curiosities such as Tibetan bronze Buddhas or images of Jesus from the "Western Ocean". There was also a market at the rear gate of the palace in Beijing held on the fourth day of every month, notorious for selling smuggled items from the imperial collection. Clunas writes that some of the operators here could be working on a very small scale and utilized shady tactics.[113]

Portraits and other sources of the early Qing suggest that the *pifeng* was a style that lasted into the early eighteenth century. According to Pomeranz, the Qing dynasty (1644–1911) was a period where fashion experienced a decline. This is refuted by Antonia Finnane who finds sources that suggest a steady consumption of fashion during this period. The source material is not as abundant, but she argues that there is enough to permit a nuanced vestimentary history other than one written based on imperial dragon robes. The poet and dramatist Kong Shangren (1648–1718) writing in Yangzhou in the 1680s wrote about "accountants, clerks, slaves, and servants" of the wealthy households of his city dressing up in flashy clothes and putting on great airs to snub others.[114] Li Dou, a great chronicler of eighteenth century Yangzhou, had much the same to say a century later. The criteria of Chinese fashion in the late imperial era were not quite the same as in Europe because cut and fit were far less significant in China than the quality and the color of the textiles. Li Dou itemized not so much the shapes and fit of what he saw around him, but the different sorts of cloth that went in and out of fashion in Yangzhou. He cataloged the silks and satins in the different colors that rapidly succeeded each other in popularity. Next to textiles, it is hairstyles on which he focuses his attention. Much like hats for men, there was a thriving market for false hairpieces and hair adornments.[115]

When the Qing assumed power in the middle of the seventeenth century, they maintained the social and political distinctions between their Chinese subjects and the other groups, the Mongols chief among them. The success of this Manchu dynasty was predicated upon ensuring the collaboration of the Chinese, particularly the scholarly class who provided the bureaucratic administration they needed. The identification of these servants of the new state was established by a new dress code and Chinese men were forced to shave the front of the head and wear the remainder in a long braid in the Manchu style. These officials now had to wear conical straw or bamboo hats adorned with red silk cords in the summer and fur-trimmed hats with blue satin in the winter. A single long robe continued to be the mark of a man of education with a high social status, but the wide sleeves of the Ming dynasty were replaced with close-fitting sleeves with horseshoe-shaped cuffs. The regulation governing dress under the Qing is notable for being directed more at keeping distinctions of rank rather than maintaining gender differences. The wife of an official wore a plaque on her outer garment that matched that of her husband, plainly demonstrating that she shared his rank. There were some marks of differentiation; some women's robes were distinguished by extra bands of ornament for noblewomen. Women's robes in general were slit at the sides, while men's were slit front and rear to allow for horseback riding.[116]

William Alexander (1767–1816), a draughtsman who accompanied Lord McCartney and his embassy to China, provided illustrations to accompany the account of the embassy written by George Leonard Staunton (1737–1801). Entitled *The Costume of China,* it was published at about the same time as another book on Chinese clothing written by George Mason who had been long resident in Canton. The latter consisted of sixty engravings of Chinese daily life based on the watercolors made by a Chinese artisan who signed his name Pu Qua. Mason's book, with text in both French and English, was aimed for a European readership that was avidly interested in China. The production of these two large expensive illustrated volumes, both called *The Costume of China*, is a testament to Europe's interest in Chinese clothing.[117] At the time the fashion for *chinoiserie* was at its height in Europe.[118] It was the arrival of oriental luxury goods in vast quantities that was key in sparking a debate about luxury.[119] The tide would turn and perception of these luxury goods as "foreign" was to build some political resistance to consuming them in the eighteenth century.

Study Questions

1 Did European consumption habits and tastes spread to Europe's colonies?
2 What does tulipmania uncover about how goods were valued by consumers in a society?
3 How did the Dutch Republic and the French monarchy differ in their ways of displaying consumption?

4 Did religious belief reinforce or conflict with consumption in the Dutch Republic and Bourbon France?
5 Was fashion a Western phenomenon in Early Modern times?

Notes

1 James Cawthorn, *On Taste* (1756). As cited in Robert A. Leath "'After the Chinese Taste': Chinese Export Porcelain and Chinoiserie Design in Eighteenth-Century Charleston", *Historical Archaeology*, Vol. 33, No. 3, Charleston in the Context of Trans-Atlantic Culture (1999), 48–61.
2 Leath, "After the Chinese Taste", 50.
3 Maxine Berg and Elizabeth Eger, eds., *Luxury in the Eighteenth Century*: *Debates, Desires and Delectable Goods* (Basingstoke, Hampshire; New York: Palgrave, 2003), 230–235.
4 Lisa Jardine, *Going Dutch: How England Plundered Holland's Glory* (New York: Harper, 2008), 14–16.
5 Jardine, *Going Dutch*, 7.
6 Jardine, *Going Dutch*, Ch. 7–8, 175–232.
7 Jardine, *Going Dutch*, 261.
8 Jardine, *Going Dutch*, 261.
9 Madeleine Jarry, *Chinoiserie: Chinese Influence on European Decorative Art, 17th and 18th Centuries* (New York: Vendome Press, 1981).
10 Anne Goldgar, *Tulipmania: Money, Honor and Knowledge in the Dutch Golden Age* (Chicago: University of Chicago Press, 2007).
11 Anne Goldgar, "Nature as Art: The Case of the Tulip" in Pamela H. Smith and Paula Findlen, eds., *Merchants & Marvels: Commerce, Science, and Art in Early Modern Europe* (New York; London: Routledge, 2002), 324–336, 325.
12 Goldgar, "Nature as Art", *Merchants and Marvels,* 325.
13 Goldgar, "Nature as Art", *Merchants & Marvels,* 330.
14 Goldgar, "Nature as Art", *Merchants & Marvels,* 331.
15 Goldgar, "Nature as Art", *Merchants & Marvels,* 332.
16 Mike Dash, *Tulipomania: The Story of the World's most Coveted Flower and the Extraordinary Passions it Aroused* (Great Britain: Indigo, 2000), 7.
17 Dash, *Tulipomania*, 78.
18 Dash, *Tulipomania*, 10.
19 Dash, *Tulipomania*, 20–21.
20 Dash, *Tulipomania*, 22
21 Ariel Salzmann, "The Age of Tulips: Confluence and Conflict in Early Modern Consumer Culture (1550–1730)" in Donald Quataert, ed, *Consumption Studies and the History of the Ottoman Empire, 1550–1922* (Albany, NY: State University of New York Press, 2000), 83–106.
22 Dash, *Tulipomania*, 43.
23 Dash, *Tulipomania*, 46–63.
24 Dash, *Tulipomania*, 75–79.
25 Goldgar, *Tulipmania*, 8–9.
26 Simon Schama, *The Embarrassment of Riches: An Interpretation of Dutch Culture in the Golden Age* (Berkeley; Los Angeles; London: University of California Press, 1988), 353–354.
27 Goldgar, *Tulipmania*, 200.
28 Goldgar, *Tulipmania*, 226.
29 Dash, *Tulipomania*, 125.
30 Dash, *Tulipomania*, 108.

31 Schama, *The Embarrassment of Riches*, 358.
32 Goldgar, *Tulipomania*, 7.
33 Dash, *Tulipmania*, 128.
34 Goldgar, *Tulipmania*, 221.
35 Dash, *Tulipmania*, 150.
36 Goldgar, *Tulipmania*, 17–18.
37 Goldgar, *Tulipmania*, 142.
38 Goldgar, *Tulipmania*, 20–25.
39 Dash, *Tulipmania*, 157–166.
40 Dash, *Tulipmania*, 150–157.
41 Goldgar, *Tulipmania*, 221.
42 Goldgar, *Tulipmania*, 258.
43 Dash, *Tulipmania*, 175.
44 Dash, *Tulipmania*, 76.
45 Goldgar, *Tulipmania*, 231.
46 Dash, *Tulipmania*, 187–193.
47 Goldgar, *Tulipmania*, 265.
48 Dash, *Tulipmania*, 188.
49 Schama, *The Embarrassment of Riches*, 364–365.
50 Oscar Gelderblom and Joost Jonker, "Amsterdam as the Cradle of Modern Futures Trading and Options Trading, 1550–1650" in William N. Goetzmann and K. Geert Rouwenhorst, eds, *The Origins of Value: The Financial Innovations that Created Modern Capital Markets* (Oxford; New York: Oxford University Press, 2005), 189–206.
51 Gelderblom and Jonker, "Amsterdam as the Cradle of Modern Futures Trading", 204.
52 Gelderblom and Jonker, "Amsterdam as the Cradle of Modern Futures Trading", 204.
53 Klaske Muizelaar and Derek Phillips, *Picturing Men and Women in the Dutch Golden Age: Paintings and People in Historical Perspective* (New Haven, CN: Yale University Press, 2003), 68.
54 Dash, *Tulipmania*, 100.
55 Celeste Brusati, *Johannes Vermeer* (New York, NY: Rizzoli 1993).
56 Wikipedia.org, Jan de Bray *The Governors of the Guild St. Luke, Haarlem 1675* http://en.wikipedia.org/wiki/File:Jan_de_Bray_002.jpg
57 Wikipedia.org, Bartholomeus van der Heist, *Sophia Trip, Wife of Balthasar Coymans,* http://en.wikipedia.org/wiki/File:Portrait_sophia_trip_wife_of_balthasar_coymans.jpg
58 Julia A. King "Still Life with Tobacco: The Archaeological Uses of Dutch Art", *Historical Archaeology* Vol. 41, No. 1, Between Art & Artifact (Society for Historical Archaeology, 2007): 6–22.
59 Schama, *The Embarrassment of Riches*, 161–166.
60 Schama, *The Embarrassment of Riches*, 297–298.
61 Schama, *The Embarrassment of Riches*, 319–320.
62 Jennifer Jones, *Sexing la Mode: Gender, Fashion and Commercial Culture in Old Regime France* (Oxford; New York: Berg, 2004), 22.
63 Daniel Roche, *The Culture of Clothing: Dress and Fashion in the Ancien Regime* (Paris, France: Maison des Sciences de l'Homme; New York, NY: Cambridge University Press, 1994), 39–41.
64 Roche, *The Culture of Clothing*, 29–41.
65 Ina Baghdiantz McCabe, *Orientalism in Early Modern France: Eurasian Trade, Exoticism and the Ancien Régime* (Oxford; New York: Berg, 2008), 250.
66 Norbert Elias, *The Court Society*, edited by Stephen Mennell (Dublin: UCD Press, 2006).

67 Roche, *The Culture of Clothing*, 185–186.
68 Joan DeJean. *The Essence of Style: How the French Invented High Fashion, Fine Food, Chic Cafés, Style, Sophistication and Glamour* (New York: Free Press, 2005), 35.
69 DeJean, *The Essence of Style*, 36–44.
70 DeJean, *The Essence of Style*, 27–48.
71 DeJean, *The Essence of Style*, 49–51.
72 DeJean, *The Essence of Style*, 53–54.
73 For a detailed account of this embassy see: Dirk van der Cruysse, *Louis XIV et le Siam* (Paris: Fayard, 1991), 373–410.
74 Most of this literature is in part reproduced by Dominique Lanni, *Le Rêve Siamois du Roi Soleil: Récits D'une Fièvre Exotique à La Cour De Louis XIV, 1660–1680* (Paris: Cosmople, 2004) most of what is not is in the bibliography of Dirk Van der Cruysse, *Louis XIV et le Siam*.
75 Cruysse, *Louis XIV et le Siam*, 383.
76 *Le Mercure galant* December 1682. As cited in Sabine Melchior-Bonnet, *The Mirror: A History* (New York: Routledge, 2001), 46.
77 Bonnet, *The Mirror: A History*, 74.
78 Dirk van der Cruysse, *Louis XIV et le Siam*, 401, gives all these items and more.
79 For more on this see Baghdiantz McCabe, *Orientalism*, chapter ten.
80 Described by Timoléon de Choisy, *Journal du Voyage de Siam*, ed. Dirk Van der Cruysse (Paris: Fayard, 1995) cited in Carolyn Sargentson, *Merchants and Luxury Markets: The Marchands Merciers of Eighteenth-century Paris* (London: The Victoria and Albert Museum, 1996), 62.
81 Baghdiantz McCabe, *Orientalism*, 258–259.
82 Joan DeJean, *The Essence of Style*, 3–5, 8–9, 6–introduction, 272.
83 Robert Fox and Anthony Turner, *Luxury Trades and Consumerism in Ancien Régime Paris: Studies in the History of the Skilled Workforce* (Aldershot, UK: Ashgate, 1998) and Maxine Berg and Helen Clifford, *Consumers and Luxury: Consumer Culture in Europe 1650–1850* (Manchester: Manchester University Press, 1999). Carolyn Sargentson's book on the *marchands merciers* is a brilliant study on the rise of luxury and its consumption in Paris and remains unique.
84 Berg and Clifford, eds, *Consumers and Luxury: Consumer Culture in Europe* is about England as are most books about luxury. Nothing for France has surpassed Charles Woosley Cole's 1939 work on Colbertisme: *Colbert and a Century of French Mercantilism*, 2nd ed. (New York: Columbia University Press, 1964).
85 A recent work illuminates the discussions of luxury during those two decades 1770–89 and the consequences of court expenditure, especially by Marie Antoinette: Caroline Weber, *Queen of Fashion: What Marie Antoinette Wore to the Revolution* (New York: Henry Holt and Co., 2006).
86 DeJean, *The Essence of Style*, 68.
87 DeJean, *The Essence of Style*, 64–69.
88 James G. McLaren, "A Brief History of Wigs in the Legal Profession", *International Journal of the Legal Profession*, 6:2 (London, England: Routledge, 1999), 241–250, 242–243.
89 Jean-Louis Flandrin, *Arranging the Meal: A History of Table Service in France*, trans. Julie E. Johnson (Berkeley: University of California Press, 2007).
90 Giorgio Riello, "Fabricating the Domestic: The Material Culture of Textiles and the Social Life of the Home in Early Modern Europe" in Beverly Lemire, ed, *The Force of Fashion in Politics and Society: Global Perspectives from Early Modern to Contemporary Times* (England: Ashgate, 2010), 41–66, 63–64.
91 Riello, "Fabricating the Domestic" in *The Force of Fashion*, 45–46.
92 Riello, "Fabricating the Domestic" in *The Force of Fashion*, 51.

93   Riello, "Fabricating the Domestic" in *The Force of Fashion*, 56.
94   Jonathan Spence, *The Chan's Great Continent: China in Western Minds* (New York: W.W. Norton, 1998), 34–35.
95   Spence, *The Chan's Great Continent*, 34–35.
96   Song Ying-Sung. Translated and annotated by E-tu Zen Sun and Shiou-chuan Sun. *T'ien-kung k'ai-wu, Chinese Technology in the Seventeenth Century* (New York: Dover Publications, 1997). All subsequent notations refer to this edition.
97   Ying-Sung, *Chinese Technology in the Seventeenth Century*, 129.
98   Ying-Sung, *Chinese Technology in the Seventeenth Century*, 109–123.
99   Ying-Sung, *Chinese Technology in the Seventeenth Century*, 35.
100 Ying-Sung, *Chinese Technology in the Seventeenth Century*, 59.
101 Kenneth Pomeranz, *The Great Divergence: China, Europe and the Making of the Modern World Economy* (New Jersey: Princeton University Press, 2000), 152–162.
102 Antonia Finnane, *Changing Clothes in China: Fashion, History, Nation* (New York: Columbia University Press, 2008), 44.
103 Gary Dickinson and Linda Wrigglesworth, *Imperial Wardrobe* (Berkeley, CA: Ten Speed Press, 2000).
104 Finnane, *Changing Clothes in China*, 45.
105 Finnane, *Changing Clothes in China*, 47.
106 Finnane, *Changing Clothes in China*, 48–49.
107 Craig Clunas, *Superfluous Things: Material Culture and Social Status in Early Modern China* (Honolulu: University of Hawaii Press, 2004), 90.
108 Francesca Bray, *Technology and Gender: Fabrics of Power in Late Imperial China*, (Berkeley CA: University of California Press, 1997), 363.
109 Clunas, *Superfluous Things*, 129–130.
110 Clunas, *Superfluous Things*, 131.
111 Clunas, *Superfluous Things*, 131–134.
112 Clunas cites illustrations from *Ideal Love Matches* by author Li Yu (1611–1680).
113 Clunas, *Superfluous Things*, 134–137.
114 Richard Strassberg, *The World of K'ung Shang-jen: A Man of Letter in Early Ch'ing China* (New York: Columbia University Press, 1983), 144. As quoted in Finnane, *Changing Clothes in China*, 54.
115 Finnane, *Changing Clothes in China*, 55.
116 Finnane, *Changing Clothes in China*, 26–27.
117 Finnane, *Changing Clothes in China*, 25.
118 Baghdiantz McCabe, *Orientalism*, 247–258.
119 Berg and Eger, eds, *Luxury in the Eighteenth Century*.

Figure 6.1 'The Bubblers Medley, or a Sketch of the Times' (1720). © Heritage Images/ Getty Images.

6   Consumption as a Global Phenomenon

Colonial Dreams and Financial Bubbles in Europe, China's Consumer Culture

As pride and luxury decrease, so by degrees they leave the Seas[1]

Few ideas have created as much controversy as Bernard Mandeville's. A Dutch physician, Mandeville is remembered as a philosopher and a satirist. After moving to London in 1705, he published *The Grumbling Hive, or Knaves Turn'd Honest*, later republished as *Fable of the Bees: or, Private Vices, Public Benefits*. The book became famous as a political satire on the social state of England. He wrote this fable much in the style of La Fontaine in France, as a moral fable describing the corruption of society. But unlike La Fontaine who condemned corruption, Mandeville argued that it was the source of wealth and public good, a necessity for a commercial culture. The beehive he describes is a thriving community until the bees are suddenly made virtuous and honest; as their desire for personal gain disappears, their hive collapses. The few survivors went on to lead solitary frugal lives in hollow trees. Mandeville implies that the bees' desires and private vices were in fact the basis of the public benefit of the hive. Controlling one's passions was detrimental to the state's commercial and intellectual progress, an idea that caused much controversy at the time. Mandeville believed that greed, considered a vice by Christianity, was in fact beneficial and led to invisible social cooperation. Mandeville argued that the basest and vilest behaviors were in fact those that produced positive economic effects. A spendthrift libertine might be viewed as greedy but in his spending he would employ tailors, servants and laborers. Adam Smith made use of some of the examples used by Mandeville. Mandeville argued that if fashion was a moral vice driven by envy and appetite, it was the "wheel that turn'd the Trade".[2] If the British were to curb their appetite and stop fulfilling their own desires, he argued, they would grow weak because, "As pride and luxury decrease, so by degrees they leave the Seas."[3]

This praise for the necessity of luxury was indeed rare in Britain in an era where discourse was mostly about the social corruption brought about by luxury. Adam Smith argued that frugality amassed capital and capital helped commerce. Frugality and luxury were key concepts during the age of revolutions.

In the British Empire, American revolutionary leader Samuel Adams cautioned that if "foppery become the ruling taste of the great, the body of the people would be in danger of catching the distemper".[4] The rise of several groups who challenged monarchs, colonial rulers and other elites meant profound changes in social structure in Western Europe and North America. Entitlement to goods, the boycott of foreign goods and the acquisition of colonial goods are all part and parcel of the major political upheavals that marked the eighteenth century. Discourse against luxury and the corruption it was associated with was key during these political upheavals in France and North America.

The Beginnings of Consumer Society

The eighteenth century was the age of major political revolutions. Entitlement to goods, the boycott of foreign goods and the acquisition of colonial goods are all part and parcel of the major political upheavals that marked the eighteenth century. Discourse against luxury and the corruption it was associated with was key during these political upheavals in France and North America. It has been argued that the age of revolutions also brought a revolution in consumption in Europe. Over thirty years ago a path-breaking book, *The Birth of a Consumer Society,* argued that the eighteenth century experienced a dramatic surge in the consumption of goods in Europe.[5] Not everyone agrees that the birth of a consumer society dates to the eighteenth century. Jan de Vries traces a sociable and inclusive urban form of luxury consumption back to the seventeenth-century Dutch Republic, where he argues a precocious consumer culture developed. He differentiates what he calls "new luxury" from "old luxury", which is a type of consumption that thrived at European courts. He argued that the republican Dutch seemed comfortable with new luxury; comfortable enough that opposition to luxury and debates about the corruption it brought never erupted as they did in eighteenth-century Britain and France.[6] In societies where luxury goods had been the guarded privilege of a small elite, discourse about corruption and luxury was part of the revolutionary discourse.[7] Kenneth Pomeranz has argued for the existence of a consumer society in China well before Europe and that the nineteenth century should be considered the period when consumer societies were born in Europe.[8]

By most accounts, the eighteenth century witnessed a deep psychic investment in the world of goods. Major questions about the relation of men, women and goods still remain unanswered despite the recent boom in consumption studies; one of the larger problems is the fact that most studies are exclusively concerned with Western Europe. If other regions have been studied, save for China and Japan, they are seen as commercial or political colonies of Europe. The relationship between European courts, companies and their colonies is perhaps a key element that created crisis and revolution in the eighteenth century. It has been argued that luxury was no less than "the keyword" that marks the eighteenth century.[9] As Maxine Berg has emphasized for England and Jan de Vries has for the Dutch, I have highlighted that most luxuries in Early Modern France were imported.[10] The relationship and discourse about these luxury goods mark the political and economic lives of all three societies.

Another aspect of the discourse about luxury and consumption is the prejudices hiding in its gendered discourse. Amanda Vickery argued that in the literature on consumption, the gulf between the producing man and the consuming female seems to survive as a trope against all evidence to the contrary. She argues that men historically have dissociated themselves from shopping but nevertheless were enthusiastic consumers of certain categories of goods. As opposed to daily expenses, these goods were often the most expensive investments of the household: horses, carriages, watches, weapons and books. It was because women were seen as running the business of everyday shopping that American patriots made such efforts to ensure female cooperation in the colonial boycott of British imports, particularly tea in the 1760s. Vickery demonstrates that, based on account books, men dominated the purchase of high-status expensive, luxury goods.[11] She also finds that the tie between women and the purchase of everyday textiles is strong and persistent in English account books. Female weakness for fine fabrics, especially silk, was not simply a cliché of eighteenth-century commentary but a reality. Yet she argues that, if these commentaries emphasized women's fetishized self indulgence in silks, linens and clothing, the same account book she studies charts a story of emotional responsibility and consumer service to the household through the on-going provision of linen garments for members of the family, especially men. On the other hand, men bought the expensive luxuries. A conspicuous object of male desire was the most sought-after masculine sign of status: the coach.[12] All three families she has studied maintained one. It was not only extremely expensive but the maintenance of "it demanded coachmen, horses, stables, feed, farriers and so on and could be ruinous".[13] The full amount would be equal not to owning a car but to owning a helicopter today. Vickery also argued that if women adored the infinite variety of textiles available to them, as a counterpart, horse furniture (saddle, tackle, leather, buckles) were equally attainable desires for men. Major redecoration of homes was also listed under male accounts.[14] She concludes that his and hers accounts tell a distinctive story of clear financial allocation within households. Despite differences, the accounts she studied underline women's material obligations to the family. Vickery concludes that it is a cruel irony that the chief self-indulgent consumer of the eighteenth century, married men, went unnoticed by scholars who invariably pointed at women and bachelors.[15] The dandies and fops in caricatures were always young bachelors. Wives' responsibility for basic provisioning, on the other hand, exposed them to accusations of vanity, extravagance and materialism. This note of caution is necessary, because as will be discussed further, popular opinion directly tied Queen

Marie Antoinette's "conspicuous consumption" to the advent of the French Revolution. Accusation of this foreign queen being at the root of French bankruptcy were convenient to mark the fact that decades earlier the most powerful of French kings, Louis XIV, had bankrupted France. The attempts made to save France from bankruptcy by creating a bank only made the deficit much graver. The creation of that first bank was a major financial bubble that created social chaos. If tulipmania has been called history's first financial bubble with the birth of derivatives, the most notorious bubble happened in France with John Law's creation of a bank that was tied to importing foreign goods.

Law's Plan for Louis XIV's Bankrupt France

Despite the fact that the reign of Louis XIV was characterized by the dominance of French culture over European courts, France itself was bankrupt when Louis died on September 1, 1715. The permanent state of war in which he kept the country contributed to heavy taxation and social and economical instability yet Louis XIV's extravagance has never been highlighted like Marie Antoinette's would be before the French Revolution. If by 1715 France had become the most powerful country and the cultural leader of Europe, the paradox was that France was bankrupt and lacked an organized financial system. By that date, both the Dutch and English had created central banks to permit large-scale government borrowing. A foreigner, John Law came to France in order to create the first central bank. A Scottish economist, adventurer and exile, Law has been called everything from a financial genius to con man extraordinaire.[16] A thorough study of Law's bank and bankruptcy was made by Edgar Faure in 1977.[17] Law was born in 1671 in Edinburgh, Scotland, to wealthy goldsmiths. He went to London for his studies where he became known for winning card games by mentally calculating the odds in his head. Through this capacity, he made a sizable amount of money gambling. Unfortunately, he also killed a man in London in a duel for the affections of a woman and was consequently imprisoned and sentenced to death. His sentence was remitted to manslaughter and he managed to escape England and reached Amsterdam in 1694. John Law began to record his own economic and monetary theories in the city that was the financial capital of Europe at the time. Hoping for a pardon, Law returned to Scotland in 1705 as an economist with a book titled *Money and Trade Considered, with a Proposal for Supplying the Nation with Money*. His argument was simple: the prosperity of a country could be increased by the amount of currency put into circulation. Considering many thinkers such as John Locke influenced him, none of the ideas in the book were new; however, he made many of these ideas into practical ones.[18] With the union of Scotland with England in 1707, he was a wanted man even in Edinburgh, now part of the new Great Britain. He left for the continent.

Economic Climate for Law's Proposal

Law was an innovator because unlike his contemporaries he argued that paper money was superior to gold and silver for creating prosperity. In his *Money and Trade* treatise, he argued that paper money should be tied to land because silver and gold fluctuated too much.[19] With paper money, greater sums of paper currency could circulate in a national economy than specie alone could permit. Traditional mercantilist thinking had always argued that the wealth of nations depended on their reserves of silver and gold and on regulation that avoided specie from leaving the country. In France, monies consisted of metallic coins of gold, silver and copper. These were called *real* money but there had long been an *ideal* or account money, the *livres tournois*, which had never had any material form. At its origin, the *livres* was set to be 490 grams of silver under Charlemagne (742–814). In reality this ideal account money, the *livres,* had never weighed 490 grams of silver because it had always fluctuated. On September 1, 1715 when Louis XIV died, the value of the *livres* in silver grams was as low as 7.90 grams. In fact, when Louis XIV died it was said to be a tearless mourning; very few lamented the passing of the King as the economic situation of France was in shambles.[20]

A major historian Pierre Goubert, in his *Histoire economique et sociale de la France,* analyzed the relationship between the high mortality between 1693 and 1720 and the "under consumption" of this period in France. In his analysis, it was due to a period of epidemics, famines and climate change. He describes people stealing cereals while they were still green, eating grass and consuming rotten meat from road kill. He links a series of poor harvests and famines to a steep rise in prices that also contributed to under consumption. Added to this, deflation also brought prices that neither remunerated producers nor incited production. It is in this atmosphere that Law was proposing his banking system to the court.[21] Additionally, France was trying to prevent money that had been altered, some of it fake, from entering its borders. But a traffic in altered and false coins could not be stopped after Louis XIV's death, despite a decree banning them.[22] Law would build his financial scheme on the hope of obtaining exotic riches through France's commercial companies, such as tobacco, pelts, gold, silver and silk from the Americas and indigo and all kinds of gems from Asia. Louis XIV's nephew, the Duc d'Orléans, became the regent of France. He had a very close relationship with England. The English throne was contested by the Stuarts and the French Regent's reign was contested by King Philip of Spain, a Bourbon, who could claim succession in France. The Regent's closeness to England might explain why he had more enthusiasm for Law's projects than Louis XIV.[23] In a letter to the Regent, written just as he came to power in December 1715, John Law argued he would make France the most powerful country and the arbiter of Europe without ever having to resort to war.[24]

Law proceeded to anticipate a massive and immediate reimbursement of France's debt. He wanted to reimburse 900 million livres immediately in 1719.

Until John Law's *Banque Royale* notes were introduced in 1719, France had never had paper currency. French citizens used specie in their everyday transactions. Law had noticed the small matter of conspicuous consumption and pleasure seeking among the French aristocracy following the lead of the King at Versailles. In his view, the gap between the "haves" and "have-nots" was staggering. Law's schemes, he argued, were to become a catalyst for bringing the classes together, or so he wrote. Indeed, he was right: when there was a run on the bank all social classes were clamoring for their money.[25]

Establishing the Banque

Louis XIV's wars and the court's lavish lifestyle had left France with three billion *livres* in debt. Hearing of Law's ideas, the regent of France for the young Louis XV invited Law to reduce debt and receive some profit from the colonies by developing the French territories of Louisiana. Law promised him he could achieve both goals. The Regent approved the establishment of a private bank first called *Banque Générale* and later to become *Banque Royale*. In 1717, the bank and the French government were closely associated when the regent ordered that all public funds be deposited by everybody in the *Banque Générale*. The payment of France's taxes in the new paper money issued by the bank was authorized. Law's ideas had been to create a bank for national finance and to make French commercial companies such as the French East and West India Companies into state companies for commerce that would exclude all private banks and investors. This would create a huge monopoly of both finance and colonial trade run by the French state. The profits of this large colonial company and of the bank were supposed to pay off France's national debt. Law was granted a charter by the regent to create the *Compagnie de Louisianne* with an exclusive lease to develop the immense French territorial holdings along the Mississippi river. The river at the time was known as the Colbert River and the territory had been named Louisiana after Louis XIV; not all of it had been explored, let alone exploited or settled.[26]

Beginnings of the Mississippi Bubble

The Regent did make some demands of John Law; Law was required to settle 6,000 French citizens and 3,000 French slaves in the American territory. To sweeten the transaction, the new company was awarded the monopoly of growing and selling tobacco. The Louisiana Company became widely known as the Mississippi Company. Law decided that its stock shares could initially be bought by French investors with only a 10 percent down payment. Thanks to this favorable term, fortunes were made overnight. Rumors ran through Paris that one of the early investors, a mere beggar, invested his life savings and made 70 million *livres* when he cashed out. It must be remembered that French Louisiana contained land that forms the present states of Louisiana,

Mississippi, Arkansas, Missouri, Illinois, Iowa, Wisconsin and Minnesota. French claims of course conflicted with the British, who had their eyes on the Ohio and Missouri river valleys. The idea of tying paper money to land was not a feasible one in France since land prices, which Law had erroneously believed to be stable, were fluctuating. With the Duc de Noailles, President of the Finance Council, the decision was made to tie paper money to a conglomeration of all French overseas companies for the Americas now joined into one called *Compagnie d'Occident*. This idea in fact made the Duc de Noailles the viceroy of an American territory eight times bigger than France. On April 6, 1717, the Company's status was formally registered as a twenty-five year monopoly on overseas commerce. In reality, it considered itself to be a perpetual privilege on all the land, sea coasts, ports and islands in the French colony of Louisiana.[27]

Subscriptions to this trade monopoly were opened immediately. The first one to invest was of course the Duc de Noailles. A new edict fixed the capital of the Company at 100 million livres. The Duc de Noailles took responsibility for the payments to investors as he was still at the head of finance. Parliament signed a decree making all of this official on December 31, 1717. The King's participation, which was as high as 40 percent of the subscription, was kept secret.[28] On January 16, 1719, the last contracts were passed. The Company had also bought the privileges of the *Compagnie du Sénégal* that ran the slave trade for 1,600,000 *livres*. This happened in December at the same time that the bank became a royal bank.[29] The bank and the *Mississippi Company* were then united into one, whereupon Law named the bank *Banque Royale*. The Regent bought out all of the stockholders of the bank, making it a royal institution. In May 1719, Law also acquired the French East India Company and the China Company and he reorganized the entire conglomerate as a new *Compagnie des Indes*, which would monopolize any and all French trade with Asia. This put all French trade globally under the Mississippi Company. Adding the taxes on tobacco to this mix of revenues, the interest rates rose to 25 percent within a few weeks.[30]

Most importantly this new bank/company was also given the right to mint new coinage and to collect French indirect taxes. The takeover of the tax system was in line with Law's views that a simplified fiscal regime would benefit the economy and encourage consumption. Law was determined to refund most of the national debt, which was the King's debt, through this new *Compagnie*; the first refund would be the King's debt for a sum of 1,200,000 *livres*.[31] The Regent ordered that the *Banque Royale*'s notes were the only legal tender in France and appointed Law as the Controller General of Finances. Effective marketing schemes greatly exaggerated the wealth and resources of the Mississippi river and of Louisiana.[32] Shares originally issued at 150 *livres* rose to 10,000 *livres* in a matter of months. It was anticipated that French America would become a vast and prosperous tobacco growing region. Since it stretched 3,000 miles from the mouth of the Mississippi to Canada, it was also thought that trade in beaver pelts would add to France's colonial riches. False rumors that gold and silver were discovered in Mississippi shot up the speculation in Paris. In January 1720, the share price rocketed to 18,000 *livres*. *Banque Royale* offices were opened in cities such as Paris, Lyon, Tours, and Amiens to facilitate the issuing of bank notes. The subscribers' money was going directly into the King's coffers and only a handful of people – among them the King, Law and the Regent – were aware of this secret part of what has been called Law's system. The King's 100,000 secret shares were worth a billion *livres* when the shares hit 10,000 *livres*. The deal became public knowledge when Law offered to buy the shares for the *Compagnie* at 900,000,000, making it an apparent good deal for the bank.[33]

The demand was enormous and the issuing of these notes caused an increase in prices and an inflationary spiral. The poverty and famines described by Pierre Goubert were the rule for most of France's population who lived with under-consumption, but some lucky speculators from the lower class did get rich. Investors were euphoric, believing that Law was a magician. In Paris stock trading was carried out on the *Rue Quincampoix* where wild scenes broke out in crowds seeking to buy Mississippi Company shares. Even the working classes sought a part in this new prosperity. Money was now easy to borrow since you only needed to put down 10 percent. Often all it took to have a bit of capital was to sell a cow. The Parisian aristocrats were the first to be shocked by the number of lower class people that wanted to invest in the bank. Both mercantile and peasant classes invested whatever small sums they could. One document tells of an individual who sent his valet with 250 shares with instructions to sell the shares at 8,000 *livres*. The valet sold them at 10,000 *livres* and made a profit of 500,000 *livres* unknown to his master. He reinvested this sum and within a few days, his net worth had risen to 2,000,000 *livres*. These stories led to such frenzied buying and selling that soldiers had to be sent to restore order. Law's own coachman found sudden wealth. One morning he showed up for work in fashionable clothes to notify Law of his termination of employment. Because of the steady rise of servants, the King decreed on 28 December 1719 that servants could not dress without signs on their liveries that indicated their master's household. These signs, called *galons*, had to be at least an inch wide, seen at the front of the livery, opposed to the back, and a third *galon* had to be seen on the sleeve. In addition, the King forbade them from wearing any silk or velvet, anything golden, buttons made of silver or silver thread. These laws would be enforced with fines to their masters and prison sentences for the servants. These sumptuary laws were also applied to craftsmen and even to master tailors, the only exception made was for the servants of foreign embassies.[34]

Popping the Mississippi Bubble

Suddenly some early investors realized that their hopes of getting rich in "Mississippi" were greatly exaggerated and began to sell their shares for gold, silver and land instead of paper money. They feared the ever-increasing production of paper notes was based on nothing. In early 1720 when two royal princes decided to cash in their shares, others decided to follow their example. The downward spiral of mistrust had begun. John Law had to resort to printing 1,500,000 *livres* in paper money to stem this tide. The sudden decline in confidence from the French aristocracy sent share prices tumbling down. Panic set in. Investors suddenly seemed to want to redeem their bank notes all at once and convert paper into specie. What has been called the "Mississippi Bubble" burst when the *Banque Royale* could no longer redeem their notes for lack of gold and silver. Those not quick enough to redeem their shares were ruined. In an effort to slow the run on the bank, clerks resorted to counting the money out very slowly, giving the money out in small denomination coins, inserting clerks in the line who would return the money they drew and by drastically reducing bank hours. At one point, the bank refused to accept anything but 10 *livres* notes. None of these schemes were able to stop the run on the bank. John Law decided he had to resort to drastic measures to restore confidence in the Mississippi Company and the bank. He ordered the public burning of the paper bank notes as they came in. He hoped to convince the shareholders that they were becoming scarce. A huge enclosure was set up outside the bank for burning the paper notes and several times a day, with great ceremony, the notes were consigned to the fire. The general public then turned on Law and would have lynched him if they could. His effigy was burned and the mere mention of his name aroused a fury of insults. John Law saved himself by hiding in a church.[35]

The Mississippi Company, despite all this, was not a swindle. It was legitimate and established for a purpose: to exploit the riches of French colonial possessions. The big mistake was the issuing of more money as demand rose for shares in the company. John Law's plans for the bank had been well thought out and were sound. His idea to issue bank notes instead of specie was also solid, as time has now proven. Despite this colossal failure, John Law was a financial genius whose idea is at the basis of modern banking. If subscriptions had ruined many shareholders, the finances of the French state were greatly improved. At the death of the Regent in 1723, there were 91 million *livres* in specie in the King's treasury. It seems not everybody lost under Law's system.[36] As has become familiar to those who know Wall Street in present times, the first big investors won. Nevertheless, the resentment against Law was real. As the author of what became known as the Mississippi Bubble, Law was held responsible and forced to flee France in 1721. France maintained control over its Mississippi colony until 1753, losing the territory to England and Spain after the Seven Years War. The lands east of the Mississippi went to England and the rest went to Spain, who returned the Mississippi territory to France thirty-seven years later under Napoleon Bonaparte in a secret deal that promised to set up Spanish rule in Italy. In 1803, Thomas Jefferson acquired this vast area for the US in the land acquisition known as the Louisiana Purchase.[37]

Britain's South Sea Bubble

As Law was attempting to refinance France's debt, the British debt in 1720 amounted to approximately 50,000,000 pounds. To finance the British debt acquisition, the South Sea Company, which since 1711 had held all the British trade with the Spanish colonies of America, expanded the number of its shares – each of which had a value of 100 pounds. The company needed to provide a mechanism for funding government debt but unlike in France, it could not establish a bank because the charter of the Bank of England made it the only joint stock bank allowed. Therefore, the company had to appear as a trading company, although it was a joint stock company whose main activity was in fact the funding of government debt. The Bank of England was founded in 1694 after at least two years of public debate. The government agreed that taxes on shipping and liquors would be earmarked specifically for the bank. The bank did not immediately fulfill the functions of a modern central bank, as it dealt with private clients, but its primary goal was to lend to the state. Its creation has been lauded as one of the main events of the financial revolution. The name South Sea, in contrast, has always been associated with failure. The bank, however, was a more outlandish and modern concept than the trading companies. Other new projects of the time were the insurance companies. In the modern developed world, they are now key components of a functioning economy. The basic principle behind these institutions is that risks are pooled. Many of the innovations of what is being called the financial revolution were debated by contemporaries just as Law's innovations were; however with hindsight most have been successful and survived.

The South Sea Company format was not an innovation. The joint stock company format had been used before by trade companies and the slave trade that the South Sea Company concentrated on was long established. Before the South Sea Company, the main English slave trader was the *Royal African Company*. It was granted a charter in 1662 to trade in slaves under the name of *Royal Adventurers*. The monopoly of the slave trade was lost when the government of 1698 was hostile to the Royal African Company. Despite setbacks, however, the company continued to ship large numbers of people across the Atlantic. The South Sea Company was granted the opportunity of the monopoly and also restructuring the government debt.[38] The company convinced shareholders of the government debt to exchange it with a new issue of stock in the company. The government was sure it would gain, as the interest payments it would pay to the company would be obtained by placing government tariffs on the goods imported from South America. The Bank of England had proposed a similar competing offer that did not prevail against the South Sea Company. Just as in France, the company set to create propaganda about the value of its potential trade in exotic goods with the new world, chiefly slaves rather than goods, which led to a speculation frenzy. The Treaty of Utrecht of 1713 granted the company a thirty-year *Asiento* (contractual permission) to supply the Spanish colonies with an unlimited number of slaves and 500 tons of goods. The company was free to set the exchange rate between shares and debt; it valued the shares well above par value. It labeled the surplus shares as the company's "profits" from the conversion of the debt to shares.[39] Britain and Holland dominated the slave trade in the early eighteenth century.

That the South Sea Company's holding of its own shares represented an asset was an innovation. The interest to be paid by the government on the debt acquired by the company was 5 percent per year until 1724 and 4 percent per year thereafter. This would imply a substantial reduction in the annual debt servicing costs for the government. "Conditional on the passage of the refunding act, the South Sea Company paid bribes to members of Parliament and to favorites of the King totaling £1.3 million".[40] Numerous members of Parliament and the government participated in stock subscriptions and most received large cash loans from the company on their shares. While these bribes add a sinister appearance to the episode, they were not a signal of fraud, as at the time bribery was not an unusual practice. Indeed, Parliament and the government supported the refunding so enthusiastically that it must have been understood as a signal that official cooperation in the South Sea Company's ventures had been purchased. To the extent that members of Parliament held shares in the company, they would have an interest in the future and prosperity of the company. Given John Law's influential theories, such equity in the South Sea Company could then have been used to undertake commercial projects that would drive the economy.[41]

Collapse of the South Sea Bubble

Suddenly, South Sea share prices collapsed from about 775 pounds on August 31 to about 290 pounds on October 1, 1720. Researchers of the episode are vague about the reason for the speed and magnitude of this decline, most generally attributing it to the appearance of a liquidity crisis. As a consequence of this collapse, Parliament passed the Bubble Act in June 1721 to ban the formation of unauthorized corporations. With the collapse of share prices, the South Sea Company faced the hostility of its shareholders and Parliament quickly turned against the company and eventually stripped the directors of their wealth.[42] Some of the decisions taken by the directors were foolish but some of the moral condemnations and arguments that appeared in the contemporary press are not convincing. There were relatively few alternative investments that offered the same flexibility as joint stock company shares. The bubble was partly due to the difficulties of adjusting to financial change, which was largely driven by competition with France. John Law and British financiers vied with one another to reconstruct their economies.[43]

Just like tulipmania, the South Sea Bubble gave rise to illustrations, pamphlets and objects. Cards were one of the most intriguing South Sea Bubble artworks. One complete set held at the Harvard University library shows various national and religious groups being ruined in the stock market including the Welsh, French and Dutch. The illustrations on the cards were also highly anti-Semitic. There is shocking silence about the slave trade. Another card points to the consumerism of the time and shows a woman in a china shop being asked by brokers if she wished to buy or sell stock. The card implies that women's stock trading was as lightly undertaken as window-shopping for luxury goods.[44] Like tulipmania and the Mississippi bubble, the South Sea bubble is remembered every time there is a financial bubble in order to prove that history repeats itself.[45] Nevertheless, historically these two financial bubbles, unlike tulipmania, mark a new era with the creation of institutions such as banks based on the profits of globalized trade in colonial goods. The easy credit they provided encouraged a rise in consumption.

Price Convergence: De Vries

Both bubbles relied on overseas trade and the import of foreign luxury goods. That some of the growing imports now depended on slave plantations controlled by the European powers is an important marker of the eighteenth century, yet in the 1720s the Atlantic trade that both bubbles advertised had not yet overtaken the Eurasian import of luxury goods. Coffee prices, as the consumption of coffee rose in Europe, help to follow this transformation from importing from Mocha to importing from European-run plantations. According to Jan de Vries, coffee prices in Europe declined substantially across the century from 1.36 guilders per Dutch pond in 1710 to 1719 to less than 0.50 guilders by the 1770s (1 pond = 494 grams).[46] However, profit margins did not decline significantly and he argues that this was because the Dutch East India Company, the VOC, followed shortly by the French East India Company, the *Compagnie des Indes*, had encouraged coffee production on territories under their direct control, such as Java for the Dutch and La Reunion for the French. This circumvented the inelastic supply of coffee at high prices from Mocha that, until these colonial plantations, had remained the unique source for coffee beans. As early as 1730, the six million pounds of coffee consumed in Europe still came from Asia but only one quarter of this coffee came from Mocha. Java had become an important producer. Coffee prices continued to fall after production rose in the Caribbean and by 1750 Asia accounted for only one quarter of Europe's coffee supply. By the 1770s, less than 10 percent of one quarter of all the coffee consumed in Europe came from Asia.

De Vries continues to argue that the history of tea prices is more straightforward. Once the port of Canton was open on equal terms to all European traders in 1701, the shipments of tea to Europe grew rapidly. By 1718, 1.6 million pounds of tea were sent to Europe. By 1784, when English trade became prominent in Canton, shipments to Europe had reached 20 million pounds a year. The price of black tea in Amsterdam fell from 6.95 guilders per pound in 1715–1718 to 0.66 guilders a pound in 1785–1789. De Vries notes that Asian goods sent to Europe were typically non-competing; for example, the pepper and spices of the sixteenth century had no direct counterpart on the market. However, when in the seventeenth century European trading companies shifted their attention to cotton textiles, porcelain and silk, matters were different. These Asian manufactured goods competed and often substituted European cloth and ceramics.[47] Moreover, the demand for these Asian manufactured goods encouraged the development of European imitations over time, as Chandra Mukerjee and Maxine Berg have argued for England and as has also been argued for France.[48] De Vries argues that the popularity of exotic goods was due to the collapse of their prices.

Criticism of de Vries: Austen and Smith

Jan de Vries' argument that the decrease of tea and other colonial goods' prices allowed for their popularity has been criticized by Austen and Smith in their article "Private Tooth Decay as Public Economic Virtue".[49] They do not deny that reductions in price in the eighteenth century due to the lower cost of production and duties for tea, sugar, and other common colonial goods played a role in the spread of consumption of these exotic goods. While they also accept the trickle-down theory, which posits that the middle classes may imitate what the aristocracy consumed and that accelerated social mobility, they find a weakness in this sort of explanation. They concede that Sidney Mintz was undoubtedly right to argue that each social group that adopted sugar, coffee and tea interpreted the meaning of these new rituals in their own way. This in fact limits the trickle-down explanation, as a new commodity meant new things to a new group of potential users. Secondly, Austen and Smith argue that because the span of time between elite and mass consumption is very long, consumption habits change markedly over the space of several generations and not always because of innovations introduced at the apex of society. In their opinion, the relationship between the sugar, tea, coffee and cocoa complex in the broader context of the pre-industrial period is centered primarily on the phenomenon of "respectability". In their definition, respectability was not a matter of simply emulating elite fashions, although that is part of it. They argue for a distinctive cultural pattern with strict guidelines for specific groups who each had their own elaborate system of "moral legitimization." They criticize looking at economic factors to look at the spread of tea or coffee and argue that even economic factors fit themselves into broader patterns of thought and action that have immediate cultural and social meaning to the participating consumer. From this standpoint, the use of commodities such as sugar, coffee and tea is not simply a sign of a socio-economic change, but is an active process of cultural construction in itself.[50]

As signs of deeper social phenomena, tea, sugar, printed cotton and other exotic goods could easily have been interchanged with other products. If one simply argues that their consumption had been a matter of fashion, they almost certainly would have been replaceable. Austen and Smith argue that if they persisted, it was because of the nature and the interpretation of these particular commodities. Tea, coffee, cocoa and sugar came to play a significant role in shaping respectability in eighteenth-century England. In a functional sense, they argue that one could say that respectability centered on a demand on the part of a certain group of people for respect from the people above them, below them and at the same level as them in society. Taking tea and sugar in certain ways – with the proper saucer, implements and at the proper time of day – was connected to a wider array of cultural practices, such as wearing the right fashionable clothes and adhering to the rules of polite behavior. This goes beyond the idea of bundling commodities together and adds morality to the usage of goods. In this theory, consumer habits are tied to modes of moral justification for the respect demanded of others. They argue that tea was especially morally significant because it was consciously consumed as a substitute for an alcoholic drink. They contrast taking sugar and tea with the immoderation and wastefulness of the excessive sugar decorations and the sweets consumed by the aristocracy. Tea drinking was a sober behavior with beneficial social consequences to British overseas trade. In Austen and Smith's view, respectability was one of the main sources of demand for the products of the early industrial revolution (cottons, table-wares, etc.) that imitated exotic products. They argue that respectability itself is not a general human condition, but a very specific cultural pattern that developed in the period immediately preceding industrialization in Britain.[51]

As early as the late seventeenth century, evidence of the damage to the physical body, including teeth, by the consumption of sugar was increasingly cited in opposition to the proponents of sugar. They argue that the habit of taking sugar in tea may have arisen out of an attempt to reconcile these perceptions. The most serious form of this confrontation came in debates over doctrines and policies generally referred to as mercantilism. Mercantilist writers were driven by their belief that volume accumulation within the country was better than the domestic consumption of colonial goods, such as sugar. It aimed to maximize balances of trade by restricting exotic imports. On the whole, there was conflict between companies and merchants who were the importers of exotic commodities and mercantilists who argued that widespread consumerism endangered society and the economy. This last position against widespread consumerism contributed to the non-zero sum view of consumerism as a public economic virtue, advanced in Adam Smith's *Wealth of Nations*, the canon of liberal economics. Among the forms of individual self-interest, sugar consumption is quite prominent. Despite Adam Smith's (1723–1790) denunciation of the inefficiency of bonded workers, other free trade economists such as Turgot argued for the rationality for the slave trade and the slave plantations to produce commodities such as sugar. The overvaluation of colonial trade by mercantilist theorists such as Adam Smith and Turgot can be understood to have had a positive impact on the development of capitalist culture. Colonial commodities and their consumers gave rise to a debate about economics that was temporarily won by the mercantilists.[52] Within the mercantilist version of proto-industrialist capitalism, African and West Indian slaves were valued not only as labor but as consumers of goods manufactured in Europe. Initially, these goods were textiles but eventually sugar, tea, cocoa and goods produced on

European-run colonial plantations played a role in the rise of proto-capitalism. Austen and Smith seem to look at a cultural explanation; economic explanations continue to be important as well. Could it be that both respectability and the price collapse played a role?[53]

Consumerism and Global Competition

De Vries has argued that Asian coffee, chiefly from Mocha, found itself head to head on the European consumer market with coffee produced in the West Indies on colonial holdings. The existence of alternatives and the practice of import substitution by European companies by growing expensive imports on colonial plantations influenced the prices at which many Asian goods could be sold in Europe. De Vries argues that globalization, what he calls a soft globalization, affected European consumers in the period primarily by increasing consumer choice. These goods reached broad European markets and encouraged new patterns of consumption as novel products integrated into daily patterns of life. De Vries argues that the impact of intercontinental trade on the European consumer should not be measured by the conversions of price for non-competing goods but by relative prices and the effective augmentation of consumer choice. In order to maintain their profit margins, European companies shifted the locus of their buying and selling activities within Asia itself. Aware that most Asian goods had vast markets within Asia, the companies tried to direct goods to markets offering the highest returns. The intra-Asian trading activities of the European trading companies brought about a measure of global level price conversions in consumer markets.[54] As the companies sought out trade with more growth potential, they changed their mix of goods for more competition both in Asia and Europe. This speaks to the fact that despite the promulgations of monopolies by the European companies, as for example the French Mississippi Company examined above, the European trading companies did not in fact enjoy monopoly power on any long-term basis – with perhaps one exception for the Dutch in the spice trade for a short period. Portuguese monopoly power on the seas only briefly interrupted the overland trade routes that had long supplied pepper and spices to Europe. Competition was the rule.

With the exception of the Dutch hold over the sources of fine spices for a period of time, all commodities were bought in competitive markets. European companies vied with one another and Asian traders for silk, spices, coffee and any goods sold on both Asian and European markets. The advantage that European companies had was exclusive access to their national consumer markets. Jan de Vries explains that it is only in this sense that they can ever have the name "monopoly companies". But even in this case, he argues that there were sole suppliers only in a limited way, as they sold their goods at auction to a number of merchants, some of them foreign, who distributed the pepper, silk, cotton, piece goods, tea and coffee. De Vries argues that conventional wisdom maintains that the restrictive policies of the monopolies not only led to high profits for the companies that exploited "the riches of the Indies" but also ensured that Asian luxuries and their New World substitutes would remain too expensive for the vast majority of each trading company's country's population, therefore never reaching the middle class. To counter this conventional wisdom, de Vries has demonstrated in his book *Industrious Revolution* that Asian cotton textiles, coffee and tea became items of everyday use among what he calls "the middling sorts" and even sometimes among the poor in eighteenth-century Western Europe.[55] As for the companies growing rich, in the case of one of the most successful, the VOC, its role as Asian Prince proved not to be a road to riches. The cost of protecting and administering its colonial territories always seemed to have exceeded revenues. De Vries argues that the English East India Company was more fortunate in its pursuit of riches as its conquests subsequent to the Battle of Plassey in 1757 in India which generated both large tax revenues and a hold on Chinese trade goods such as tea, cotton and opium. From 1760 to 1784, the EIC was successfully able to avoid sending silver shipments from Europe to China.[56] Before that date, tea had to be bought exclusively with silver and many countries in Europe were trying to conserve silver.

Domesticating Exotic Commodities

Conserving gold and silver was a must for Early Modern economic thinkers. It was often argued that foreign imports hurt the domestic economy. In this form of economic thinking, agricultural innovation was also important to protect domestic production against imports from the "Indies". This too had a long tradition among French botanists. The most famous of such thinkers is Carl Linnaeus, to whom we owe the classification system of the natural world that is still used today. He is also best remembered for "taming the exotic", for *acclimatation*. The term hides the enormous scale of his ambitions as he incrementally and slowly adapted plants to new and colder environments that would allow him, or so he hoped, to plant exotic Chinese tea as far north as Lapland. Tea was only the most famous of his many experiments. He is quoted: "Nature has arranged itself in such a way that each country produces something especially useful; the task of economics is to collect from other places and cultivate such things that don't want to grow [at home] and can grow [there]."[57]

Carl Linnaeus is universally remembered for his classification system based on Joseph Pitton de Tournefort's classification of plants, but his Swedish titles of nobility were received for his economic ideas in service to the commercial goals of Sweden. Economically, Linnaeus was cameralist; in an insightful article, Lisbet Koerner analyzed how Linnaeus "considered nothing more important than to close that gate [to the China trade], through which all silver of Europe disappears".[58] She writes that he was well aware that East India companies made sure that Europe's consumers had all sorts of Asian goods, even if they were on the black market.[59] Even in the eighteenth century, these mercantilist views prevailed after they had been philosophically attacked both in England and France. His agenda was argued in terms of "Europe", not simply

Sweden. Cameralists, like mercantilists, had a zero sum view of international economics and viewed trade and finance as largely parasitic on agriculture. Also like mercantilists, they argued that precious metals ought to be conserved within national borders. Yet free trade was not among cameralist doctrines, instead they hoped to replace expensive foreign imports with domestic substitutes. One such product was "French coffee" imported into Sweden. Indeed Linnaeus considered coffee a French national product that was harmful to Sweden's economy.[60]

Consumers Imagining Coffee as Ottoman or French

Why was coffee perceived as French in Sweden? In France, coffee remained imagined as an Ottoman drink save some exceptions that pointed to Persians and Armenians. Coffee's African origins were silenced in every part of this discourse in France. Africa only emerged in eighteenth-century paintings that represented Africa by black slaves handing coffee to the aristocracy, notably in a famous picture of Madame de Pompadour receiving coffee painted by Vanloo (1705–1765), "La sultane prenant le café".[61] This was one of many illustrations of French elite women as sultanas.[62] Depicting a black slave serving coffee was more a tie to the European slave trade than to Africa itself. This silence on the African origins of coffee replicates the silence on the slave trade, until a century later in the 1770s.

There were several stages of "commodity indigenization" that coffee underwent as an exotic good in France to become French.[63] The French colonial enterprise eventually used its knowledge of coffee and coffee growing gained under Louis XIV to grow coffee in its colonies. Less than a decade after the death of Louis XIV, the French succeeded in creating a thriving crop of beans in Martinique. Until then, coffee was an expensive "oriental" good imported to France. The image of Africans serving coffee only appeared after the colonial success of coffee in the French Caribbean. Partly because of colonial plantations, patterns of coffee consumption changed dramatically over time, yet coffee was adopted as an expensive, rare exotic luxury before it became a colonial good, making a purely economic explanation for its indigenization insufficient. It was prized because it was an oriental luxury and that elusive element of "taste" and fashion played a role in its spread.[64] Coffee would continue to be marketed as an oriental luxury long after it was grown in the Caribbean, pointing to the fact that its oriental provenance was important to its image. Coffee was considered "oriental" within France long after it became a French colonial product in Martinique after 1723. The rest of Europe would start to think of it as French.

Swedish Consumption of "French" Coffee

By the middle of the eighteenth century, France was the major European producer of coffee thanks to its colonial production. Linnaeus wanted Sweden to find a substitute for "French coffee". In his mind, coffee imports were both a moral and a medical hazard to Sweden's well-being: "There are still living the most trustworthy old people, who assure us that [coffee] was brought into [Sweden] by travelers returning from France, and infecting our people with this, as with other foreign customs."[65] Koerner points out that the idea that exotic customs and foreign goods were "infectious" was an idea shared by some philosophers. Linnaeus bemoaned a capital outlay of a thousand Swedish *thalers* for the drink; he listed the "conspicuous consumption" brought about by coffee by listing the necessities it engendered: the silver pot, the Chinese porcelain cups, a round table painted and lacquered, a hand-held coffee bean grinder made of steel, silver trays and linen cloth. This was written exactly in the year that Louis XV placed his multiple orders for coffee pots in gold at Versailles. While Linnaeus argued that Europeans, and not simply Swedes, should abandon such immorally wasteful forms of sociability as drinking coffee, Linnaeus and his wife not only owned all of the aforementioned objects for their afternoon coffee parties, but had their own custom-made porcelain service painted with *Linnaea borealis*.[66] Like many European elites in this period, the Swedish elite imitated the French court. Linnaeus saw these habits as French yet they were already his own habits. This did not stop him from advocating for the substitution of cheaper "over-burned" goods such as peas and beechnuts for imported coffee presumably for other Swedes – not for those, like himself, that were part of the elite.[67]

Before Linnaeus' tea plants in Lapland, another Chinese product of considerable economic importance had been the object of French experimentation. Silk had been the main culprit of Europe's expenditure in gold and silver. The ideas of Olivier de Serres (1539–1619) on the domestication of the mulberry tree on French territory were pioneering.[68] Olivier de Serres, a Protestant, wrote a book on estate management called *Le théâtre d'agriculture* (1600). Serres argued that land had to be managed and used for the profit of its owners, a sentiment that was not germane to Catholic views of nature. His most ambitious commercial project was growing mulberries in colder climates. Most probably, Linnaeus had known of the French experiments directly through his travels in France but also through a German thinker considered the father of cameralism, Heinrich Gottlieb von Justi (1720–1770), who like many of his French predecessors participated in the *rêve chinois*.[69]

European Exports of Opium for Chinese Tea

Swedish, French, German and English attempts to grow tea in Europe failed. To substitute silver payments for Chinese tea and conserve bullion within Europe, it was important to find something that the Chinese would buy. China only accepted silver as payment for tea. However, opium was the only substitute that was in demand. The tea so cherished by consumers in England was imported in large part thanks to the opium trade of the English East

India Company. In the eighteenth century, the EIC traded British woolens and Indian cottons for Chinese tea, porcelain and silk. Because of its high consumption, tea imports became the largest single item in Britain's trading account. Conversely, the export of British and Indian goods to China began to decline and trade imbalance between Britain and China occurred as a result. The shortage of silver to pay for the tea imports forced the British to seek other commodities to compensate for the loss. In large part, the East India Company could avoid shipments of silver to China through the new position it had acquired in India after defeating the Mughals in 1757. Not only had the Company gained access to the large amount of bullion held by the Mughal court, but it would soon surpass the Dutch East India Company as the main long-distance trader of opium by planting opium poppies in India.[70]

Om Prakash demonstrates that the involvement of the English East India Company in the Bihar opium trade was initially limited. The English conquest of Bengal, initiated in 1757 with the defeat of the Nawab's forces at the battle of Plassey and completed in 1765 with the acquisition of revenue collection rights, brought about a dramatic change in their situation. Because of political leverage, the English were now in a position to coerce opium producers and suppliers; this was done by important individual English company servants operating in a private capacity trying to assume a monopoly right in the opium trade of a given area. Initially there were many failures, but there was a drastic change in 1773 when the English Company at Calcutta decided to assume the opium monopoly rights for itself. The company was to organize the supply of the drug on an exclusive basis and then arrange for its sale through public auctions held at its headquarters in Calcutta.[71]

Given that at the time of the British takeover of Bengal the Dutch East India Company was the single biggest buyer of opium in the world market, the existence of a monopoly was hardly likely to have been passed over.[72] The Dutch second in command, Gregorius Herklots, suggested that, against the usual 400–450 chests that the Dutch used to be able to obtain in the 1770s, the EIC could now agree to provide 800 chests of opium to the Dutch company. Since the English needed to finance their supercargo at Canton in China without having to send silver, they asked if the Dutch could arrange for the payment of the opium at Canton. Thereafter, it would be the Dutch bringing specie to China to acquire opium from the English. The amount of opium mentioned in this trade was between 800 and 1,000 chests on an annual basis. Herklots sent a very vague reply, as this arrangement did not appeal to the Dutch and was never put into practice. From then on, the Dutch quota was reduced.[73]

The English company chose to restrict opium growing to Bihar and Banaras and to discontinue it in Bengal. It appointed two opium agents to oversee cultivation in the fields. The formal legislation defining this new principle of cultivation and trade was set out under regulation VI of 1799. This edict, although supplemented by several Acts in the nineteenth century, continued to regulate opium production and marketing in India until the early twentieth century. Through the edict, all private cultivation of the opium poppy was banned. Peasants were therefore forced to cultivate a specific amount and plot of land and deliver its entire opium production at a fixed price to English agents. If a peasant failed to cultivate the full amount that he was required to, he was obliged to pay back pro-rata three times the value of the advance for the shortfall. If a peasant decided to be in the business of producing opium, he had no option but to work for the Company.[74]

According to Prakash, the opium enterprise in India was clearly a great advantage to the English East India Company as well as to the private English traders engaged in the opium trade. Many, but not all, of these traders were servants of the Company. The opium revenues rose from a low value of 14,256 English pounds in 1774–1775 to 49,572 English pounds in 1778–1779 and to 78,300 English pounds in 1783–1784, although the next year they fell to 53,348 English pounds. As a proportion of total Bengal revenues, however, the revenue of opium was estimated to be 5.2 percent in 1792.[75] The Company's direct involvement in the opium business in Bihar put it in a very advantageous position in the export of increasing opium amounts to China. It is this trade in opium that stopped the drain of specie from Bengal to China to pay for the tea procured for the European market. The main consumers of opium were in China while the main consumers of Chinese tea were the British. Consumers of tea in London were not aware of its tie with the opium trade. Many colonial products, especially sugar, would clearly be associated with the slave trade and abolitionist movements would call for boycotts. The only protests in Europe about opium were from rival merchants; it was not a banned drug as the notions of drugs we hold today are not applicable to the eighteenth century where there was no concept of addiction and certainly no legislation against the sale or use of drugs.[76]

Tea and the Culture of Trade of China

In China, all foreign traders were confined to Canton where rigid restrictions were imposed through the practice of Co-hong, a guild of Chinese merchants, the sole recognized agency between foreign and Chinese merchants. The Hongs were the only merchants licensed by the Chinese Emperor. They were made responsible not only for all business deals with foreigners, but for their debts and behavior. Merchants were traditionally despised by the Mandarin class in China. The Hong merchants were under the jurisdiction of a local governor and a customs officer, who was required to pay a large sum every year to the court. The first British ambassador to China, Lord George Macartney (1737–1806), a distinguished diplomat and colonial administrator, set sail for China in September 1792 and the voyage lasted nearly a year. On board the ship, Macartney carried £15,000 worth of presents from the East India Company, the highlight of which was a planetarium with the latest astronomical technology from Europe to be presented to the Emperor of China. His mission to Emperor

Qianlong to make a trade agreement failed. European traders could not get tea directly from Chinese producers. They had to deal with China's commercial infrastructure. Tea did not exist elsewhere until the English began to produce it in quantities in India in the nineteenth century.[77]

Well into the 1890s, China still exported more tea than any other country in the world. In the eighteenth century, tea had to be purchased with silver as this was the only payment that China accepted. If enough opium could be sold to China to pay for the cost of tea, it would eliminate the bullion drain from Europe. Beyond that, it would reduce the cost of tea. Another advance was the establishment of an East India Company factory in Canton in 1716 that gave British factors direct access to China. Between 1700 and 1706, EIC tea imports jumped from 20,000 to 100,000 pounds annually. In 1760, the EIC paid duties in Great Britain on 5,000,000 pounds of tea. In 1767, they exported 6,000,000 pounds of tea from China. This shift that had taken place in trade in calicoes and tea was to the detriment of the Dutch. The Chinese "junk trade" based largely at the Fujian and Shantou ports had come to serve all the needs of the VOC center at Batavia. Between 1728 and 1733, the Dutch Company tried six expeditions into China to try and reserve itself a direct link between Europe and China. The British had found a way of overcoming this problem by virtue of their high position in India.[78]

In the 1780s, the European trading companies imported into Europe about a pound of Asian trading goods for every European inhabitant. Jan de Vries calculates that this composite bundle of Asian goods had a wholesale value of about 0.625 guilders (or just over 1 English shilling). He concludes that the average consumption of Asian commodities per household was between 2.5 and 3 Dutch guilders wholesale in the year 1780. This represented at least a week's earnings of a manual worker in England or Holland. Another approach to measure the significance of Asian trade in Europe is to look at the percentage of Asian imports as a percentage of total imports. In the 1770s, the cumulative value of British, French and Dutch imports from Asia was about 11 percent of their combined total imports. By value, New World imports exceeded those from Asia by a factor of almost three. Moreover, if the imports of other European countries, especially the Iberian empires, were to be included, New World imports would be even larger. De Vries argues that by volume the difference must have been even greater as the per-ton value of Asian goods in the 1770s was probably double that of the plantation products from the New World.[79] Asian trade, however, was never marginal and de Vries argues that its greatest impact was to stimulate new European consumer wants. In the eighteenth century, while spices and tea always remained Asian luxury goods, Caribbean coffee and sugar as well as European produced silk, porcelain and cotton textiles all managed to limit, or even eliminate, competing Asian goods from Europe's consumer markets. Consumerism has been seen as a Western phenomenon that Asia produced and Europe consumed. Just as with the gender bias that men produced and women consumed, this prejudice needs some examining.[80]

Consumerism is Not Only a Western Phenomenon

A scholar of China has tried to eliminate this contrast between a booming, consuming, active Europe and a stagnant China – a contrast termed "the Great Divergence". By revisiting the data, Kenneth Pomeranz cautions that it is important to limit the view that there was a boom in everyday luxuries in Europe before the mid-nineteenth century. He argues that if the list of new consumer goods, foods, textiles, beverages and exotic objects reaching Europe after 1400 was dazzling, their use spread rather slowly until at least the late eighteenth century. He makes a comparison with the consumption of the drug foods in China wherein he points out that even England, the largest consumer of tea in Europe, consumed only one pound of tea per person per year *circa* 1800. Even after prices fell dramatically as late as 1840, the English tea drinker consumed 1.4 pounds of tea per capita. Tea consumption reached about 5 pounds per person only as late as 1880, while for the rest of Europe tea consumption figures were far lower. Non-Russian Europe reported about 22 million pounds of tea per year in the 1780s. This would suggest that the whole European continent consumed 2 ounces per person and non-English Europe considerably less per year. Even in 1840 it remained at 4 ounces a year per capita; in contrast Pomeranz demonstrates that Chinese consumption of tea was significantly higher. Wu Chengming has estimated that the Chinese domestic tea trade was at about 260 million pounds in 1840. If there were 380 million Chinese people at this date, this would be just under eleven ounces per capita. He concedes that just concentrating on tea consumption – as tea was a Chinese product – is an unfair comparison to gauge Chinese consumption levels. There are no figures for tobacco but both Staunton and Macartney, British envoys to China in 1793, were struck by how much tobacco the Chinese smoked. Even in the case of sugar, Pomeranz argues that a European advantage emerges much later than the eighteenth century. Although English consumption was already about four pounds per person by 1700, and had reached eighteen pounds per person by the 1800s, the rest of Europe was far behind. A good estimate for continental Europe in 1800 is about two pounds per capita, which would roughly match Braudel's estimate of one kilo per person in France in 1788.[81]

He also points out that despite slave labor and cheaper sugar prices, consumption was not on a steady upward trend throughout Europe. Pomeranz points out that, as Sidney Mintz has argued, sugar was not just any commodity. Exchanged by kings and popes, it had a social mystique that had been built up for centuries in Europe before the newly discovered tobacco, tea or cocoa. Sugar was eagerly promoted by mercantilist governments who stood to gain from its increased consumption. Pomeranz argues that given all this and the fact there is a fifty-year pause in the growth of consumption between 1750 and 1800 – at a time of high economic prosperity – positing the "birth of a consumer society" in Europe before 1850 is seriously misleading.[82] Pomeranz also argues that before 1850 we mostly have an English consumer revolution and not a European one. He warns against using the general term "Europe" for what is really an exceptional situation in England. The most important part of his work is to try and dismiss what many scholars have called "the Great Divergence" between Europe and China. Most famously, David Landes has argued that economic growth was specific to Europe and that it stagnated in China after the year 1000.[83] Pomeranz takes issue with this thesis by looking at both the production and the consumption of food drugs such as sugar, tea and tobacco in China.

Pomeranz points out that sugar had important ritual and medicinal uses among the elite in China as early as the Tang dynasty. In the Song dynasty, the use of sugar among the rich had spread beyond special occasions. In the sixteenth and seventeenth centuries, certain European visitors commented on how much more common sugar use was among the elite than their more common counterparts. Sugar use on special occasions seemed to have reached the general population. An account from Guangdong province *circa* 1680 tells us that sugar was modeled into the shapes of people, animals and buildings and that sugarplums were a crucial part of weddings. This was true whether the bride was rich or poor, but the wealthy could prepare feasts where several thousands of jars of sugarplums were served. The amount of sugar distributed was said to affect the experience the bride would have when she gave birth. Another source Pomeranz quotes from roughly the same period notes that the Pope ate sugar biscuits on New Year's Day. On the other hand, in China the large amounts of candied fruits were such an essential ritual at a wedding that some families were ruined by trying to meet this need.[84]

There are no totals for Chinese sugar consumption in the mid eighteenth century. But as Pomeranz finds remarkably high estimates of production, he calculates consumption through population figures. A vast majority of Chinese sugar was grown in Guangdong, Fujian (including Taiwan) and Sichuan. Without including the figures for Taiwan, the production was 104 million pounds in 1720. He estimates that the average output per acre on Guangdong for sugarcane was 2,400 pounds. Pomeranz corrects these figures with recent work done by Robert Marks, who suggests that half of Guangdong's cultivated land was non-grain crops. Sugarcane probably occupied more land than any other non-grain. If it was not the first, it was the second (behind mulberries) or at least the third. Taking even one-tenth of the figure for Guangdong's non-grain crops circa 1753, he finds 280,000 acres and gives 672 million pounds of sugar per year for Guangdong. Adding Taiwanese cane production, the total he gives is 776 million pounds in 1750, without considering Sichuan. With China's population in 1750, probably between 170 million to 225 million, this would suggest a per capita sugar consumption of 3.8 to 5 pounds per year.[85] Pomeranz adds that if other Chinese production is considered, it would add at least half a pound a year. These estimates of sugar consumption for China far exceed the European average for 1750 (2.2 pounds per capita per year) and even 1800 (2.6 pounds per capita per year).[86]

In China, overall per capita consumption of "drug foods" certainly grew more slowly, if it did not in fact shrink. Pomeranz argues that it is not enough to note that Europe could have conceivably followed China's path, where consumption preceded Europe. What needs to be explained is the divergence that did eventually occur in consumption. China's post-1750 population growth was heavily concentrated in poor areas and therefore national averages of consuming luxury goods would have declined. This was especially true of sugar, since eighteenth-century sugar consumption was concentrated in three prosperous regions connected to sugar fields by water transport: Lingan, the southeast coast and the Lower Yangtze.[87] But population trends explain only part of the divergence in consumption. Consumption of cotton cloth, for instance, was not geographically concentrated like that of sugar but there is still evidence of a decline in cotton output in northern China. The structure of trade in these new "everyday luxuries" differed in significant ways in China; sugar, tobacco and tea were overwhelmingly domestic products. They competed for land used for food production. The drug food trade did not produce significant revenues for the state in China and it was in the hand of fairly small merchants who had relatively low profit margins. Consequently, contrarily to Europe, there were no particularly powerful interests promoting the increased consumption of these goods.[88]

Pomeranz points out that if moralists in Japan, the Ottoman Empire and India argued against the consumption of these goods, unlike in China, they did so against powerful interests who encouraged increased consumption. He posits that even with all the propaganda from revenue hungry officials, merchants, colonial planters, slave owners and companies with monopolistic privileges, consumption rose slowly in most of continental Europe and among the poor British until the great price decline of the nineteenth century.[89] Pomeranz's argument goes directly against McKendrick's theory that a consumer society was born in eighteenth century Europe, as is quoted at the beginning of this chapter. As such, and because it tries to do away with European and especially British exceptionalism, Pomeranz's work has generated a lot of debate. All groundbreaking work generates academic debate; it remains that some of his analysis has helped diffuse the idea of a European economic advantage.

Arguments against the Existence of Consumerism in Asia

Pomeranz's critics argue that the "Great Divergence" between Europe and Asia was well underway to Europe's advantage before 1800. They believe that, contrary to the claims made by Pomeranz and other world historians such as Parthasarathi, the prosperous part of Asia between 1500 and 1800 was similar to the poorer stagnant regions of southern, central and eastern Europe. They continue to argue for the advantage of northwestern Europe in great part by comparing silver wages. For Pomeranz's critics, high silver wages in northwestern Europe were not simply a monetary phenomenon, but a sign of high productivity in trade and high consumption. However, Pomeranz is not alone; world historians such as Andre Gunder Frank, with his famous book

ReOrient, have also argued that the Yangtze delta in China, southern India and other parts of Asia witnessed the same level of development by 1800 as the most developed parts of Europe, such as Britain and the Netherlands. Their critics argue that, despite the fact that New World silver passed through Spain, wage leadership passed from south to north, with India showing the most rapid growth in wages earned. They use the gap between "silver wage" and the "grain wage" as an indicator of the level of development in north-western Europe. Their argument is that looking at these wages for Europe confirms the well-known tendency for both wages and prices to be higher in developed economies. They argue that despite the high grain wages empha-sized by world historians that have argued against the "Great Divergence", the most advanced parts of Asia had very low silver wages and low levels of urbanization. Based on the pattern of silver wages in Europe, they argue that 1) northwestern Europe saw substantial silver wage growth with Britain over-taking the Netherlands during the eighteenth century, 2) southern Europe knew considerable fluctuations and lower growth in silver wages, 3) in central and eastern Europe there were also substantial fluctuations in sliver wages and only weak growth significantly at a lower level than northwestern Europe in 1500, 4) there was a strong positive correlation between silver wage growth and urbanization ratio in northwestern Europe, and 5) real consumption wages may have risen through increased consumption of non-agricultural goods, even if high silver wages in northwestern Europe did not translate into high grain wages before the nineteenth century.[90]

The "Industrious Revolution" was proposed by Jan de Vries[91] as a solution to the paradox that, despite the consistency of real daily wage rates in Europe during the Early Modern period, evidence from probate inventories after death and other evidence that documents consumption, one finds "an ever-multiplying world of goods, a richly varied and expanding material culture, with origins going back to the seventeenth century and exhibiting a social range extending far down the hierarchy".[92] For de Vries, the household is a unit through which he sees a maximization of utility, a reallocation of labor from non-market to market activities. A reduction of leisure time helped the households increase consumption of market-supplied goods. He sees the rise of this consumerism not simply because of the relative lowering of the prices of goods, but also as a consequence of changing tastes. If the living standards of northwestern European households increased through the falling of the prices of manufactured goods, rather than through an increased consumption of basic things such as grain, it is likely that development was spread unevenly. Clearly the wages of skilled artisans were higher and had a larger surplus over basic food needs than those of unskilled laborers. During the Early Modern period, the relative price of luxuries was declining. These goods were available to the top 20 percent of the highest wage earners.[93] Although Frank and Pomeranz's critics recognize that the wage and price data available for Asia is not as complete and clear as the European data, they still think it important to try a systematic analysis of the existing data. Chiefly they find that the scale of the silver wage difference between Britain and Asia during the seventeenth and eighteenth centuries was very large. They argue that this difference was so large that it is difficult for them to imagine how their conclusion could be overturned by any conceivable form of data correction. Without wanting to participate in this debate here, it is still important to be aware of it. Some historians continue to firmly believe in the European advantage and especially argue for Britain and the Netherlands as exceptional societies with high urbanization, high silver wages and a high level of consumption. Broadberry and Gupta argue that the advanced parts of Asia in 1800 were on the same level of development as some poorer parts of the European periphery.[94]

Consumption as Societal Classifier

Pomeranz's work does not only concentrate on drug foods, but also addresses the issue of the rise of fashion in the West. Asia has been viewed as a society where there was little change in clothing and the rise of fashion in Europe has also bolstered theories of Europe's exceptional development and consumerism. Pomeranz tries to close the breach. He classified arguments about the rise of "luxury" and "consumer" society in Europe after 1400 into two groups. One group of scholars concentrated on drugs. Another group concentrated on luxury consumption among the very wealthy, emphasizing the employment of durable manufactured objects such as silks, mirrors, furniture and carpets that replaced earlier ways of expressing status. The sociologist Werner Sombart called this "objectification of luxury". Sombart's work on the rise of capitalism, although discredited after his political adherence to Nazism, is still cited for his ideas on consumption and luxury. He posited "luxury is any expenditure that goes beyond necessity" and there are two kinds of luxury: quantitative and qualitative.[95] They can appear together but qualitative luxury means a refinement of the goods consumed. For Sombart, the desire for luxury can be traced to sexuality and therefore consumption has unconscious or libidinal motives as well as a rational motive.[96] Canons of taste were important in imitating the elite and it has been argued that the rise of "fashion" dictated that even those who owned large amounts of luxury goods still experienced a desire for them as socially necessary.

In an argument familiar by now, high status consumption patterns were imitated by lesser folk. This consumption was further encouraged by new conceptions of the self and a fluidity in social structure that allowed not only for the nouveau riche but for the "middling sort" and even the poor to use their money to claim new social status. Consumption begins at the top but emphasizes the transformation of luxuries into everyday goods for the middle class and eventually the poor. Even if it might include small objects, this form of argument is usually about the drug foods: sugar, cocoa, tobacco and tea. Pomeranz points out that although the two overlap, for scholars who focus on the upper class luxuries, objects such as furniture, china or clothing, there is an emphasis on industrialization that there isn't for scholars who look at the consumption of drug foods. He hypothesizes that an internally generated European advantage may seem more plausible for more durable goods, furniture, silverware, linens and so on. But he cautions that even here we have to look closely at China and Japan before we accept such an advantage. While Pomeranz concedes that sources such as probate inventories are scarce for Asia, he argues that elite consumption seems roughly comparable across a number of societies between 1400 and 1800. In Europe, China, Japan and India one finds a striking increase in home furnishings, elaborate clothing, eating utensils and collectibles among the wealthy. In all of these societies, the display of material possessions became a more important determinant of status. The importance of personal retinues as a sign of status declined in these societies, as Norbert Elias has long argued for France. Many elite families across these societies in Asia participated in this luxury consumption but Pomeranz concedes that consumption was not exactly similar in any two societies.[97]

Controlling Wealth and Society

Pomeranz points out that dichotomies arise between societies in which commodities and markets determine social relationships and other societies where social exchanges are for the pursuit of gain. On one hand, there are societies in which social status governs consumption and people are concerned with social reciprocity based on status, while others are driven by profit. He argues that these dichotomies give rise to the idea that Europe became materialistic first and that the rest of the planet had not crossed this divide. This also leads to the false conclusion that "materialism" and "economic man" had to be introduced from the outside to non-European societies. He credits Arjun Appadurai's theories for framing these issues more subtly. In a theory that has become very well known, Appadurai denies dichotomy and creates a continuum that links "fashion systems", on the one hand, to the "coupon" or "license systems" on the other. In this definition, fashion systems have an enormous number of status-conferring goods that circulate in society. These status-conferring goods may be purchased by anyone with enough money to acquire them. In the fashion system, the immediate transmutability of money into status is only limited by the ever-shifting social rules of elites that shape taste. They, as the elite, decry some consumer behaviors as "vulgar" and others as "refined". In the coupon system, on the other hand, important and often sacred items can only be legitimately possessed and exchanged by those who have the social license to hold them or buy them.[98] He calls societies with the licensing system, or coupons system, "societies devoted to stable status displays in exploding commodity contexts, such as India, China, and Europe in the premodern period".[99] Appadurai even found some coupon goods in the contemporary West and avoids making total dichotomies between societies. He avoids the argument of consumerism being subsumed under a unique Western individualism.[100] A coupon system, by definition, has the purpose of discouraging imitation of a higher status group's consumption by the social groups below them. In the fashion system, the elite proceeds not by forbidding such imitations but by shifting to new goods and to maintaining power through imposing their taste.

Pomeranz argues that although the phenomenon of consumption is best documented for various regions of Western Europe, Renaissance Italy, Golden Age Spain and the Dutch Republic, the rise of consumer society was not unique to France and England. Craig Clunas has shown that upper class homes in China during the Ming dynasty (1368–1644) were crammed with paintings, sculptures, fine furniture and other goods. He finds that, just as in Europe, it became important to have the right to own luxury goods. He has shown that, for example, it became important to own elegantly carved beds in wealthy Chinese families well before the same desire for elaborately carved beds existed in Europe.[101] The very rich might have owned different beds and chairs for the different seasons of the year. Prestigious pieces were produced by great artists and they were increasingly commodified, as they were available to anyone with enough money. Clunas has argued that the wealthy could increasingly be converted to status through consumption alone rather than buying office, land or education for their children. Published Chinese guidebooks began to offer decorating advice on how to display such objects properly. Some books showed older elites how to reassert their status through taste while other manuals targeted the *nouveaux riches*, advising them on the proper way to acquire and display their new objects.[102]

The early Ming state promulgated various sumptuary laws in order to regulate dress, tableware and the use of various objects by different social groups. These laws seemed to have very little effect and soon became outdated; only one new item was added to these laws after 1500, despite the fact that new luxuries proliferated.[103] Clunas points out that sumptuary laws continued to be promulgated in seventeenth-century Italy, Spain and in other European societies. Clunas finds that similar evidence can be deduced for Muromachi and Tokugawa Japan where complaints from moralists and a series of ineffective sumptuary laws list all kinds of luxuries being inappropriately used by people of the wrong rank. In eighteenth-century Japan, sumptuary laws had strict rules against gold, silver and ivory decorations in the homes of peasants and there were complaints about how samurai and even daimyo had been ruined attempting to keep up appearances. Peter Burke, a specialist in European consumerism, is one of the few Europeanist scholars who has concluded that Chinese and Japanese developments are strikingly contemporaneous to the ones in Western Europe.[104]

Consumerism in India

Kenneth Pomeranz points out that Indian evidence is more ambiguous. Not so much because of the lack of luxury in India, but for lack of evidence of an emerging "fashion system" with the broad participation of many classes. There is more evidence in India of an established, older "coupon system" than there is for Western Europe or East Asia. It seems likely that consumerism, though certainly present, made less headway in India than in East Asia.[105] C. A. Bayly has described how the Kashmir shawl had become a universal symbol of aristocracy in the Indo-Persian world. Muslim emperors had developed special institutions for the reception, grading and storing of the shawls. Kashmir shawls were closely tied into the diplomatic tribute systems of both the Iranian and Indian empires. In the courts of North India, the shawl remained a widely used form of honorific currency that marked status. In Lucknow in the 1770s, the ruler Jahandar Shah gifted shawls regularly to both his servants and supporters. Members of the royal family distributed vast numbers of shawls and items of brocade work during weddings and other festivals in the city of Benares.[106]

C.A. Bayly has suggested that the importance of consumption by the elites was further enhanced by the low level of demand from the mass population. In his view, this was a reflection not only of widespread poverty, but of the limited needs in a tropical climate. He argues that the sharp distinction between ordinary and luxury demand was a consequence of the influence of cultural models on patterns of consumption. The expensive and luxurious kingly style of behavior was one of several culturally accepted styles. Next to it coexisted princely, merchant and peasant styles that emphasized frugality. Socially highly placed Brahmins shunned any conspicuous display. The giving and taking of gifts would involve them in undesirable social relations with others who were below their high caste. In their religious texts, the Jain were opposed to luxurious clothing and housing and to the maintenance of large bodies of servants. Among the great peasant castes, the Jats, Kunbis and Kurmis, a strong ascetic and parsimonious style was advocated. C.A. Bayly points out, however, that there were innumerable exceptions to these rules. Merchants indulging in expensive habits and regal Brahmins were to be found all over different communities. Because of this, he posits that neither the economic nor the social historian of India can take consumption patterns in the diverse society of India as a given. Even wealthy groups such as the Marathas continued, for a considerable time even after their conquest, to stick to ascetic patterns of consumption during the zenith of their power. It was not until the 1770s and 1780s that a real consumer class developed among the Marathas and later among the Sikhs. Palace building and luxury consumption were then financed by hoards of bullion that had been hoarded in more insecure days. This new consumption signaled an important social change that transformed warriors into settled rulers living in kingly style, giving acquiescence in the still powerful culture of Mughal court ritual that encouraged and practiced the consumption of luxury goods.[107]

Asian Urbanization and Consumerism

In China, the main exporter of these goods, as in Europe, the dynamics of human consumption changed in response to changes in income and shifts in taste. China had a long experience of extensive commercialization and integration into the international trading economy. Chinese historians have argued that the level of technology in eleventh century China was comparable to that of Europe in the early eighteenth century. The other argument for the rise of consumption has been the proliferation of urban centers in Europe. Both China and Japan were also highly urbanized societies: by the Ming Dynasty (1368–1644) there were 4,500 market towns in China. The Japanese capital of Edo grew from a fishing village to a city of a million inhabitants by the end of the eighteenth century. The necessary conditions of urbanization in Asia depended on three interrelated conditions. In a centralized political empire, it was almost axiomatic that the imperial capital would serve as a model. Secondly, very active long-distance trade and the dominance of merchants and bankers strengthened the importance of social consumption and economic production. A strong association between religion, cultural life and market towns was the third condition. Long-distance trade in the world of the Indian Ocean and the Mediterranean was arguably held together according to K.N. Chaudhuri by the urban pool of Canton, Malacca, Calicut, Cambay, Hormuz, Aden, Alexandria and Aleppo. It is also important to use Fernand Braudel's concept of the urban typology to extend the role of towns even further and to include a hierarchy of smaller towns in this equation. The influence of major cities such as Constantinople, Damascus, Baghdad, Delhi or Peking occupied a rank at the very top of this spatial hierarchy. The next in order would be the regional city followed by provincial and district towns. Only great capital cities such as Cairo, Isfahan or Agra should unquestionably be placed at the first category in this hierarchy because of political, economic and cultural prominence. These cities were all major producers and consumers of luxury goods.[108] The millionaire bankers of the port of Surat financed trade to Delhi, Agra, Bijapur, Golconda, Mocha, Hormuz and Bandar Abbas in Persia. They also lent money to European East India Companies.[109]

K.N. Chaudhuri has argued that the great merchants acted directly as bankers to states. Even if centralized empires exercised little control over the international economic transactions of merchants, they benefited from their profits that permitted the development of state capitalism. He has argued that the mining and redistribution of large quantities of gold and silver from the New World and Japan accelerated the growth of liquidity in the Indian Ocean and eased the problem of supporting a metallic currency. The role played by European merchants in the Indian Ocean as agents of monetary redistribution was a crucial one. The internal adjustment of Europe's new demand for Asia's luxury goods broke down the relative insularity of the Chinese economy and made the economies of the Middle East and India even more open than they were. The final stage in the dynamic movements in the Indian Ocean was reached during the second half of the eighteenth century when British military and naval power fused with European technology to turn India into a colonial territory.[110] As Jan de Vries has argued, the Battle of Plassey in 1757 was the turning point that made British trade in India profitable for the first time.[111]

Eighteenth-century China was a civilization that was close to its peak in forms of cultural accomplishments and wealth. It had a large "leisure class" which we find portrayed in works of Qing literature where a lot of people seem to have little to do but to entertain themselves or be entertained by others. One thing is clear: in his work *The Scholars*, Wu Jingzi tells heartbreaking stories about the thousands of hopeful members of the literati desperately studying, hoping to rise through China's strict examination system. What Wu depicts is that this traditional system of provincial examinations, which was the only way that a scholar became an official, was near impossible. With large numbers of candidates and very few offices available, the high level of competition naturally meant a high level of failure in the exams. This resulted in high unemployment and frustrations among the best-educated and most affluent people of the country. Ichisada Miyazaki, in his classic study on the Chinese examination system estimated that only 1 in 3,000 actually was able to secure a civil service position. This relative lack of opportunity amongst the most ambitious, traditional elite was a major problem. Later, many of China's rebels sprung from the ranks of failed examination candidates. In the years between the beginning of the eighteenth century and the third decade of the nineteenth century, a culture of opium use was created in this leisure class in China. Even though forbidden, the consumption of opium became entrenched and since this culture was associated with the elite, it became an object of emulation for the lower classes. Like the consumption of most other drugs, there was a tendency for the practice to move down the social scale as opium became cheaper and more readily available.[112] Sydney Mintz showed a similar phenomenon with sugar and Jessica Warner has shown a similar spread in the case of gin for eighteenth century Britain.[113]

Asia had well developed consumer markets and this meant product differentiation in the production of ceramics and silk. High quality ceramics were distinguished by studio marks and would have been made for private consumers in the Chinese middle market. Similarly, silks, though functional, were also made in special qualities and designs for the middle market. In India, luxury markets based around the Mughal courts reflected a diverse and well-developed consumer culture. Fashionable clothing was mainly expressed in color, patterning, embroidery, pleating and various types of ornament and accessories, sashes, slippers and jewelry. China, Japan and India provided long-standing models of highly urbanized commercial societies providing for an early flowering of consumer culture well before Europe.[114] Chinese ceramics sold to sixty-four foreign destinations and textiles to eighty-five different destinations and this was beyond China's own domestic consumer market. China traded in metal products, gold, silver, copper and iron with another 134 destinations. During the Ming Dynasty, China had very few imports such as horses, medicinal herbs, and chiefly metals – especially silver bullion. China, followed by India, was the main supplier of industrial manufactured goods to the world. China's main barter product to the spice islands was Indian piece goods acquired in its own well-developed triangular trade. China also had extensive trade with Japan and the South China Seas. Chinese ships taking goods to Japan in the Ming period averaged 298.4 tons. Those traveling to west Asia with Chinese goods had a larger loading capacity of 955 tons.[115] During the Ming period, 130 Chinese government registered vessels traveled overseas ever year. The China Manila trade, Manila being the main port for silver, was also extensive.

In Manila, China's constant demand for silver bullion was met by Spanish galleons bringing in silver from the New World and buying Chinese silks and porcelains as well as Asian spices. The Chinese traded very great quantities of porcelain on these Asian markets before and after the Europe market opened to them. In 1645 alone, 229,000 pieces of porcelain were sold within the year to the Japanese and another 300,000 to the Arabs via the Dutch. In the first half of the seventeenth century, more than half of the exports from China went to South Sea markets but those sent to Europe were of better quality. By the end of the seventeenth century, Europe's share of Chinese ceramic exports was around 31 percent. From Japan, through the small trading factory of Deshima on Hirado island, Kakeimon ware was exported followed by Imari ware later.[116] The bulk of these Japanese exports also went to the South Seas and only 10 percent went to European consumers. China shipped silk to the Dutch in Batavia for re-export to Japan along with silk from Bengal, India. In exchange, China bought cotton textiles from India, spices, sandalwood and timber. The Indian cotton textile trade faced a constant demand on Asian markets. It produced and fine-tuned for the specialized taste of highly diversified consumers. The trade in textiles and ceramics between Asia and Europe that became more important in the eighteenth century was organized on trading routes already well frequented by Asian merchants. The European consumer was therefore simply added on to the highly developed Asian markets for Chinese, Japanese and Indian goods. Maxine Berg nevertheless argues that European demand caused a shock in the case of China when the Dutch traded a million pieces of porcelain at the very end of the seventeenth century. The effect of this European consumer demand on Chinese trade was a shift from a more diversified trade of consumer goods to a narrow trade based only on silk and porcelain.[117]

A Global Consumption: Calicoes

Between the thirteenth century and 1800, there was a steady expansion of cotton textile consumption around the world. Cotton textiles displaced hemp, linen, wool and other competing fibers from Japan and China to Europe and North America. In these centuries, the majority of cotton textiles that criss-crossed the globe had their origins in the Indian subcontinent, which was the preeminent center for cotton manufacturing in the world.[118] There is an ongoing debate amongst historians about what is called the "de-industrialization" of India, as the industrialization of Britain took place.[119]

Printed Indian cottons and calicoes did not only inspire fashions in Europe, but had a major influence on Japanese dress. In "Japan Indianized", Fujita Kayoko demonstrates that there was a deep Indian influence on Japanese fashions between the sixteenth and nineteenth centuries. In Japanese visual artworks, as early as the seventeenth century, one sees foreign Portuguese missionaries and traders dressed in European style, made of Indian fabrics with stripes and checkered patterns. These Indian textiles had an influence on Japanese textile production. Based on the example of imports, craftsmen started producing both cotton and silk textiles in a variety of striped and checkered patterns. In 1736, striped cotton textiles (706,600 *ryô* in silver for 698,747 pieces) were the second-most important commodity shipped from the central market in Osaka. The Indian motifs of stripes were found in the urban societies of Edo, among merchants and craftsmen. Tie-dyeing and embroidery were the most common design techniques for Indian cotton textiles at the beginning of the seventeenth century. The importation of Indian printed and painted textiles re-shaped the art of dyeing in Japan. As in many other parts of the globe during this period, the Japanese also tried to copy colorful Indian textiles, but the process of imitation was not a smooth one. Japan had long benefited from Chinese technology. Therefore, the transfer of weaving and dyeing technologies was not direct and relied on manuals imported from China. As fashion conscious consumers in urban Japan constantly sought new trends, there was high demand for Indian cotton textiles as top-end luxury goods.[120] That demand did not end with the establishment of a domestic cotton manufacturing industry in the eighteenth century.

Over the course of the eighteenth century, the huge potential of Asian manufactures emerged as cotton became an even larger component of dress and furnishing across the world. Cotton became a vehicle both for style and functional utility across social ranks. For Indian merchants, the growth of a new European market represented just another form of negotiations on the colors, patterns and textures that they had formerly been selling in Asia. Beverly Lemire quotes Braudel who observed "fashion is also a search for a new language to discredit the old"; the manufacturers of India were the intermediaries who brought a new visual language to Europe.[121] They helped nurture the craze for Indian textiles that ensued in the Netherlands, England and France. By 1700, English merchants and tradesmen, both wealthy and middle class, draped vibrant calicoes over their beds and windows. This fashion, however, would precipitate a crisis as European governments tried to protect their own manufacturers and printing industries that were now embellishing plain Indian cotton cloth domestically.[122] The cloth embellished in Britain imitated Indian motifs, albeit motifs that had already been transformed by the European market.

Maxine Berg has shown that in India, the Coromandel chintzes of the early period had Persian or Deccani motifs but that by the end of the seventeenth century artisans were using pattern books sent from England, Holland and France. The English East India Company merchants in the eighteenth century wanted to avoid risk. They willingly accepted pattern books from Europe to India, but insisted that the Indians work "their own fancy".[123] This imitation of European patterns was not a novelty in China or India. For centuries, artisans in both cultures had adapted to the demand in very diversified markets in Eurasia. Asian imitations of European forms were combined with Oriental themes that became a product designed for world markets in the eighteenth century. To protect European textile weavers and printers, there were many prohibitions against importing printed calicoes in Europe. Britain promulgated outright prohibition of printed calicoes in 1700.[124]

The fashion for *indiennes*, as calicoes were called in French, did not disappear despite other European prohibitions in London and in the Dutch Republic in the early eighteenth century. Robert Chenciner writes that many enterprising men in France and elsewhere tried to penetrate the secret of madder dyeing. It would have been easier had they read that – in their possession of Canada – there was another way of obtaining red; as early as 1603, Samuel Champlain had praised a brilliant American red dye he called Micmac red. In 1670, Sister Marie de l'Incarnation wrote down the simple technique it required, which was equally ignored. In contrast to her less involved method, the techniques used for dyeing with madder could take up to a month or more for one piece of cloth, explaining the value and price of these printed cottons. Oriental products were highly prized and the nun's description of how the Indians painted porcupine quills is once again a case of gathering information on plants and spices to no avail. It was, as was much of the information gathered abroad, completely ignored in France.[125] The fear of foreign products, of exotic goods hurting the economy of France, took over after Colbert's mitigating influence to assuage French hostility to foreigners and the foreign had disappeared. The court began by taxing imported cotton cloth, a measure the Marseillais protested as they said it restricted French industries' progress. As a result of this misguided policy, the remaining Marseillais artisans left for Tuscany and later competed with Marseilles' production.[126]

Olivier Raveux has studied the French production of *indiennes*, as calicoes were called.[127] As a consequence of breaks in transmission and the difficulty of dyeing with madder, there was not just one moment when there was a transfer of technology, but several. After the departure of the skilled Armenians and Marseillais artisans from Marseilles in 1687, there was a long gap to recuperate lost knowledge and there were other examples of transference of similar technologies at the height of the fashion for *indiennes*. A simplified recipe of this oriental technique was reached by J. C. Flashat after years of study. Flaschat was sponsored to travel and live in Edirne (Adrianople), a center for Turkish red dye in the eighteenth century. He returned to France and according to Schaefer set up a dyeing factory devoted to dyeing with madder in Saint Chamond near Lyons in 1748, exactly a century after the Marseillais had first tried but failed to copy *indiennes*. To run the dye factory he brought his entire team with him from the Ottoman Empire: two dyers from Adrianople, two tinsmiths *étameurs* from Constantinople one of whom made high end coffee pots, a Persian spinner, and from Smyrna a thummer or *arçonneur* who fluffed up cotton. An Indian *brodeur au tamis* was left behind as he refused to come to France, but he taught Flaschat his art of making sieves, and the team was completed with two Armenian vitriol makers from Cyprus. Flaschat's trip was subsidized by Henri Betrin, Minister of Finance, as is clear from the preface to his treatise on dyeing, published in 1766 in Lyons.[128] A royal edict of 1704 now allowed the Dutch to bring in their goods, among them several dyes, including madder. This was not to France's advantage nor would it benefit the Marseillais. Though the process of dyeing with madder had been developed entirely empirically, it was considered a "secret" process achieved by Claude Berthollet (1748–1822). The many details of this transfer of techniques are the domain of textile historians, many of whom concur that Europe had turned to Asia to integrate superior manufacturing techniques that set its own technological progress in motion. "Oriental" techniques carried through a series of merchant networks marked the beginning of European industrialization.[129] It can be argued that fashion for things oriental was the impetus behind these economic transformations in French manufacturing and that consumer demand for oriental luxury goods drove this transformation.

Discussion of consumption became a focus for a much larger public than just mercantilists and philosophers, perhaps because the consumption of luxuries went far beyond the nobility. If the increased consumption of exotic and domestic luxuries challenged the Catholic belief that luxury was a sin, the fierce political debates they sparked were not about sin but about the disastrous economic effects on France of a higher influx of foreign luxury goods. This opened debates on colonization, on the slave trade and on the legislation of domestically manufacturing the imitations of exotic imports.[130] It has been argued by John Shovlin that middling elites were concerned about their rank and place and that this new competition for the consumption of luxuries was an element in creating the debate that led to the Revolution.[131] There were no fewer than 2,869 titles appearing between 1750 and 1789 about economic subjects. Jean Claude Perrolt has argued that this was a higher production than any form of literature, including novels.[132] The peak of this production was in 1789 with 804 titles, yet as Shovlin puts it, these debates have attracted surprisingly little notice. The Catholic debate about sin and luxury receded to some degree and gave way to a concern for the national good rather than concern for one's soul. In this moral and patriotic debate about national wealth, the consumer of foreign luxury came under fire.

Study Questions

1 Is the discourse about consumption a gendered discourse?
2 What forms of arguments have been offered by scholars for the spread of exotic goods to a larger and larger group of consumers?

3 Did commodities produced on colonial plantations through slave labor, such as coffee, overtake Asian imports in Europe in the eighteenth century?
4 Was consumption a Western phenomenon? What arguments have been made to demonstrate that it was not?
5 What are the difficulties for studying consumption in a vast territory like India?

Notes

1 Bernard Mandeville, *The Fable of the Bees and Other Writings*, E.J. Hundert, ed. (Indianapolis: Hackett Publishing, 1997), in Kate Haulman, *The Politics of Fashion in Eighteenth-century America* (Chapel Hill: University of North Carolina Press, 2011), 1.
2 Mandeville, *The Fable of the Bees*, 28 in Haulman, *The Politics of Fashion*, 1.
3 Mandeville, *The Fable of the Bees*, 33 in Haulman, *The Politics of Fashion*, 1.
4 Samuel Adams to James Warren, October 20, 1778, in Paul H. Smith, Gerard W. Gawalt, Rosemary Fry Plakas, Eugene R. Sheridan, and Ronald M. Gephard, eds., *Letters of Delegates to Congress, 1774–1789,* CD ROM (Summerfield, FL, 1998) in Haulman, *The Politics of Fashion in Eighteenth-Century America*, 1.
5 Neil McKendrick, John Brewer and J. H. Plumb, *The Birth of a Consumer Society: the Commercialization of Eighteenth-century England* (Bloomington: Indiana University Press, 1982).
6 Jan de Vries, "Chapter 3" in *Luxury in the Eighteenth Century: Debates, Desires and Delectable Goods*, Maxine Berg, Elizabeth Eger, eds. (Basingstoke, Hampshire; New York: Palgrave, 2003).
7 Ina Baghdiantz McCabe, *Orientalism in Early Modern France: Eurasian Trade, Exoticism and the Ancien Régime* (Oxford; New York: Berg, 2008), 268–197.
8 Kenneth Pomeranz,*The Great Divergence: China, Europe, and the Making of the Modern World Economy* (New Jersey: Princeton University Press, 2000).
9 Berg and Eger, *Luxury in the Eighteenth Century*.
10 Berg and Eger, *Luxury in the Eighteenth Century*; Jan de Vries, *The Industrious Revolution: Consumer Behavior and the Household Economy, 1650 to the Present* (Cambridge: Cambridge University Press, 2008); Baghdiantz McCabe, *Orientalism*.
11 Amanda Vickery, "His and Hers: Gender, Consumption and Household Accounting in Eighteenth-century England", *Past and Present* (2006) 1 (suppl 1): 12–38, 29.
12 Vickery, "His and Hers", 33.
13 Vickery, "His and Hers", 33.
14 Vickery, "His and Hers", 34.
15 Vickery "His and Hers", 37.
16 John E. Sandrock, "John Law's Banque Royale and the Mississippi Bubble". Accessed 18 September 2013. http://www.google.com/url?sa=t&rct=j&q=&esrc =s&source=web&cd=1&ved=0CCAQFjAA&url=http%3A%2F%2Fwww.thecur rencycollector.com%2Fpdfs%2FJohn_Laws_Banque_Royale.pdf&ei=ZYxFUKq xGMm36gHQxoGACQ&usg=AFQjCNHezfya7qm3KRRVm47N7tdceydTQA
17 Edgar Faure, *La Banqueroute de Law, 17 Juillet 1720* (Paris: Gallimard, 1977).
18 Faure, *La Banqueroute de Law*, 49.
19 Faure, *La Banqueroute de Law*, 50–51.
20 Faure, *La Banqueroute de Law*, 110–111.
21 Faure, *La Banqueroute de Law*, 67.
22 Faure, *La Banqueroute de Law*, 108, decree of August 23, 1716.
23 Faure, *La Banqueroute de Law*, 99–109.
24 *Lettre au régent (décembre 1715)* in Faure, *La Banqueroute de Law*, 120.

25 Faure, *La Banqueroute de Law*, 247.
26 James S. Pritchard, *In Search of Empire: the French in the Americas, 1670–1730* (Cambridge, UK; New York: Cambridge University Press, 2004).
27 Faure, *La Banqueroute de Law*, 132.
28 Faure, *La Banqueroute de Law*, 153.
29 Faure, *La Banqueroute de Law*, 134.
30 Faure, *La Banqueroute de Law*, 148.
31 Faure, *La Banqueroute de Law*, 223.
32 Peter M. Garber, *Famous First Bubbles: The Fundamentals of Early Manias* (London; Cambridge, MA: The MIT Press, 2000), 195–203.
33 Faure, *La Banqueroute de Law*, 241.
34 Faure, *La Banqueroute de Law*, 247.
35 Faure, *La Banqueroute de Law*, 247.
36 Faure, *La Banqueroute de Law*, 613.
37 James E. Lewis, *The Louisiana Purchase: Jefferson's Noble Bargain?* (Charlottesville, VA: Thomas Jefferson Foundation, 2003).
38 Helen J. Paul, *The South Sea Bubble: An Economic History of its Origins and Consequences* (London; New York: Routledge, 2011), 37–39.
39 Garber, *Famous First Bubbles*, 104–122.
40 Garber, *Famous First Bubbles*, 111.
41 Garber, *Famous First Bubbles*, 104–122.
42 Garber, *Famous First Bubbles*, 104–122.
43 Paul, *The South Sea Bubble*, 87.
44 Paul, *The South Sea Bubble*, 93.
45 Paul, *The South Sea Bubble*, 160.
46 Jan de Vries, "The Limits of Globalization in the Early Modern World", *The Economic History Review,* 63, 3 (2010), 720.
47 De Vries "The Limits of Globalization in the Early Modern World", 721–22.
48 Baghdiantz McCabe, "Domesticating the Exotic: Imports and Imitation", Chapter 8 in *Orientalism in Early Modern France*, 205–230. Berg and Eger, "Asian Luxuries and the Making of the European Consumer Revolution", Chapter 16 in *Luxury in the Eighteenth Century*, 228–244.
49 Ralph A. Austen and Woodruff D. Smith, "Private Tooth Decay as Public Economic Virtue: The Slave-Sugar Triangle, Consumerism, and European Industrialization", *Social Science History*, Vol. 14, No. 1 (Spring 1990): 95–115.
50 Austen and Smith, "Private Tooth Decay as Public Economic Virtue", 105.
51 Austen and Smith, "Private Tooth Decay as Public Economic Virtue", 107.
52 Austen and Smith, "Private Tooth Decay as Public Economic Virtue", 105–119.
53 Austen and Smith, "Private Tooth Decay as Public Economic Virtue", 110.
54 De Vries, "The Limits of Globalization in the Early Modern World", 723. Tables of profit margins for the Dutch, English and French East India Companies are also available in his work *Industrious Revolution.*
55 De Vries, *Industrious Revolution*, 154–164, 181–185.
56 De Vries, "The Limits of Globalization in the Early Modern World", 727.
57 Lisbet Koerner, "Linnaeus' Floral Transplants", *Representations*, No. 47, Special Issue: National Cultures before Nationalism (Summer, 1994): 144–169, 147.
58 Koerner, "Linnaeus' Floral Transplants", 147.
59 Koerner, "Linnaeus' Floral Transplants", 147.
60 Koerner, "Linnaeus' Floral Transplants", 144–169.
61 Carl Vanloo, *La sultane prenant le café*, Ermitage Museum, Saint Peterburg.
62 For Oriental disguises, see chapter 9 in Baghdiantz McCabe, *Orientalism in Early Modern France.*
63 This work has been done for colonial encounters, but this is not the case of coffee and France, which makes the question even more interesting and complex to

solve. Marshall Sahlins coined the term "commodity indigenization" to demonstrate that non-Western cultures did not passively accept European goods but incorporated them after transforming them to something more familiar, applying their own terms, in ways that were consistent with their cultures: Marshall Sahlins, "Cosmologies of Capitalism: The Trans-Pacific Sector of 'the World-System'," *Proceedings of the British Academy* 74 (1988): 1–51. Jordan Goodman uses Sahlins's model to help account for tobacco's success in Europe: Jordan Goodman, *Tobacco in History: The Cultures of Dependence* (London: Routledge, 1994), 41–42.

64　For the social aspects of taste formation see Wolfgang Schivelbusch, *Tastes of Paradise: a Social History of Spices, Stimulants, and Intoxicants* (New York: Pantheon Books, 1992) and Bianca Maria Rinaldi, *The "Chinese Garden in Good Taste": Jesuits and Europe's Knowledge of Chinese Flora and Art of the Garden in the 17th and 18th Centuries* (München: Meidenbauer, 2006).

65　Cited by Koerner, "Linnaeus' Floral Transplants", 157–8.

66　The *Twin Flower*, a very small plant that is found worldwide in northern forests, and which was his favorite plant, which he named for himself: LINNAEA *(linA'a)* BOREALIS, borealis meaning, of the northern forest.

67　Koerner, "Linnaeus' Floral Transplants", 157.

68　Olivier de Serres, *Le théâtre d'agriculture et mesnage des champs* (Paris : Jamet Métayer, 1600).

69　Johanna M. Menzel, "The Sinophilism of J. H. G. Justi," *Journal of the History of Ideas* 17, No. 3 (June, 1956): 300–310.

70　Om Prakash, "Opium Monopoly in India and Indonesia in the Eighteenth Century", *Indian Economic Social History Review* 1987 24:63.

71　Prakash, "Opium Monopoly in India and Indonesia in the Eighteenth Century", 66.

72　Prakash, "Opium Monopoly in India and Indonesia in the Eighteenth Century", 67.

73　Prakash, "Opium Monopoly in India and Indonesia in the Eighteenth Century", 77.

74　Prakash, "Opium Monopoly in India and Indonesia in the Eighteenth Century", 69.

75　Prakash, "Opium Monopoly in India and Indonesia in the Eighteenth Century", 70.

76　Hans Derks, *History of the Opium Problem: the Assault on the East, ca. 1600–1950* (Leiden; Boston: Brill, 2012).

77　Carl Trocki, *Opium, Empire and the Global Political Economy: a Study of the Asian Opium Trade, 1750–1950* (London; New York: Routledge, 1999), 40–42.

78　Trocki, *Opium, Empire and the Global Political Economy*, 40–42.

79　De Vries, "The Limits of Globalization in the Early Modern World", 728.

80　Kenneth Pomeranz, *The Great Divergence: China, Europe and the Making of the Modern World Economy* (New Jersey: Princeton University Press, 2000), 192.

81　Pomeranz, *The Great Divergence*, 117.

82　Pomeranz, *The Great Divergence*, 119.

83　David Landes, *The Wealth and Poverty of Nations: Why Some are so Rich and Some so Poor* (New York: W.W. Norton, 1998).

84　Pomeranz, *The Great Divergence*, 119.

85　Pomeranz, *The Great Divergence*, 121.

86　Pomeranz, *The Great Divergence*, 122.

87　Pomeranz, *The Great Divergence*, 123.

88　Pomeranz, *The Great Divergence*, 124–125.

89　Pomeranz, *The Great Divergence*, 124.

90　Stephen N Broadberry and Bishnupriya Gupta, "The Early Modern Great Divergence: Wages, Prices and Economic Development in Europe and Asia, 1500–1800", *International Macroeconomics and Economic History Initiative* (London: Centre for Economic Policy Research, 2005).

91　Jan de Vries, "Between Purchasing Power and the World of Goods: Understanding the Household Economy in Early Modern Europe" in John Brewer and

Roy Porter, eds., *Consumption and the World of Goods* (London: Routledge, 1993), 85–132, 107.

92 Jan de Vries, "The Industrial Revolution and the Industrious Revolution", *Journal of Economic History*, 54, (1993): 249–270, 257.

93 Broadberry and Gupta, "The Early Modern Great Divergence", 10–11.

94 Broadberry and Gupta, "The Early Modern Great Divergence", 2.

95 Werner Sombart, *Liebe, Luxus und Kapitalismus* New edn. (Wagenbach, 1992), 92.

96 Sombart, *Liebe, Luxus und Kapitalismus*, 92.

97 Pomeranz, *The Great Divergence*, 114–127.

98 Pomeranz, *The Great Divergence*, 128.

99 Arjun Appadurai, "Introduction: Commodities and the Politics of Value", *The Social Life of Things: Commodities in Cultural Perspective* (Cambridge: Cambridge University Press, 1986), 25 (emphasis in original) as quoted in Pomeranz, *The Great Divergence*, 129.

100 Pomeranz, *The Great Divergence*, 129.

101 Craig Clunas, *Superfluous Things: Material Culture and Social Status in Early Modern China* (Honolulu: University of Hawaii Press, 2004), 54–55.

102 Clunas, *Superfluous Things*, 8–39.

103 Clunas, *Superfluous Things*, 151.

104 Peter Burke, "*Res et Verba:* Conspicuous Consumption in the Early Modern World" in Brewer and Porter, eds., *Consumption and the World of Goods*, 148–161.

105 Pomeranz, *The Great Divergence*, 132.

106 C.A. Bayly, *Rulers, Townsmen and Bazaars: North Indian Society in the Age of British Expansion, 1770–1870* (Cambridge; New York; Melbourne: University of Cambridge, 1983), 59.

107 Bayly, *Rulers, Townsmen and Bazaars*, 60–62.

108 K.N. Chaudhuri, *Asia Before Europe: Economy and Civilization of the Indian Ocean from the Rise of Islam to 1750* (Cambridge, England; New York: Cambridge University Press, 1990.), 343–344.

109 Chaudhuri, *Asia Before Europe*, 359.

110 Chaudhuri, *Asia Before Europe*, 387.

111 De Vries, "The Limits of Globalization in the Early Modern World", *The Economic History Review*, 63, 3 (2010), 710–733.

112 Trocki, *Opium, Empire and the Global Political Economy*, 92.

113 Jessica Warner, "The Life and Times of 'Mother Gin' 1720–1751: Images of Mothers and Alcohol on the Eve of the Industrial Revolution". A paper delivered at the International Congress on the Social History of Alcohol, London, Ontario, May 13–15, 1993.

114 Berg and Eger, *Luxury in the Eighteenth Century*, 232.

115 Berg and Eger, *Luxury in the Eighteenth Century*, 233.

116 Berg and Eger, *Luxury in the Eighteenth Century*, 234.

117 Berg and Eger, *Luxury in the Eighteenth Century*, 235.

118 Introduction in Giorgio Riello and Prasannan Parthasarathi, eds., *The Spinning World: A Global History of Cotton Textiles, 1200–1850* (Oxford; New York: Oxford University Press, 2009), 1.

119 David Clingingsmith and Jeffrey G. Williamson, "Deindustrialization in 18th and 19th Century India: Mughal Decline, Climate Change and Britain's Industrial Ascent" (Cambridge: National Bureau of Economic Research, 2005), 209–234.

120 Fujita Kayoko, "Japan Indianized: The Material Culture of Imported Textiles in Japan, 1550–1850" in Riello and Parthasarathi, eds., *The Spinning World*, 181–203, 190–199.

121 Beverly Lemire, "Revising the Historical Narrative: India, Europe, and the Cotton Trade, c. 1300–1800" in Riello and Parthasarathi, eds., *The Spinning World*, 205–226, 222–223.

122 Lemire, "Revising the Historical Narrative" in *The Spinning World*, 222–223.

123 Berg and Eger, *Luxury in the Eighteenth Century*, 239.

124 Berg and Eger, *Luxury in the Eighteenth Century*, 240.

125 Baghdiantz McCabe, *Orientalism*, 226.

126 Baghdiantz McCabe, *Orientalism*, 227.

127 Olivier Raveux, "Spaces and Technologies in the Cotton Industry in the Seventeenth and Eighteenth Centuries: The Example of Printed Calicoes in Marseilles", *Textile History* 36, 2 (November, 2005): 131–145.

128 Baghdiantz McCabe, *Orientalism*, 227.

129 "Le rôle joué par les espaces méditerranéens et orientaux au début de l'industrialisation occidentale, à la faveur des stratégies marchandes en même temps que s'ébauche l'image d'un Orient conservatoire de techniques et pourvoyeur de savoir-faire," is cited by Raveux from L. Hilaire-Pérez, "Cultures techniques et pratiques de l'échange entre Lyon et le Levant: inventions et réseaux au XVIIIe siècle," *Revue d'Histoire Moderne et Contemporaine* 49, no. 1 (2002), 113.

130 Joseph J. Spengler, "The Physiocrats and Say's Law of Markets," *Journal of Political Economy* 53, no. 3 (September 1945): 193–211.

131 John Shovlin, *The Political Economy of Virtue: Luxury, Patriotism and the Origins of the French Revolution* (New York: Cornell University Press, 2006).

132 Jean Claude Perrot, *Une histoire intellectuelle de l'économie politique au XVIII-XIIIième siècle* (Paris: Editions de l'Ecole des hautes études en sciences sociales, 1992). See all this and more discussed in the newest book in English on the subject: John Shovlin, *The Political Economy of Virtue: Luxury, Patriotism, and the Origins of the French Revolution* (Ithaca: Cornell University Press, 2006).

THE DESTRUCTION OF TEA AT BOSTON HARBOR

Figure 7.1 Boston Tea Party in 1773, Nathaniel Currier, lithograph, (c. 1846).
© Glasshouse Images/Alamy.

7 Resisting Exotic Luxuries
Simplicity and Boycotts in the Age of Revolutions

I began my reform with my finery … I gave up my gold trimmings and white stockings, I took a short wig, I laid aside my sword, I sold my watch … I left *le monde* and its pomp. I renounced all finery: no more sword, no more watch, no more white stockings, gold trimmings, hairdo.[1]

Michael Kwass describes Jean Jacques Rousseau's renunciation of his sartorial luxuries during the winter of 1751. A bed-ridden and delirious Rousseau, facing the possibility of his own death, resolved to live more simply. Kwass contends that Rousseau's reform was putting his own philosophy into practice. "He was turning his back on the luxury and artifice of Parisian high society and embracing a virtuous and authentic mode of living."[2] That Rousseau kept his wig is full of meaning according to Micheal Kwass. In the seventeenth and eighteenth centuries, the wig was the aristocratic ornament of old regime Europe, which marked high birth and status. It was worn by the privileged few. Nevertheless, in the eighteenth century wigs were worn by the "commonest of heads".[3] It was not uncommon for the guild of wigmakers to open shops in relatively small towns. Daniel Roche and Laurence Fontaine have described how peddlers acted as intermediaries in markets and fairs to channel urban consumer goods beyond the capital of Paris.[4] The wig had become so common in eighteenth-century France that it was suggested that it was no longer an exclusive marker of class or even an article of luxury.[5] Michael Kwass argues that the diffusion of the wig illuminates a large-scale transformation in consumption. Although fine fabrics remained beyond the reach of the majority of the population, cheaper secondary accessories became popular. Studies have demonstrated that this middle zone of consumption became increasingly crowded with clothing, furniture and household furnishings in France and England. Kwass argues that the example of the wig brings into focus other goods, hygienic accessories such as toiletries or what we would call personal care products today and portable accessory objects. There was a fashion for snuff boxes, canes, fans, watches and umbrellas.[6] The author of "Big Hair: A Wig History of Consumption of Eighteenth-Century France" contends that Norbert Elias' theory of emulation is not enough to explain the diffusion of the wig. He credits the agency of self-proclaimed experts, "taste leaders", who participated in the century's flourishing public sphere. He recognizes two groups: the first includes writers, *philosophes* and fashion critics and the second group was engaged in the relatively new business of advertisement. Along with well-known Parisian newspapers such as the *Mercure de France*, France had around forty provincial newspapers engaged in advertising. Kwass argues that there was a major change in the discussion of wigs, a change in values strong enough to evoke a new age of consumption. Instead of status being central, it was the concept of convenience, "*la commodité*", that was central to eighteenth-century luxury.[7] Joan DeJean, in her book *The Age of Comfort*, has also argued that this language of convenience was employed to define consumer goods. Her book concentrates on architecture, on the creation of rooms new to the eighteenth century such as the dining room, and on the creation of comfortable furniture.[8]

It has been argued that far from being an object of Veblen's style of conspicuous consumption, the post-Louis XIV wig was, according to taste leaders, an accessory of convenience. Michael Kwass is tempted to interpret this shift towards smaller, more convenient wigs as an early sign of what J.C. Flügel has coined "the great masculine renunciation"; after the French Revolution, the men of the bourgeoisie rejected extravagant dress in favor of a dark, simple, sober costume to symbolize the denial of pleasure and the acceptance of duty, self control and work.[9] Women became the principal agents of conspicuous consumption by wearing ostentatious clothing. Historians have pushed Flügel's theory further by arguing for greater sexual differentiation and a clearer division between a male public sphere and a female private sphere. Nevertheless, Flügel's thesis is rejected because Kwass argues that new short wigs aimed to renounce pleasure and that on the contrary they were meant to enhance pleasure and set fashions. Beyond convenience, the highest value stressed by taste leaders was the concept of nature. This concept dear to the *philosophe*, especially Rousseau, spilled into the commercial world.[10]

The French court itself was deeply influenced by the new philosophy. Historians accepting a new modern consumption born away from the court tend to stress the role of writers, merchants and publicists. Many have argued for a new modern form of consumption that was no longer court-driven. Nevertheless, other historians continue to look at the French court itself for the "taste leaders" of the eighteenth century. Caroline Weber's work on Marie Antoinette's wardrobe successfully integrates both arguments. If a major role is played by the Queen, then her *marchande de mode*, Rose Bertin, is a towering figure.[11] The Queen was not alone in being accused of giving in to excessive desires; women were often seen as the sole consumers of luxury goods.

Women's Love of Luxury

The Catholic Church had long favored asceticism and its influence was still important in eighteenth-century Paris where some of the most important philosophical debates about luxury took place. In French texts, the diatribe against luxury was often a diatribe against women's irresistible attraction to the boutiques of the *marchandes de modes*. Jennifer Jones has argued that in the later eighteenth century, a conceptual framework was constructed that made it possible to think of the excessive desire to consume as a particularly feminine trait, a weakness shared by all women from Queen Marie Antoinette to the fishmongers of the marketplace. She quotes the chief of police of Paris, Nicolas Desessarts, equating moral corruption with the infinite number of fashion boutiques and their decorative shop windows that he saw as a source of danger. "What young woman has the strength to shield her eyes, when everyday she sees the production of genius of the *Marchandes de mode*?"[12] The large number of women going in and out of dress shops built a new fear in many observers that this sort of fervent consumption was a threat to domestic peace and prosperity. Desessarts' fears are the example of a construction of a new ideology that linked women to consumption but also showed a new understanding for the contagion of fashion. Jennifer Jones argues that while moralists might have traced women's love of luxury back to the Garden of Eden before the eighteenth century, Desessarts' views do not only point at women being weak, but at a new temptation: the fashion boutiques along the streets of eighteenth century Paris. Shopping had power over them. To Desessarts, the source of danger was the boutique itself, which seduced women with new kinds of decorations, providing a haven for frivolity, luxury and over-consumption. A popular eighteenth-century saying about women was "dress of velvet, belly of bran" which implied that the desire to consume fashion was often against the cost of food for themselves and their families.[13]

In the 1740 manuscript entitled "The Superiority of Men Over Women Or the Inequality of the Two Sexes" the author complained that women wanted to have what other women had, no matter the price, even if their children might die of hunger, so that they "will have bellies of luxury and clothing of silk".[14] Although there were debates about luxury earlier, it is only in the early eighteenth century in the wake of Mandeville's *Fable of the Bees*, popularized by Voltaire, that the debate on luxury heated up in France. Jones argues that part of this debate was to pull away from the traditional discourse against expenditures forbidden by one's social station. The traditional argument was that luxuries would cause social disorder, the ruin of families and sexual debauchery. In the newer discourse, luxury was simply defined as the commercial exchange to obtain any desired, but not necessary, commodity. Luxury in this modern definition was neither good nor evil. It was up to the individual to assess this commercial exchange for the health and happiness of the individual or society at large. Nevertheless, even in the driest philosophical treaties, the physiocrats would still stray away from the virtues of agriculture to condemn the love for luxury of women and make them stand for the core of the problem for French society. The association of women and luxury was not unique to the eighteenth century. Saints Augustine and Jerome had lashed out against the luxuries of the women of Rome.[15]

Jennifer Jones argues that if most critics were not opposed to ostentatious display in itself, as the magnificence of kings and courts was condoned, they were still opposed to any display of wealth that was inappropriate to one's social station. This form of critique expressed worries that luxury would upset the social hierarchy. Critics also worried in the 1770s and 1780s that women's love of luxury would lead to depopulation. The physician Samuel August Tissot explained that when a society is obsessed with luxury, it will restrict the number of births in order not to distribute wealth among many children. He also believed that luxury produced dissolute lives that ruined people's health, rendering them sterile, or that it produced sickly children. In this light, luxury was presented as a problem for society at large. The gravest effects of women's love of luxury were on the private sphere of family and domesticity; with their love for trinkets they would neglect their duties as housekeepers, mothers, and wives.[16]

The eighteenth century debate on the danger of women's desire for luxury, however, concerned a much broader group of women than the aristocracy. Many texts on luxury also lashed out at the ostentation of butchers and barge women. Jennifer Jones argues that increasingly in the second half of the eighteenth century, women's desire for luxury was attributed not only to their vanity and desire for political clout, but to their frivolity, the desire for novelty and to their enslavement to the new commercial deity: *la mode*. Luxury, therefore, was not driven solely by women's lust for power and social status, but also by their lust for novelties available in the shops of Paris. The *philosophes* set aside blaming it all on Eve and instead started researching the scientific basis of women's love for all that was new. They forged new beliefs in the gender specific liveliness of women's visual senses and imagination to justify their views of women as prime consumers. In other words, women's heightened senses, as opposed to men's, allowed objects to create desires they could not resist. Alongside the traditional model that equated luxury with sin, this new model attributed women's attraction to luxury goods to a specific female psychology. Women now had to battle window displays, fashion magazines and business cards in the bustling commercial city of Paris. We should not imagine that shopping was what it is today. Shopping for fashion was relatively new. The wealthy ordered their clothing to measure through tailors and seamstresses who came to their homes and delivered. Fashion accessories such as ribbons and lace completed these wardrobes and were provided by *marchandes de modes* who made daily rounds of the cities' wealthiest quarters with baskets brimming with bows, scarves, jewelry and gloves.[17]

Joan DeJean has argued that shopping in the modern sense was invented in Paris in the last two decades of the seventeenth century.[18] Before the mid eighteenth century, most Parisian shops would be unrecognizable to the modern consumer; boutiques were often street-side stalls or small stands. Each neighborhood had its own seamstresses, tailors and mercers to serve the needs of the local clients. Many of the best *marchandes de modes* and dealers in luxury fashions congregated in the most elegant quarters of Paris in close proximity to the wealthy; until the middle of the eighteenth century, the *Palais de Justice* was the most fashionable place to shop in Paris. Indeed shop windows had become an art. Guilds continued to regulate the luxury trade. As Steven Kaplan demonstrates, one of the six luxury guilds of Paris, the mercers, and their shops had climbed to the very top of the hierarchy of the guilds through hubris, sheer snobbery and their pride in selling almost everything and manufacturing nothing, which unlike other guilds, put them above artisans and gave them the status of merchants.[19]

It could also be rightly argued that their right to sell imported goods gave them the unique power to sell foreign objects against those made by French artisans in other guilds without the stamp of the guild. In a sense their imports broke the monopoly the guilds each held on their own craft in France, which was true for many things such as furniture, porcelain and jewels. It could be further argued that their rise to power was closely tied to their customers' passion for the foreign and exotic and its domestic imitations. In the quarrels among guilds, the rise of the mercers was an important phenomenon that changed the social order. Merchants rose through the ranks of society through newly acquired wealth. The creation of a fashion press also contributed to this debate.[20] Daniel Roche has long demonstrated that the *Ancien Régime* was a culture of appearance and that you were what you wore; rising through the ranks meant an increased consumption of luxury goods and dress.[21] Daniel Roche's pioneering work already pointed to the eighteenth century as a turning point for consumption and clothing.[22] The education of merchants and their social rise also led to their public participation in economic debates.[23] The rise of consumption in eighteenth century Paris, the feminization of fashion and culture, the breaking of class and gender barriers, the rise of the crafts related to fashion, the extinction of sumptuary laws, the excesses of Marie Antoinette and their surprising ties to subsequent Revolutionary dress codes have been brilliantly studied in some recent works.[24]

Marie Antoinette as Taste Leader

Caroline Weber's seminal study of Marie Antoinette's frenetic consumption and its social consequences highlights the importance of the sartorial traditions of the *Ancien Régime*. Marie Antoinette's wardrobe history highlights the political meaning of defying traditional conventions. Jennifer Jones and Joan DeJean have both demonstrated that Louis XIV was an arbiter of fashion and taste for Europe, and after his reign, *la mode* was a major French export. Jones explores the royal creation of a Parisian tradition of *coiffeurs* and *couturiers*, who for the next century dictated much of Europe's fashion. French fashion went well beyond European courts. Jones has shown how the Sun King exerted domestic political control of his courtiers through dictating sartorial fashion and devoting much of his long reign (1654–1715) to harnessing the artifice of Frenchness. Through French customs and fashions he strove to extend his power – politically, economically and culturally – throughout France and across Europe. He did so by asserting a distinctively French style, by deploying the artifice of fashion for the purpose of court spectacles and by disciplining fickle fashion to the theater of absolutism.[25] Louis XIV would remain unmatched in his political use of fashion until Marie Antoinette, Louis XVI's queen, would be called *"la reine de la mode"*. This unfortunately was not a queenly role in France. French kings had counted on their mistresses to set fashion.[26]

Louis XVI was the first king in many centuries not to have a mistress, so his Austrian Queen Marie Antoinette was forced to fill the void. In popular imagination she became both queen and mistress – thereby joining, as only the king should, both reproductive and sexual power in one body. Traditionally, a century earlier when modern fashion was born with fashion dolls and engravings, it was Louis XIV's mistresses that held sexual power and had led the court's fashion. Under the old King Louis XV, Madame du Barry, his last mistress, continued to make fashion at court while Marie Antoinette was still the Dauphine of France. The power of the male monarch rested on two "economies": one of reproduction and another of sexuality. Mistresses were a royal tradition in France and the King distinguished himself from others by having as many as he pleased. The most famous mistress of Louis XIV had made fashion at court and had even gone so far as to introduce other beautiful women such as Mademoiselle de Fontanges to the King. Mademoiselle de Fontanges' hairstyle was imitated by the entire court when Louis XIV vocally admired the fact that she had made a ponytail that threw her curls on her face.[27] The fashion magazine *Le Mercure galant* and the private letters of the King's sister-in-law the Duchess d'Orléans revealed the ways in which aristocratic women around Louis XIV had participated in the construction of French fashion culture. The relationship of aristocratic women to court costume and French dress marked the long enduring ideological power of Louis' sartorial system.[28] The role of "taste leader", which had always been assumed by several mistresses, now fell to one woman: the Queen of France.

The sartorial order of the French court was well in place since the century when Marie Antoinette crossed the French border to marry the Dauphin of France in 1770. She was subjected to the grand ceremony of the *Remise*, where she was to leave Austrian dress and customs behind to be fitted into what had been defined as French court dress. The new category of "Frenchness" crafted by Louis XIV extended across classes and was a unifying gesture where clothing marked participation in the nation. Marie Antoinette knew all about French fashion as scores of fashion dolls had been arriving in Vienna as soon as she had turned thirteen, wearing miniature versions of the robes and gowns proposed for her by the foreign minister of France. When she crossed the French border at fourteen, the future Queen had accumulated a spectacular trousseau-dowry of sumptuous gowns. The observer Pierre Saint Amand wrote that the Austrian archduchess became something of a miniature mannequin prepared carefully for the enjoyment of the court at Versailles. In a book devoted to Marie Antoinette's wardrobe, Caroline Weber writes that the fourteen-year-old Dauphine was much like a *poupée de mode*, the fashion dolls that the French shipped internationally; she was to serve as a valued object of exchange between two nations in order to foster goodwill. Marie Antoinette's transformation into a living, breathing fashion doll allowed her to participate actively in the magic of sartorial transformation. This transformation subjected her to the exacting standards of French court dress. At the court of Versailles, clothing was the currency of social acceptance and political survival. In fact, the foreign minister himself, the Duc de Choiseul, a strong advocate of the union, had stipulated that her wardrobe be overhauled as a necessary pre-condition for the royal match.

The Empress of Austria spared no expense to make her daughter worthy of becoming a Bourbon bride. At a time when the wardrobe of an entire working class French family had an average value of 30 *livres*, that of an aristocratic couple's wardrobe was worth somewhere between 2,000 and 5,000 *livres*; the Empress spent a staggering 400,000 *livres* on her youngest daughter's trousseau-dowry before her arrival in France. This amount exceeded the sums the Empress had spent for all her other daughters combined. It was important for Choiseul that every garment purchased be made in France, to support the important French silk industry. Choiseul and his emissaries also suggested alterations to Marie Antoinette's physical person. During the marriage preparations, he noticed that her teeth were crooked and sent a French doctor to straighten them. These operations were excruciating, performed without anesthesia and required three long months. In many ways she was prepared to be the ultimate fashion doll.[29]

Despite these dictates, the new Dauphine had a mind of her own. Marie Antoinette broke the strict etiquette of French dress by riding astride "like a man"; she sat for an equestrian portrait that is now lost. Her attempt to stage herself, both in the painting and in real life, as a mighty, manly horseman created a lot of hostility against her at court. It was understood as an act of defiance and an assertion of authority. Several decades earlier, Louis XIV's breeches and boots in an equestrian portrait had forced the King's detractors to accept his authority. Voltaire had written that until that moment the Sun King had been little respected. To see the Austrian Dauphine dressed in much the same way, posing as the Sun King's female descendant, was even more shocking as her husband, the future King, had recently refused to have himself depicted in such a heroic manner. To make matters worse, in Brun's equestrian portrait of Marie Antoinette, the future Louis XVI appears as a tiny figure in the background, also on horseback but eclipsed by his wife commanding in king-like pose. Ironically, at first dressing and riding like a man seemed to serve her well. Her authority began to be respected and she began to be imitated. It is only later that this reversal of royal gender roles would come back to haunt her with accusations of debauchery, lesbianism and a brazen thirst for power hurled against her several years before the French Revolution. Even when she was a Dauphine, because her marriage was not consummated, she was attacked with malicious gossip at court.[30] As long as brazen sexuality at court was represented by Madame du Barry, Marie Antoinette's breeches and her limited sexual power received exemption from the people's ire.[31]

When Marie Antoinette gave birth, the people of France contended that the King was impotent and that she had given birth to a bastard. Pages and pages were produced against Marie Antoinette to destroy the legitimacy of the King, especially after Marie Antoinette gave birth to a boy who would be the heir to the French throne.[32] Louis XVI's crippling sexual reticence when he became the King of France was well known. He was not interested in his wife and had no mistresses. He seemed perfectly happy to grant his wife the traditional main mistress' privileged financial position, if not her sexual functions.[33] Marie Antoinette's sartorial ostentation became an essential part of her political campaign for increased popularity and prestige. Like her equestrian cross-dressing, the parties she now organized imbued her with an aura of influence that she otherwise sorely lacked. The top of the hierarchy was invited to these parties, accepting her as a center of gravity. The Queen, in the absence of any direct political power or any hope for maternity, had chosen to showcase her power through consumption. Cécile Berly has argued that it is exactly when Marie Antoinette became the Queen of France in 1774 that she became the Queen of fashion.[34]

According to Weber, the Queen's parties established her as a leader in the realm of fashion, who set the tone at Versailles. As the main "taste leader" at court, she had a huge following. Egged on by the aristocrats she was close to, Marie Antoinette set her sights on Paris, one of Europe's largest cities and undisputed center of fashion. As discussed above, in the city of Paris the *marchandes de modes,* female fashion merchants, had opened shop. This period was what Daniel Roche has described as an absolute revolution in clothing.[35] Capitalizing on women's appetite for diversity and novelty, the *marchandes de modes* offered their services. This profession was a talent that, under the law, could only be practiced by the all male mercers' guild and their wives. Most *marchandes de modes* were married to mercers. In October 1773, Rose Bertin, an unmarried twenty-four-year-old woman defied the law by setting up shop as a *marchandes de modes* on the *rue Saint-Honoré*. Her shop was exotically named *The Grand Mogul*, referencing Asian emperors to symbolize the fashion for exotic goods that gripped Paris.[36] The social groups enjoying exotic luxury goods were well beyond the court and extended to the bourgeoisie.[37] Carolyn Sargentson's work on the mercers and their shops has shown that as they had the privilege to sell oriental wares or luxuries, such as paintings and mirrors, they became a powerful guild. She has demonstrated the steady socio-economic rise of the guild of mercers during this period. This is the same period where one also found not only prosperous merchants but also artisans enjoying some leisure in the theatre or the fancy *cafés* of the *Palais Royal*.[38] Her new boutique boasted large windows filled with displays that were designed to divert foot traffic from the *Palais Royal*, then the center of fashion. Weber's discussion of Marie Antoinette's dress maker (Rose Bertin), and hair dresser,

Léonard, with their privileged access to court point to the same social mobility.

The Grand Mogul and the Pouf

Rose Bertin's windows displayed all kinds of baubles that hid the place's true purpose; once inside, *The Grand Mogul* had fashion displays of complete one-of-a-kind outfits covered with all kinds of accessories. Caroline Weber has found that at some point this boutique housed 280 such dresses, each one heavily trimmed by Rose Bertin. Collectively, these would be valued at half a million *livres*. Bertin presided over her team of elegantly clothed shop girls. Among the most celebrated accessory offered by Rose Bertin in the early months of 1774 was a wild headdress called the *pouf*. Bertin had developed it in conjunction with a fashion hairdresser, Monsieur Léonard. The *pouf* was built on a scaffolding of wire, gauze, horsehair, real hair and its own tresses. It was a high edifice heavily covered with powder in which, amid the curls, Bertin and Léonard could lodge elaborate miniature still lifes to commemorate an event or ceremony. An early adopter of the *pouf*, the Duchess de Chartres was such a fan of Rose Bertin that she presented her to the Queen of France in the spring of 1774.[39] Marie Antoinette placed both Rose Bertin and Léonard on her payroll and adopted the *pouf* as her signature look. Despite disapproval from the court, she began traveling to Paris two or three times a week to show off her new look. Initially, the once inconceivable sight of the Queen mingling freely with her subjects evoked elated reaction from the population of Paris. The Queen's female subjects were delighted and Paris witnessed an outbreak of copycat *poufs* across the city.[40]

Some of these headdresses paid direct homage to the Queen, such as a *pouf* showing a rising sun over a wheat field, which was an allusion to the reign's inauguration. Soon *poufs* towered with ostrich and peacock feathers that sometimes measured up to three feet high. Suddenly these exotic feathers were terrifically expensive and were the hair accessory of choice for the wealthy. Marie Antoinette favored both and soon she was imitated all over Europe. Marie Antoinette nicknamed Bertin "*ministre des modes*" and devoted a good part of her budget to ordering from *The Grand Mogul* in Paris. In 1780, she had ordered 108,000 *livres* of goods from the store. In the wake of this, Bertin acquired a sinister reputation while the Queen acquired debts at *The Grand Mogul* that the King paid for without batting an eyelash. Entire families were condemned to living very tightly in order to follow fashion.[41] Marie Antoinette was committed to her new role as standard-bearer for Parisian fashions. Marie Antoinette had much in common with her astute Bourbon ancestor Louis XIV who had employed forty wigmakers to maintain him in unrivaled splendor.[42] Instead of shunning the limelight and staying hidden away like France's prior queens, Marie Antoinette actively sought the limelight and proclaimed her power with her voguish coiffeurs. Perhaps most shockingly of all, breaking the tradition which required any of the sovereign's purveyors to cut all ties with other patrons, she allowed both Bertin and Léonard to retain their shops and their clients in the capital of Paris. Her dissociation from her narrowly prescribed queenly role would prove devastating both for her reputation as a Queen and her husband's regime. Weber finds that in 1776 Marie Antoinette spent 100,000 *livres* on accessories alone even though she had an allowance of 120,000 *livres* on all her clothing.[43]

Rose Bertin always refused to provide detailed accounts. Beyond the court, Bertin and the Queen achieved a monumental international influence and French clothing exports received a tremendous boast.[44] In their rise, Bertin and Léonard had broken class prerogatives into which they had been born and this threw fuel on the fires of resentment against the lavish ways of the monarchy. That Bertin was so close to the Queen of France and could touch her, as if she were nobility, was an inversion of power in the French court system. Sovereigns were given the divine right to rule and only those of princely blood could live in such proximity to them. By all accounts, Marie Antoinette continued to commit sartorial mistakes. In 1776, she declared that she would rather see the King spend her money on warships for France than on more diamonds for herself. Yet, as Weber points out, she had immediately appeared in public with an obviously expensive replica of a warship called *la Belle Poule* perched on her head. Although innocent, ten years later, her alleged guilt in the diamond necklace affair consolidated her reputation for greed. A number of pornographic pamphlets depicted the Queen's sexual decadence and affirmed her status as the queen of vice. Her beloved expensive ostrich feathers now figured in a print called *la Poule d'Autruyche* where the Queen was depicted as an ostrich complete with Marie Antoinette's head swallowing the gold of France. There is one letter different between ostrich "*autruche*" in French and Austria "*Autryche*". She was condemned as Austria's creature and as the head of the hard lined French royalists who tried to suppress the revolution in France.[45]

Petit Trianon: The Queen's Return Back to Nature

It is also in this time, in the spring of 1774, that the King decided to offer the Queen of France her own palace, the *Petit Trianon*. This was now a marble palace, which replaced the destroyed porcelain one. The Queen looked at it as her personal retreat and followed the new percepts of Rousseau to go back to nature. The Queen's views on nature, however, demanded huge expenditure: for example, the *Petit Trianon*'s gardens were destroyed to make a new garden in the English style that cost at least 150,000 *livres*.[46] The court was scandalized by the expenditure and turned against her. Excluded from the parties where the Queen was dressed as a lemonade seller and her friends as farmers, the courtiers were nevertheless aware that a party given to honor the King at the *Petit Trianon* had cost the enormous sum of 400,000 *livres*.[47] Among the hens and the sheep, she started wearing her new and more relaxed muslin outfit, the *gaulle*. From 1774 to 1780 the dresses ordered by the Queen were still in expensive velvet, brocade and silk, the flowing *gaulle* took the constraints of the corset and court dress away.[48] It created a scandal.

The fashion for muslin dresses reached France via the Creole women of Saint-Domingue who had settled in Paris. The back to nature dress that Marie Antoinette adopted was not synonymous with economy despite appearances. The textile was very costly even if less costly than brocades and silk.[49] Her portrait painted in 1783 dressed in a *gaulle* by Elizabeth Vigé-Lebrun was exhibited at the Salon. At this yearly public exhibition, where her portraits appeared regularly, the Queen was reproached for posing in her underwear, but the *gaulle* was going to play an even more destructive role for Marie Antoinette's reputation; she began to be called "Madame Déficit". Not only was her dress considered underwear, but it was also a foreign outfit on a foreigner; she was blamed for bankrupting France. Most paradoxically, as she aimed for simplicity, it was at this point that she was reproached for her prior consumption. For political reasons, to show economy, she had shed her diamonds, feathers and brocades. They were required for proper French court dress since Louis XIV. Marie Antoinette was accused of wasting money on foreign imports at the exact time she tried to be frugal, but once again she had broken tradition. The only measure taken to appease the wild rumors about her was to publicly ban imports of muslin from England and the Levant trade.[50]

Weber shows how after a certain date Marie Antoinette could do no right. If stimulating domestic industry was patriotic and seen as part of the augmentation of the wealth of the nation, initially her huge orders of silk from the Lyon silk industry were seen as positive. After this fiasco even her orders were only interpreted as laying waste to a French industry, because she capriciously required new colors of silk.[51] As exotic imported luxuries, or their more affordable French copies, became part of more households, a philosophical debate arose about class, hierarchy and government. The French economy was still largely agrarian; people's living conditions had worsened drastically after a bad harvest and the snowy winter of 1774–1775 had led to one of the worst harvests in memory. That spring, a scarcity of food and the misguided reforms by the King's controller general, Turgot, impelled the starving people throughout France to stage riots known as the "Flour Wars". 5,000 people charged the gates of Versailles, accusing the monarchs of hoarding grain and bread. The brutality with which they were met left a scar, as the summary tribunals and exemplary hanging were not easily forgotten.[52]

Against the backdrop of the Flour Wars, Marie Antoinette's status as a style icon turned against her. The people started accusing her of all manner of horrors. Whereas her plumes and baubles had inspired admiration and awe, they now raised questions about her morality and concern for the French people. Popular distaste might have been exacerbated by the fact that flour was a main ingredient in the powder that was used to coat her *poufs*. Historians have now established that she never uttered the famous phrase "Let them eat cake" (*"qu'ils mangent de la brioche"*) but there were many missteps. Only one study by Georges Lefebvre *La Grande Peur de 1789* cites this phrase as hers, but only to refute it.[53] The King by this date was seen as responsible for the distribution of flour and he was even called the Baker King. That famine was rife was seen as the direct responsibility of the court. An impolitic decision was made by Rose Bertin to have the Queen celebrate the Flour Wars with a powdered headdress called *coiffure à la revolte*. Marie Antoinette's status as leader of fashion completely changed from enchanting to suspect. The "Flour Wars" cast her frivolity into public view.[54] In keeping with etiquette, a French queen changed her clothes at least three times a day: a formal dress for mass, a *déshabillé* for hours of intimacy and a gala dress for the evening, However, Marie Antoinette's indulgences had her wardrobe associated with the greed of a king's mistress rather than a queen's. In particular, her costly hairstyles had her associated with the famous Madame de Pompadour, Louis XV's mistress. To accommodate a climate of criticism and curb revolt, at this time the Queen greatly curbed her expenditure and stopped aspiring to lead French fashion.[55]

The Queen abandoned silk around 1780 and was followed very promptly. According to Joan DeJean in the middle of the 1780s a young woman, Henriette-Lucy Dillon, was given a hugely expensive trousseau before her marriage to the future Marquis de la Tour du Pin in which there was not a single silk dress. Joan DeJean argues that this was a perfect indication of how the cotton craze had transformed French fashions. Elsewhere in Europe, upper class women only used chintz, calicoes and floral cottons inside, as a *robe de chambre*. In France, the finest ladies did not hesitate to wear painted cotton in public. There were some criticisms of indecency. Cotton was called "the Indian material" and the "next-to-nothing fabric". DeJean argues that the lighter the cotton got, as in muslin or gauze, the more embraced by French fashions it became. These were prohibited fabrics but cotton spread through the ranks of society as no other fabric ever had. The fashion industry was the reason for the French's first embrace of Indian cotton textiles.[56] Joan DeJean argues for an age of comfort not only with this new form of looser clothing but because of the various inventions that made rooms more informal and gave seats increased support for the body.[57]

Ending a marked leave of absence from the world of fashion, Marie Antoinette stepped out on July 14, 1790 before 400,000 people to celebrate the first anniversary of the Bastille's fall. For this event, she had selected a simple white cotton dress not unlike those that all female attendees had been required to wear along with a tricolor sash. Yet, she nevertheless chose to accessorize her gown with a headpiece of graceful tricolor feather and matching ribbons. This dress seemed to affirm her revolutionary sympathies. She had also dressed the Dauphin accordingly. This was in contrast to the King who remained impartial with his fancy breeches and glittering jacket; he still wore the plumed hat of court culture. On that day, she still triumphed and the revolutionaries still treated her as their loyal queen of fashion-but this was never to happen again. In secret, she corresponded with her brother in

Austria and other monarchs throughout Europe for help to pull France "back from the abyss".[58] Towards the end of 1790, the King and Queen of France concluded that they had little choice but to escape the *Tuilleries* with their family and flee. Revolutionary journalists now sat up and took notice of Bertin's renewed regular presence at the Queen's side. In January 1791, the revolutionary journalist Camille Desmoulins wrote a description of Marie Antoinette as, "That Fury who has detached all the snakes from her hair and turned them loose on the French Nation."[59] Royalist historians have portrayed the Queen as a traitor in order to restore the King's reputation. That she was allowed to assist in the meeting of the King's counsel did not help her reputation as an intriguer that destroyed the monarchy.[60]

Weber remarks that none of the attacks deterred the Queen as she selected clothes for her impending journey away from France. In her new royalist-hued ensembles she saw the many prerogatives that she hoped to recapture. Unbeknownst to Marie Antoinette, there was political support from at least one unexpected source, *Le Journal de la mode et du goût*, whose editor had initially been enthusiastic over the Revolution's sartorial accomplishments and its drive for this simplicity. He had, however, grown increasingly anxious as simplicity equated with patriotism, had now created havoc in the important French luxury industry. The trend towards plain inexpensive fabrics was a terrible blow to the French silk manufacturers. Ironically the white dresses of the Revolutionary period had much in common with the much maligned *gaulle* in their simplicity. The popular dress was now causing rampant unemployment and poverty in many sectors of the French economy. The fashion business in the capital had also terribly suffered from the mass emigration of wealthy aristocrats, many of whom left Paris without paying their debts. Few Parisian fashion purveyors survived this turn of events; even the great Rose Bertin who stayed afloat was owed a great deal of money, several million *livres*, by the Queen herself.[61]

France had a century old tradition of protectionism to protect its silk industry and its manufacturers against foreign imports. Despite the mercantilist arguments against foreign imports, Indian cotton and foreign muslins were there to stay. The debate in France against foreign luxuries had some similarities to the ones taking place in England and in the prosperous Dutch Republic.[62] In Europe, and also in colonial North America, the debates about imported luxuries were dominant ones in foreign policy as well as in the domestic sphere. As is well-known, many French thinkers had much in common with their peers across the English Channel, not least of all Montesquieu whose views on the social utility of commerce as a civic virtue were not far from the arguments of those supporting the Hanoverian regime in England.[63] Debates on luxury and commerce either questioned or justified the political status quo. Luxury, argued Montesquieu, was necessary for monarchies to prosper. During revolutions, luxury and exotic wares were the first to come under attack. During the American Revolution, English imports came under attack with the homespun movement in North America, just as in England there was a long tradition of discourse against foreign goods to protect the English economy. This English discourse once adopted in its colonies turned against England in North America. Another discourse joined this xenophobic one: an appeal to morality. Not only were luxuries attacked because they were foreign, but because they were immoral.

Morality and Clothing

The French monarchy had set court fashion on a European scale. Aileen Ribeiro demonstrates that in England, despite much criticism, French fashion ruled the eighteenth century. Novels and periodicals disseminated ideas of gentility and good manners. The theme of an article in *The Spectator* in 1712 was that one should not complain of the time spent on fashion because one had to remember what a prodigious number of people the fashion industry maintained and the large circulation of money it occasioned. Of course, it was bemoaned that most of this money ended up in France. There is much comment throughout eighteenth-century England that the English were far too keen to abase themselves before a country "which has infected all the Nations of Europe with its Levity".[64] *The Spectator* poked fun at the English dress-makers who inspected the fashion dolls that arrived from Paris, despite the Anglo-French war. French fashion often gave rise to sarcastic comments; fashion magazines of the 1740s are full of accounts of the accidents that befell women that were described as the "tubs of hoops". Women had to practice walking in the hoops that France had made fashionable. *The Female Spectator* (1744) described how women had to enter public assemblies with a kind of skip and jump and throw their enormous hoops almost at the faces of those who passed them by. *The Enormous Abomination of the Hoop-Petticoat*, was written by a certain A.W. who made sure to clarify that he was neither a Methodist nor a Quaker. He felt compelled to write about the hoops because they took up too much room: women, because of this garment, have become a public nuisance in streets, coaches and at church. He also decries the foolish expense of so much silk and other costly materials with which women had skewed and molded their bodies into shapes quite contrary to nature. He continued to see the skirts as indecent because when a woman had to lift her skirts to get out of the mud, the wind caused them to be thrown up over her head.[65]

Several plays criticized foreign imports of lace from the Flanders and silk from France and bemoaned that it was hopeless to dissuade the English from the patronage of foreign finery. The clergy got involved in the arguments. Learned clerics like the Bishop of Llandaff published attacks on French *modes*. Bishop George Berkeley joined the attack on foreign imports by starting a campaign to encourage the consumption of Irish silks and linens. He believed that this would help the English and Irish economies. In *The Querist* (1735) he wondered, "Whether it be true, that Two Millions are yearly expended by England in foreign Lace and Linnen?"[66] In the next generation,

John Wesley and his Methodist field preachers argued that spending large sums of money on dresses was to steal from God, for it meant that there is less to spend on children and the poor. Wesley gave about 40,000 sermons as he traveled around the kingdom. Most of his remarks were directed at women's dress. He wished them to avoid a bold and immodest look created by the profusion of ribbons, gauze or linen about their heads. Although he was very quick to condemn fashion as sinful, Wesley did not give any positive suggestions as to what a godly woman should wear.[67]

London Fashion: Imitating Paris

London was the largest city in Europe, with a population of over one million people. Aileen Ribeiro points out that there was a common belief that the women who spent too much on their clothes might be inclined to a life of idle frivolity or even prostitution. Bishop Berkeley was among those who believed that the folly of fashion may lead to many other follies such as the derangement of domestic life, absurd manners, neglect of wifely duties, bad mothers and the general corruption of women. By the middle of the century, under the prevailing influence of France, the influence of French rococo, the sensual language of the rituals of dressing and undressing, became a kind of witty strip tease. Rococo dress involved a passion of light reflecting silks covered with three-dimensional lace, ribbons and flowers. Scraps of fabrics mixed with feathers and jewels formed tiny headdresses called pom-poms after Madame de Pompadour, Louis XV's mistress. In the magazine *The World,* a certain Adam Fitz-Adam bemoaned that not only was his food disguised in the dressing of French cookery, but that his womenfolk had also taken to French red. By red he meant *rouge*, reddened cheeks, a part of the many cosmetics that accompanied this form of dress. If, by the middle of the century, hoops had disappeared except at the English court, women's hair had begun to rise. A kind of scented paste was needed to hold this increasingly high edifice along with lots of false hair needed to give this new hairdo its necessary bulk. By now it was clear that it was none other than Marie Antoinette's *pouf*. In the mid 1770s, Miss Delaney (cited by Ribeiro) called the wearers of the hairstyle preposterous Babylonian heads towering in the skies, a vogue she attributed to "influenza of the brain".[68]

Lady Louisa Stuart remembered that the ostrich feathers in the hairdo were attacked as immoral and that the unfortunate wearers of feathers were mobbed, hissed at and almost pelted at wherever they appeared. In spite of the war between England and France, there remained considerable communication of the fashions between the two countries. Paris remained a mecca for the well-dressed visitor, including the English, even though men were increasingly turning to London for tailoring. For women, the 1770s saw a growing divergence in the difference between formal and informal dress. Marie Antoinette's famous *gaulle* was going to eclipse a fashion for amplifying bottoms and bosoms. Court hip pads and back bustles created a full bouncy effect over the buttocks and to enlarge their bosoms, women either wore false rubber bosoms, starched linen or gauze kerchiefs. The *Morning Herald* on 29 May 1786 advised women who wanted to visit the Vauxhall to avoid wearing their anterior and posterior protuberances. The complaint was that women took up too much room.[69]

Rousseau's influence for nature and the famous muslin dress advocated by his followers soon emphasized the truly natural body. Horace Walpole complained that informal dresses looked like dressing gowns, but more serious critics state that the flimsy muslins were too thin to be decent. When the American Abigail Adams visited Paris in 1784, she found fashionable Parisians not to be averse to what she calls a state of nature, showing flesh. She was shocked to find the widow of the celebrated philosopher Helvétius in a very revealing chemise, as the *gaulle* was also called. What also amazed the severe Mrs. Adams was the overriding importance attached to fashion. In her condemnation of fashion, she was not alone. Mary Wollstonecraft, in her *A Vindication of the Rights of Women* (1792), argued after visiting Paris during the revolution that women should exercise their minds as well as their bodies. But for her fashion was not to be part of a woman's preoccupation. She wrote "an air of fashion is but a badge of slavery", a belief which many feminists hold dear today.[70] By the mid 1790s, in imitation of an imagined revered, heroic, classical past the Revolution had induced many fashionable French women to adopt short sleeve white muslin gowns, roman style sandals and short cropped curls. Greco-roman fashion as it was imagined took hold. Even when fashion magazines were banned, fashion never stood still during the Revolution. Embracing a body-mind dualism, Wollstonecraft had employed the four-stage theory of human history to explain in racialized terms why certain bodies were drawn to fashion. Not only had she said that women were slaves to their bodies, but she had stated "A strong inclination for external ornaments ever appears in barbarous states".[71]

According to this view, enlightened societies and civilized states had moved beyond the stage of following fashion. The revolution had its fashion: the Greco-roman styles adopted by Parisian women evoked the idea of republic, of civilization. Paradoxically, it was not viewed that way; according to Louis-Sébastien Mercier, women "were dressed *à la sauvage*, with clinging semi-transparent muslin gowns, worn over flesh-colored body stockings, with naked breasts, bare arms and bare feet".[72] People in England watched with fascination and horror as events unfolded during the French Revolution. It was easy for moralists in England to link what was viewed as savage dress to an alien republic and political system that had abolished the monarchy. The semi-naked neoclassical dresses were described as highly immoral in British fashion magazines. The ladies magazines for 1794 describe a young man meeting a young woman dressed this way and assuming that she is a prostitute. He propositions her only to be rebuffed. He discovers the next day that she is the same girl that his mother has arranged for him to marry.[73]

Dressing the Revolution

As Lynn Hunt has argued in France "dress, with both its freedoms and constraints, turned out to be one of the most hotly contested arenas of revolutionary cultural politics".[74] She has argued that French Revolutionaries veered between two extremes in their views about clothing: they hoped to erase all of the hierarchical rules imposed by the old regime to make sure that there was free choice. On the other hand, they aimed to obtain a consensus by enforcing new regulations about personal adornment. She gives the example of the red, white and blue cockade that had appeared on men's hats as early as 16 July 1789. Wearing them had been a spontaneous gesture signaling support for the new regime. On July 5 1792, the Legislative Assembly ordered all men to wear the cockade by law; women were excluded from this law. Women's clubs, such as the Society of Republican and Revolutionary Women took matters in hand for women's dress and demanded that all women wear the cockade. Over this, in the summer of 1793 a "cockade war" broke out between club militants and market women who made it a point of pride to rip off the cockades to show their disdain for these female Jacobines in their mimicry of men.[75] Conflicts over women's fashions ended in a simultaneous declaration of freedom of dress and the suppression of women's political organizations.

Lynn Hunt argues that the declaration of freedom of dress grew out of motives much more complicated than a simple break with old regime sumptuary laws because as Daniel Roche has demonstrated, these laws had long been disregarded.[76] Revolutionaries wanted to install a new system of signs marking divisions. Democracy, especially in practice, created tensions about various forms of social and gender differentiation that extended to dress.[77] Festivals instituted a new kind of functional division that moved away from the old calendar. To read new distinctions, some forms of markings were proposed but not taken up, such as priests wearing a badge on their left breast reading: "Priest suspected of sedition". Others suggested that prostitutes wear special colors, or that soldiers wear gold stars on their clothing over the spots of their wounds.[78] The sumptuary laws that had once helped signal distinction and social rank for both men and women in the old regime gave way to a new code of masculine sameness and female difference.

The history of fashion shows that ornate dress had been a class, rather than a gender, prerogative since the fifteenth century a class prerogative protected by law in most European countries. As Jennifer Jones has argued, the eighteenth century was a transitional century in which commercial fashions had replaced sumptuary laws well before the French Revolution. Most fashion historians seem to notice and agree that major changes took place for men's clothing in the eighteenth century. None of them so far have given solid explanation for the "great male renunciation" as to why men gave up their long hair, their wigs and their elaborate dress. Class distinction within male dress blurred while class distinction between women's dress became much clearer. Women's dress still carried messages of social distinction while men's dress began to shun them. Lynn Hunt quotes Philippe Perrot for his view on trousers; they constitute a rare exception of fashion from below moving up the social scale. Trousers had been worn by workingmen and now all men wore trousers, stopped wearing wigs, stopped using makeup and stopped using ornamentation. Even if this did not happen overnight, it was grounds for the famous painter David to start marking sketches in 1792 of a new national male costume.[79] In 1794, David actually designed a national costume with a combination of Renaissance and antique motifs. Although the government never manufactured these new civil national uniforms, an engraving was reproduced in *La Décade philosophique*, which carried lengthy discussions of dress in the summer of 1794. The legitimacy of the government seemed to depend on being able to represent itself visually among the population.[80]

Resistance to fashions and textiles could also mean resistance to imperial rule, as in the American Revolution. By the treaty of Utrecht of 1713 Britain had attained the status of the leading commercial and imperial power with a hegemonic standing navy to maintain external security and internal stability. Its considerable armed forces supported and imposed England's policy of aggressive mercantilism pursued in order to increase its shares and gains at the expense of European rivals. English mercantilism formed the context for the import of three textiles that appeared to have been central to the development of domestic production: finished cloth from India, linen yarn from Ireland, and bales of raw cotton cultivated, cleaned and ginned on slave plantations in the Caribbean and in the Americas. These key imports became fundamental commodities for a textile industry that counted on selling to a multitude of customers in Britain's colonies.[81] North America was a favored market of customers keen to copy English manners and style.

American Colonies

David Armitage and T. H. Breen have noted that eighteenth-century writers seem uncertain how best to describe Britain's relations with its many overseas possessions. It is without enthusiasm that they employ the concept of "empire" because it carried uncomfortable baggage from ancient history and clashed with the blessing of living under a balanced constitution. They spoke of a commercial empire but the innovated eighteenth-century discourse was not trade, but rather a commerce organized around expanding markets for Britain's new manufactured goods: it was an empire of consumer colonies. The rapid growth of a consumer-oriented economy sparked curiosity on both sides of the Atlantic Ocean with Americans looking at eighteenth-century England with admiration for its cosmopolitan culture.[82] In their re-evaluation of the metropolitan culture, colonial Americans would almost certainly have taken note of a new social group in Britain, the middle class. Educated, professional and prosperous people with no claim to inherited privilege had established themselves as a "polite" and "commercial" society. They articulated a claim to respected social standing in dramatically visible ways, by consuming imported luxury goods.[83]

This rising middle class studied and copied the manners of its betters, celebrating consumer fads, purchasing new goods and clothing and populating trendy spas in European resort towns. As an American colonist would have soon noticed, the members of this self-confident group in England energized an impressive new consumer domestic marketplace. Small English manufacturing centers managed to turn out consumer items in unprecedented quantities. Prosperous Englishmen and women much like their American counterparts bought what they had seen advertised in an expanding and commercial press. Of course, there are debates about whether this "consumer revolution" overstates the pace of change, but at least for McKendrick and his followers it is clear that objects, which for centuries had been privileged possessions of the rich few, came to be within the reach of a larger part of society.[84]

T. H. Breen writes that, as one might anticipate, Benjamin Franklin played masterfully on the theme of infinite consumer promise for the Americans. In his essay entitled, "The Increase of Mankind" (1751), he held out the growth of colonial demand as the proper index to America's important standing within the British Empire. He had no doubt that, if an upward trend of consumption continued in the American colonies, then the concept of "mutual dependence" might take on a new meaning. Mid-century, the promise of commercial parity seemed a possibility and an aim for the future. For future Americans, Franklin believed, consumption would be the way to ensure British respect. Although mid-century Americans appreciated the many benefits that came with imperial commerce since they fancied themselves as the freest and most prosperous European colonists in the empire, nevertheless, frequently they grumbled that they found it hard to participate in this balance of trade. For the provincial consumers, the purchase of huge quantities of British goods created a chronic imbalance of payments, as the cash required was in short supply. From a colonial perspective, it seemed to Americans that they had to work harder just to maintain this fiction of commercial reciprocity. William Smith, a political figure in New York City, wrote that buying goods "obliged to send abroad all the cash we acquire, and as fast as we acquire it".[85] American consumers gradually began to regard themselves as indispensable to the genuine interests of what they considered the mother country. The arguments still remained that the British respected the colonists precisely because the Americans had proven themselves to be loyal consumers. By consuming so many manufactured articles, colonists reinforced a growing feeling of empowerment within the commercial empire.[86] The road to resistance and boycotts would be a long one, but only people who had come to take "galloping consumption" for granted could have fully comprehended its political and revolutionary implications.[87]

Breen paraphrases the poet Carl Sandburg, writing "in the life histories of obscure Americans the consumer revolution came to the mainland colonies on little cat's feet."[88] By which he means that the market drew energy from countless small transactions that he traces through the surviving account books. He found that colonists generally entered a village store looking for specific items such as an ivory cone, some pins or a piece of cloth. The charge for these goods seldom exceeded several shillings. From 1741 to 1746, most customers demanded the same range of household goods; they took home shoe buckles, snuffboxes, pen knives, knee buckles, iron kettles and writing papers. He looks at the records of a certain Allen MacLean who operated a general dry goods store in Hartford Connecticut. Breen writes that unlike some storekeepers in Philadelphia, MacLean did not seem to lure customers into his shop with allure of free coffee. Nor did the Hartford merchant seem to have special glass windows such as the ones commonly used in large towns and cities by milliners, stationers and watchmakers. Accounts of actual shopping during this period were extremely rare; the fullest description comes from the pen of an English traveler, Madam Knight. Although she was a rather condescending observer, Knight recorded in detail the conversation that she overheard. She reported that the first question asked by the shopkeeper was about the intended method of payment. Spanish, Massachusetts or Native American money were used, but some customers arrived with goods such as agricultural products while other consumers expected to be able to negotiate on credit. Beef and pork, corn and other goods were used as payment. Hard money of course, especially silver, was the most desired form of payment and got buyers the best deals. The issue of debt seems to loom large in Knight's observations. She observed that most customers were meek and quiet because they were indebted to the shopkeeper. Breen dismisses this as he argues that there was enough competition so that, if customers did not find what they wanted, they could turn to the competition.[89] But it is not these small items that have attracted the attention of historians. Perhaps the most studied British import to the colonies is tea while the second most important studied episode is resistance to English textile imports through the homespun movement.

It is often believed that resistance to British goods resulted from anger at taxation without representation. Breen demonstrates that the Stamp Act was received negatively not so much for the duty collected, but for the realization that the colonists were not equal to the British and that even before the outbreak of violent resistance in 1765 to the Stamp Act, colonists were eager to keep continued access to the comforts of life that had brought them so much happiness while reducing their dependence on England and becoming more self-reliant. It was not so much due to the mounting debt – but more like anyone's intent to have one's cake and eat it too – Americans were not yet prepared to contemplate radical changes in their comfortable lifestyle. They pledged to be frugal, more diligent and more self-reliant. Breen remarks that this is not yet a politicization of manufactured goods, but a voicing of public opinion on the household and on the ability and willingness of women to produce a supply of cloth sufficient to free colonial families from dependence on store bought textiles. Soon, women discovered that they had a voice in revolutionary politics. But on the other hand, one might note that attacks on "Laces, ribbons and gaudy flowers" in the discourse against imported luxurious directly touched the lives of women.[90] The discourse was about popular consumer sacrifice.

Breen points out that it is during such a mindset that extraordinary episodes of conspicuous consumption occurring during moments of genuine bereavement came to the attention of the Massachusetts House of Representatives. Funerals had become fashionable events with imported luxurious scarves, gloves and rings from England. Even the wine was imported. The Massachusetts House of Representatives in 1741 decreed that only six individuals could wear gloves, that no imported wine was to be served and that if these guidelines were broken a fine would be levied. The willingness of the rich to abide by these rules portrayed a dedication to the common cause. The white imported gloves worn only at funerals became a symbol of lavish and unnecessary spending. If one had to purchase a pair for a single event, they had better be made in the colonies. It was especially important for the rich to follow suit so as to set a good example for the lower classes to imitate. The dead were now remembered for the sensible and patriotic funerals that they left this earth with.[91]

A Boston town meeting in Faneuil Hall once produced an exhaustive list of every item imported from England that was to be boycotted. The publication of these lists in newspapers, and the distribution to other cities and colonies, brought colonists together who beforehand might have stayed distant due to religious and ethnic differences which were now secondary to the non-importation movement. Three years after the Townshend Revenue Act of 1767, it was repealed, all but for the duties on tea. Colonists again bought the consumer goods that they had fought hard against in the non-consumption movement. Based on the Navigation Acts which prohibited foreign ships from entering the New World ports, the colonists assumed that Britain would be granted a privileged consumer market in return for only conducting trade with the mother country. The Acts, which made a non-competitive market less advantageous for the colonists, broke this contract in the eyes of the colonists. Second-rate goods being sent to the colonies, after likely being rejected in Britain, added insult to the injury, as colonists felt taken advantage of. They realized that an out-right non-consumption would clearly transmit the colonists' message to Britain, while domestic production would help independence.[92]

Breen demonstrates that even if merchants had helped repeal the Stamp Act by no longer ordering certain consumer goods, laymen began to realize that they could not be the ones to control the non-importation agreements.[93] Oversight committees and town meetings were now to become the supervisor of their specific communities, ensuring that everybody in the population adhered to the non-importation agreement. This grassroots enforcement allowed general information about compliance to be public and colonists quickly adapted to rituals of publicly shaming and ostracizing anyone who did not support the movement.[94] Lists of names of shamed individuals were regularly publicly reprinted to ensure that the population was aware of those it had to ostracize from the community. Colonists were even using force to extort confessions from the merchants. The lightest punishment was long lectures when communities were not enraged enough to partake in the usual punishment of tar and feathers in the name of the common good. This did not mean that fashion disappeared. A new fashion appeared in its stead, humble dress made from cloth spun domestically was virtuous.[95]

In March 1770, the British Parliament finally repealed the legislation that had sparked colonial resistance. The Townshend Acts and its five laws had the purpose of raising revenue from the colonies to pay the salaries of British governors and judges in the colonies so that they would be independent. The Townshend Acts had been met with resistance in the colonies, prompting the occupation of Boston by British troops in 1768 that eventually resulted in the Boston massacre of 1770. In the aftermath of the Boston Massacre, most of the new taxes were repealed. One provision survived: a tax on tea remained on the statute books. Breen writes that less appreciated at this moment of dejection was how Americans had constructed in imitation "a nation that was not yet a nation".[96]

Sartorial Imitation for Power: Clothed in Robes of Sovereignty

In *Clothed in Robes of Sovereignty*, Benjamin H. Irvin studied the symbols and images necessary to craft the ceremonies of a newly sovereign America. A remarkable episode he retells demonstrates that despite the impact of the homespun movement, homespun clothing was not seen as appropriate for power. One evening in the summer of 1774, sometime before the "Grand Continental Congress" was scheduled to convene, an unexpected visitor knocked at the door of Samuel Adams' family home in Boston. Interrupting their dinner, the family discovered that the visitor was a tailor who had been sent to dress Samuel Adams. When asked why he was there and who had sent him, the tailor refused to explain. After some discussion, Adams consented to let the tailor take his measurements. Once the tailor left, another unexpected visitor knocked at the door. It was the best hatter in Boston, who once again presented himself without revealing who sent him. The evening continued to be interrupted by a stream of surprise visitors. The hatter was succeeded by a shoemaker who was then succeeded by a wigmaker. Sometime later, a big trunk appeared on the doorstep of the Adams' family home. It was addressed to Mr. Samuel Adams and it contained a suit of splendid clothes. The items sent to him completely broke with the homespun propaganda of the age. The new wardrobe sent to Adams consisted of two pairs of shoes of the highest quality, a set of silver shoe buckles, six pairs of high-end silk hose, a set of gold knee buckles, a set of gold sleeve buttons, and a gold-headed cane. Included were also a red cloak, a new wig and a very elegant hat. The trunk was delivered anonymously but after examining all of this sartorial splendor, Adams noticed a liberty cap embossed on each of his new buttons. He concluded that it had been sent to him by Boston's Sons of Liberty, who knew that the Continental Congress would not be the kind of venue where Adams could show up with his "notoriously threadbare wardrobe".[97] Samuel Adams would emerge as a very important and influential figure in this very first Continental Congress. During the long summer of 1774, popular support for commercial opposition had been heightened and congressmen were urged to adopt the continental boycott.[98]

By boycotting British goods, Whig organizers intended to bring political pressure to bear on Parliament for telling it to acknowledge American liberties and privileges. The most effective acts passed for this boycott were the Articles of Association. Benjamin H. Irvin argues that, although its fundamental purpose was political in nature, Congress' Association bore tremendous implications for American society and culture. Most importantly, the Association called an abrupt halt to the phenomenon that historians have now called the "consumer revolution". Beginning in the 1720s, North America's colonists had imported and consumed increasing quantities of European goods and commodities such as furniture, silver, fabric, tea, chocolate and coffee. In the five decades preceding Congress' Articles of Association, the American per capita consumption of British goods alone rose almost 50 percent. The consumer revolution refashioned the material landscape of British North America by providing new objects for the expression of their social status. Benjamin H. Irvin posits that the consumer revolution had accustomed certain classes of British colonists to the possession, use and display of imported manufactured items, as was manifest, for example, in Samuel Adams new suit of clothing.[99] Yet, Adams wore his new suit to participate in a non-consumption campaign that promoted "frugality, economy, and industry".[100]

In the Articles of Association lay tremendous irony because for ten years the American resistance movement had drawn support from people such as artisans, mechanics, sailors and dog hands who willingly suffered losses to contribute to the boycott. Without the enthusiastic support of ordinary people, Irvin writes, the Sons of Liberty could not have rocked the British Empire.[101] Nevertheless, the pursuit of sartorial refinement, the display of rich possessions and the cultivation of genteel manners was what had given political legitimacy to the Continental Congress.[102] Many of the New England delegates claimed to not put much stock in the riches of this world, but even the sober and stern congressmen of New England were carried away with the pretenses of their new office. Samuel Adams' new suit of clothes can demonstrate both the importance of Congress and the importance of fashion as a social and political marker of status. Irvin argues that Adams began to grasp the sartorial implication of this self-representation very quickly after a few months in office.[103]

The Boston Tea Party

Benjamin Carp has studied one of the most remarkable episodes of this revolt against British goods. Boston's continued consumption of tea during non-importation convinced British Parliament that an American tea market still existed and that the Tea Act would be beneficial.[104] The Tea Act furthered the abhorred Townshend Act and also gave exclusive trading rights to the monopolistic EIC officials.[105] The Tea Act gave the East India Company an unfair competitive advantage in selling tea in America. In the month of October, a New York author who called himself "HAMPDEN" published a series of essays called "The Alarm". He wrote that the American colonies would be forced to overpay for Asian goods. Although the Tea Act actually lowered the price of tea, he argued that this was merely a seductive trick designed to get Americans to accept an offensive law. The EIC could eventually set any price it wanted with its new privileges. Even with the duty paid on EIC tea, its new low price would threaten all American tea traders with stiff competition. The fact that Governor Thomas Hutchinson's sons were the carriers of the tea made the whole situation more insidious. As a result, Bostonian anger at tea imports seems to have been more personal or even tribal. Their hatred of the local governor was transferable to his sons and extended family and amplified political resistance to the tea arriving in the harbor. The Boston Son's of Liberty were also feeling significant pressure from their counterparts in New York and Philadelphia to stand fast and prevent the tea from landing. A writer in New York reminded his audience of the non-importation agreement respecting tea, but the Bostonians had not given a good account of themselves thus far, as they had never completely abstained from importing tea. Benjamin Carp asks that if importers of tea were enemies to commerce and liberty, then what did that make the merchants and consumers of Boston? A Philadelphia correspondent warned the Bostonians that if they continued to accept tea, it would confirm the many prejudices against them. The Boston town meeting and a writer for the Boston Gazette were forced to acknowledge that while other colonies had observed the non-importation agreement and bought tea only from Holland, Boston's record was not unblemished. Bostonians tried to make excuses. Boston's government, they said, had friends (pirates) who were willing to import legal tea.[106]

Benjamin Carp describes how thousands of people were packed into the Old South Meeting House, the only building in town large enough for the crowd. The discussion was about the tea that had just arrived in Boston harbor aboard the *Dartmouth*.[107] All goods were removed from the *Dartmouth* except for the tea, which neither the consignees, the ship owner, the governor nor the captain would take responsibility for. There were a total of four ships holding tea now in Griffin's Wharf. Rumors of Captain Hall trying to leave the harbor forced Governor Hutchinson to place the soldiers on command. To boycott the import visibly a secret group, the Sons of Liberty, agreed to board the ships and destroy the tea on board. They dressed as Indians. While the meeting continued, "Mohawks" entered the Old South Meeting House with war cries and shouts. Because the majority of leaders were still at the meeting, they were able to resist blame for being part of the invasion that was to follow. As a large group of Mohawks approached the Wharf, many wondered if the soldiers would intervene. Without instruction from Hutchinson, the military did nothing. The captains and others manning the ships did little to stop the Mohawks. In addition to those unloading the tea, certain individuals were charged with ensuring no inside smuggling occurred. They were careful that no other cargo on the ships was damaged. As for other details, most stories and numbers regarding the Tea Party are hard to verify.[108]

Some information is clear: most Tea Party members were politically active or had social relationships that pressured them to be a part of the resistance. Poor shoemakers unloaded tea next to Harvard graduates; almost all of society was somehow affected by and invested in the Tea Party. The members of the North End Caucus were particularly tied to the tea ships in either the nightly watch or the Tea Party itself. Other Tea Party members were active in clubs, had met even Freemasons. Men in the building trades were definitely participants in the Tea Trade. Those with elaborate disguises were better known individuals, while teenage boys and un-ranked individuals sometimes didn't bother with disguises at all. The eighteen chiefs who spoke an unintelligible language were clearly the most recognizable or close to the leadership. Most, with hours' notice, merely rubbed soot on their faces. As soon as the destruction was done, the Mohawks returned home silently and without further rioting or noise.[109] The disguises allowed the participants to cover their own identities and blame the Indians. Bostonians had used scapegoats so often in the past that the other colonies knew of the common strategy. In Maine, New Hampshire and Boston rioters had donned Indian garb before. While colonists enjoyed the humor behind their disguises, Britain's situation was further complicated by how to view and treat the colonists.[110]

According to Carp the first news of the Tea Party was not too shocking, but as more ships arrived with rejected tea, Britain was shocked at how widespread the resistance was. Trade in and out of Boston, besides food, fuel and military supplies, was prohibited. Benjamin Carp argues that although tea was the symbol of the resistance, many British goods were now being boycotted as well. A Massachusetts Provincial Congress met as an independent state government to discuss arms, militia and commanders. The Revolutionary War had begun. The Boston Tea Party led to the war of American Independence and that alone has been enough to ensure its fame, but Carp argues that this was in some ways an accident of history because New York City and Philadelphia radicals were the ones in the forefront in the fight against the Tea Act.[111]

T. H. Breen nevertheless argues that tea was not enough to mobilize a nation. Imagining a new nation required greater sacrifice from American consumers than forgoing its favorite beverage. In the immediate aftermath of the Boston Tea Party and the Intolerable Acts, all colonists from Georgia to New Hampshire expressed solidarity with the Bostonians. But during the summer of 1774, the tide of public opinion demanded a harsher form of consumer resistance, that of a demonstration of popular virtue, a total denial of British imported goods. Breen writes that the number of people involved is impossible to estimate but that these men and women were at the vanguard for the final push for American Independence. He contends that the influence of the Boston radicals has been exaggerated and that people in other parts of America took the manifestos pouring out of Boston with a grain of salt.[112] The colonists who responded to Boston's call in 1774 were consciously repudiating the empire of goods, imported articles, the cloth, the ceramics, the buttons and the furniture that had served as markers of British identity and that had flooded the homes of American colonists. These goods became politically charged in the 1760s and 1770s. When the colonists finally decided that they could do without the "Baubles of Britain", they destroyed their vital socio-cultural bond with the mother country.[113]

Clothing played a large part in political imagination during the American Revolution. Benjamin Rush, president of the United Company of Philadelphia for Promoting American Manufactures, argued "people who are entirely dependent upon foreigners for food or clothes must always be subject to them".[114] George Washington had assured his London merchants in 1765 that once domestic manufacturing became widespread in the colonies, the luxuries sent from England could be dispensed with.[115] As Michael Zakim writes in "Sartorial Ideologies: From Homespun to Ready-Made":

> planting, harvesting, sheering, cleaning, drying, rippling, wetting, braking, hackling, dyeing, separating, and combing, and only then spinning for three weeks and then weaving for another to produce the six yards of cloth necessary for a plain dress, to be made with material inferior to imported goods from England or the continent – this was the stuff of virtuous politics.[116]

In 1767, the *Boston Gazette* congratulated Ebenezer Hurd of Connecticut for having made no less than 500 yards of linens and woolens. This form of rhetoric allowed observers to gauge the respective dedication of their neighbors to the patriotic cause of the revolution. The homespun cause brought an end to business as usual; the growing amount of imported luxury manufactured goods reaching North America. This was a trade so large that it led Adam Smith to call America "a nation of customers". They bought English cultural refinement with their clothes, furniture and many other luxury goods. American concern about these fine clothes was nothing new. As early as 1722, Benjamin Franklin was already bemoaning the "Pride of Apparel" that had overtaken the colonies. The rise of fashionableness, Franklin had complained, had allowed people to envy one another's destruction; he meant that as they imitated fashions they hated each other while they aspired to a similitude of manners. Franklin's views had a puritanical legacy that was not far from the Methodist critiques that were circulating in England. During the years preceding the American Revolution, industry and economy were seen as the antidote to British rule. Homespun cloth would ensure American Independence, it was argued. The *Boston Gazette* reported in 1768 that a number of women from South Kingston, Narragansett, dressed in home-spun manufactures had been invited to the house of a gentleman of the first rank. There were reports from several towns in the northeast, Providence, Ipswich, Beverly and Boston among them, of the gatherings of Daughters of Liberty to spin in public displays designed to save freeborn Americans, who should not submit to the thoughtless emulation of metropolitan fashions inimical to liberty.[117]

The patriotic boycott of British goods first organized in response to the Sugar and Stamp Acts had opened up new opportunities for commerce in domestic manufacturers. But over a decade later, the Continental Congress', "non-importation, non-consumption, and non-importation" policy in 1774 was less concerned with ascetic self-denial than with the urgent encouragement of a new national economy. Zakim writes that non-consumption did not mean anti-consumption and that American agriculture, arts and manufactures, especially that of wool, were especially encouraged through the advocacy of domestic consumption. Homespun proved to be a good business venture. In New York City, American-made woolens were rumored to be selling for three times their original value. A Chester county farmer actually protested when the Stamp Act was repealed. Profit was the happy result of this virtuous coordination of private and public. It was argued that a homespun economy would rectify imperial corruption by supporting an alternative commercial logic, a democratic one that was not monopolized by a government or a company. Zakim points out that when sophisticates appeared in Boston and Charleston bereft of their silks and their English woolens, they celebrated the coarseness that was once the sign of social marginality, the dominion of workers and servants. This new love for the homespun did not mean that it never solicited distaste. Zakim quotes Alexander Hamilton's diaries where he is struck by the homely effect of homespun clothing on his landlady. Making the homespun a symbol of civic membership was a consciously leveling moment where rich and poor turned to the domestic spinning wheel without regard for their status. Zakim contends that concerns about luxury and admonitions for frugality did not abate after American independence. In the wake of a huge influx of British goods, there were calls to renew the pre-war boycott of British imports and chastisements and criticisms of citizens wearing foreign dress were common. From across the political spectrum, Thomas Paine exhorted Americans to stop being servile imitators of foreign fashions.[118]

Zakim points out that when Virginia's state legislature commissioned a sculpture of George Washington from Jean-Antoine Houdon in the 1970s, a debate over his costume erupted; an earlier commission had him dressed in classical robes. It so happens that the new French republic made such a choice when they had commissioned a design for a national uniform from Jacques-Louis David for its *citoyens*. David had chosen classical drapery with some semblance of the Renaissance guilds. Zakim quotes Washington writing to Jefferson, questioning how the toga is popularly invoked to symbolize civic virtue and in writing that "a servile adherence to the garb of antiquity might not be altogether so expedient".[119] The inauguration of Washington's statue excited considerable public comment. The statue was dressed in homespun clothes but it was written that the cloth was such fine fabric that it was universally mistaken for a foreign manufactured superfine cloth. Washington had recently visited the Hartford Woolen Company in Connecticut and had solicited a sample of their best cloth. Zakim writes that Washington then ordered a suit to be made of this cloth that he purposely wore to the inaugural ceremonies together with American made silk stockings and plain silver show buckles.[120] Zakim concludes that the homespun movement had never been a utopian protest and that its prosaic nature was the key to its success as a symbol of the American Revolution because the homespun had augured American progress.

Kate Haulman argues that fashion and dress served as a partisan cudgel in the political culture of the American Revolution, as Federalists and Democratic Republicans tarred each other with the brush of fashion. Accusing Federalist men of being "aristocrats" was powerful imagery that conjured visions of "a brocade-clad languid male figure, embodying Federalists as monarchical, elitist, and corrupt".[121] George Washington's move from his homespun clothing worn at the inauguration in 1789 to wearing imported velvet at a time when his own administration championed American manufactures did not help. In turn, Federalists accused their rivals, Democratic Republicans, of being too foreign, too French and too foppish. As David Waldstreicher states, "Thanks to the Republican antiaristocratic politics of style and the Federalist repression of 'Jacobinism,' partisan causes had been equated with everything, including dress, manners, and religion".[122] In addition, competing versions of Republicanism animated the "style wars" of the 1790s mapped onto political positions over the French Revolution and the conflict between France and England.

As of July 1792 in France, the French Legislative Assembly required all men to wear the tricolor cockade to replace the white of the *Ancien Regime*. Men and women in the United States adopted the knotted tricolor ribbons in their show of solidarity for the French Revolution. The tricolor ribbons appeared on the clothing of women of various ranks. In 1793, when the Revolution's radical turn disheartened some American supporters, the black of the traditional English cockade rivaled the tricolor to demonstrate loyalty to the Federalists. Kate Haulman argues that even as certain elements of dress became explicitly political in the age of revolutions, fashion's cultural politics placed it, and its followers, beyond the bounds of citizenship. Discourse about fashion prescribed an independence of dress for the nation often charging Anglo-American women for the creation of this independence and freedom of dress. Fashion writers insisted on a national mode that would be simple and ornament free. However, just as they were advocating this "true taste" they continued to cast fashion as feminine, unreasonable, tyrannical and enslaving.[123]

McKendrick has pointed out that England was Europe's most developed consumer society.[124] The debate over fashion is overshadowed by a larger one about the relative contributions of foreign and domestic consumption to fuel Europe's industrialization. Britain's empire was a vast consumer market for its goods. Scholars have emphasized the growing prominence of Atlantic markets in the eighteenth century. Ralph Davis' research on exports demonstrates that English exports rose two and half times in value between 1701 and 1774, but that exports to Africa and the Americas alone jumped six fold. Fueled by the slave trade, exports to Africa from England, mostly textiles, grew impressively. The expansion of Britain's American trade was the most dramatic, with a twenty-fold export to the West Indies and North America. By 1797–1798 the Americas took nearly 60 percent of English exports as opposed to just 10 percent in 1700-1701. The importance of British trade to America only lent power to America's boycott of British consumer goods during the Revolution.[125]

Spain's Imperial Fashion System

Spain was a major competitor and wanted to supersede English fashion in the Americas. During this period, Spanish economic writers, government authorities and merchants wanted to meet the demand from colonial consumers with products from Spain. By offering Spanish products, they were hoping to promote their own national values in order to colonize. Several pamphlets predicted great profits to be made from the sale of calicoes in the American colonies such as *Discurso sobre el luxo de la señoras* (Discourse on the Luxury of the Ladies, 1788). The anonymous author of the *Discourse on the Luxury of the Ladies* predicted that 5.5 million women would readily spend 118 million *reales de vellón* on fashion and luxury goods. The business of fashion used vice to foster the virtue of patriotism by strengthening the bonds between the Spanish monarchy and its colonies in America. A belief in the power of clothing to instill Spain's moral values across all racial lines is reflected in eighteenth-century *casta* paintings. These paintings were idolized paintings of interracial couples with their children. Made in Mexico, they depicted the Spanish *casta* system. It was a culturally constructed taxonomy based on color that depicted the different racial types that resulted from the relatively new mixing of Indian, African and Spanish populations. These portraits usually comprised sixteen different combinations of couples and their children. The *casta* system had been created to maintain a social hierarchy and the clothes worn by the subjects were key markers of their ethnic and racial identity: a wealthy Spaniard might not only be identified by his white skin, but also by the outfit he was wearing for status, such as a *banyon* coat, which was imported from India and made of fine chintz. By the 1770s and 1780s, such coats came directly from Spain, where they had become fashionable.[126]

   At the same time, the greater availability of Indian cotton textiles in the Spanish colonies posed a threat to the racial hierarchy of the *casta* system. Economic societies argued that if all inhabitants of the Americas should embrace Spanish textiles and style it would confuse the social order. The monarchy ruled that only Spaniards and *criollos* were allowed to wear the finest cotton fabrics imported from Spain. Spanish cloth, as the norm and the ideal, remained powerful even in the closing days of the empire and reflected the efforts of the Spanish monarchy to maintain both order and profit from the empire in the late eighteenth century. The Indian calicoes were considered a threat because they instilled a taste for foreign fashion that might cool the ties that bound the colonies to Spain. Only wealthy Spaniards were allowed to wear Indian cloth, while Spanish cotton cloths were for the Indians. Ultimately, Spain's efforts completely failed as all of Spanish America opened the floodgates to foreign fashions and to English cottons.[127]

Plantation Slaves as Buyers in the Consumer Market

Recent scholarship has dramatically changed our understanding of the ways in which slaves in the Americas participated in market culture and consumerism. If by the middle of the eighteenth century in Virginia masters generally supplied slaves with food and clothing that met their basic needs, most slaves gained access to the world of goods by selling their own surplus agricultural commodities, mainly vegetables, eggs and poultry. Ann Smart Martin asserts that those slaves that came from West Africa were no strangers to market sales and market relations. She cites as an example the Yoruba expression "*aye l'oya*" ("the world is a marketplace"). She stresses that the economic system that they were part of is not so well documented or understood in Virginia but that the sheer quantity of market regulations implies a strong African-American presence in the market. A committee was appointed in 1764 to examine the problem of slaves selling food in the markets and other public places. Nine years later, "Indians, mulattoes or negroes Bound or free", were banned by law from selling food, beer, or liquor.[128] The repeal of this law in 1783 suggests that slaves and other marginal groups had become too important in the supply of food for this prohibition to hold. The debate about controlling slave activity in the market continued and most commonly there was a requirement that owners should give slaves written permission to sell foodstuffs in order to control the sale of stolen food.[129]

Slave participation in the marketplace went beyond the sale of food. Martin opens her chapter on African Americans as consumers with Richard Stith's slave named Suckey purchasing a looking glass and a ribbon at John Hook's store. She paid for these goods by supplying four pounds of cottonseed. Martin, as a material culture researcher, began to ask questions about the role of enslaved men and women as players in the world of goods. She asserts that the experience of slaves in the retail trade presents a profound paradox; slaves could appropriate commodities even as they could be appropriated as commodities themselves. The paradox is clear since the same account books bearing their names as customers could also record their own sale to a new owner. The same merchant could serve them, sell them ribbons and other goods, and own them.[130]

Martin finds that among the slaves that entered the marketplace in central Virginia, men outnumbered women by approximately three to one. She also notices that the most active traders were either quite old or young adults who did not have children yet. This indicates that families with young children probably consumed what they grew, and this form of auto-consumption is one of the forms of consumption that is hardest to document. Slaves had knowledge and practice in vending produce and poultry, which allowed them to become small entrepreneurs and obtain ready cash to buy consumer goods. However, the nature of slaves' access to consumer goods and the items they chose remains largely undocumented. Martin stresses that this is a testimony to the uneasiness and ambivalence that such slave activity produced among whites. Early in the eighteenth century, illicit trade between slaves and poor whites had provoked Virginia lawmakers to legislate that slaves obtain written permission to trade. George Washington himself worked to identify local whites who had received stolen foodstuffs in the vicinity of Mount Vernon. He even tried to prevent his own former carpenter's daughter from opening a store. Washington argued that "her shop wd. be no more than a receptacle for stolen produce by the Negroes".[131]

Some stores attempted to construct a business system that tried to separate white and black customers as a way of accommodating both worlds. But the system ended up blurring the racial identity of the customer. A merchant named Anne Frame kept separate day books for blacks and whites but made mistakes by occasionally recording entries into the wrong book. She was an exception. Clearly every other eighteenth-century merchant had integrated slave transactions into the same accounting system as their other customers.[132] In addition to Suckey's purchases of a mirror and a ribbon, John Hook's 1773–1775 mercantile ledgers report purchases made by thirteen slaves. Most of the transactions he recorded involved small amounts – be it for blacks or whites. Martin finds that for the most popular commodities, both customer groups exhibited nearly identical purchasing patterns. Just as for the whites, rum was the overwhelming choice of the slaves. Slaves also purchased sweeteners to provide a bit of flavor to an otherwise repetitive diet. Inexpensive mirrors, ribbons, hats and textiles were also popular purchases. Ann Martin notes that what is most surprising is that the better quality textiles made up a higher percentage of slave purchases. The forms of payment listed for these purchases prove a remarkable flexibility from the merchants. This demonstrates a willingness to accept slaves as active economic players in the consuming world. For example, John Hook's records extend credit; Suckey had purchased her goods in February and John Hook credits her for partial payment ten months later. Slaves paid most often with the value of their own time and labor. Suckey paid by giving four pounds "cotton in ye seed".[133] The labor of picking seeds out of cotton fiber raised the value of a pound of cotton fourfold. A slave named London used the same form of payment; through cottonseed, he purchased clothing, rum, sugar and even a necklace.[134]

Martin studies another ledger kept by John Hook in the early nineteenth century: she finds that there are purchases made by thirty-five slaves. But unlike the group of slaves coming to his New London store over thirty years earlier, half of these slave customers were owned by Hook himself on his plantations. The account of John Hook's slave named Will reflects the range of market activities for one of these slaves. Will had the largest account and his purchases alone represented 17 percent of all the slave debt in the ledger. Debt was not unusual, most other customers also bought on credit. The page begins with a two-pound debt for which Will delivered 145 pounds of tobacco to the store in payment. In August 1807, Will purchases a wool hat and some household ceramics, including a dozen plates. In February 1808, he stopped in for a knife. In April, he bought a pair of cotton cards. The next day he paid with 630 pounds of tobacco, but John Hook deducted one-third of that payment towards rent. Among the 110 slaves listed in the inventory of Hook's estate on his death in 1809, six males and five females had family groups. The names of the male heads of household appear at least once in the ledger with lengthy lists of purchases. The sole female account belongs to a woman who was the head of the household herself. This extensive inventory has allowed Ann Martin to analyze slave consumption patterns as households – a task that can seldom be achieved for the poor whites of Virginia.[135]

Martin was able to uncover that the activity of African American women was very limited except for Phoebe, the only named black woman in John Hook's ledger. Like white people's store accounts, these slave purchases reveal preferences. The slave community she studies bought many textiles and items of clothing from Hook's store, over 90 percent of the purchases. The motives for these purchases were complex; however, shedding the discomfort of the basic coarse clothing provided by owners was probably very high on the list. A comparison was made to wearing the kind of shirt provided to the feeling of having a hundred or more chestnut burrs on one's chest. Comfort was not the only incentive: descriptions from white observers reveal the care with which slaves cultivated their appearance. Indeed, Martin contends that some owners used the special regard that slaves had for clothing as a means to reward and punish the slaves they owned. Household goods constituted a second major category of goods that slaves purchased. Many of them survive in the archeological record. Although scholarly debates still rage over how these things were acquired, John Hook's accounts indicate that they were purchased. The mirrors, knives, forks and straight pins all belong to the growing tide of consumer goods "and the changing behaviors that formed the heart of the consumer revolution".[136] The dozen plates purchased by Will would be of no use for the browned corn that was the slave diet. They indicate that he had adopted separate portions of multiple foods – an idea embedded in the Anglo-American food ways of his owners. Similarly, knives and forks indicate the adoption of European taboos against eating with one's hands. The fact that many archeological sites have unearthed teacups and saucers at slave sites further emphasizes the importance of slave participation in the Anglo-Virginian consumer world.[137]

Ann Smart Martin contends that mirrors are in many ways the most magical of consumer goods because they had special powers that transcended their role as a manufactured product. By the late eighteenth century, Virginian merchants could offer their customers very inexpensive face mirrors as well as large wall mirrors. Suckey could purchase one of the small face mirrors for two and a half shillings. Among the wealthy, the large mirrors belonged to the realm of fashion and night lighting. Middling Virginia households increasingly placed mirrors over the fireplace in the best room of the house, allowing it to reflect back its furnishings. Mirrors also played a significant role in amplifying the available light but Martin argues that Suckey only had one foot in that world. Even if mirrors belonged to European culture, they also had a deep resonance in West African culture. They functioned in a Bakongo ritual tradition, which valued light. Mirrors permitted entry into another world. Martin contends that African American slaves, like their African ancestors, believed that mirrors could capture, attract and repel spirits. Mirrors buried outside the house or standing next to doors could flash back evil spirits who wanted to cross the threshold. Mirror glass also has a history among eighteenth-century African Americans. Archeologists have recovered mirror glass in numerous slave quarters. Martin focuses the spotlight on Suckey to assess the ways in which she fit into the black and white worlds that she inhabited. She comes to the conclusion that Suckey was likely a black woman in a white household when she purchased a consumer good that was imbued with these extraordinarily complex meanings.[138] Martin concludes that a store and its consumer culture brought together many who did not "belong together" socially; slaves stood at the same counter as the wife of the wealthiest planter.[139] If it is very important to notice slave participation in the world of goods, it is more so to point out that their participation was on a deeply unequal basis.

Blood in the Sugar

In the latter part of the eighteenth century abolitionist movements in the revolutionary period advocated that all men were equal. After centuries of the slave trade and slavery, an English coalition of men and women merged into an anti-slavery movement, which Elizabeth Abbott compares to "a hybrid spider propelled by unmatched legs".[140] She describes each leg as formed by members of the following groups: working class men and women; black residents in England; West Indian slaves, free blacks of color; West Indian missionaries; Quaker and other religious men; politically minded reformers; anti-protectionist free traders. Starting from the 1750s, Abbott finds that from time to time over the more than half a century of anti-slavery efforts, a leg would shrivel away. In response to these abolitionist movements, the West Indian committee formed in about 1775, developed a powerful lobby for the sugar trade. The guilt-inducing theme of "blood as sugar", an abolitionist favorite, was used to counter this West Indian lobby's economic fear mongering.[141] A number of pamphlets were created; one of them identified anyone who ate sugar as "the grand cause of all the horrible injustices".[142] Some important literary figures espoused abolitionism; most famously Samuel Johnson, author of the first

English dictionary had a lifelong hatred of slavery.[143] The Quaker William Fox calculated that for every pound of West Indian sugar, consumers could be considered as consuming two ounces of human flesh. Abbott argues that the abolitionist propaganda of "blood as sugar" inverted African cannibalism by attributing it to whites consuming sugar. To a Christian audience, it also echoed transubstantiation, wine as Christ's blood. The abolitionists in England decided to boycott sugar. William Fox had calculated that if every family accustomed to consuming five pounds of sugar and rum combined in a week abstained from slave-grown sugar, the family could save one African from slavery every twenty-one months; every nineteen and a half years, eight families together would save 100 Africans. London debating societies also borrowed the topic and published several pamphlets to dissuade consumers from any longer consuming an "Article of Luxury that is polluted with the blood of innocent Fathers, Mothers and Children". Both well-to-do families and working class families abstained. In the early stages of the boycott, abolitionist propaganda coincided with the price of English sugar rising during the Revolution of 1791 on French-held Saint-Domingue. About 300,000 English people abstained from consuming West Indian sugar; this abstaining was usually a family matter that was decided by the female head of household.[144] From her village of Chesham, one such head of household, Lidya Hardy, wrote to Equiano that in the village there were more people that drank tea without sugar than those who sweetened their tea.[145]

Equiano's had become a household name in England. His published work was the most famous and successful of the testimonials of the African victims of the slave trade. Equiano's "The Interesting Narrative of the Life of Olaudah Equiano, or Gustavus Vassa, the African (1789)" was a seven-shilling pamphlet. The success of this pamphlet by a former slave was due to what historian Adam Hochschild has argued to be "the first great political book tour".[146] Equiano traveled all over England selling his pamphlet and advancing the cause of abolitionism. Equiano also accused planters, greedy for cheap sugar, of destroying Africa's rich and peaceful societies. Abolitionism spewed out advertisements, newspaper articles, letters and pamphlets to persuade editors to publish and support abolitionism. One supporter of the cause traveled with a very grim show and tell: handcuffs, shackles, thumb screws and a tool to pry open the mouths of slaves attempting suicide by starvation. Both abolitionist and pro-slavery groups distributed cheap or free pamphlets, some of them with terrifying images.[147]

In fact, the sugar boycott brought about by abolitionists harmed the English sugar business far less than the fact that sugar was in short supply because of war in the sugar islands between the English and the French. West Indian sugar had become increasingly expensive. Nevertheless, they very successfully linked sugar to slavery and pointed out the individual consumers' complicity in perpetuating slavery by purchasing sugar. Elizabeth Abbott writes that by acknowledging women's power in buying, using and serving sugar, women became participants in the campaign that until then largely excluded them from the political sphere. Moreover, since that first political boycott involving women, boycotting as an economic weapon would become a standard feature of major justice campaigns for women in the political sphere.[148]

Abolitionism suffered many defeats and faced formidable opposition from the West Indian interest. The West Indian plantation owners and their representatives were diligently dealing with Parliament offering counter evidence, denials and justification for the continuation of slavery to grow sugar. Their preferred tactic was to favorably compare the lives of the slaves with those of England's wretched workers. But their strongest argument was that sugar was a mainstay of the British Empire because of its economic power. Yet another West Indian tactic was to justify slavery by portraying Africans as savage. When the French-held sugar plantation of Saint-Domingue (today Haiti) erupted and insurrection spread to the West Indies, they declared that it was interference with slavery that had led to what they considered "such horrors" as the victory of 1791 that brought slaves their freedom. The economic pressure on Parliament did not stop, writes Abbott, the English public from admiring heroic black slaves of Saint-Domingue. That the revolt was against the French plantation owners helped the price of English Jamaican sugar to rise as France's imports dried up. The revolt was influenced by the ideas of the French Revolution; liberty, equality and fraternity were the ideas espoused by the leader Toussaint L'Ouverture and his followers.[149] The poet Wordsworth assured Toussaint L'Ouverture, that "thou hast great allies; / Thy friends are exaltations, agonies, / And love, and man's unconquerable mind".[150] Nevertheless, if abolitionists sympathized with the slaves, they also deplored the violent tactics of the revolution. After a period of freedom, slavery was reinstated on the island in 1793 by the English. In January 1807, the Abolition Bill made its sixteenth appearance on the political scene in England. The House of Commons debated it passionately, but the Bill finally passed 115–15 in the Commons and 41–20 in the House of Lords. It became law in March 1807.[151]

In North America, as early as 1696, the Quakers began a campaign to abolish slavery and the first anti-slavery society was founded by Benjamin Franklin in 1774.[152] In 1775, the same year that the West Indian lobby of plantation owners was formed in London, the Pennsylvania Society for Promoting the Abolition of Slavery (PAS) was founded. Although Quakers had been active in abolitionism, this was the first formal Quaker anti-slavery society. Benjamin Franklin would become its honorary president in 1787. Although slavery was not abolished in Pennsylvania, the Gradual Emancipation Act was passed in 1780. The Act freed the future children of slaves but those born prior to the date of the Act remained enslaved for life. This Act of gradual emancipation became the model for other Northern states in the newly independent territories of North America, except for the states of Vermont and Massachusetts.[153] Vermont abolished slavery in its 1777 constitution that banned slavery and made it unlawful.[154] Some years later, in 1783, the Massachusetts Judicial Court also ruled that slavery was illegal based on its own previous

1780 constitution that proclaimed freedom for all, therefore all slaves were to be immediately freed.[155] Slavery did not disappear despite all this legislation. The war to keep their American colonial holdings was fought in great part because of the fear of losing the most lucrative business in the British Empire: sugar. The colonies were also the largest market for English consumer goods, a trade that had grown by 2,000 percent in the eighteenth century. Much of the North American colonies were tied to the sugar trade and saw the West Indies as a natural extension of their trading world. For example, in New England, the Brown family from Providence had made a fortune in the West Indian trade of sugar and rum, most of it illegal, by funding privateers during the war between England and its enemies France and Spain.[156]

Profits from sugar and rum not only led to the conspicuous consumption of the sugar barons on their island estates, but also to the construction of mansions and "follies" in England. A son of the Beckford family (large estate owners in Jamaica) was not only one of the largest art collectors in the world, but when he returned to England he was raising towers and digging grottos to enhance the unprecedented splendor of the aptly named *Splendens*, his English estate. Most of the spending done for all these worldly goods was already largely dependent on huge debts for many of the wealthy sugar growers. Display and consumption had become a way of life, no matter the cost. Largely run by attorneys, these absentee landlords were concerned with acquiring respectability and rank through display despite their many debts.[157] In the wake of revolutions and boycotts, the wealthy strived more than ever to display the triumph of a world of goods. After the turn of the century, the habits and spending of the wealthy inspired Thorstein Veblen to call the nineteenth century the age of conspicuous consumption.

Study Questions

1   What was the economic relationship of Britain with its colonies?
2   How did this relationship affect consumption patterns and political consciousness among European settlers in the North America?
3   How did the thoughts of Jean-Jacques Rousseau on simplicity and nature shape Marie Antoinette's conception of her sartorial consumption? What were its consequences?
4   What was the political meaning of boycotting commodities such as tea and sugar? Give two examples discussed in the chapter.
5   What role did credit play in eighteenth-century consumption and the marketplace? Discuss examples of debt and credit.

Notes

1   Jean-Jacques Rousseau, *Oeuvres complètes*, 5 vols. (Paris, 1959), 1: 363; Rousseau, *Oeuvres complètes* de J. J. Rousseau, 4 vols. (Paris, 1852), 1: 409.

Translation by Michael Kwass. As cited in Michael Kwass, "Big Hair: A Wig History of Consumption of Eighteenth-Century France" *The American Historical Review* Vol. 111, No. 3 (Oxford University Press, June 2006), 631–659, 631.

2 Kwass, "Big Hair", 631.
3 Kwass, "Big Hair", 634.
4 Kwass, "Big Hair", 637.
5 Kwass, "Big Hair", 634–635.
6 Kwass, "Big Hair", 640.
7 Kwass, "Big Hair", 644.
8 Joan DeJean, *The Age of Comfort: When Paris Discovered Casual—and the Modern Home Began* (New York: Bloomsbury, 2009).
9 J. C. Flügel, *The Psychology of Clothes* (London, 1950), 110–119, as cited in Kwass, "Big Hair", 650.
10 Kwass, "Big Hair", 651.
11 Caroline Weber, *Queen of Fashion: What Marie Antoinette Wore to the Revolution* (New York: Henry Holt and Co., 2006).
12 Nicolas-Toussaint Lemoyne Desessarts, *Dictionnaire universel de police (1785–1789)* as quoted in Jennifer Jones, *Sexing la mode: Gender, Fashion and Commercial Culture in Old Regime France* (Oxford; New York: Berg, 2004), 145.
13 Jones, *Sexing La Mode*, 146.
14 Jones, *Sexing La Mode*, 146.
15 Jones, *Sexing La Mode*, 147.
16 Jones, *Sexing La Mode*, 148.
17 Jones, *Sexing la Mode*, 150–151.
18 Joan DeJean, *The Essence of Style: How the French Invented High Fashion, Fine Food, Chic Cafés, Style, Sophistication and Glamour* (New York: Free Press, 2005), 12–14.
19 Steven Laurence Kaplan, *La fin des corporations*, trans. Béatrice Vierne (Paris: Fayard, 2001).
20 See Jones, *Sexing La Mode* and Weber, *Queen of Fashion*.
21 Daniel Roche, *Histoire des choses banales: naissance de la consommation dans les sociétés traditionnelles (XVIIe-XIXe siècle)* (Paris: Fayard, 1997).
22 Daniel Roche, *La culture des apparences: une histoire du vêtement, XVIIe–XVIIIe siècles* (Paris: Fayard, 1989). Roche, *Histoire des choses banales.*
23 Daniel Roche, *France in the Enlightenment* (Cambridge, MA: Harvard University Press, 1998), 164–72.
24 Clare Haru Crowston, *Fabricating Women: The Seamstresses of Old Regime France, 1675–1791* (London: Duke University Press, 2001); Jennifer Jones, *Sexing La Mode*; Caroline Weber, *Queen of Fashion.*
25 Jones, *Sexing la Mode*, 9.
26 Cécile Berly, *La Reine Scandaleuse: idées reçues sur Marie-Antoinette* (Paris: Cavalier bleu, 2012), 73–83.
27 DeJean, *The Essence of Style*, 29–30.
28 Jones, *Sexing la Mode*, 11–12.
29 Weber, *Queen of Fashion*, 14–16.
30 Berly, *La Reine Scandaleuse*, 112–113.
31 Weber, *Queen of Fashion*, 81–85.
32 Berly, *La Reine Scandaleuse*, 115.
33 Weber, *Queen of Fashion*, 100.
34 Berly, *La Reine Scandaleuse*, 73.
35 Weber, *Queen of Fashion*, 100–102.
36 Ina Baghdiantz McCabe, *Orientalism in Early Modern France: Eurasian Trade, Exoticism and the Ancien Régime* (Oxford; New York: Berg, 2008), 220–222.
37 Jones, *Sexing La Mode*, 11.

38 Carolyn Sargentson, *Merchants and Luxury markets: the Marchands Merciers of Eighteenth-century Paris* (Malibu, CA: Victoria and Albert Museum in association with the J. Paul Getty Museum, 1996).
39 Weber, *Queen of Fashion*, 104.
40 Weber, *Queen of Fashion*, 106.
41 Berly, *La Reine Scandaleuse*, 94.
42 DeJean, *The Essence of Style*, chapter 1.
43 Weber, *Queen of Fashion*, 118.
44 Weber, *Queen of Fashion*, 121.
45 Weber, *Queen of Fashion*, 209.
46 Berly, *La Reine Scandaleuse*, 96.
47 Berly, *La Reine Scandaleuse*, 98.
48 Berly, *La Reine Scandaleuse*, 78.
49 Berly, *La Reine Scandaleuse*, 79.
50 Weber, *Queen of Fashion*, 159–192.
51 Weber, *Queen of Fashion*, 159.
52 Weber, *Queen of Fashion*, 113.
53 Berly, *La Reine Scandaleuse*, 104.
54 Weber, *Queen of Fashion*, 112–114.
55 Weber, *Queen of Fashion*, 118–123.
56 DeJean, *The Age of Comfort*, 216–217.
57 DeJean, *The Age of Comfort*, 219.
58 Weber, *Queen of Fashion*, 225.
59 Weber, *Queen of Fashion*, 229.
60 Berly, *La Reine Scandaleuse*, 144.
61 Weber, *Queen of Fashion*, 241.
62 For debates in England and in the Dutch Republic, see Maxine Berg and Elizabeth Eger, *Luxury in the Eighteenth Century: Debates, Desires and Delectable Goods* (Basingstoke, Hampshire; New York: Palgrave, 2003).
63 Albert O. Hirschman, *The Passions and the Interests: Political Arguments for Capitalism before its Triumph* (Princeton: Princeton University, 1977).
64 *The Spectator*, 19 July 1712 as quoted in Aileen Ribeiro, *Dress and Morality* (London: Berg, 2003), 96.
65 Ribeiro, *Dress and Morality*, 97.
66 Bishop George Berkeley, *The Querist*, Dublin 1735–1737. Part I. Query 80 as quoted in Ribeiro, *Dress and Morality*, 101.
67 Ribeiro, *Dress and Morality*, 103.
68 Ribeiro, *Dress and Morality*, 106.
69 Ribeiro, *Dress and Morality*, 114.
70 Ribeiro, *Dress and Morality*, 117.
71 Kate Haulman, *The Politics of Fashion in Eighteenth-century America* (Chapel Hill: University of North Carolina Press, 2011), 219.
72 M. Evelyn (attr.) *Mundus Muliebris: or, The Ladies Dressing-Room unlock'd*, ed. J. L. Nevinson, London 1977 as quoted in Ribeiro, *Dress and Morality*, 117.
73 Ribeiro, *Dress and Morality*, 118.
74 Lynn Hunt, "Freedom of Dress in Revolutionary France" in Sara Melzer and Kathryn Norberg, eds., *From the Royal to the Republican Body: Incorporating the Political in Seventeenth and Eighteenth-century France* (Berkeley; Los Angeles; Oxford: University of California Press, 1998), 224–249, 224.
75 Hunt, "Freedom of Dress in Revolutionary France", in *From the Royal to the Republican Body,* 225.
76 Daniel Roche, *La Culture des apparences: Une Histoire du vêtement (XVIIe–XVIIIe siècle)* (Paris: Fayard, 1989), 54. In Hunt, "Freedom of Dress in Revolutionary France", *From the Royal to the Republican Body*, 228.

77 Hunt, "Freedom of Dress in Revolutionary France", *From the Royal to the Republican Body,* 233.
78 Hunt, "Freedom of Dress in Revolutionary France", *From the Royal to the Republican Body,* 234.
79 Hunt, "Freedom of Dress in Revolutionary France", *From the Royal to the Republican Body,* 237.
80 For more see Lynn Hunt, "Freedom of Dress in Revolutionary France", *From the Royal to the Republican Body,* 224–249, 224.
81 Patrick O'Brien "The Geopolitics of a Global Industry: Eurasian Divergence and the Mechanization of Cotton Textile Production in England", in Giorgio Riello and Prasannan Parthasarathi, eds., *The Spinning World: A Global History of Cotton Textiles, 1200–1850* (Oxford; New York: Oxford University Press, 2009), 351–365, 355–356.
82 T. H. Breen, *The Marketplace of Revolution: How Consumer Politics Shaped American Independence* (Oxford; New York: Oxford University Press, 2004), 72.
83 Breen, *The Marketplace of Revolution,* 78–79.
84 Breen, *The Marketplace of Revolution,* 81.
85 William Smith, *The History of the Late Province of New York ...* (New York Historical Society *Collections*, vol. 4, pt. 2, 1829) as quoted in Breen, *The Marketplace of Revolution,* 98.
86 Breen, *The Marketplace of Revolution,* 99.
87 Breen, *The Marketplace of Revolution,* 101.
88 Breen, *The Marketplace of Revolution,* 127.
89 Breen, *The Marketplace of Revolution,* 129–131.
90 Breen, *The Marketplace of Revolution,* 210.
91 Breen, *The Marketplace of Revolution,* 213–216.
92 Breen, *The Marketplace of Revolution,* 235–242.
93 Breen, *The Marketplace of Revolution,* 246.
94 Breen, *The Marketplace of Revolution,* 254–259.
95 Breen, *The Marketplace of Revolution,* 262–266.
96 Breen, *The Marketplace of Revolution,* 291.
97 Benjamin H. Irvin, *Clothed in Robes of Sovereignty: The Continental Congress and the People Out of Doors* (New York: Oxford University Press, 2011), 25.
98 Irvin, *Clothed in Robes of Sovereignty,* 24–25.
99 Irvin, *Clothed in Robes of Sovereignty,* 28–30.
100 Irvin, *Clothed in Robes of Sovereignty,* 30.
101 Irvin, *Clothed in Robes of Sovereignty,* 37.
102 Irvin, *Clothed in Robes of Sovereignty,* 39.
103 Irvin, *Clothed in Robes of Sovereignty,* 42–43.
104 Benjamin Carp, *Defiance of the Patriots: the Boston Tea Party and the Making of America* (New Haven: Yale University Press, 2010), 82.
105 Carp, *Defiance of the Patriots,* 79.
106 Carp, *Defiance of the Patriots,* 82–83.
107 Carp, *Defiance of the Patriots,* 96.
108 Carp, *Defiance of the Patriots,* 109–131.
109 Carp, *Defiance of the Patriots,* 132–138.
110 Carp, *Defiance of the Patriots,* 141–159.
111 Carp, *Defiance of the Patriots,* 187–218.
112 Breen, *Marketplace of Revolution,* 318–319.
113 Breen, *Marketplace of Revolution,* 329.
114 As quoted in Michael Zakim, "From Homespun to Ready-Made" *The American Historical Review* 106.5 (2001): 81 accessed 23 Jul. 2012, 1553–1586, 1554. <http://www.historycooperative.org/journals/ahr/106.5/ah0501001553.html>.
115 Zakim, "From Homespun to Ready-made", 1556.

116 Zakim, "From Homespun to Ready-made", 1556.
117 Zakim, "From Homespun to Ready-made", 1555.
118 Zakim, "From Homespun to Ready-made", 1567.
119 Zakim, "From Homespun to Ready-made", 1567.
120 Bagnall, *Textile Industries*, 102–103; Bishop, *American Manufactures,* 418; William L. Stone, *History of New York City* (New York, 1872), 303–304; Clark, *History of Manufactures*, 46, 366, 448 in Zakim, "From Homespun to Ready-made", 1568.
121 Haulman, *The Politics of Fashion in Eighteenth-Century America*, 222.
122 Waldstreicher, *In the Midst of Perpetual Fetes: The Making of American Nationalism, 1776–1820* (Chapel Hill, NC: Published for the Omohundro Institute of Early American History and Culture, Williamsburg, Virginia by the University of North Carolina Press 1997), 203 as quoted in Haulman, *The Politics of Fashion in Eighteenth-century America*, 222–223.
123 Haulman, *The Politics of Fashion in Eighteenth-Century America*, 222–224.
124 Neil McKendrick, John Brewer and John Harold Plumb, *The Birth of a Consumer Society: The Commercialization of Eighteenth-century England* (Bloomington: Indiana University Press, 1982).
125 Robert S. DuPlessis, "Cottons Consumption in the Seventeenth and Eighteenth-century North Atlantic" in Riello and Parthasarathi, eds., *The Spinning World*, 227–260.
126 DuPlessis, "Cottons Consumption".
127 DuPlessis, "Cottons Consumption".
128 Ann Smart Martin, *Buying into the World of Goods: Early Consumers in Backcountry Virginia* (Baltimore: Johns Hopkins University Press, 2008), 174.
129 Martin, *Buying into the World of Goods*, 174–175.
130 Martin, *Buying into the World of Goods*, 173.
131 Martin, *Buying into the World of Goods*, 176.
132 Martin, *Buying into the World of Goods*, 178–179.
133 Martin, *Buying into the World of Goods*, 180.
134 Martin, *Buying into the World of Goods*, 180.
135 Martin, *Buying into the World of Goods*, 181.
136 Martin, *Buying into the World of Goods*, 185.
137 Martin, *Buying into the World of Goods*, 185.
138 Martin, *Buying into the World of Goods*, 192.
139 Martin, *Buying into the World of Goods*, 186–192.
140 Elizabeth Abbott, *Sugar: A Bittersweet History* (London; New York: Duckworth Overlook, 2009), 225.
141 Abbott, *Sugar: A Bittersweet History*, 238–239.
142 Abbott, *Sugar: A Bittersweet History*, 239.
143 Matthew Parker, *The Sugar Barons: Family, Corruption, Empire, and War in the West Indies* (New York: Walker & Co., 2011), 316.
144 Abbott, *Sugar: A Bittersweet History*, 239–241.
145 Abbott, *Sugar: A Bittersweet History*, 239–241.
146 Abbott, *Sugar: A Bittersweet History*, 236.
147 Abbott, *Sugar: A Bittersweet History*, 236–237.
148 Abbott, *Sugar: A Bittersweet History*, 241.
149 Marc Aronson and Marina Tamar Budhos, *Sugar Changed the World: A Story of Magic, Spice, Slavery, Freedom, and Science* (Boston, MA: Clarion Books, 2010), 83–84.
150 Abbott, *Sugar: A Bittersweet History*, 243.
151 Abbott, *Sugar: A Bittersweet History*, 245.
152 Parker, *The Sugar Barons*, 317.

153 A. Leon Higginbotham, Jr., *In the Matter of Color: Race & the American Legal Process* (New York: Oxford University Press, 1978), 310.
154 Robert William Fogel and Stanley L. Engerman, *Time on the Cross: The Economics of American Negro Slavery* (New York; London: W.W. Norton, 1995), 33–34.
155 Higginbotham, *In the Matter of Color: Race & the American Legal Process*, 91.
156 Parker, *The Sugar Barons*, 318.
157 Parker, *The Sugar Barons*, 337–344.

Bibliography

Abbott, Elizabeth. *Sugar: A Bittersweet History*. London; New York: Duckworth Overlook, 2009.

Agnew, Jean-Christophe. "Coming Up for Air: Consumer Culture in Historical Perspective". In John Brewer and Roy Porter, eds, *Consumption and the World of Goods*. New York; London: Routledge, 1993, 23–25.

Aignan, François. *Le preste médecin ou Discours physique sur l'etablissement de la Medicine. Avec un traité du caffé & du thé de France selon le système d'Hippocrate*. Paris: chez Laurent D'Houry, 1696.

Allsen, Thomas. *Culture and Conquest in Mongol Eurasia*. Cambridge, UK; New York: Cambridge University Press, 2001.

Al-Jaziri, Bibiothèque nationale Ms. arabe no. 4590 al-Jaziri, 'Abd al-Qadir ibn Muhammad al Ansari al Hanbali 'Umdat al al-sawfa fi hill al-qawha', n.d.

Anderson, Virginia DeJohn. *Creatures of Empire: How Domestic Animals Transformed Early America*. Oxford; New York: Oxford University Press, 2004.

Anjomand, Saïd. "Coffeehouses, Guilds & Oriental Despotism: Government & Civil Society in late 17th–early 18th Century Istanbul and Isfahan, and as seen from Paris & London". *European Journal of Sociology*, 45, no.1 (2004): 23–42.

Appadurai, Arjun. "Introduction: Commodities and the Politics of Value". *The Social Life of Things: Commodities in Cultural Perspective*. Cambridge: Cambridge University Press, 1986.

Arnold, Lauren. *Princely Gifts and Papal Treasures: The Franciscan Mission to China and its Influence on the Art of the West, 1250–1350*. San Francisco: Desiderata Press, 1999.

Aronson, Marc and Marina Tamar Budhos, *Sugar Changed the World: A Story of Magic, Spice, Slavery, Freedom, and Science*. Boston, MA: Clarion Books, 2010.

Articles for the execution of the Statutes of Apparel, and for the reformation of the outrageous excess thereof grown of late time within the realm, devised upon the Queen's Majesty's commandment, by advice of her Council, 6 May 1562. Westminster, London Available from: <http://elizabethan.org/sumptuary/ruffs-hose-swords.html>

Audigier, François. *La Maison réglée, et l'art de diriger maison d'un grand seigneur & autres, tant à la Ville qu'à la Campagne, & le devoir de tous les Officiers, & autres Domestiques en général. Avec la Véritable Méthode de faire toutes sortes d'Essences, d'Eaux de Liqueurs, fortes & rafraîchissantes, à la mode d'Italie. Ouvrage utile et nécessaire à toutes sortes de personnes de qualité, gentilshommes de Province, étrangers, bourgeois, officiers de grandes maisons, limonadiers & autres marchands de liqueurs*. Paris 1962 or counterfeit of same edition. Reprint, Amsterdam: Paul Marret, 1967.

Austen, Ralph A. and Woodruff D. Smith. "Private Tooth Decay as Public Economic Virtue: The Slave-Sugar Triangle, Consumerism, and European Industrialization". *Social Science History*, Vol. 14, No. 1 (Spring 1990): 95–115.

Baghdiantz McCabe, Ina. *The Shah's Silk for Europe's Silver: The Eurasian Trade of the Julfa Armenians in Safavid Iran and India.* Atlanta, Georgia: Scholar's Press, 1999.

——*Orientalism in Early Modern France: Eurasian Trade, Exoticism and the Ancien Régime.* Oxford; New York: Berg, 2008.

Baghdiantz McCabe, Ina, Gelina Harlaftis and Ionna Minoglu, eds. *Diaspora and Entrepreneurial Networks 1600–2000.* Oxford: Berg, 2005.

Barkan, Ömer Lütfi. "The Price Revolution of the Sixteenth Century: A Turning Point in the Economic History of the Near East". Justin McCarthy, trans., *International Journal of Middle East* Studies 6 (1975): 3–28. Quoted in Şevket Pamuk, "The Price Revolution in the Ottoman Empire Reconsidered", *International Journal of Middle East Studies,* Vol. 33, No.1 (February 2001): 69–89.

Barrera-Osorio, Antonio. "Empiricism in the Spanish Atlantic World". In James Delbourgo and Nicholas Dew, eds, *Science and Empire in the Atlantic World.* New York; London: Routledge, 2008, 177–202.

Barthes, Roland. *Mythologies.* Translated by Annette Lavers. New York: Farrar, Straus, Giroux, 1972.

——*The Fashion System.* New York: Hill and Wang, 1983.

Baudrillard, Jean. *Système des Objets.* New York; London: Verso, 1996.

Baudry, Jean. *Jean Nicot.* Lyon: La Manufacture, 1988.

Bayly, C. A. *Rulers, Townsmen and Bazaars: North Indian Society in the Age of British Expansion, 1770–1870.* Cambridge; New York; Melbourne: Cambridge University Press, 1983.

——"'Archaic' and 'Modern' Globalization in the Eurasian and African Arena, ca. 1750–1850". In A. G. Hopkins, ed. *Globalization in World History.* New York, NY: W.W. Norton & Company, 2002, 45–72.

Berg, Maxine and Helen Clifford. *Consumers and Luxury: Consumer Culture in Europe 1650–1850.* Manchester: Manchester University Press, 1999.

Berg, Maxine and Elizabeth Eger, eds. *Luxury in the Eighteenth Century: Debates, Desires and Delectable Goods.* Basingstoke, Hampshire; New York: Palgrave, 2003.

Berly, Cécile. *La Reine Scandaleuse: idées reçues sur Marie-Antoinette.* Paris: Cavalier blue, 2012.

Bermingham, Ann and John Brewer, eds. *The Consumption of Culture, 1600–1800: Image, Object, Text.* London; New York: Routledge, 1995.

Bonny, Richard. *The European Dynastic States, 1494–1660.* Oxford: Oxford University Press, 1991.

Bourdieu, Pierre. *Distinction: A Social Critique of the Judgment of Taste.* London: Routledge and Kegan Paul, 1984.

——*Reproduction in Culture, Education, Society.* Beverly Hills, CA: Sage, 1977.

Braudel, Fernand. *Civilization materielle, économie et capitalisme: XVe–XVIIIe siècle.* Paris: A. Colin, 1979.

Bray, Francesca. *Technology and Gender: Fabrics of Power in Late Imperial China.* Berkeley CA: University of California Press, 1997.

Breen, T. H. *The Marketplace of Revolution: How Consumer Politics Shaped American Independence.* Oxford; New York: Oxford University Press, 2004.

Bretschneider, Emil. *History of European Botanical Discoveries in China.* Hamburg: SEVERUS Verlag, 2011.

Brewer, John and Roy Porter, eds. *Consumption and the World of Goods.* New York; London: Routledge, 1993.

British Library Board. "1500s Food" Last accessed February 21, 2012. Available from: http://www.bl.uk/learning/langlit/booksforcooks/1500s/1500sfoods.html

Broadberry, Stephen N. and Bishnupriya Gupta. "The Early Modern Great Divergence: Wages, Prices and Economic Development in Europe and Asia, 1500–1800". *International Macroeconomics and Economic History Initiative.* London. Centre for Economic Policy Research, Volume 59, Issue 1 (February 2006): 2–31.

Brook, Timothy. "Smoking in Imperial China", S. Gilman and X. Zhou, eds., *Smoke: A Global History of Smoking.* London Reaktion Books, 2004. Quoted in Charles C. Mann, *1493, Uncovering the New World Columbus Created.* New York: Alfred A. Knopf, 2011, 84–91, 164–165.

Brusati, Celeste. *Johannes Vermeer.* New York: Rizzoli, 1993.

Burke, Katherine Strange. "A Note on Archaeological Evidence for Sugar Production in the Middle Islamic Periods in Bilād al-Shām". *Mamluk Studies Review* 8/2 (University of Chicago, 2012): 109–118.

Burke, Peter. "*Res et Verba:* Conspicuous Consumption in the Early Modern World". In John Brewer and Roy Porter, eds., *Consumption and the World of Goods.* New York; London: Routledge, 1993, 148–161.

Butel, Paul. *Histoire du Thé.* Paris: Presses Universitaires de France, 1997.

Campbell, Colin. "Consumption and the Rhetorics of Need and Want". *Journal of Design History,* Vol 11, No. 3 (Oxford University Press, 1998): 235–246.

Campbell, Mary Baine. *Wonder and Science: Imagining Worlds in Early Modern Europe.* Ithaca; London: Cornell University Press, 1999.

Carp, Benjamin. *Defiance of the Patriots: the Boston Tea Party and the Making of America.* New Haven: Yale University Press, 2010.

Chaudhuri, K. N. *The Trading World of Asia and the English East India Company 1660–1760.* Cambridge; New York: Cambridge University Press, 1978, 131–4. Cited in Lemire, Beverly. "Fashioning Cottons: Asian Trade, Domestic Industry and Consumer Demand, 1660–1780", in Giorgio Riello and Peter McNeil, eds., *The Fashion History Reader: Global Perspectives.* Abingdon, Oxon; New York: Routledge, 2010, 197.

——*Asia Before Europe: Economy and Civilization of the Indian Ocean from the Rise of Islam to 1750.* Cambridge, England; New York: Cambridge University Press, 1990.

Clapham, Sir John Harold, Michael Moïssey Postan and Edwin Ernest Rich, eds. *The Cambridge Economic History of Europe.* Cambridge: Cambridge University Press, 1941.

Clarence-Smith, Gervase and Steven Topik, eds. *The Global Coffee Economy in Africa, Asia and Latin America, 1500–1989.* New York: Cambridge University Press, 2003.

Clifford, James. *The Predicament of Culture: Twentieth Century Ethnography, Literature, and Art.* London: Yale University Press, 1988.

Coron, Sabine and Bibliothèque de l'Arsenal Staff. *Livres en bouche: cinq siècles d'art culinaire français, du quatorzième au dix-huitième siècle.* Paris: BNF, Hermann, 2001.

Clunas, Craig. "Modernity Global and Local: Consumption and the Rise of the West". *AHR* 104, no. 5 (December, 1999): 1497–1511.

——*Superfluous Things: Material Culture and Social Status in Early Modern China.* Honolulu: University of Hawaii Press, 2004.

——"Splendour and Excess in Ming China". In Frank Trentman ed. *The Oxford Handbook of the History of Consumption.* Oxford: Oxford Universty Press, 2012, 51–52.

Coe, Sophie D. and Michael D. Coe. *The True History of Chocolate*. New York: Thames and Hudson, 2007.

Cole, Charles Woosley. *Colbert and a Century of French Mercantilism*, 2nd ed. New York: Columbia University Press, 1964.

Colley, Linda. *Captives: Britain, Empire and the World 1600–1850*. London: Pantheon, 2002.

Colomb, Claude. *Question de médecine proposée par Messieurs Castillons et Foque, docteurs de la faculté d'Aix, à Monsieur Colomb, pour son agrégation au collège des médecins de Marseille, sur lesquelles on doit disputer le 27 février 1679 dans la salle de la Maison de Ville*. Dissertation. Marseille, 1679.

Cook, Harold J. *Matters of Exchange: Commerce, Medicine, and Science in the Dutch Golden Age*. New Haven, CN: Yale University Press; 2008.

Coustou, Josée Balagna. *Arabe et humanisme dans la France des derniers Valois*. Paris: Editions Maisonneuve et Larose, 1989.

Cowan, Brian William. *The Social Life of Coffee: The Emergence of the British Coffeehouse*. New Haven, CN: Yale University Press, 2005.

Cowan, Brian. "New Worlds, New Tastes". In Paul Freedman ed., *Food: The History of Taste*. Berkeley: University of California Press, 2007, 197–232.

Crosby, Alfred. *The Columbian Exchange: The Biological Consequences of 1492*. Westport, CT: Greenwood Press, 1972.

Curta, Florin. "Merovingian and Carolingian gift giving". *Speculum 81, 3* (2006): 670–699.

Dalby, Andrew. *Dangerous Tastes: The Story of Spices*. Berkeley: University of California Press, 2002.

Dash, Mike. *Tulipomania: The Story of the World's most Coveted Flower and the Extraordinary Passions it Aroused*. Great Britain: Indigo, 2000.

Davidson, Hilary. "Fashion in the Spanish Court". In Giorgio Riello and Peter McNeil, eds., *The Fashion History Reader: Global Perspectives*. Abingdon, Oxon; New York: Routledge, 2010, 169.

De Blègny, Nicolas. *Le bon usage du thé du caffé et du chocolat pour La préservation & pour La guérison des maladies*. Paris: Estienne Michallet, 1687.

De Choisy, Timoléon. *Journal du Voyage de Siam*, ed. Dirk Van der Cruysse. Paris: Fayard, 1995. Cited in Carolyn Sargentson, *Merchants and Luxury Markets: The Marchands Merciers of Eighteenth-century Paris.* London: The Victoria and Albert Museum, 1996, 62.

De Filippis, Marybeth. "Margrieta van Varick's East Indian Goods". *The Magazine Antiques* (September 2009), accessed October 24, 2012. http://www.themagazinean tiques.com/articles/margrieta-van-varicks-east-indian-goods-a-possible-influence-on-colonial-american-silver/

De la Roque, Jean. *Voyage de l'Arabie heureuse: par l'Ocean oriental, & le détroit de la mer Rouge, fait par les françois pour la premiere fois, dans les années 1708, 1709 & 1710; avec la relation particuliere d'un voyage fait du port de Moka à la cour du roi d'Yemen, dans la seconde expedition des années 1711, 1712 & 1713; un memoire concernant l'arbre & le fruit du café, dressé sur les observations de ceux qui ont fait ce dernier voyage; et un traité historique de l'origine & du progrès du café, tant dans l'Asie que dans l'Europe; de son introduction en France, & de l'établissement de son usage à Paris*. Paris: A. Cailleau, 1716.

——*A Voyage to Arabia Felix (1708–1710); and, A Journey from Mocha to Muab (1711–13); and, A Narrative Concerning Coffee; and, An Historical Treatise Concerning Coffee*. Cambridge; New York: Oleander, 2004.

De Roover, Raymond. "New Facets on the Financing and Marketing of Early Printed Books". *Bulletin of the Business Historical Society*, Vol. 27, No. 4 (Dec., 1953), 222–226.

De Rouvroy, Louis, duc de Saint-Simon. *Mémoires*. Edited by Yves Coirault. Paris: Gallimard. 1984. Cited in Jennifer Jones, "Clothing and the Courtier" in Giorgio Riello and Peter McNeil, eds., *The Fashion History Reader: Global Perspectives*, Abingdon, Oxon; New York: Routledge, 2010, 168.

De Serres, Olivier. *Le théâtre d'agriculture et mesnage des champs*. Paris : Jamet Métayer, 1600.

De Thévenot, Jean. *Relation d'un voyage fait au Levant*. Paris: L. Billaine, 1665–1684.

De Vries, Jan. "The Industrial Revolution and the Industrious Revolution". *Journal of Economic History*, 54 (1993): 249–270.

——*The Industrious Revolution: Consumer Behavior and the Household Economy, 1650 to the Present*. Cambridge: Cambridge University Press, 2008.

——"The Economic Crisis of the Seventeenth Century after Fifty Years". *Journal of Interdisciplinary History* Vol. 40, No. 2 (2009): 151–194.

——"The Limits of Globalization in the Early Modern World". *The Economic History Review*, 63, 3 (2010): 710–733.

DeJean, Joan. *The Essence of Style: How the French Invented High Fashion, Fine Food, Chic Cafés, Style, Sophistication and Glamour*. New York: Free Press, 2005.

——*The Age of Comfort: when Paris Discovered Casual – and the Modern Home Began*. New York: Bloomsbury, 2009.

Derks, Hans. *History of the Opium Problem: the Assault on the East, ca. 1600–1950*. Leiden; Boston: Brill, 2012.

Desessarts, Nicolas-Toussaint Lemoyne. *Dictionnaire universel de police (1785–1789)*. Quoted in Jennifer Jones, *Sexing la Mode: Gender, Fashion and Commercial Culture in Old Regime France*, Oxford; New York: Berg, 2004, 145.

Dickinson, Gary and Linda Wrigglesworth. *Imperial Wardrobe*. Berkeley CA: Ten Speed Press, 2000.

Diffie, Bailey W. and George D. Winius. *Europe and the World in the Age of Expansion*. Book 1, Foundations of the Portuguese Empire, 1415–1850. Minnesota: University of Minnesota Press, 1977.

Douglas, Mary and Baron Isherwood. *The World of Goods: Towards an Anthropology of Consumption*. New York: WW Norton, 1979.

Dufour, Philippe Sylvestre. *De l'usage du caphé, du thé, et du chocolat*. Lyon, 1671. Reprint, Lyon: Jean Girin & B. Riviere, 1685.

DuPlessis, Robert S. "Cottons Consumption in the Seventeenth and Eighteenth-century North Atlantic". In Riello and Parthasarathi, eds., *The Spinning World: A Global History of Cotton Textiles, 1200–1850*. Oxford; New York: Oxford University Press, 2009, 227–260.

Elias, Norbert. *La société de cour*. Paris: Flammarion, 1993.

——*The Civilizing Process: Sociogenetic and Psychogenetic Investigations*. Translated by Edmund Jephcott. Malden, MA; Oxford, England; Victoria, Australia: Blackwell Publishing, 2000.

——*The Court Society*. Edited by Stephen Mennell. Dublin: UCD Press, 2006.

Ellis, Markman. *The Coffee-house: A Cultural Study*. London: Phoenix, 2005.

Enthoven, Victor. "An Assessment of Dutch Transatlantic Commerce, 1585–1817". In Johannes Postma and Victor Enthoven, eds., *Riches from Atlantic Commerce: Dutch Transatlantic Trade and Shipping, 1585–1817*. Leiden: Brill Academic Publishers, 2003, 385–445.

Evelyn, John. *Diary*, Vol. 3, 460. Cited in Charlotte Jirousek, "Ottoman Influences in Western Dress". In Faroqhi and Neumann, *Ottoman Costumes*. Istanbul, Turkey: EREN Press, 2004, 231–251.

Evelyn, M. (attr.) *Mundus Muliebris: or, The Ladies Dressing-Room unlock'd*. Edited by J. L. Nevinson, London 1977.

Faroqhi, Suraiya and Christoph K. Neumann. *Ottoman Costumes: From Textile to Identity*. Istanbul, Turkey: EREN Press, 2004.

Faure, Edgar. *La Banqueroute de Law, 17 Juillet 1720*. Paris: Gallimard, 1977.

Febvre, Lucien and Henri-Jean Martin. *The Coming of the Book: The Impact of Printing, 1450–1800*. London; New York: Verso, 1976.

Félibien, André. *Les Divertissements de Versailles, donnés au retour de la conquête de la Franche-Comté en 1674*. Paris: Imprimerie Royale, 1676.

Ferguson, Niall. *The Ascent of Money: A Financial History of the World*. New York: Penguin Press, 2008.

Findlen, Paula. *Possessing Nature: Museums, Collecting, and Scientific Culture in Early Modern Italy*. Berkeley; Los Angeles; London, University of California Press: 1994.

——"Possessing the Past: The Material World of the Italian Renaissance". *AHR* 103, no. 1 (February 1998): 83–114.

——*Early Modern Things*. New York: Routledge, 2012.

Finnane, Antonia. *Changing Clothes in China: Fashion, History, Nation*. New York: Columbia University Press, 2008.

Flandrin, Jean-Louis, "Distinction through Taste". In Philippe Ariès and Georges Duby, eds., *A History of Private Life*. Cambridge, MA: Belknap Press of Harvard University Press, 198 1991 Vol. III, 265–308.

——*Arranging the Meal: A History of Table Service in France*. Translated by Julie E. Johnson. Berkeley: University of California Press, 2007.

——and Montanari, Massimo, eds. *Histoire de l'alimentation*. Paris: Fayard, 1996.

Flügel, J. C. *The Psychology of Clothes*. London, 1950, 110–119. Cited in Michael Kwass, "Big Hair: A Wig History of Consumption of Eighteenth-Century France" *The American Historical Review* Vol. 111, No. 3, Oxford University Press (June 2006).

Fogel, Robert William and Stanley L. Engerman. *Time on the Cross: The Economics of American Negro Slavery*. New York; London: W.W. Norton, 1995, 33–34.

Fox, Robert and Anthony Turner. *Luxury Trades and Consumerism in Ancien Régime Paris: Studies in the History of the Skilled Workforce*. Aldershot, UK: Ashgate, 1998.

Frank, Caroline. *Objectifying China, Imagining America: Chinese Commodities in Early America*. Chicago: University of Chicago Press, 2011.

Friedman, Milton. *A Theory of the Consumption Function*. Princeton: Princeton University Press, 1957.

Galland, Antoine. *De l'origine et du progés du café*. Caen: 1699; Reprint, Paris: L'écrivain voyageur, 1992.

Garber, Peter M. *Famous First Bubbles: The Fundamentals of Early Manias*. London; Cambridge, MA: The MIT Press, 2000.

Geertz, Clifford. "Ethos, World-View and the Analysis of Sacred Symbols." *Antioch Review* (Winter 1957–1958): 421–437.

——*The Interpretation of Cultures: Selected Essays*. New York: Basic Books, 1973.

Gelderblom, Oscar and Joost Jonker. "Amsterdam as the Cradle of Modern Futures Trading and Options Trading, 1550–1650." In William N. Goetzmann and K. Geert Rouwenhorst, eds., *The Origins of Value: The Financial Innovations that*

Created Modern Capital Markets. Oxford; New York: Oxford University Press, 2005, 189–206.

Glamann, Kristof. *Dutch-Asiatic Trade, 1620–1740.* Copenhagen: Danish Science Press, 1958.

Goldgar, Anne. "Nature as Art: The Case of the Tulip". In Pamela H. Smith and Paula Findlen, eds., *Merchants & Marvels: Commerce, Science, and Art in Early Modern Europe.* New York; London: Routledge, 2002, 324–336.

——*Tulipmania: Money, Honor and Knowledge in the Dutch Golden Age.* Chicago: University of Chicago Press, 2007.

Goldthwaite, Richard. *The Building of Renaissance Florence: An Economic and Social History.* Baltimore: Johns Hopkins University Press, 1980.

——"The Medici Bank and the World of Florentine Capitalism". *Past & Present* 114. Oxford University Press on behalf of the Past and Present Society (February 1987): 3–31.

——*The Structural Transformation of the Public Sphere: An Inquiry into a Category of Bourgeois Society.* Translated by Thomas Burger. Cambridge, MA: MIT Press, 1989.

——*Wealth and the Demand for Art in Italy, 1300–1600.* Baltimore, MD: Johns Hopkins University Press, 1993.

——*The Economy of Renaissance Florence.* Baltimore: Johns Hopkins University Press, 2009.

Goodman, Jordan. *Tobacco in History: The Cultures of Dependence.* London: Routledge, 1994.

Goodman, Jordan, Paul E. Lovejoy and Andrew Sherratt., eds., *Consuming Habits: Global and Historical Perspectives on how Cultures Define Drugs.* Second edition. London; New York: Routledge, 2007.

Grieco, Alen J.; Odile Redon, and Tomasi Lucia Tongiorgi. *Le monde végétal (XII– XVII siècles): savoirs et usages sociaux.* Saint-Denis: Presses universitaires de Vincennes, 1993.

Grieco, Alen J. "Les plantes, les regimes vegetariens et la melancolie à la fin du Moyen Age et au debut de la Renaissance italienne". In Alen J. Grieco, Odile Redon, and Tomasi Lucia Tongiorgi, *Le monde végétal (XII-XVII siècles): savoirs et usages sociaux.* Saint-Denis: Presses universitaires de Vincennes, 1993, 11–29.

Grivetti, Louis E. "Medicinal Chocolate in New Spain, Western Europe and North America". In *Chocolate: History, Culture and Heritage.* Translated by Louis E. Grivetti and Howard-Yana Shapiro. Hoboken, NJ: Wiley, 2009, 67–89.

Grotius, Hugo. *Mare Liberum.* Leiden, 1609.

Hamilton, Earl J. *War and Prices in Spain, 1651–1800.* Cambridge, MA: Harvard University Press, 1947.

Harrison, Peter. "Original Sin and the Problem of Knowledge in Early Modern Europe". *Journal of the History of Ideas* 63.2 (April 2002): 239–259.

Haru Crowston, Clare. *Fabricating Women: The Seamstresses of Old Regime France, 1675–1791.* London: Duke University Press, 2001.

Hattox, Ralph. *Coffee and Coffeehouses: The Origins of a Social Beverage in the Medieval Near East.* Seattle: University of Washington Press, 1985.

Haulman, Kate. *The Politics of Fashion in Eighteenth-century America.* Chapel Hill: University of North Carolina Press, 2011.

Heller, Sarah Grace. *Fashion in Medieval France.* Cambridge; Rochester, NY: Brewer, 2007.

——"Birth of Fashion". In Giorgio Riello and Peter McNeil, eds., *The Fashion History Reader: Global Perspectives*. Milton Park, Abingdon, Oxon; New York: Routledge, 2010.

Higginbotham, A. Leon. Jr., *In the Matter of Color: Race & the American Legal Process*. New York: Oxford University Press, 1978.

Hilaire-Pérez, L. "Cultures techniques et pratiques de l'échange entre Lyon et le Levant: inventions et réseaux au XVIIIe siècle". *Revue d'Histoire Moderne et Contemporaine* 49, no. 1 (2002), 113.

Hirschman, Albert O. *The Passions and the Interests: Political Arguments for Capitalism before its Triumph*. Princeton, NJ: Princeton University Press, 1977.

Hopkins, A. G., ed. *Globalization in World History*. New York, NY: W.W. Norton & Company, 2002.

Hunt, Allen. "A Short History of Sumptuary Laws". In Giorgio Riello and Peter McNeil, eds., *The Fashion History Reader: Global Perspectives*. Abingdon, Oxon; New York: Routledge, 2010, 43–59.

Hunt, Lynn. "Freedom of Dress in Revolutionary France". In Sara Melzer and Kathryn Norberg, eds., *From the Royal to the Republican Body: Incorporating the Political in Seventeenth and Eighteenth-century France*. Berkeley; Los Angeles; Oxford: University of California Press, 1998, 224–249.

Hunter, Michael (September 2004; online edition May 2006). "Ashmole, Elias (1617–1692)". *Oxford Dictionary of National Biography*, London: Oxford University Press.

Hyde, Elizabeth. *Cultivated Power: Flowers, Culture, and Politics in the Reign of Louis XIV*. Philadelphia: University of Pennsylvania Press, 2005.

İnalcik, Halil. "Servile Labor in the Ottoman Empire". In A. Ascher, B. K. Kiraly, and T. Halasi-Kun, eds., *The Mutual Effects of the Islamic and Judeo-Christian Worlds: The East European Pattern*. Brooklyn, N.Y.: Brooklyn College, 1979, 25–43.

——and Donald Quataert, eds. *An Economic and Social History of the Ottoman Empire, 1300–1916*. New York, NY: Cambridge University Press, 1994.

Innis, Harold. *The Fur Trade in Canada*. Toronto: University of Toronto Press, 2001.

Irvin, Benjamin H. *Clothed in Robes of Sovereignty: The Continental Congress and the People Out of Doors*. New York: Oxford University Press, 2011.

Irvine, Jonathan. *Diasporas Within a Diaspora: Jews, Crypto-Jews, and the World of Maritime Empires 1540–1740*, Brill's Series in Jewish Studies. Boston: Brill, 2002.

Jacob, Margaret C. "Mental Landscape of the Public Sphere: A European Perspective". ECS 28:1 (Fall 1994). In Brian Cowan, *The Social Life of Coffee: The Emergence of the British Coffeehouse*. New Haven, CN: Yale University Press, 2005, 96.

Jardine, Lisa. *Worldly Goods: A New History of the Renaissance*. London: MacMillan, 1996.

——*Going Dutch: How England Plundered Holland's Glory*. New York: Harper, 2008.

Jarry, Madeleine. *Chinoiserie: Chinese Influence on European Decorative Art, 17th and 18th Centuries*. New York: Vendome Press, 1981.

Jirousek, Charlotte. "Ottoman Influences in Western Dress". In Faroqhi and Neumann, *Ottoman Costumes*. Istanbul, Turkey: EREN Press, 2004, 231–251.

Jones, Jennifer. *Sexing la Mode: Gender, Fashion and Commercial Culture in Old Regime France*. Oxford; New York: Berg, 2004.

Josten, C. H. *Elias Ashmole (1617–1692). His Autobiographical and Historical Notes, his Correspondence, and Other Contemporary Sources Relating to his Life and Work.* Vol I. Oxford: Clarendon Press, 1966.

Kafescioğlu, Çiğdem. *Constantinopolis/Istanbul: Cultural Encounter, Imperial Vision, and the Construction of the Ottoman Capital.* University Park, Pennsylvania: Pennsylvania State University Press, 2009.

Kaiser, Thomas. "The Evil Empire? The Debate on Turkish Despotism in Eighteenth-Century French Political Culture". *The Journal of Modern History* 72, no. 1, New Work on the Old Regime and the French Revolution: A Special Issue in Honor of François Furet (Mar., 2000): 6–34.

Kaplan, Steven Laurence. *La fin des corporations.* Translated by Béatrice Vierne, Paris: Fayard, 2001.

Kayoko, Fujita. "Japan Indianized: The Material Culture of Imported Textiles in Japan, 1550–1850". In Giorgio Riello and Prasannan Parthasarathi, eds. *The Spinning World: A Global History of Cotton Textiles, 1200–1850.* Oxford; New York: Oxford University Press, 2009, 181–203.

Kelly, James C. and Barbara Clark Smith. *Jamestown, Quebec, Santa Fe: Three North American Beginnings.* New York: Smithsonian Books, 2007.

Keynes, John Maynard. *The General Theory of Employment, Interest, and Money.* London: Macmillan, 1936.

Killerby, Catherine Kovesi. *Sumptuary Law in Italy 1200–1500.* Oxford: Clarendon Press; New York: Oxford University Press, 2002.

King, Julia A. "Still Life with Tobacco: The Archaeological Uses of Dutch Art". Historical Archaeology Vol. 41, No. 1, Between Art & Artifact (*Society for Historical Archaeology,* 2007): 6–22.

Kiple, Kenneth F. and Kriemhild Conee Ornelas. *The Cambridge World History of Food, Volume I.* Cambridge: Cambridge University Press, 2000.

Klooster, Wim. "An Overview of Dutch Trade with the Americas, 1600–1800". In Johannes Postma and Victor Enthoven, eds., *Riches from Atlantic Commerce: Dutch Transatlantic Trade and Shipping, 1585–1817.* Leiden: Brill Academic Publishers, 2003, 368–84.

Koeppe, Wolfram. "Collecting for the Kunstkammer". In Heilbrunn Timeline of Art History. New York: The Metropolitan Museum of Art, 2000. Available at: http://www.metmuseum.org/toah/hd/kuns/hd_kuns.htm (accessed October 2002)

Koerner, Lisbet "Linnaeus' Floral Transplants". *Representations,* No. 47, Special Issue: National Cultures before Nationalism (Summer, 1994): 144–169.

Krohn, Deborah L.; Peter N. Miller, and Marybeth de Filippis. *Dutch New York between East and West: The World of Margrieta van Varick.* New York: Bard Graduate Center, Decorative Arts, Design History, Material Culture: New-York Historical Society; New Haven: Yale University Press, 2009.

Kuntz, Marion Leathers. *Guillaume Postel, Prophet of the Restitution of All Things: His Life and Thought.* The Hague; Boston: Nijhoff; Hingham, MA: Kluwer Boston, 1981.

Kwass, Michael. "Big Hair: A Wig History of Consumption of Eighteenth-century France". *The American Historical Review* Vol. 111, No. 3. Oxford University Press (June 2006): 631–659.

Landes, David. *The Wealth and Poverty of Nations : Why Some are so Rich and Some so Poor.* New York: W.W. Norton, 1998.

Lanni, Dominique. *Le Rêve Siamois du Roi Soleil: Récits D'une Fièvre Exotique à La Cour De Louis XIV, 1660–1680.* Paris: Cosmople, 2004.

Lauterwald, Alexander. *Colloquium Philosophicum* [unfoliated, 16r-v]. In Tara E. Nummedal "Practical Alchemy and Commercial Exchange". In Pamela H. Smith, Paula Findlen, eds., *Merchants & Marvels: Commerce, Science, and Art in Early Modern Europe*. New York; London: Routledge, 2002.

Leath, Robert A. "'After the Chinese Taste': Chinese Export Porcelain and Chinoiserie Design in Eighteenth-Century Charleston." *Historical Archaeology*, Vol. 33, No. 3, Charleston in the Context of Trans-Atlantic Culture (1999): 48–61.

Lemire, Beverly. "Domesticating the Exotic: Floral Culture in the East India Calico Trade with England, c. 1600–1800". in *Textile: A Journal of Cloth and Culture*, I/I (2003): 65–85.

——"Revising the Historical Narrative: India, Europe, and the Cotton Trade, c. 1300–1800". in Giorgio Riello and Prasannan Parthasarathi, eds. *The Spinning World: A Global History of Cotton Textiles, 1200–1850*. Oxford; New York: Oxford University Press, 2009.

——"Fashioning Cottons: Asian Trade, Domestic Industry and Consumer Demand, 1660–1780". In Giorgio Riello and Peter McNeil, eds., *The Fashion History Reader: Global Perspectives*. Abingdon, Oxon; New York: Routledge, 2010.

——ed. *The Force of Fashion in Politics and Society: Global Perspectives from Early Modern to Contemporary Times*. England: Ashgate, 2010.

Lewis, James E. *The Louisiana Purchase: Jefferson's Noble Bargain?* Charlottesville, VA: Thomas Jefferson Foundation, 2003.

Mackie, Louise W. "Ottoman kaftans with an Italian identity". In Suraiya Faroqhi and Christoph K. Neumann, eds., *Ottoman Costumes: From Textile to Identity*. Istanbul, Turkey: EREN Press, 2004, 219–229.

Macfarlane, Alan and Iris Macfarlane. *Green Gold: The Empire of Tea*. London: Ebury, 2003.

Maguelonne, Toussaint-Samat. *A History of Food*. Chichester, West Sussex, UK; Malden, MA: Wiley-Blackwell, 2009.

Mair, Victor H. and Erling Hoh. *The True History of Tea*. London; New York: Thames & Hudson, 2009.

Mandeville, Bernard. *The Fable of the Bees and Other Writings*. E.J. Hundert, ed., Indianapolis: Hackett Publishing, 1997.

Mann, Charles C. *1493, Uncovering the New World Columbus Created*. New York: Alfred A. Knopf, 2011.

Martin, Ann Smart. *Buying into the World of Goods: Early Consumers in Backcountry Virginia*. Baltimore: Johns Hopkins University Press, 2008.

Marx, Karl. *Capital: A Critique of Political Economy*, Volume I. New York: Vintage Books, 1976.

Massialot, François. *Nouvelle instruction pour les confitures, les liqueurs, et les fruits : avec la maniere de bien ordonner un dessert, & tout le reste qui est du devoir des maîtres d'hôtels, sommeliers, confiseurs, & autres officiers de bouche : suite du cuisinier roïal & bourgeois : egalement utile dans les familles, pour sçavoir ce qu'on sert de plus à la mode dans les repas, & en d'autres occasions. Seconde édition, revûë, corrigée, & beaucoup augmentée*. Paris: Chez Charles de Sercy, 1698.

Matthee, Rudi. "Exotic Substances: The Introduction and Global Spread of Tobacco, Coffee, Cocoa, Tea, and Distilled Liquor, Sixteenth to Eighteenth Centuries". In Roy Porter and Mikuláš Teich, eds., *Drugs and Narcotics in History*. Cambridge, UK: Cambridge University Press, 1995, 26.

Mauss, Marcel. *The Gift: The Form and Reason for Exchange in Archaic Societies.* London: Routledge, 1900.

McCants, Anne E.C. "Porcelain for the Poor: the Material Culture of Tea and Coffee in Eighteenth Century Amsterdam". In Paula Findlen, ed., *Early Modern Things.* New York: Routledge, 2012.

McLaren, James G. "A Brief History of Wigs in the Legal Profession". *International Journal of the Legal Profession*, 6:2. London, England: Routledge, 1999, 241–250.

McCracken, Grant. *Culture and Consumption: New Approaches to the Symbolic Character of Consumer Goods and Activities.* Bloomington: Indiana University Press, 1990.

McKendrick, Neil, ed. *Historical Perspectives: Studies in English Thought and Society.* London: Europa, 1974.

——with John Brewer, and J. H. Plumb, eds., *The Birth of a Consumer Society: The Commercialization of Eighteenth-century England.* Bloomington: Indiana University Press, 1982.

McWilliams, James E. *A Revolution in Eating: How the Quest for Food Shaped America.* New York: Columbia University Press, 2005.

Meadow, Mark A. "Merchants and Marvels: Hans Jacob Fugger and the Origins of the *Wunderkammer*". In Pamela H. Smith, Paula Findlen, eds., *Merchants & Marvels: Commerce, Science, and Art in Early Modern Europe.* New York; London: Routledge, 2002.

Melchior-Bonnet, Sabine. *The Mirror: A History.* New York: Routledge, 2001.

Melzer, Sara and Kathryn Norberg, eds. *From the Royal to the Republican Body: Incorporating the Political in Seventeenth and Eighteenth-century France.* Berkeley; Los Angeles; Oxford: University of California Press, 1998.

Menzel, Johanna M. "The Sinophilism of J. H. G. Justi". *Journal of the History of Ideas* 17, No. 3 (June, 1956): 300–310.

Mentges, Gabriele. "European Fashion (1450–1950)". *European History Online (EGO).* Mainz: Institute of European History (IEG) (2011). Available from: http://ieg-ego.eu/en/threads/models-and-stereotypes/the-spanish-century/gabriele-mentges-european-fashion-1450-1950

Menzhausen, Ingelore. *Early Meissen porcelain in Dresden.* New York: Thames and Hudson, 1990.

Messar, Ellen. "Potatoes (White)". In Kenneth F. Kiple and Kriemhild Conee Ornelas eds., *The Cambridge World History of Food, Volume I.* Cambridge: Cambridge University Press, 2000, 187–201.

Mintz, Sidney W. *Sweetness and Power: The Place of Sugar in Modern History.* New York, NY: Viking, 1985.

Molà, Luca. *The Silk Industry of Renaissance Venice.* Baltimore: Johns Hopkins University Press, 2000.

Monardes, Nicolas. *Segunda parte del libro des las cosas que se traen de nuestras Indias Occidentales, que sirven al uso de la medicina; do se trata del tabaco, y de la sassafras, y del carlo sancto, y de otras muchas yervas y plantas, simientes, y licores que agora nuevamente han venido de aquellas partes, de grandes virtudes y maravillosos effectos.* Seville: Alonso Escrivano, 1571.

——*Joyfull Newes out of the Newe Founde Worlde wherein is declared the rare and singuler vertues of diverse and sundrie hearbes, trees, oyles, plantes, and stones, with their applications, aswell for phisicke as chirurgerie, the daied beyng well applied bryngeth suche present remedie for all deseases, as maie seme altogether incredible: notwithstanding by practize founde out, to bee true: also the portrature of the saied hearbes, very aptly described.* 1577. Translated by John Frampton. 2 vols. London: Constable and Co. Ltd; New York: Alfred A. Knopf, 1925.

Montanari, Massimo. *The Culture of Food.* Translated by Carl Ipsen. Oxford, UK; Cambridge, MA: Blackwell, 1994.

Muizelaar, Klaske and Derek Phillips. *Picturing Men and Women in the Dutch Golden Age: Paintings and People in Historical Perspective.* New Haven, CN: Yale University Press, 2003.

Mukerji, Chandra. *From Graven Images: Patterns of Modern Materialism.* New York: Columbia University Press, 1983.

Musgrave, Toby. *An Empire of Plants: People and Plants that Changed the World.* London: Cassell; New York: Sterling Publishing Co., 2000.

Norton, Marcy. *Sacred Gifts, Profane Pleasures: A History of Tobacco and Chocolate in the Atlantic World.* Ithaca and London: Cornell University Press, 2008.

Nummedal, Tara E. "Practical Alchemy and Commercial Exchange in the Holy Roman Empire". In Pamela H. Smith, Paula Findlen, eds., *Merchants & Marvels: Commerce, Science, and Art in Early Modern Europe.* New York; London: Routledge, 2002.

O'Brien, Patrick. "The Geopolitics of a Global Industry: Eurasian Divergence and the Mechanization of Cotton Textile Production in England". In Giorgio Riello and Prasannan Parthasarathi, eds., *The Spinning World: A Global History of Cotton Textiles, 1200–1850.* Oxford; New York: Oxford University Press, 2009, 351–365.

Oviedo y Valdés, Gonzalo Fernández de. *La historia general de las Indias.* Seville, 1535.

Pamuk, Şevket. "The Price Revolution in the Ottoman Empire Reconsidered". *International Journal of Middle East Studies,* Vol. 33, No.1 (February 2001): 69–89.

Parker, Matthew. *The Sugar Barons: Family, Corruption, Empire, and War in the West Indies.* New York: Walker & Co., 2011.

Paul, Helen J. *The South Sea Bubble: An Economic History of its Origins and Consequences.* London; New York: Routledge, 2011.

Peck, Linda Levy. *Consuming Splendor: Society and Culture in Seventeenth Century England.* Cambridge: Cambridge University Press, 2005.

Pepys, Samuel. *Diary.* Robert Latham and William Matthews, eds., London: Bell & Hyman, 1970, VII 373.

Perrot, Jean Claude. *Une histoire intellectuelle de l'écomomie politique au XVIII-XIIIième siècle.* Paris: Editions de l'Ecole des hautes études en sciences sociales, 1992.

Perry, William Martin. *Hunting Law and Ritual in Medieval English Literature.* D.S. Brewer: Cambridge, 2006.

Pietsch, Ulrich. *China, Japan, Meissen: The Dresden Porcelain Collection.* Translated by Ulrich Boltz, Munich: Deutscher Kunstverlag, 2006.

Pincus, Steven. "Coffee Politicians Does Create: Coffeehouses and Restoration Political Culture". *Journal of Modern History 67* (December 1995), 828–29. Quoted in Brian William Cowan. *The Social Life of Coffee: The Emergence of the British Coffeehouse.* New Haven, CN: Yale University Press, 2005.

Pocoke, Edward. *The Nature of the Drink Kahue, or Coffee, and the Beery of which it is made Microform/Described by an Arab Phistian.* Oxford: Henry Hall, 1659.

Polo, Marco. *The Travels of Marco Polo.* 3 Vols. New York: Dover Publications, 1903. Vol. 1, Book 1.

——*The Travels of Marco Polo.* Translated by Ronald Latham, New York: Penguin, 1958.

Pomeranz, Kenneth. *The Great Divergence: China, Europe and the Making of the Modern World Economy.* New Jersey: Princeton University Press, 2000.

Le porte-feuille galant, ouvrage mêlé de prose et de vers. Avec plusieurs questions sérieuses et galantes. Paris: Jean Moreau, 1700.

Porter, Roy and Mikuláŝ Teich, eds. *Drugs and Narcotics in History.* Cambridge, UK: Cambridge University Press, 1995.

Prakash, Om. "Opium Monopoly in India and Indonesia in the Eighteenth Century", *Indian Economic Social History Review* 24:63 (1987), 65–66.

Pritchard, James S. *In Search of Empire: the French in the America, 1670–1730.* Cambridge, UK: New York: Cambridge University Press, 2004.

Puga, Rogério Miguel. "The Presence of the 'Portugals' in Macau and Japan". In Richard Hakluyt *Navigations, Bulletin of Portuguese/Japanese Studies*, Vol. 5. Lisbon, Portugal: Universidade Nova de Lisboa, 2002, 81–115.

Quataert, Donald, ed. *Consumption Studies and the History of the Ottoman Empire, 1550–1922.* New York: Albany State University of New York Press, 2000.

Quellier, Florent. *La Table des Français: Une Histoire Culturelle (XV–début XIX siècle).* Rennes: Presses Universitaires de Rennes, 2007.

Rambert, Gaston. *Histoire du Commerce de Marseille Publié par la chambre de commerce de Marseille en sept Tomes.* Paris: Plon, 1953–57.

Raveux, Olivier. "Spaces and Technologies in the Cotton Industry in the Seventeenth and Eighteenth Centuries: The Example of Printed Calicoes in Marseilles". *Textile History* 36, N.2 (November, 2005): 131–145.

Ribeiro, Aileen. *Dress and Morality.* London: Berg, 2003.

Riello, Giorgio. "Fabricating the Domestic: The Material Culture of Textiles and the Social Life of the Home in Early Modern Europe". In Beverly Lemire, ed, *The Force of Fashion in Politics and Society: Global Perspectives from Early Modern to Contemporary Times.* England: Ashgate, 2010, 41–66.

Riello, Giorgio and Prasannan Parthasarathi, eds. *The Spinning World: A Global History of Cotton Textiles, 1200–1850.* Oxford; New York: Oxford University Press, 2009.

Riello, Giorgio and Peter McNeil, eds. *The Fashion History Reader: Global Perspectives.* Abingdon, Oxon; New York: Routledge, 2010.

Riello, Giorgio; Peter McNeil, Glenn Adamson and Sarah Teasley, eds. *Global Design History.* New York: Routledge, 2011.

Riello, Giorgio and Peter McNeil. "Fashion and Social Order: the Early Modern World". In Glenn Adamson and Sarah Teasley, eds., *Global Design History.* New York: Routledge, 2011, 85–93.

Rinaldi, Bianca Maria. *The "Chinese Garden in Good Taste": Jesuits and Europe's Knowledge of Chinese Flora and Art of the Garden in the 17th and 18th Centuries.* München: Meidenbauer, 2006.

Rimsky-Korsakoff Dyer, Svetlana. *Grammatical Analysis of the Lao Ch'i-ta: With an English Translation of the Chinese Text.* Canberra: Faculty of Asian Studies Australian National University, 1983), 430–431. Cited by Craig Clunas in *The Oxford Handbook of the History of Consumption*, ed. Frank Trentman (Oxford: Oxford Universty Press, 2012), 51.

Ritchie, Robert C. *Captain Kidd and the War Against the Pirates.* Cambridge, MA, 1986.

Roche, Daniel. *Histoire des choses banales: naissance de la consommation dans les sociétés traditionnelles (XVIIe–XIXe siècle).* Paris: Fayard, 1997.

——*La culture des apparences: une histoire du vêtement (XVII – XVIII siècle)*. Paris: Fayard, 1989.

——*The Culture of Clothing: Dress and Fashion in the Ancien Regime*. Paris, France: Maison des Sciences de l'Homme; New York, NY: Cambridge University Press, 1994.

Roche, Daniel. *France in the Enlightenment*. Cambridge, MA: Harvard University Press, 1998.

Rolandsen, Unn Malfrid H. *Leisure and Power in Urban China: Everyday Life in a Chinese City*. Abingdon, Oxon; New York, NY: Routledge, 2001.

Rousseau, Jean-Jacques. *Oeuvres complètes*, 5 vols. Paris, 1959, 1: 363; Rousseau, *Oeuvres complètes* de J. J. Rousseau, 4 vols. (Paris, 1852), 1: 409.

Runciman, Steven. *The Fall of Constantinople 1453*. Cambridge: Cambridge University Press, 1965.

Salzmann, Ariel. "The Age of Tulips: Confluence and Conflict in Early Modern Consumer Culture (1550–1730)". In Donald Quataert, ed, *Consumption Studies and the History of the Ottoman Empire, 1550–1922*. Albany, NY State University of New York Press, 2000, 83–106.

Sahlins, Marshall. "Cosmologies of Capitalism: The Trans-Pacific Sector of 'the World-System'". *Proceedings of the British Academy* 74 (1988): 1–51.

Sandman, Alison. "Mirroring the World: Sea Charts, Navigation, and Territorial Claims in Sixteenth-Century Spain". In Pamela H. Smith, Paula Findlen, eds., *Merchants & Marvels: Commerce, Science, and Art in Early Modern Europe*. New York; London: Routledge, 2002, 83–108.

Sandrock, John E. "John Law's Banque Royale and the Mississippi Bubble". Accessed 18 September 2013. Available at: http://www.google.com/url?sa=t&rct=j&q=&esrc =s&source=web&cd=1&ved=0CCAQFjAA&url=http%3A%2F%2Fwww.thecurrency collector.com%2Fpdfs%2FJohn_Laws_Banque_Royale.pdf&ei=ZYxFUKqxGMm3 6gHQxoGACQ&usg=AFQjCNHezfya7qm3KRRVm47N7tdceydTQA

Sargentson, Carolyn. *Merchants and Luxury Markets: The Marchands Merciers of Eighteenth-century Paris*. Malibu, CA: Victoria and Albert Museum in association with the J. Paul Getty Museum, 1996.

Savary des Brûlons, Jacques. *Dictionnaire universel de commerce: d'histoire naturelle, & des arts & métiers*. Paris: Estienne et fils, 1723.

Schama, Simon. *The Embarrassment of Riches: An Interpretation of Dutch Culture in the Golden Age*. Berkeley; Los Angeles; London: University of California Press, 1988.

Schivelbusch, Wolfgang. *Tastes and Paradise: A Social History of Spices, Stimulants, and Intoxicants*. Translated by David Jacobson. New York: Pantheon Books, 1992.

Schmidt, Benjamin. *Innocence Abroad: The Dutch Imagination and the New World, 1570–1670*. Cambridge: Cambridge University Press, 2001.

——"The Dutch Atlantic From Provincialism to Globalism". In Jack P. Greene and Philip D. Morgan, eds. *Atlantic History: A Critical Appraisal*. Oxford; New York: Oxford University Press, 2009, 163–189.

Shovlin, John. *The Political Economy of Virtue: Luxury, Patriotism and the Origins of the French Revolution*. New York: Cornell University Press, 2006.

Simoons, Frederick J. *Food in China: A Cultural and Historical Inquiry*. Boca Raton, FL: CRC Press, 1991.

Smith, Adam. *An Inquiry into the Nature and Causes of the Wealth of Nations*. New York: Random House, 1937.

Smith, Paul H., Gerard W. Gawalt, Rosemary Fry Plakas, Eugene R. Sheridan, and Ronald M. Gephard, eds., *Letters of Delegates to Congress, 1774–1789*, CD ROM Summerfield, FL, 1998.

Smith, Pamela H. and Paula Findlen, eds. *Merchants & Marvels: Commerce, Science, and Art in Early Modern Europe*. New York; London: Routledge, 2002.

Smith, William. *The History of the Late Province of New York from its Discovery, to the Appointment of Govener Colden, in 1762*. New York Historical Society *Collections*, vol. 4, pt. 2, 1829. Quoted in Breen, T. H. *The Marketplace of Revolution: How Consumer Politics Shaped American Independence*. Oxford; New York: Oxford University Press, 2004, 98.

Studnicki-Gizbert, Daviken. *A Nation upon the Ocean Sea: Portugal's Atlantic Diaspora and the Crisis of the Spanish Empire, 1492–1640*. Oxford; New York: Oxford University Press, 2007.

Sombart, Werner. *Liebe, Luxus und Kapitalismus*. New edn. Wagenbach, 1992.

——*Le bourgeois: contribution à l'histoire morale et intellectuelle de l'homme économique moderne*. Translated by Dr. S. Jankélévitch, Paris: Payot, 1926.

——*Luxury and Capitalism*. Ann Arbor: University of Michigan Press, 1967.

Spence, Jonathan. *The Chan's Great Continent: China in Western Minds*. New York: W.W. Norton, 1998.

Spengler, Joseph J. "The Physiocrats and Say's Law of Markets". *Journal of Political Economy* 53, no. 3 (September 1945): 193–211.

Strassberg, Richard. *The World of K'ung Shang-jen: A Man of Letter in Early Ch'ing China*. New York: Columbia University Press, 1983.

Strieder, Jacob and Norman Scott Brien Gras, eds. *Jacob Fugger: Merchant and Banker of Augsburg, 1459–1525*. Translated by Mildred H. Hartsough. Washington, D.C.: Beard Books, 2001.

Taylor-García, Daphne Vanessa. *The Emergence of Racial Schema in the Americas: Sexuality, Sociogeny, and Print Capital in the Sixteenth Century Atlantic*. Berkeley: University of California, 2008.

Thomas, Hugh. *The Slave Trade*. New York, NY: Touchstone Books, 1999.

Thornton, John. *Africa and Africans in the Making of the Atlantic World, 1400–1800*. Cambridge; New York: Cambridge University Press, 1998.

Toomer, G. J. *Eastern Wisdom and Learning: The Study of Arabic in Seventeenth Century England*. Oxford: Clarendon Press, 1996.

Trentmann, Frank, ed. *The Oxford Handbook of the History of Consumption*. Oxford: Oxford University Press, 2012.

Trocki, Carl. *Opium, Empire and the Global Political Economy: a Study of the Asian Opium Trade, 1750–1950*. London; New York: Routledge, 1999.

Tuchscherer, Michel. "Coffee in the Red Sea Area from the sixteenth to the nineteenth century". In Gervase Clarence-Smith and Steven Topik, eds., *The Global Coffee Economy in Africa, Asia and Latin America, 1500–1989* (New York: Cambridge University Press, 2003, 51–52.

Ukers, William Harrison. *All about Coffee*. New York: The Tea and Coffee Trade Journal Company, 1935.

Van den Broecke, Marcel. *Ortelius' Theatrum Orbis Terrarum (1570–1641)*. Utrecht: Utrecht University, Royal Dutch Geographical Society, 2009.

Van der Cruysse, Dirk. *Louis XIV et le Siam*. Paris: Fayard, 1991.

Veblen, Thorstein. *The Leisure Class: An Economic Study in the Evolution of Institutions*. New York; London: Macmillan, 1899.

Vickery, Amanda. "His and Hers: Gender, Consumption and Household Accounting in Eighteenth-century England". *Past and Present* (2006) 1 (suppl 1): 12–38.

Vigié, Marc and Muriel Vigié. *L'herve à Nicot: Amateurs de tabac, fermiers généraux et contrebandiers sous l'Ancien Régime.* Paris: Fayard, 1989.

Vryonis, Speros. *Byzantium and Europe.* New York: Harcourt, Brace & World, 1967.

Warner, Jessica. "The Life and Times of 'Mother Gin' 1720–1751: Images of Mothers and Alcohol on the Eve of the Industrial Revolution". A paper delivered at the International Congress on the Social History of Alcohol, London, Ontario, May 13–15, 1993.

Weber, Caroline. *Queen of Fashion: What Marie Antoinette Wore to the Revolution.* New York: H. Holt, 2006.

Weber, Max. *Protestant Ethic and the Spirit of Capitalism.* Translated by Talcott Parsons. London: G. Allen & Unwin Ltd., 1930.

Weinberg, Bennett Alan and Bonnie K. Bealer. *The World of Caffeine: The Science and Culture of the World's Most Popular Drug.* London, Routledge, 2002.

Welch, Evelyn. *Shopping in the Renaissance: Consumer Cultures in Italy 1400–1600.* New Haven, CN: Yale University Press, 2005.

Wills, John E. *1688: A Global History.* New York: Norton, 2001.

Winter, Joseph C., ed. *Tobacco Use by Native Americans: Sacred Smoke and Silent Killer.* Norman: University of Oklahoma Press, 2000.

Wong, R. Bin. *China Transformed: Historical Change and the Limits of European Experience.* Ithaca and London: Cornell University Press, 1997.

Ying-Sung, Song. *T'ien-kung k'ai-wu, Chinese Technology in the Seventeenth Century.* Translated and annotated by E-tu Zen Sun and Shiou-chuan Sun. New York: Dover Publications, 1997.

Zakim, Michael. "From Homespun to Ready-made". *The American Historical Review* 106.5 (2001): 81 (Accessed 23 Jul. 2012), 1553–1586, 1554. http://www.historycoope rative.org/journals/ahr/106.5/ah0501001553.html. Zega, Andrew and Bernd H. Dams. *Palaces of the Sun King: Versailles, Trianon, Marly: The Châteaux of Louis XIV.* New York: Rizzoli, 2002.

Index